Ultimate Redis for High-Performance Applications

Master Redis Data Structures, Scripting, Scaling, Monitoring, Replication, and Clustering for High Performance Applications

Karnish Master

www.orangeava.com

First Published: Feburary 2026

Published By: Orange Education Pvt Ltd, AVA®

Address: 9, Daryaganj, Delhi, 110002, India

275 New North Road Islington Suite 1314 London,

N1 7AA, United Kingdom

ISBN (PBK): 978-93-49887-81-7

ISBN (E-BOOK): 978-93-49887-65-7

Scan the QR code to explore our entire catalogue

www.orangeava.com

Get a Free eBook

We hope you're enjoying your recent book purchase! Your feedback is incredibly valuable to us and helps other readers discover books that truly make a difference.

If you found this book useful or enjoyable, we'd greatly appreciate it if you could leave a short review with a 5-star rating on Amazon. Your review supports our work and allows us to reach more learners worldwide.

As a thank-you, we're happy to offer you a **free digital copy of this book** plus a **30% discount code** for your next purchase on our official websites:

www.orangeava.com

www.orangeava.in (For the Indian Subcontinent).

☑**How it works:**

Leave your review on Amazon, take a screenshot of the confirmation or use the following link to submit the claim and email it to **info@orangeava.com.** Once received the required detail, we will send your rewards within 24 hours, **along with one month free subcription to the book on AVA SkillShelf!**

Claim Form
https://rebrand.ly/4d2477

Thank you for your support—it truly means a lot to us.

Enjoy 1 Month of Free Access to AVA SkillShelf!

The future belongs to lifelong learners. With AVA SkillShelf, you go beyond reading books and start building real, job-ready skills curated by industry experts.

Your membership unlocks **200+ learning products** covering AI, Cloud, Python, Cybersecurity, Data Science, DevOps, and more—all in one platform. Our bestselling technical books are transformed into structured courses designed for practical, real-world application.

Learn directly from experienced professionals and published authors, with no filler—just actionable insights. Earn **verified digital certifications** to strengthen your CV, LinkedIn profile, and professional credibility.

Learn anytime, anywhere, on any device, at your own pace. Ideal for students, professionals, career switchers, and tech leaders.

For full access to all current and future courses, choose our **Annual Membership**. Simply scan the QR to get started!

For 1 month Free access, simply refer to the steps on the previous page titled: Get a Free ebook!

https://www.avaskillshelf.com/

Downloading the code bundles and colored images

Please follow the links or scan the QR codes to download the
Code Bundles and Images of the book:

https://github.com/ava-orange-education/Ultimate-Redis-for-High-Performance-Applications

The code bundles and images of the book are also hosted on
https://rebrand.ly/1099a0

In case there's an update to the code, it will be updated on the existing GitHub repository.

Errata

We take immense pride in our work at **Orange Education Pvt Ltd**, and follow best practices to ensure the accuracy of our content to provide an indulging reading experience to our subscribers. Our readers are our mirrors, and we use their inputs to reflect and improve upon human errors, if any, that may have occurred during the publishing processes involved. To let us maintain the quality and help us reach out to any readers who might be having difficulties due to any unforeseen errors, please write to us at :

errata@orangeava.com

Your support, suggestions, and feedback are highly appreciated.

Dedicated to

My Beloved
Grandmother, Godavariben Master (Baa).

My Loving Parents,
Mr. Mahendra Master and Mrs. Ashvina Master.

My Dear Sister,
Mrs. Ridhi Abhishek Panchal,
And

My Loving Wife,
Kinjal.

About the Author

Karnish Master brings over 14 years of experience in the technical domain, having worked on diverse projects across multiple industries. Beginning his career in Mumbai in 2011, he has steadily grown into a seasoned database and technology professional. In his current role as an Associate Director, he focuses on designing and maintaining reliable, scalable, and high-performance data platforms that support critical business operations.

Karnish has strong expertise across relational (RDBMS), NoSQL, and analytical databases, with hands-on experience in MySQL, MongoDB, Redis, Exasol, Sphinx, and Elasticsearch. His work spans database management, performance optimization, data modeling, and high-availability architectures. He has a particular interest in caching and search technologies, and often combines them with well-structured database designs to deliver systems that are both fast and robust.

In addition to his database skills, Karnish is proficient in PHP, shell scripting, Python, and Lua scripting, among other technologies. This blend of programming and database knowledge enables him to bridge the gap between applications, infrastructure, and data, and to implement end-to-end solutions that are practical, maintainable, as well as aligned with real-world needs.

Karnish is also the creator of mysqlgyan, a knowledge-sharing initiative that includes a blog at www.mysqlgyan.com and a YouTube channel named "mysqlgyan". Through these platforms, he shares tutorials, best practices, and lessons learned from real projects, with a focus on making database topics accessible to students, aspiring engineers, and working professionals. He also creates unboxing and review videos focused on gadgets and everyday technologies, offering practical insights and user-focused perspectives on the tools people use daily.

Beyond his technical work, he has a strong interest in teaching, mentoring, and technical writing. He enjoys breaking down complex concepts into clear, structured explanations that can be directly applied in day-to-day work. This book on Redis certainly reflects that philosophy.

About the Technical Reviewer

Bhushan Nikhar is a technology leader and enterprise architect with over 14 years of experience in software development and architecture, specializing in cloud-native systems, distributed computing, and emerging technologies. His core expertise lies in technical, solution, and enterprise architecture—applied across AWS, Azure, and Google Cloud platforms.

Bhushan has designed and led large-scale systems in banking, financial services, healthcare, retail, and e-commerce, with a focused emphasis on scalable data platforms and intelligent automation. Having delivered impactful AI/ML solutions throughout his career, he currently serves as an Enterprise Architect for a leading U.S. bank's credit card business, where he also mentors internal teams in AI and cloud transformation.

As a recognized reviewer for industry publications, Bhushan has contributed to multiple technical books, reflecting his commitment to advancing the global developer and architecture community. He is deeply passionate about cultivating technical excellence within teams and envisions India emerging as a global hub for next-generation deep tech innovation.

Acknowledgement

Writing this book has been a long, intense, and deeply rewarding journey, and I would not have reached the finish line without the support, guidance, and encouragement of many people.

First and foremost, I would like to thank my family. My late grandmother, Godavariben Master (Baa), who has been a constant source of blessings and inspiration throughout my life, and her values continue to guide me every day. My father, Mr. Mahendra Master, and my mother, Mrs. Ashvina Master, who have always believed in me, and taught me the value of hard work, honesty, and perseverance. My sister, Mrs. Ridhi Panchal, who has supported me in more ways than she will ever admit, and my wife, Kinjal, who has been my pillar of strength - patiently standing by me through late nights, drafts, rewrites, and endless "just one more chapter" moments. This book is as much theirs as it is mine.

I owe a deep debt of gratitude to my mentors, who shaped my career and thinking at every stage:

- Mr. Sunny Shende, who gave me my first chance, and quite literally taught me what a database is.
- Ms. Meeta Bilimoria, who opened my eyes to the world of APIs and their implementations, connecting databases with real-world applications.
- Mr. Piyush Naik, the then AVP – Talent Acquisition, who first reached out with a job opportunity, and has continued to support my career ever since.
- Mr. Tope Iluyomade, under whom I began my journey as a DBA. Working with him gave me the discipline and mindset needed for serious database work.
- Mr. Vijay Mehta, who placed a bet on me with just a phone call, and trusted me enough to recruit me without a formal interview.

I am equally grateful to my friends who have been much more than just colleagues:

- Akshat Puranik, who has stood by me since school days, and remained steady through every up and down.
- Ankit Patodi, whom I met during my first job, and has mentored, supported, and stood by me ever since.
- Ashwin Sawai, who has been a constant source of support and inspiration.

Special thanks goes to my technical reviewer, Bhushan Nikhar, whose detailed feedback, suggestions, and critical eye made this book more accurate, clearer, and practical, and last but not the least, to you, my Readers for picking up this book, and investing your valuable time and trust in me!

Preface

This Book was Born out of Real-world Work with Redis:

Over the years, Redis has evolved from being seen primarily as a "nice-to-have cache" to becoming a core building block in production systems—powering leaderboards, session stores, queues, rate limiters, analytics, and more. At the same time, many developers, DBAs, DevOps engineers, and students either use Redis only as a simple key-value store or hesitate to adopt it more broadly because the ecosystem appears complex and fragmented.

The Goal of This Book:

To take readers from their first contact with Redis all the way to running, monitoring, troubleshooting, and scaling it confidently in production step-by-step with practical examples.

This preface provides a brief tour of how the book is structured, and how it can be used effectively.

This Book is Designed for:

- Developers and Software Engineers who want to use Redis for more than basic caching.
- DBAs and Data Engineers who need to understand Redis architecture, replication, clustering, and troubleshooting.
- DevOps/SREs responsible for keeping Redis healthy, observable, and highly available in production.
- Students and Enthusiasts looking for a structured, end-to-end understanding of Redis - from fundamentals to advanced use cases.

No prior Redis expertise is required. Basic familiarity with databases and command-line usage is helpful, but each concept is introduced gradually, and reinforced with practical examples.

How the Book has been Organized:

The book can be read from start to finish as a guided journey, or consulted selectively depending on the reader's current needs.

Foundations: Understanding Redis and Its Data Model

Chapter 1. Introduction to Redis and Its Core Concepts

The opening chapter sets the stage. It answers fundamental questions such as: What is Redis? Where does it fit among other databases? Why is it worth learning? Readers explore Redis at a high-level, understand the benefits of learning it, and see where it sits in the broader database ecosystem. A comparison with traditional RDBMS systems and other NoSQL databases provides a clear mental model for why Redis is the right tool.

Chapter 2. Redis Data Structures and Their Uses

Once the basic idea of Redis is established, attention shifts to how Redis stores and organizes data. This chapter walks through the core Redis data types - Strings, Sets, Sorted Sets, Lists,

Hashes, and other specialized structures - and explains practical use cases for each. The chapter concludes with key points to remember and a short recap.

Installing and Using Redis in Practice

Chapter 3. Getting Redis up and Running on Various Platforms

Concepts become concrete in this chapter through hands-on setup. Readers learn how to install Redis on Linux, CentOS, Ubuntu, macOS, and Windows. The chapter covers securing Redis, verifying installations, applying basic configuration, and troubleshooting common issues. The content is written so that a working Redis instance can be set up on any of the covered operating systems. Key points and a concise conclusion help reinforce what has been done.

Chapter 4. Data Management in Redis with Popular Scripting Languages

With Redis up and running, the focus shifts to connecting real applications. This chapter explains how to connect to Redis, and perform data management operations using popular scripting languages. It demonstrates how to move from basic CLI usage to programmatic access, and presents best practices for reliable and maintainable data management in Redis.

Observability and Monitoring

Chapter 5. Monitoring Redis for Optimal Performance - Part 1

Reliable systems require observability. This chapter introduces the built-in monitoring tools that Redis provides, and extends into third-party tools such as RedisInsight and Prometheus with Grafana. Readers learn what to monitor, how to monitor it, and how to interpret key metrics to keep Redis responsive and healthy.

Chapter 6. Monitoring Redis for Optimal Performance - Part 2

This chapter covers Datadog and the ELK (Elasticsearch, Logstash, Kibana) stack for collecting and analyzing Redis logs and metrics. It also discusses how to choose a monitoring solution, how to set up alerts and notifications, and presents the best practices for Redis alerting. The emphasis is on moving from passive observation to proactive incident prevention.

Extending Redis with Lua

Chapter 7. Lua Scripting with Redis for Enhanced Functionality

Redis becomes especially powerful when combined with Lua scripting. This chapter focuses on advanced capabilities enabled by Lua such as conditional logic, batch processing with loops, working with hashes, implementing rate limiting, comparing pipelining and Lua scripting, error handling, and caching complex computations. The basic Lua script format is recapped, and then expanded into reusable patterns that can simplify application logic as well as reduce round trips.

High Availability, Replication, and Failover

Chapter 8. Mastering Redis Replication - Part 1

High availability begins with replication. This chapter explains how Redis replication works conceptually, shows how to set up a basic master-replica configuration, and reviews key replication settings in *redis.conf*. Readers learn how to verify replication status, and understand the overall replication flow from master to replica.

Chapter 9. Mastering Redis Replication – Part 2

Building on Part 1, this chapter introduces Redis Sentinel for automatic failover. It walks through setting up Sentinel, testing automatic failover, using replicas for read scaling, and dealing with common issues. The chapter closes with advanced tips and best practices based on real operational experience, helping readers design resilient setups.

Scaling Horizontally with Clustering and Sharding

Chapter 10. Redis Clustering and Sharding for Scalability and Availability

This chapter explains Redis Cluster from the ground up: core architecture, hash slots, and sharding behavior. It guides readers through setting up a Redis Cluster step-by-step, adding and removing nodes, and understanding failover and high availability in cluster mode. Additional sections cover securing Redis cluster communication, client-side behavior, handling redirection (MOVED and ASK), limitations and trade-offs, monitoring and maintenance, performance tuning for large-scale clusters, and best practices.

Keeping Redis Healthy When Things Go Wrong

Chapter 11. Troubleshooting Redis Issues

No production system is free from problems. This chapter introduces a structured approach to troubleshooting Redis. Topics include connection and authentication issues, performance and resource problems, including data integrity and consistency concerns. A dedicated section addresses cluster and advanced scenarios such as network partitions, replication lag, and Lua scripting pitfalls. The chapter concludes with guidance on analyzing Redis logs and metrics to identify the root causes quickly and reliably.

Redis in the Cloud and Beyond

Chapter 12. Running Redis on Cloud Platforms

Modern deployments often run Redis in the cloud using managed services. This chapter explores how to set up and configure Redis on major cloud platforms such as: Amazon Web Services (ElastiCache), Google Cloud Platform (MemoryStore), and Microsoft Azure (Azure Cache for Redis). It explains the basics of each managed offering, and compares managed versus self-hosted Redis in the cloud, highlighting trade-offs, and helping readers choose what best fits their environment.

Chapter 13. Best Practices and Advanced Use Cases

The final chapter brings the journey together. It presents advanced Redis use cases and best practices for running Redis in production. It also introduces Redis 8, highlighting new features and enhancements that are relevant for modern applications. A dedicated section covers backing up Redis and protecting critical data, including backup validation. The book then closes with the "Final Words: Closing the Book, Opening Possibilities," shifting the focus from the content to how readers can apply what they have learned in their own systems and careers.

DID YOU KNOW

Did you know that Orange Education Pvt Ltd offers eBook versions of every book published, with PDF and ePub files available? You can upgrade to the eBook version at **www.orangeava.com** and as a print book customer, you are entitled to a discount on the eBook copy. Get in touch with us at: **info@orangeava.com** for more details.

At **www.orangeava.com**, you can also read a collection of free technical articles, sign up for a range of free newsletters, and receive exclusive discounts and offers on Print Books and eBooks.

PIRACY

If you come across any illegal copies of our works in any form on the internet, we would be grateful if you would provide us with the location address or website name. Please contact us at **info@orangeava.com** with a link to the material.

ARE YOU INTERESTED IN AUTHORING WITH US?

If there is a topic that you have expertise in, and you are interested in either writing or contributing to a book, please write to us at **business@orangeava.com**. We are on a journey to help developers and tech professionals to gain insights on the present technological advancements and innovations happening across the globe and build a community that believes Knowledge is best acquired by sharing and learning with others. Please reach out to us to learn what our audience demands and how you can be part of this educational reform. We also welcome ideas from tech experts and help them build learning and development content for their domains.

REVIEWS

Please leave a review. Once you have read and used this book, why not leave a review on the site that you purchased it from? Potential readers can then see and use your unbiased opinion to make purchase decisions. We at Orange Education would love to know what you think about our products, and our authors can learn from your feedback. Thank you!

For more information about Orange Education, please visit **www.orangeava.com**.

Table of Contents

CHAPTER 1

Introduction to Redis and Its Core Concepts

Introduction

In this chapter, we will address Redis and its key aspects. This includes exploring how Redis distinguishes itself from other NoSQL databases, while highlighting its unique strengths and advantages. Then, we will take an in-depth look at Redis architecture, and uncover the key mechanisms behind its impressive speed and performance. By the end of this chapter, you will have a clear understanding of how Redis functions, why it is exceptionally fast, and why developers around the world rely on it for a wide range of applications. Finally, we will discuss how mastering Redis can be a transformative skill, whether your goal is to enhance application performance, manage data more effectively, or build real-time systems.

Structure

This chapter will cover the following topics:

- Exploring Redis
- Benefits of Learning Redis
- Redis Core Concepts and Ecosystem Overview
- Comparing Redis with Other Databases
    - Redis and RDBMS
    - Redis and other NoSQL Databases

Exploring Redis

Redis, short for **Remote Dictionary Server**, is an open-source data structure server designed for efficient storage and management of various data structures. **It belongs to the NoSQL database category, which is known as key-value stores**. This is where data is organized into key-value pairs. Each key acts as a unique identifier, and is used to retrieve the corresponding value, which can be of different types supported by Redis. This structure is known for its simplicity and speed, which makes Redis a great choice for applications that need quick data lookups and flexible data management.

One of the standout features of Redis is its exceptional speed. This performance comes from **storing and serving data directly from memory (RAM)**, which is significantly faster than using traditional disk storage. While Redis does offer data durability by persisting data to disk, all read operations are handled from the in-memory copy, while allowing real-time data access.

Because of its fast access capabilities, **Redis is commonly used as a cache**. In this role, it temporarily stores frequently accessed data, enabling faster retrieval and improving the overall performance of applications that rely on immediate access to data.

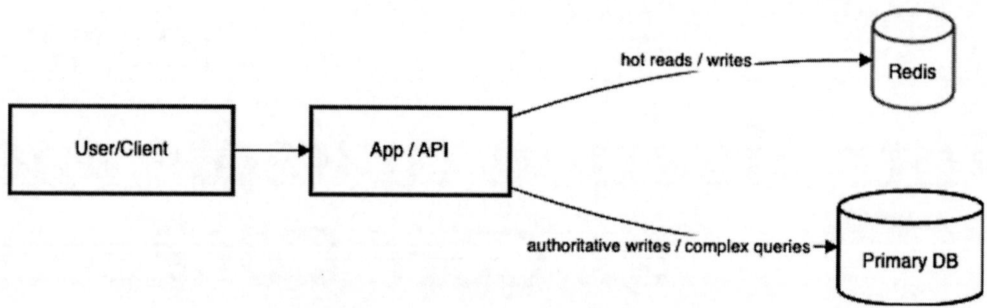

***Figure 1.1**: Where Redis Fits in a Typical Stack*

Benefits of Learning Redis

In today's world, where everything moves fast and data is at the heart of it all, managing information efficiently and in real time is more important than ever. That is where Redis comes in. As a high-speed, **in-memory data store**, Redis is perfect for handling the kind of demands modern applications need, whether it is lightning-fast data access, real-time analytics, or handling massive amounts of traffic. Learning Redis gives you the tools to boost your application's performance and tackle some of the biggest challenges in today's tech landscape with ease.

Exceptional Speed

One of Redis's defining features is its incredible speed. Unlike traditional databases that store data on disk and rely on frequent reads and writes to slower storage systems, **Redis stores all its data in memory** (**RAM**). This design allows Redis to access and modify data almost instantaneously, which results in sub-millisecond response times.

This speed is critical for real-time applications where delays in data processing can lead to poor user experiences. For example:

- **Web applications use Redis to manage session data**, while ensuring that a user's interactions are processed instantly without delays.
- Gaming leaderboards leverage **Redis to update scores in real-time,** and give players immediate feedback.
- Financial platforms use **Redis to handle real-time analytics to enable** instant decisions and insights, such as in algorithmic trading or fraud detection.

Additionally, Redis's **single-threaded** event-driven model ensures that each operation completes without the overhead of multiple threads competing for resources. This makes Redis extremely efficient for handling thousands of requests per second, which is why it is commonly used in high-traffic systems where performance is paramount. With **sub-millisecond latency**, Redis not only enhances user experience but also enables applications to scale and remain responsive under heavy loads. This makes it the go-to choice for developers building real-time, high-performance systems.

Versatile Data Structures

Redis is incredibly versatile because it supports a variety of data structures beyond just simple key-value pairs. You can use Redis to store not only plain text or numbers, but also complex data like lists, sets, and hashes. For example, you can use lists to manage ordered data like a to-do list, sets to handle unique items such as user IDs, and hashes to store objects with multiple fields like user profiles. This variety allows Redis to tackle a wide range of tasks, from simple data storage to complex operations like ranking and real-time analytics, all in a way that is both flexible and efficient.

Scalability and High Availability

Redis excels in scalability and high availability, which makes it a robust solution for large-scale and mission-critical applications.

- **Scalability: For scalability, Redis supports clustering**, which allows you to distribute data across multiple servers. This means that as your application grows and requires more capacity, you can easily add more nodes to the cluster to handle increased load and store more data. Redis also features automatic data sharding that splits the data across different nodes, while ensuring that no single node becomes a bottleneck.
- **High Availability:** In terms of high availability, **Redis provides replication and failover mechanisms**. You can set up one or more replicas of a primary Redis instance to create a redundant system. If the primary fails, one of the replicas can be promoted to primary automatically, which ensures that your data remains accessible and minimizes downtime. **Redis Sentinel**, a built-in high-availability solution, monitors your Redis instances, handles failover, and provides automated recovery processes. These features collectively ensure that Redis remains reliable and performs well, even as your application's demands increase or in the event of server failures

Efficient Caching

Redis is highly effective as a caching layer due to its in-memory storage and rapid access speeds. Caching involves storing copies of frequently accessed data in a fast, temporary storage system to reduce the load on primary databases and improve response times. Redis excels at this because it keeps all data in RAM, which allows for extremely quick retrieval compared to traditional disk-based storage.

In practical terms, this means that Redis can cache the results of complex queries, user sessions, or API responses, which enables your application to access this data almost instantly rather than repeatedly querying a slower database. For example, a web application might use Redis to cache user profiles, so every time a profile is requested, it can be fetched from Redis rather than reloaded from a slower database. Additionally, Redis supports various eviction policies (**like LRU - Least Recently Used or LFU - Least Frequently Used**) to manage memory efficiently, while automatically removing old or less frequently accessed data as needed.

This efficient caching capability reduces database load, speeds up application performance, and enhances user experience by providing faster access to data.

Real-Time Analytics

Redis is great for real-time analytics because it handles large amounts of data super quickly. Since it stores everything in memory, it can process and retrieve data almost instantly. This is perfect for applications that need up-to-the-minute insights and updates.

With Redis, you can easily manage and analyze data that is time-sensitive, like tracking user activity on a website or monitoring live performance metrics. For example, Redis can keep track of the number of active users or update real-time stats with ease. It uses data structures like sorted sets and HyperLogLog to help with these tasks. Sorted sets help rank and query data efficiently, making them ideal for things like leaderboards. HyperLogLog is great for counting unique items, like visitors, as they do not use much memory.

Redis also has a **feature called Streams** that is designed for handling continuous data flows. This lets you manage and process logs or event streams in real-time, thereby making it easy to create data pipelines that can handle data as it comes in.

Overall, Redis's speed and advanced data structures make it a powerful tool for performing complex analytics and providing real-time insights quickly, which is crucial when you need immediate data processing.

Lightweight and Easy to Use

Redis is known for being both lightweight and easy to use, which makes it an attractive choice for developers looking for a straightforward, high-performance data store.

- **Lightweight:** Redis has a minimalist design that keeps it simple and efficient. It does not require heavy dependencies or complex configurations, which implies that it can run smoothly on modest hardware. This lightweight nature allows Redis to start up quickly and use minimal system resources. This is ideal for applications where performance and responsiveness are critical.
- **Easy to Use:** Redis is designed with user-friendliness in mind. Its commands are simple and intuitive, which makes it easy for developers to interact with the database. For example, commands like **SET** and **GET** are straightforward for basic operations, while more advanced features like lists, sets, and sorted sets are also easy to learn and use. The Redis documentation is comprehensive and well-organized as it provides clear examples and explanations that help users get up to speed quickly.

Additionally, Redis's configuration is straightforward, with a single configuration file that allows for easy adjustments to settings. Its client libraries are available for almost every major programming language and allow developers to integrate Redis seamlessly into their existing tech stacks without significant overhead.

Overall, Redis's lightweight nature and ease of use mean that developers can deploy it quickly, maintain it easily, and focus on building and scaling their applications without getting bogged down by complex database management tasks.

Broad Language Support

Redis boasts broad language support, which makes it highly adaptable and accessible for developers working with different programming environments. This wide compatibility is a key factor in Redis's popularity and utility.

Redis provides client libraries for nearly every major programming language, including but not limited to **Python, JavaScript, Java, Ruby, PHP, C#, Go, and C++**. This extensive support ensures that developers can seamlessly integrate Redis into their applications, regardless of the programming language they are using. Each client library is designed to interact with Redis's core functionalities while adhering to the conventions of the respective language, which makes it easy to work with Redis's data structures and commands.

For instance:

- **Python:** The `redis-py` library is a popular choice that supports a range of Redis features and integrates well with Python applications.
- **JavaScript:** The `ioredis` and `node-redis` libraries provide robust solutions for Node.js applications and allow for easy asynchronous operations.
- **Java:** Libraries like **Jedis** and **lettuce** offer comprehensive support for Java applications, which cater to different performance needs and API preferences.

- **PHP:** The **`PhpRedis`** extension is a commonly used library for PHP, which provides a fast and feature-rich way to interact with Redis.

In addition to official libraries, **there are community-supported and third-party libraries that extend Redis's reach to more niche or emerging languages**. This ensures that even as new programming languages and frameworks emerge, Redis remains a viable option for a wide range of projects.

Overall, Redis's broad language support means developers can leverage its powerful capabilities across various platforms and ecosystems, facilitating easier adoption and integration into diverse development environments.

Industry-Wide Adoption

Redis has achieved widespread adoption across various industries due to its robust performance, reliability, and versatility. Many leading companies rely on Redis to power critical aspects of their systems and applications, which further demonstrates its effectiveness and trustworthiness.

- **E-Commerce:** Online retail giants and e-commerce platforms utilize Redis to enhance user experience by speeding up search queries, personalizing recommendations, and managing shopping cart data. Companies like Shopify leverage Redis to handle large volumes of concurrent user interactions and maintain responsive user interfaces.
- **Financial Services:** In the finance sector, Redis is employed for real-time transaction processing, fraud detection, and analytics. Its ability to handle high-speed data operations makes it ideal for trading platforms and financial applications where milliseconds matter.
- **Gaming:** The gaming industry benefits from Redis's ability to manage real-time leaderboards, player statistics, and session data.
- **Media and Entertainment:** Streaming services and media platforms use Redis to cache content, manage user sessions, and provide personalized recommendations.
- **Healthcare:** In healthcare, Redis supports applications that require real-time processing of patient data, management of electronic health records, and analysis of medical imaging. Its speed and reliability contribute to better patient outcomes and streamlined operations.
- **IoT and Smart Devices:** Redis's ability to handle high-velocity data streams makes it suitable for Internet of Things (IoT) applications. It helps in managing real-time data from sensors and devices, while supporting applications that need immediate insights and responses.

Overall, Redis's industry-wide adoption highlights its versatility and effectiveness in addressing diverse requirements across different sectors. Its proven track record with some of the world's leading companies underscores its capability to handle high-performance demands and complex data management challenges.

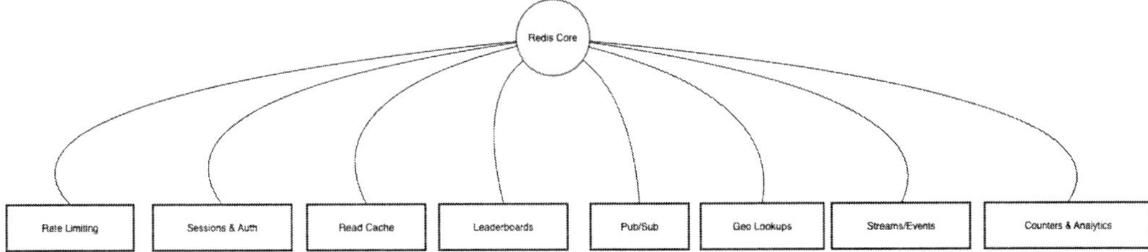

Figure 1.2: *Common Redis Use Cases at a Glance*

Redis Core Concepts and Ecosystem Overview

Redis architecture is built to deliver exceptional performance, flexibility, and scalability, which makes it ideal for a wide range of use cases. At its core, Redis executes core command processing in a single-threaded, event-driven model, but it is much more than that. Its architecture includes various components and features that expand its abilities to manage data efficiently, ensure persistence, and handle distributed workloads. In this section, we will break down the key aspects of Redis architecture to give you a clear understanding of how it works and why it is so effective for modern applications.

In-Memory Data Storage

Redis primarily stores data in memory (RAM), which allows for ultra-fast read and write operations. This in-memory approach is what gives Redis its sub-millisecond latency, thus making it ideal for real-time applications.

- **Data Durability:** While Redis stores data in memory, it can also persist data on disk through two methods:
- **Snapshot (RDB):** This method periodically creates snapshots of the dataset and stores them on disk. This method is fast but may lose some recent data during a crash.
- **AOF (Append-Only File):** This method logs every write operation in real-time, allowing Redis to recover the most recent dataset after a failure.
- **Combination:** Redis also offers a combination of both RDB and AOF to balance between performance and persistence.

Single-Threaded Event Loop

Redis uses a single-threaded event-driven model, which makes its execution path simple and predictable. This design allows Redis to handle thousands of operations per second without the overhead of context switching and thread synchronization found in multi-threaded systems.

Although Redis is single-threaded, its efficiency comes from the fact that it operates in memory and is optimized to perform operations quickly without blocking.

Data Structures

Redis offers a diverse range of data structures that extend its functionality beyond a simple key-value store. It supports Strings for basic text, numbers, or binary data; Lists for ordered collections useful in queues or tasks; Sets for unique, unordered items ideal for memberships or tags; Sorted Sets for ranking data with associated scores, perfect for leaderboards; Hashes for field-value pairs, suitable for objects or user profiles; Bitmaps and HyperLogLog for efficient memory use in tasks like counting unique elements or bit-level operations; and Streams for managing real-time log-like data flows. This variety enables Redis to handle a wide array of complex data management scenarios.

Replication

Redis supports primary-replica replication, where data is copied asynchronously from a primary node to one or more replica nodes. This allows for redundancy, load balancing, and failover capabilities.

Primary: This is the primary node that handles all write operations.

Replica: These are replicas of the primary node, which handle read-only queries. Replicas can be promoted to primary in the event of a failure.

Redis Clustering

Redis offers horizontal scaling through clustering, where the dataset is partitioned across multiple Redis nodes. This allows Redis to handle larger datasets and higher throughput.

Sharding

Data is automatically divided among multiple nodes in the cluster. Each node holds a subset of the data, which helps in scaling Redis horizontally without overloading any single node.

Cluster Management: Redis Cluster automatically manages failover, while ensuring that the system remains highly available even if some nodes fail.

Redis Sentinel

Redis Sentinel is a system designed to monitor Redis instances, provide automatic failover, and notify when failures occur. If the primary node goes down, Sentinel will promote one of the replica nodes to the primary, ensuring minimal downtime.

Monitoring: Sentinel continuously checks the health of primary and replica nodes.

Automatic Failover: If the primary fails, Sentinel will elect a new primary and redirect traffic to it.

Notification: Alerts admins of any issues in the Redis environment.

Note: *Redis Sentinel is used with standalone or replicated Redis setups and is not used with Redis Cluster, which has its own built-in failover mechanism.*

Security

Redis includes several security features such as **access control lists** (ACLs), password-based authentication, and TLS encryption for secure communication between Redis instances and clients. This ensures that data is protected, especially in sensitive applications.

Pub/Sub Messaging

Redis supports a publish/subscribe messaging system that enables real-time communication between different parts of an application. Clients can subscribe to channels, and when a message is published to the channel, all subscribers receive it instantly. This is useful for notifications, chat applications, and real-time event-driven architectures.

Note: *Redis Pub/Sub is not durable and does not guarantee delivery. For replayable or reliable messaging, Redis Streams should be used.*

Redis Modules

Redis is extensible via modules, which allow developers to add custom functionalities to Redis without modifying the core. Popular modules include:

- **`RedisGraph`:** A graph database module for handling complex graph data
- **`RediSearch`:** A full-text search engine for searching through large datasets
- **`RedisJSON`:** Enables handling and querying JSON data directly within Redis

- **RedisTimeSeries**: Specifically designed for handling time-series data

In summary, Redis's architecture is designed to be fast, scalable, and highly available. Its in-memory nature, flexible data structures, and robust support for replication, clustering, and persistence make it a powerful tool for a variety of applications like real-time analytics and caching.

Comparing Redis with Other Databases

When you are deciding on a database for your project, it can feel overwhelming with all the options out there. From traditional relational databases like MySQL and PostgreSQL to newer NoSQL options like MongoDB and Cassandra, each one has its own strengths. Redis stands out because it is an in-memory key-value store, known for being incredibly fast and flexible. But how does Redis really compare to these other databases?

In this section, we will break it down in simple terms, so you can understand where Redis excels, where it might fall short, and when it makes sense to choose it for your project. By comparing Redis with other databases, you will have a clearer idea of whether it is the right choice for what you need.

Redis and RDBMS

Before we delve into the comparison between Redis and RDBMS, it is important to understand what an RDBMS is. **Relational Database Management System (RDBMS)** is a type of database management system that stores data in a **structured, tabular format.**

Redis and Relational Database Management Systems (RDBMS) fundamentally differ in their data storage and access methodologies. Redis is an **in-memory data structure** store that prioritizes speed, keeping data in RAM to facilitate rapid access. On the other hand, RDBMSs use disk-based storage with a structured schema consisting of tables, rows, and columns, and rely on SQL for handling complex queries and maintaining data integrity.

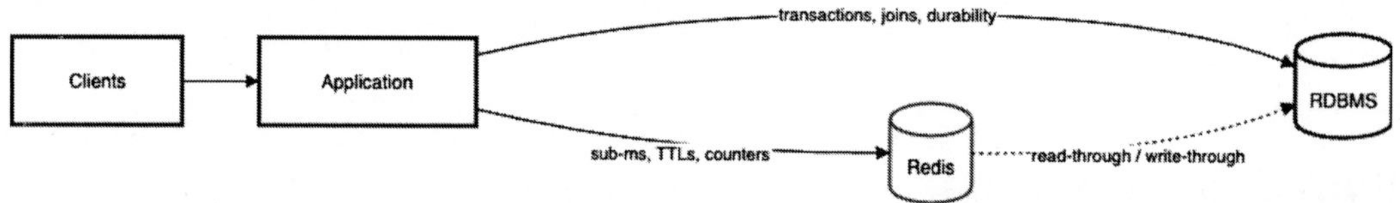

***Figure 1.3**: Redis vs RDBMS: Roles in One Architecture*

There are many differences between Redis and RDBMS, but let us focus on the key distinctions:

Redis	RDBMS
Stores data primarily in memory (**RAM**)	Stores data on **disk**
Uses a **key-value** data model and supports various in-memory data structures	Uses a **tabular** data model with structured tables, rows, and columns
Does not use **SQL**	Uses **SQL** (Structured Query Language)
Is **schemaless**	Uses a **fixed schema**
Does not enforce **referential integrity**	Supports **referential integrity**

***Table 1.1:** Redis vs RDBMS*

When to Choose Redis Instead of an RDBMS

Use Redis when your workload is real-time, simple to model, and throughput/latency are the top priorities:

- **Ultra-Low Latency Reads/Writes (<1ms)**: Personalization, ad targeting, feature flags, gaming state
- **Caching Hot Data**: Query results, rendered pages, computed views to offload your primary DB
- **Ephemeral/Session State**: Login sessions, OAuth tokens, shopping carts, rate windows with TTLs
- **Rate Limiting and Counters**: API throttling, quotas, download limits (atomic INCR/EXPIRE)
- **Real-Time Rankings**: Leaderboards, scoreboards, "`most viewed/liked`" (Sorted Sets)
- **Lightweight Messaging and Eventing**: Fan-out notifications, live feeds (Pub/Sub), or Streams for durable pipelines
- **Streaming Analytics and Sketches**: Approximate counts and top-K, percentiles (HyperLogLog, Top-K, TDigest)
- **Geospatial Lookups**: Nearby stores/drivers with modest query complexity (GEO* commands)
- **Distributed Coordination**: Locks, semaphores, queues, once-only tasks (with care for correctness)
- **Read Scaling with Replicas**: Offload reads and place replicas close to users

Rule of Thumb: Pick Redis when you need speed, TTLs, and real-time features, and your data does not require complex joins or strict relational constraints. Keep an RDBMS for durable, relational, transactional data and **combine the two when you want the best of both.**

Redis and Other NoSQL Databases

Since our primary focus is on Redis, we will not dive deeply into other NoSQL databases. However, it is important to have a basic understanding of the key concepts and types of NoSQL databases to put Redis into context and better appreciate its role and features.

NoSQL databases differ significantly from traditional relational databases in several ways. The term NoSQL stands for **"Not Only SQL"** indicating that these databases do not rely on the structured, SQL-based relational model for storing and retrieving data. Instead, NoSQL databases offer more flexible approaches to data storage, which makes them better suited for handling unstructured or semi-structured data, scaling easily, and accommodating high-volume applications. By understanding the general characteristics of NoSQL databases, we can better understand why Redis, as a key-value store, fits into this category and how it differs from other database solutions.

Types of NoSQL

Before we get into the different types of NoSQL databases, let us quickly go over what makes NoSQL different from the traditional databases you might be more familiar with. Unlike relational databases, which store data in tables with rows and columns, NoSQL databases are much more flexible. They can store data in various formats, which makes them ideal for handling large amounts of messy or unstructured data. NoSQL databases are also designed to easily scale up and manage lots of traffic, which is why they are so popular in today's fast-paced applications. In the next sections, we will break down the main types of NoSQL databases, while explaining their strengths and when it makes sense to use each one. This will help you figure out which type of NoSQL database might be the best fit for your needs.

Here is an introduction to the different types of NoSQL databases:

- **Key-Value Stores:** Key-value stores are a type of NoSQL database where data is stored as a collection of key-value pairs. Each key is unique, and it is used to retrieve the associated value. This simple model allows for efficient data retrieval and is well-suited for applications requiring high-speed access to discrete pieces of data. Key-value stores are commonly used for caching, session management, and real-time data processing.

  Examples of key-value stores **include Redis and Amazon DynamoDB.**

- **Document Stores:** Document stores are a type of NoSQL database that stores data in flexible, semi-structured formats, typically JSON, BSON, or XML. Each document is a self-contained unit of data that can have a dynamic schema, which allows for varied and evolving data structures. This model supports complex querying and indexing and is suitable for applications with diverse and nested data. Document Stores are commonly used for content management systems, user profiles, and catalogs.

  Examples of document stores include MongoDB and CouchDB.

- **Columnar Stores:** Columnar stores are a type of NoSQL database that organizes data by columns rather than rows. This format is optimized for read-heavy operations and analytics, as it allows for efficient querying and aggregation of large datasets. By storing data in columns, these databases can quickly access and process specific attributes without scanning entire rows. Columnar Stores are commonly used in data warehousing, business intelligence, and large-scale analytical applications.

  Examples of columnar stores include ClickHouse and Vertica.

- **Graph Databases:** Graph databases are a NoSQL database designed to handle and query data with complex relationships. They store data as nodes (entities) and edges (relationships), while enabling efficient exploration and analysis of interconnected data. This model is ideal for applications that require deep relationship analysis, such as social networks, recommendation engines, and fraud detection.

  Examples of graph databases include Neo4j and Amazon Neptune.

- **Multi-Model Databases:** Multi-model databases are NoSQL databases that support multiple data models within a single database engine. This versatility allows users to work with different data types such as documents, graphs, key-value pairs, and columns, all in one system. Multi-model databases provide flexibility and enable complex use cases by integrating various data handling capabilities.

  Examples of multi-model databases include ArangoDB and Couchbase.

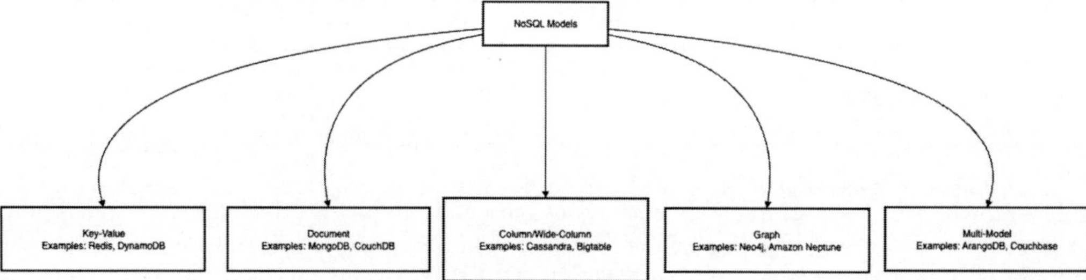

Figure 1.4: *NoSQL Landscape by Model*

When to Choose Redis Instead of Other NoSQL Databases

Pick Redis (among NoSQL options) when:

- You need sub-millisecond responses for hot paths (sessions, feature flags, carts, rate limits, leaderboards).
- Data is short-lived or lifecycle-driven (TTL/expiry first-class) and exists as tokens, windows, locks, and ephemeral state.
- You rely on atomic counters and real-time math (INCR, INCRBYFLOAT, HyperLogLog, Top-K, TDigest) for quotas, trending, and percentiles.
- Ranking and real-time ordering matter (Sorted Sets) for scoreboards, "`most viewed`," and top-N feeds.
- Lightweight messaging/pipelines fit (Pub/Sub, Streams) without operating a separate broker.
- Simple geo lookups are enough (GEO radius/box) without complex geospatial analytics.
- Operational simplicity (small footprint, easy replication, managed cloud options) is a priority.
- (Optional with Redis Stack) You want JSON + secondary search + vector search in the same runtime.

Prefer another NoSQL when:

- You need rich ad-hoc queries/aggregations over large JSON docs (document stores like MongoDB).
- You require massive, long-retention time-series writes/reads with disk-oriented economics (wide-column stores like Cassandra, or TS-focused engines).
- Your workload is relationship-heavy (multi-hop graph traversals, path queries) → graph databases (for example, Neo4j).
- Your dataset vastly exceeds RAM, and ultra-low latency is not required; a disk-first NoSQL will be more cost-efficient.

Rule of Thumb: Among NoSQL choices, choose Redis when the win comes from speed, expirations, atomic primitives, and real-time ranking/messaging; choose a document/column/graph store when you need deeper querying, very large disk-resident data, or complex relationships.

Comparison of Redis with Some Popular NoSQL

When you are choosing a NoSQL database for your project, it is important to compare the options to make sure you are picking the right one. Redis is often praised for its speed and simplicity as an in-memory key-value store, but other NoSQL databases like MongoDB, Cassandra, and Neo4j offer their own unique advantages. For example, MongoDB is great for storing documents, Cassandra excels at handling huge amounts of distributed data, and Neo4j is known for its ability to manage complex relationships using graph-based storage.

By comparing Redis with these popular alternatives, you will get a clearer picture of how each one performs in terms of speed, scalability, and how well they fit different types of projects. This way, you can make a more informed decision about which database will work best for your needs.

Here are some basic comparisons to help you better understand the differences:

- **Redis and MongoDB**

Redis	MongoDB
In-memory storage with on-disk persistence	**On-disk storage** by default
Key-value store	BSON (**Binary JSON**) documents
Supports atomic operations and transactions (MULTI/EXEC), but **does not support traditional rollback**. Rollback must be managed in the application code	**Supports ACID transactions,** including multi-document transactions with rollback.

Table 1.2: *Redis vs MongoDB*

- **Redis and Cassandra**

Redis	Cassandra
Key-value store	**Wide-column** store
The server-side scripting in Redis is done through **Lua**	There is **no server-side scripting** in Cassandra
Does not support **MapReduce**; relies on in-memory structures and external processing	Integrates with **Hadoop/Spark ecosystems for MapReduce-style analytics**

Table 1.3: *Redis vs Cassandra*

- **Redis and Neo4j**

Redis	Neo4j
Key-value store	The primary database model is a **Graph DBMS**
Does not use **foreign keys**	Uses **explicit relationships between nodes**
Atomic operations; supports transactions via MULTI/EXEC, but without traditional rollback.	Neo4j is **fully ACID-compliant**.

Table 1.4: *Redis vs Neo4j*

Conclusion

In this chapter, we have laid the groundwork for understanding Redis by exploring its core concepts and how it fits into the larger database landscape. We started by diving into what Redis is and compared it to other databases to show how Redis differs from traditional relational databases (RDBMS) and other NoSQL options. These comparisons highlight the unique strengths of Redis, such as its speed and flexibility, especially in handling real-time data. We also examined Redis architecture, giving you a peek into how its in-memory design makes it a powerful tool for performance-driven applications. Finally, we discussed the key benefits of learning Redis; while emphasizing why it is a valuable skill for developers looking to build modern, scalable systems.

By understanding these key aspects, you are now better equipped to see how Redis can be applied in various projects and why it stands out as a go-to solution for handling high-performance data tasks. This foundation will serve you well as we continue to explore more advanced topics in the chapters to come.

CHAPTER 2

Redis Data Structures and Their Uses

Introduction

In this chapter, we will take a deep dive into the fundamental data structures that form the backbone of Redis, which is a versatile and high-performance in-memory database. Redis provides a diverse set of data types, each specifically tailored to handle different use cases. It allows you to choose the best approach for your particular data storage and retrieval needs. Whether you are managing simple key-value pairs or more complex collections, Redis's rich selection of data structures enables you to build efficient, scalable, and high-performing applications. By understanding these core structures, you will gain the tools necessary to optimize your application's data handling, improving both speed and resource utilization.

We will thoroughly explore Redis's core data structures - **strings, hashes, lists, sets, and sorted sets,** unpacking their characteristics and demonstrating how to use them effectively. Strings serve as the simplest and most fundamental data type, while hashes allow you to store and retrieve field-value pairs, which are perfect for representing objects or storing metadata. Lists, sets, and sorted sets add further complexity and power, enabling more advanced operations such as sorting, ranking, and managing unique collections of data. By delving into each structure, you will learn not only how to implement them in your applications but also how to choose the right data type for different scenarios, which ensures that you can leverage Redis to its full potential.

By the end of this chapter, you will have a comprehensive understanding of Redis's data structures and will be equipped with the knowledge to apply them to a variety of practical data management challenges. Whether you are building real-time analytics platforms, caching solutions, or other data-intensive applications, this knowledge will empower you to tackle complex problems with confidence, while harnessing the full capabilities of Redis to enhance the performance and scalability of your systems.

Structure

This chapter will cover the following topics:

- Introduction to Redis Data Types
    - Strings
    - Sets
    - Sorted Sets
    - Lists
    - Hashes
    - Other Redis Data Types

Introduction to Redis Data Types

Redis offers a wide array of specialized data types, each designed to provide both flexibility and high performance when managing diverse forms of data. Unlike traditional databases, **Redis operates primarily in memory**, which allows for lightning-fast data access and manipulation. This in-memory nature gives Redis a significant edge in use cases where **speed and scalability are paramount**, such as real-time analytics, caching, message queuing, and high-throughput event processing. Its ability to handle massive volumes of data at incredible speeds makes it a go-to solution for modern, performance-intensive applications.

Each data type in Redis is crafted to solve specific challenges, while giving developers the freedom to select the most efficient structure for their needs. Whether it is simple key-value storage, managing complex sets of geospatial data, or processing streams of real-time events, Redis enables not just storage but optimized data handling. By leveraging Redis's advanced capabilities, developers can build systems that go beyond data storage to deliver enhanced performance and responsiveness.

With Redis's in-memory architecture and versatile data structures, you can create fast, scalable applications that efficiently manage both small and large datasets, while ensuring low-latency responses even under heavy loads. Understanding these data types unlocks the full potential of Redis and makes it a critical component in the development of high-performance systems.

Let us explore each data type in detail:

Strings

Strings are the most fundamental and versatile data type in Redis, and are capable of storing a sequence of bytes. This means they can accommodate a wide range of data formats, **including plain text, numbers, JSON objects, and even binary data such as images, videos, or serialized objects**. The flexibility of Redis Strings makes them an ideal choice for numerous use cases like simple caching, value storage, counting, managing user sessions, or supporting key-value APIs. With a **maximum size limit of 512 MB**, Redis Strings have ample capacity for handling large data payloads efficiently.

One of the key strengths of Redis is that its keys and string values are binary-safe, which implies that they can store and retrieve binary data without any risk of corruption. This ensures that non-text files or encoded objects are handled reliably, while preserving the integrity of the data throughout its lifecycle. Additionally, Redis offers a rich set of commands to manipulate string values, which can enable operations such as incrementing numeric values or appending new data. This combination of simplicity and power makes Redis Strings a highly effective tool for building fast, scalable systems that need to manage diverse data formats efficiently.

Try it:

```
# Store a single book ID & book name
redis-cli SET book:1001 "Redis Essentials"

# Retrieve the stored book name
redis-cli GET book:1001                    # -> "Redis Essentials"

# Store multiple books at once
redis-cli MSET book:1002 "High-Performance Redis" book:1003 "Redis Cookbook"

# Fetch multiple book names
redis-cli MGET book:1001 book:1003         # -> ["Redis Essentials","Redis Cookbook"]
```

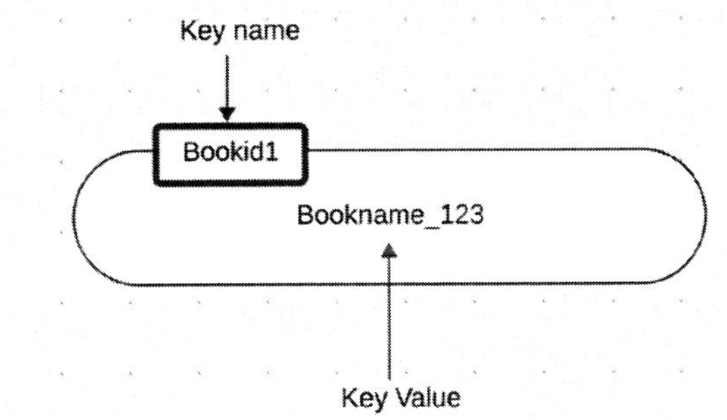

Figure 2.1: *An Example of a Redis String*

Key Features of Redis Strings

- **Simple Key-Value Storage:** Redis strings serve as a versatile **key-value** store, where each key is associated with a string value. These values can store a wide range of data types, including text, numbers, and even binary data, thereby making Redis strings ideal for various use cases.
- **Efficient Operations:** Redis strings support fast and efficient operations, such as incrementing values, appending data, and retrieving substrings. This efficiency makes strings particularly useful for tasks like **counting, caching, storing configuration settings, and managing tokens**.
- **Supports Binary Data:** Redis strings are **binary-safe**, meaning they can store any type of binary data, including images, videos, and serialized objects, without risk of data corruption. This flexibility ensures that Redis can handle both text and non-text data seamlessly.

Common Use Cases for Redis Strings

- **Caching Simple Key-Value Pairs:** Redis strings are ideal for caching straightforward key-value pairs, such as storing user session data or frequently accessed information.
- **Implementing Counters and Rate-Limiters:** With built-in support for atomic increment operations, Redis strings are perfect for creating counters, such as tracking page views, and for implementing rate-limiters to control the frequency of requests.
- **Storing and Retrieving Tokens or Short-Lived Data:** Redis strings are commonly used to store temporary data like tokens, one-time passwords (OTPs), or other short-lived information that needs fast access and quick expiration.
- **Caching Configuration Settings:** Simple configuration values can be efficiently cached using Redis strings, which makes them easily accessible for applications that need to retrieve settings frequently without querying a slower backend database.

Watch Out For:

- Very large values (hundreds of KB/MB) that consume RAM and slow the network. Prefer smaller values or store big blobs elsewhere and cache a pointer.
- Doing read-modify-write in your app can create race conditions. Use atomic commands like INCR, APPEND, and GETSET.

Summary

Redis strings provide a flexible and efficient way to store a wide range of data types, from simple text and numbers to complex binary data. Their versatility makes them an essential building block for various tasks, including caching, counting, session management, and even more advanced use cases like real-time analytics and token handling. Whether you are working with small data values or managing larger payloads, Redis strings offer the speed and reliability needed for high-performance, scalable applications. As a core data structure in Redis, they play a vital role in any system that demands fast, efficient data management.

Sets

Redis sets are a collection of unique strings, **meaning no duplicates are allowed**. They are perfect for storing data when each item must be distinct, like tracking user IDs, tags, or other unique values. Sets in Redis are highly efficient as they offer quick additions, removals, and membership checks in constant time, even with large datasets. This makes them ideal for use cases like managing collections of unique elements, handling memberships, or performing operations like intersection, union, and difference across multiple sets.

Another advantage of Redis sets is their ability to perform powerful set-based operations, such as calculating intersections or unions between different sets. This makes them particularly useful for tasks like finding common friends in social networks, recommending items, or filtering data based on multiple conditions. With their combination of speed, scalability, and built-in set operations, Redis sets offer a versatile solution for managing unique data efficiently.

Try it:

```
# Sets - Practical Example (books : book1, book2, book3)
# Add unique book names to a set
redis-cli SADD books book1 book2 book3

# List all books in the set (order not guaranteed)
redis-cli SMEMBERS books

# Count how many unique books are in the set
redis-cli SCARD books
```

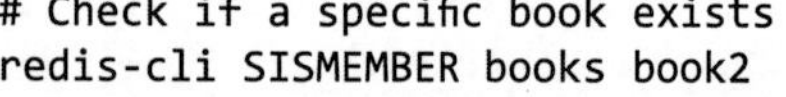

```
# Check if a specific book exists
redis-cli SISMEMBER books book2          # -> (integer) 1 means "present"
```

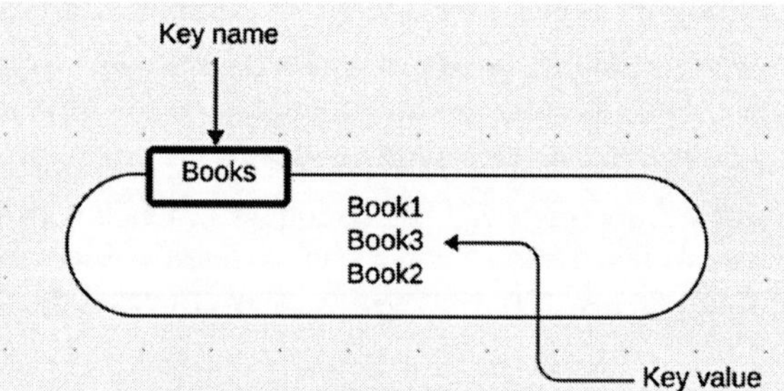

Figure 2.2: *An Example of a Redis Set*

Key Features of Redis Sets

- **Unique Elements:** Sets automatically ensure that every value is **unique**. If you try to add a duplicate, it is ignored. Therefore, you do not have to worry about repeats.

- **Unordered Collection:** Unlike lists, sets **do not keep the order of the elements**. When you add items to a set, they are stored without any particular sequence, and when you retrieve them, they may come back in a different order.
- **Fast Membership Checks:** Redis sets are great for quickly checking whether an item is already part of the set. This is useful for tasks like **managing unique IDs, ensuring no duplicates, or tracking who belongs to a group**.
- **Powerful Set Operations:** Redis comes with built-in commands to perform common set-based operations:
- **Union:** This combines two or more sets into one, while collecting all the unique elements.
- **Intersection:** This helps us find the elements that are shared between two or more sets.
- **Difference:** This identifies what is in one set but not in another. These operations are quick and efficient, even when you are dealing with large sets.
- **Random Operations:** Since sets are unordered, Redis allows you to retrieve or remove random elements. You can get a random item from the set or pop one out, which can be helpful for applications that need random selection, like picking winners in a raffle.
- **Scalability:** Redis sets can manage millions of unique elements without slowing down. Whether you are adding, removing, or checking if an item exists, Redis performs consistently well, even with large sets.
- **Memory Efficiency:** Redis optimizes the way sets are stored. Small sets use less memory, and larger sets are handled efficiently, so that they remain fast and do not consume too much memory.

Common Use Cases for Redis Sets

- **Storing Unique Items**: Redis Sets are ideal for storing collections where uniqueness is critical, such as user IDs, email addresses, or tags, ensuring that no duplicate entries exist.
- **Tagging Systems**: Sets are well-suited for implementing tagging or categorization systems, which enable you to efficiently group items under different tags.
- **Group Membership Management**: Redis Sets make it easy to manage group memberships and ensure that each member is unique, allowing for fast membership lookups and operations.
- **Social Networks**: In social media applications, Sets are perfect for representing relationships like followers or friends, while ensuring fast updates and retrieval of connections.
- **Real-Time Analytics**: Redis Sets are highly useful for tracking unique events in real-time, such as counting unique visitors or user actions, as they provide quick and accurate results for real-time metrics.

Basic Commands Used in Set Data Type in Redis

- **SADD**: This adds a new element to the set. If the element already exists, it will not be added again, which maintains the uniqueness of the set.
- **SREM**: This removes a specified element from the set, if it exists.

- **SISMEMBER**: This checks if a specific element is a member of the set, while returning a confirmation of its presence or absence.
- **SINTER**: This returns the intersection of two or more sets, while providing the elements that are common across all specified sets.
- **SCARD**: This returns the size of the set, while indicating the number of unique elements it contains.
- **SMEMBERS**: This retrieves all the members of the set stored at the specified key, allowing you to view the entire collection of unique elements.

Watch Out For:

- Big set operations (**SINTER, SUNION, SDIFF**) over large sets are costly; run off-peak or precompute results.
- Cardinality surprises: millions of members will use real memory, therefore keep an eye on SCARD and memory usage.

Summary

Redis Sets offer a powerful and efficient way to store collections of unique data. Whether you are dealing with small sets or large-scale datasets, they deliver fast performance while supporting advanced operations like unions, intersections, and differences. This versatility makes them ideal for a wide range of use cases, such as managing unique IDs, handling user permissions, tracking tags, and even more complex tasks like building recommendation systems, social networks, and real-time analytics. By ensuring data uniqueness and enabling efficient large-scale operations, Redis Sets provide a flexible and reliable solution for organizing and managing distinct data within your applications.

Sorted Sets

Redis sorted sets are a powerful variation of sets, where **each element is associated with a score**. This allows the elements to be **automatically ordered based on these scores**. Unlike regular sets, which are unordered, sorted sets maintain their elements in a precise, sorted sequence, which makes them an excellent choice for use cases that require ranking or prioritizing data. For instance, they are perfect for implementing leaderboards, tracking high scores in games, or managing ranking systems in competitive scenarios. Sorted sets are particularly valuable in cases where **you need to continuously update and retrieve items based on their priority or value**, with the elements dynamically sorted as new scores are assigned.

One of the key features of Redis sorted sets is that the scores are represented as floating-point numbers, which gives you fine-grained control over the ranking and order of elements. This allows for highly precise sorting and ensures that even minor changes in scores result in accurate positioning. Redis sorted sets also come with a rich set of operations, which consists of retrieving elements based on their rank, removing elements according to their score, and efficiently finding the top or bottom items within the set. These operations make sorted sets ideal not only for leaderboards, but also for scenarios like managing time-sensitive data, scheduling tasks based on priority, or handling any situation where ordered data needs to be queried flexibly.

With their ability to efficiently manage large datasets while maintaining optimal performance, Redis sorted sets are a crucial tool for real-time applications that require organized and ranked collections of data. Whether you are dealing with user rankings, scheduling systems, or other data that needs continuous sorting and retrieval, Redis sorted sets provide the functionality and scalability needed to handle complex, high-performance requirements.

Try it:

```
# Sorted Sets - Practical Example (books : book1=100, book2=200, book3=300)

# If you ran the Sets example earlier with key "books", delete it to avoid type
conflicts.
redis-cli DEL books

# Add books with scores (for example, popularity or ranking points)
redis-cli ZADD books 100 book1 200 book2 300 book3   # -> (integer) 3

# View all books in ascending score order
redis-cli ZRANGE books 0 -1 WITHSCORES
# -> 1) "book1" 2) "100" 3) "book2" 4) "200" 5) "book3" 6) "300"

# View all books in descending score order (top first)
redis-cli ZREVRANGE books 0 -1 WITHSCORES
# -> 1) "book3" 2) "300" 3) "book2" 4) "200" 5) "book1" 6) "100"

# Check a specific book's score
redis-cli ZSCORE books book2
# -> "200"
```

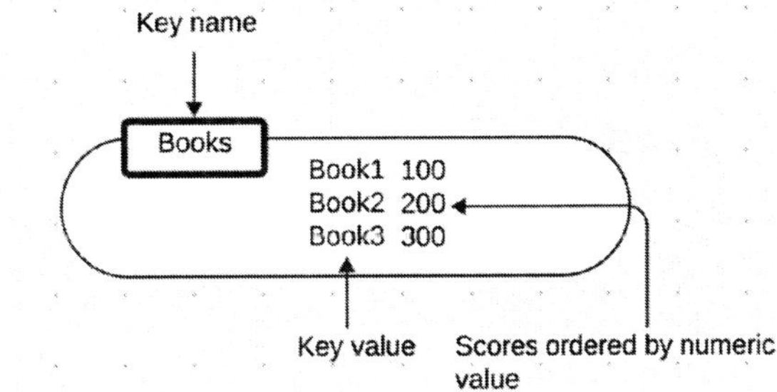

Figure 2.3: *A Redis Sorted Set*

Key Features of Redis Sorted Sets

- **Score-Based Sorting:** Every element in a sorted set has an associated score. The elements are automatically sorted by these scores, so you can easily access the highest or lowest scores, or retrieve a range of elements based on their scores.
- **Unique Elements:** Each element in the sorted set is unique, although multiple elements can have the same score. The uniqueness applies to the elements themselves, not their scores.
- **Efficient Retrieval by Score:** Sorted sets allow you to quickly fetch elements based on their scores. You can grab the top or bottom entries or even select elements that fall within a specific score range, all with minimal performance impact.
- **Rank-Based Access:** You can access elements by their rank in the set. For instance, you can retrieve the top 10 elements or find out the position of a specific element based on its score.
- **Score Updates:** When an element's score changes, Redis automatically updates the sorted set to reflect the new order. This makes sorted sets highly dynamic and well-suited for real-time applications.

- **Efficient Memory Usage:** Redis optimizes the way sorted sets are stored, so even with a large number of elements, operations like adding, removing, or updating items remain fast and memory-efficient.

Common Use Cases for Redis Sorted Sets

- **Leaderboards:** Sorted sets are often used in gaming or competitive apps to keep track of player scores and rankings in real-time. The automatic sorting makes it easy to display the top performers at any given moment.
- **Task Prioritization:** You can use sorted sets to manage tasks based on priority or deadlines. Tasks with higher priority or closer deadlines will naturally rise to the top, allowing you to handle them first.
- **Real-Time Analytics:** Sorted sets are great for tracking trends, like keeping a real-time list of the most popular products, most active users, or highest-performing metrics over time.
- **Event Scheduling:** Sorted sets can be used to store and retrieve events based on their scheduled times, as they can ensure that events are processed in the correct order.
- **Ranking Systems:** In applications where you need to continuously rank items (like users, products, or content) based on a specific metric, sorted sets provide a fast and efficient solution.

Basic Commands Used in Sorted Set Data Types in Redis

- **ZADD:** This adds an element to the sorted set with an associated score. If the element already exists, its score is updated.
- **ZRANGE:** This retrieves elements from the sorted set within a specified range, ordered by their scores in ascending order.
- **ZRANK:** This returns the rank (position) of a specified element in the sorted set, with the ranking based on the ascending order of scores.
- **ZREVRANK:** This returns the rank of a specified element in the sorted set, but in descending order, which shows its position based on reverse score ranking.

Watch Out For:

- Frequent score updates on huge leaderboards add CPU/memory overhead.
- Range queries return time grows with how many items you ask for. Do not fetch massive ranges in hot paths.
- Old items accumulate; **prune with ZREMRANGEBYSCORE or ZREMRANGEBYRANK.**

Summary

Redis Sorted Sets are a powerful and flexible data structure designed to manage data that requires storage in a specific order based on scores. Whether you are building leaderboards, scheduling tasks, or tracking real-time analytics, Sorted Sets offer an efficient solution for handling dynamic, ordered data. One of their key strengths is the ability to add, remove, or update elements while automatically maintaining the correct order based on their scores, which makes them ideal for real-time applications that need to manage ranked data or time-sensitive tasks.

In addition to their automatic sorting capabilities, Redis Sorted Sets allow for efficient querying. You can retrieve elements within specific score ranges or by their rank to get quick access to data in both ascending and descending orders. This makes Sorted Sets perfect for use cases like ranking systems, time-based event tracking, and complex querying scenarios where ordering is critical. By supporting fast insertion, deletion, and ranking operations, Redis Sorted Sets are an invaluable tool for managing ordered collections and ensuring your data remains accessible and organized even in high-performance environments.

Lists

Redis Lists are a versatile and fundamental data structure that allows you to store and manage ordered sequences of strings. They provide efficient and fast methods for adding, removing, and retrieving elements from both the beginning and the end of the list, making them ideal for a variety of use cases such as message queues, task scheduling systems, and real-time data pipelines. One of the key characteristics of Redis Lists is their **ability to maintain the exact order of elements as they are added**, which ensures that you can access data sequentially or in reverse order as needed. This is critical for processing data in a controlled, orderly fashion.

A significant advantage of Redis Lists is their ability to function as either a queue (FIFO) or a stack (LIFO), which gives developers the flexibility to implement diverse workflows based on their application requirements. Whether you need to process tasks in the order they are received (FIFO) or handle the most recent tasks first (LIFO), Redis Lists can accommodate both approaches seamlessly. Additionally, Redis Lists are optimized for performance, which allows for fast insertion and removal operations while working with large datasets. Operations like **LPUSH, RPUSH, LPOP, and RPOP** are designed to handle high-throughput scenarios efficiently. This makes them suitable for applications that demand real-time processing capabilities.

Redis also provides advanced commands like BLPOP and BRPOP, which enable blocking operations. These commands are particularly useful for scenarios where you need to wait for new data to be added to the list, allowing Redis Lists to power real-time systems, asynchronous processing, and task scheduling workflows. For instance, they can be used in messaging systems where consumers wait for new tasks or messages to appear in the list. The combination of speed, flexibility, and support for real-time operations makes Redis Lists a powerful and essential tool for building dynamic, high-performance applications that are capable of handling time-sensitive data and tasks.

Try it:

```
# Lists - Practical Example (books:list : book1, book2, book3)

# Using the same "books" theme as Sets/Sorted Sets, but a separate key to avoid type
conflicts.

# Create a list of books (append to tail)
redis-cli RPUSH books:list book1 book2 book3    # -> (integer) 3

# View the full list (0 -1 means all elements)
redis-cli LRANGE books:list 0 -1                # -> ["book1","book2","book3"]

# Add a book to the head (front) of the list
redis-cli LPUSH books:list book0                # -> (integer) 4
redis-cli LRANGE books:list 0 -1                # -> ["book0","book1","book2","book3"]

# Remove from the head (FIFO queue behavior)
redis-cli LPOP books:list                       # -> "book0"

# Remove from the tail (LIFO/stack behavior)
redis-cli RPOP books:list                       # -> "book3"
```

```
# Current length of the list
redis-cli LLEN books:list                  # -> for example, (integer) 2

# Get a specific item by index (0-based)
redis-cli LINDEX books:list 0              # -> "book1"
```

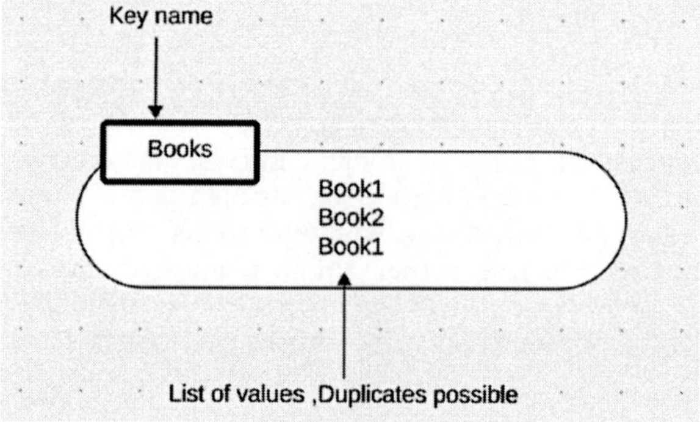

Figure 2.4: *A Redis List*

Key Features of Redis Lists

- **Maintains Order:** Lists keep track of the order in which you add elements, so you can easily retrieve them in the same order or reverse order when needed.
- **Fast Additions and Removals:** You can quickly add elements to either end of a list. Use **LPUSH to add items to the front** and **RPUSH to add them to the back**. Similarly, you can remove items from both ends using LPOP or RPOP. These operations are fast, no matter how large the list is.
- **Flexible Size:** Lists grow automatically as you add more elements, so you do not need to worry about setting a size limit. Redis handles it efficiently, even with millions of elements.
- **Get a Range of Elements:** With Redis, you can retrieve a specific range of items from the list using the LRANGE command. This is handy when you want to access a part of the list, like the first 10 elements or a section in the middle.
- **Works as Queues or Stacks:** Redis lists can act like a queue (where you add items at the end and remove them from the front) or a stack (where you push and pop items from the same end). This makes them versatile for different types of data processing.
- **Real-Time Operations:** Redis lists also support blocking commands, like BLPOP and BRPOP, which wait until new data is added before returning a result. This makes them perfect for real-time applications like message or task queues.
- **Efficient Use of Memory:** Redis stores lists in a compact way, so even when you have a large number of items, it optimizes memory usage to keep things running smoothly.
- **Access by Index:** You can access specific items in the list by their position with the LINDEX command. This is helpful if you need to retrieve an item from a particular spot in the list.

Common Use Cases for Redis Lists

- **Task Queues:** Redis Lists can be used to manage tasks in a job queue where tasks are added to one end of the list and processed from the other, while ensuring efficient task execution in a first-in, first-out (FIFO) manner.

- **Message Queues:** Lists are ideal for building messaging systems and process messages in the exact order they are received, maintaining the sequence for reliable communication.
- **Logs and Event Tracking:** Since Redis Lists preserve the order of elements, they are perfect for storing logs or tracking events that need to be recorded in a sequential manner.
- **Real-Time Data Streams:** Redis Lists are well-suited for handling real-time data streams such as chat messages or live feed updates, while ensuring that items are processed in the precise order they arrive, which is essential for real-time applications.

Basic Commands Used in List Data Structure in Redis

- **LPUSH**: Adds a new element to the head (beginning) of the list, which allows you to insert elements at the front
- **RPUSH**: Adds a new element to the tail (end) of the list, ensuring elements are appended to the back
- **LPOP**: Removes and returns the element from the head of the list, retrieving and removing the first element
- **RPOP**: Removes and returns the element from the tail of the list, retrieving and removing the last element
- **LLEN**: Returns the current length of the list, indicating how many elements are stored
- **LMOVE**: Moves an element from one list to another, allowing for automatic transfer between lists, either from the head or the tail
- **LTRIM**: Trims a list down to a specified range of elements, removing all elements outside the specified range, which is useful for managing list size

Watch Out For:

- Random access (LINDEX on long lists) is O(N) and can get slow.
- Unbounded lists grow forever as latency creeps up. Trim them regularly with LTRIM.
- Heavy blocking pops (BLPOP/BRPOP) with many consumers can become chatty; therefore, monitor latency.

Summary

Redis Lists provide a simple yet powerful way to manage ordered collections of data. With their ability to quickly add and remove items from both ends, Redis Lists can function as either queues or stacks, making them highly versatile for a wide range of applications. Whether you are handling task queues, logging events, or processing real-time data streams, Redis Lists offer a fast, flexible solution for organizing and managing your data efficiently. Their combination of speed and ease of use makes them an essential tool for applications requiring ordered data processing and real-time data management.

Hashes

Redis hashes are akin to small dictionaries or objects and allow you to store multiple field-value pairs under a single Redis key. This structure is particularly effective for organizing data with various attributes, such as user profiles or product details, where consolidating related information is beneficial. By encapsulating multiple fields within a single key, hashes provide a streamlined approach to managing complex data structures, thereby facilitating efficient storage and retrieval operations.

Each field within a Redis hash is a string, and together, they form a comprehensive data record. For example, to store a user's information, you might create a hash with fields like username, email, and age. This method enables you to access or modify individual attributes without affecting the entire data structure, while offering flexibility and precision in data management.

Moreover, Redis hashes are memory-efficient and provide fast access to individual fields. The number of fields you can include in a hash has no practical limits other than available memory, which makes them suitable for a wide range of applications.

Try it:

```
# Hashes - Practical Example (books:ID with fields: bookid, bookname)
# Optional: start clean
redis-cli DEL books:1001 books:1002 books:1003

# Create book records as hashes
redis-cli HSET books:1001 bookid 1001 bookname "Redis Essentials"            # -> 2
redis-cli HSET books:1002 bookid 1002 bookname "High-Performance Redis"      # -> 2
redis-cli HSET books:1003 bookid 1003 bookname "Redis Cookbook"              # -> 2

# Read a single field
redis-cli HGET books:1002 bookname                      # -> "High-Performance Redis"

# Read multiple fields at once
redis-cli HMGET books:1001 bookid bookname              # -> "1001" "Redis Essentials"

# Read all fields/values for a book
redis-cli HGETALL books:1003

# Update a field (rename a book)
redis-cli HSET books:1002 bookname "High-Performance Redis (2nd Edition)"
# -> 0 or 1 depending on overwrite
redis-cli HGET books:1002 bookname
# -> "High-Performance Redis (2nd Edition)"

# Check if a field exists
redis-cli HEXISTS books:1003 bookname                   # -> (integer) 1

# Remove a field (example)
redis-cli HDEL books:1003 bookname                      # -> (integer) 1
redis-cli HGETALL books:1003                            # shows remaining fields

# Delete an entire book record (hash)
redis-cli DEL books:1003                                # -> (integer) 1
```

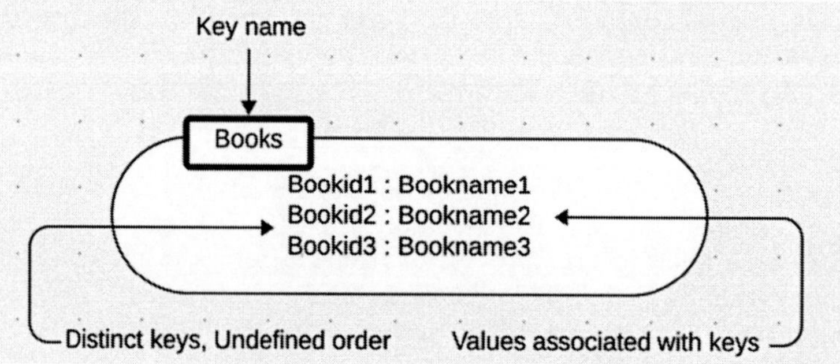

Figure 2.5: *An Example of a Redis Hash*

Key Features of Redis Hashes

- **Access Specific Fields:** With Redis hashes, you can work with individual fields without fetching the entire set of data. This means you can easily get, update, or delete specific values without touching other fields, which saves memory and improves performance.
- **Memory Efficiency**: Redis optimizes how hashes are stored, which makes them more efficient when you have many fields with small values. This is especially helpful for saving memory in large datasets.
- **Perfect for Storing Objects**: If you have data with multiple attributes, like a user's name, age, and email, Redis hashes provide a convenient and efficient way to store everything in one place.

Common Use Cases for Redis Hashes

- **Storing User Profiles:** Redis Hashes are ideal for storing structured data like user profiles, where fields such as name, age, and email are stored as individual key-value pairs within the hash.
- **Managing Product Details:** You can use Redis Hashes to manage product information and store attributes like product name, price, and stock levels efficiently. This allows for quick updates and retrieval.
- **Tracking App Settings or Configurations:** Redis Hashes are also well-suited for tracking application settings or configurations and enabling the storage and management of key-value pairs that represent different configuration options or preferences.

Basic Commands Used in Hash Data Structure in Redis

- **HSET**: Sets a field-value pair within the hash, while creating or updating the value associated with a given key
- **HGET**: Retrieves the value of a specified field from the hash, thus allowing for quick lookups
- **HMGET**: Returns multiple values for specified fields within the hash and enables efficient retrieval of multiple fields at once
- **HINCRBY**: Increments the value of a specified field by a given amount and is useful for counters or accumulating values within a hash

Watch Out For:

- Giant fields or many large values remove the memory savings of hashes.
- HGETALL on big hashes can be heavy. Fetch only the fields you need with HMGET.
- Very long field names waste memory; keep them short but clear.

Summary

Redis Hashes provide a simple and efficient way to store and manage structured data with multiple fields, such as user profiles or product details, all under a single key. They allow you to interact with individual fields, optimizing memory usage and enabling fast retrieval of specific information without fetching the entire data set. Whether you are building user management systems, tracking inventory, or managing application configurations, Redis Hashes offer a powerful solution for organizing and accessing structured data in real-time. Their flexibility, combined with Redis's in-memory speed, makes them ideal for applications that require frequent updates or partial data retrieval, ensuring both high performance and scalability.

Other Redis Data Types

In addition to the commonly used data types like Strings, Sets, Sorted Sets, Hashes, and Lists, Redis offers several specialized data types designed to handle more complex and specific use cases. These include **Bitmaps, Bitfields, HyperLogLog, Geospatial indexes, and Streams**. Each of these data types serves a unique purpose, allowing Redis to go beyond traditional database tasks and handle scenarios like approximate counting, geolocation-based queries, real-time event streams, and memory-efficient data storage. These advanced structures enable developers to tackle challenges such as efficiently tracking large datasets, managing geospatial information, or processing high-throughput streams of data. In this section, we will introduce these Redis data types, explain how they function, and explore practical examples of how they can be applied to solve various real-world problems, while adding more depth and flexibility to your Redis toolkit.

Bitmap

Although Redis **does not have a dedicated "bitmap" data type**, bitmaps are **implemented on top of strings**. They allow you to treat a string as a sequence of bits. This enables efficient bitwise operations and the ability to compactly store and manipulate large amounts of binary data, all within Redis's native string structure. Bitmaps are particularly useful for use cases like tracking user activity (for example, presence or absence on a given day), managing feature flags, or implementing high-performance counters where each bit represents a specific state (on or off).

One of the key advantages of using bitmaps is the ability to store vast amounts of binary data in a memory-efficient way, which makes them ideal for scenarios where you need to track millions of entries with minimal overhead. Redis provides commands like SETBIT, GETBIT, and BITCOUNT to manipulate and analyze bitmaps, which allows for quick and efficient querying. This makes bitmaps a powerful tool for applications that require fine-grained tracking or state management, all while maintaining Redis's speed and scalability.

Basic Commands Used in Bitmaps in Redis:

- **SETBIT**: Sets the value of a bit at a specific offset to either 0 or 1, while allowing you to manipulate individual bits in a string
- **GETBIT**: Retrieves the value of the bit at a given offset and enables you to check the state of a specific bit within the string
- **BITOP**: Performs bitwise operations (such as AND, OR, XOR, and NOT) on one or more strings, while enabling efficient manipulation of multiple bitmaps at once
- **BITCOUNT:** Counts the number of bits set to 1 in a given range, which is commonly used for analytics such as counting active users or flags

Bitfields

Bitfields in Redis offer a powerful way to manipulate and store compact binary data within a string. While Redis does not have a native "bitfield" data type, the BITFIELD command allows you to treat **strings as arrays of integers**, where each integer can have a specified bit width (ranging from 1 to 64 bits). This feature enables you to perform efficient bit-level manipulations, which makes Redis particularly useful for use cases that require packing and managing multiple integer values within a single string.

The flexibility of Redis bitfields is particularly valuable in scenarios where you need to efficiently store and modify small, fixed-width values, such as status flags, user permissions, or even gaming statistics. With commands like BITFIELD, you can easily set, get, or increment integer values within a string, all while maintaining minimal memory usage. This makes bitfields ideal for applications that require high-performance, low-memory solutions for storing and managing structured binary data.

Basic Commands Used in Bitfields in Redis:

- `BITFIELD`: Allows you to atomically set, increment, or read one or more integer values within a binary string and offers powerful bit-level operations within a compact structure
- `BITFIELD_RO`: A read-only variant of the **`BITFIELD`** command, which allows you to read values without modifying the data. This is useful when you need to retrieve bitfield values without altering the underlying binary string

HyperLogLog

The HyperLogLog is a specialized probabilistic data structure in Redis that allows you to **estimate the cardinality** (that is, the number of unique elements) of a large set without storing all the individual elements. This makes it extremely memory efficient, especially when dealing with massive datasets. HyperLogLog provides an approximate count of distinct elements with a small and predictable margin of error, which makes it ideal for use cases where exact precision is not necessary, but memory efficiency is critical.

This structure is particularly useful in scenarios like tracking the number of unique visitors to a website, counting unique actions in an application, or monitoring distinct events over a long period. Redis's implementation of HyperLogLog allows you to quickly compute these estimates while using minimal memory, even when the underlying dataset contains millions or billions of elements. With commands like PFADD and PFCOUNT, you can easily add elements and retrieve the estimated cardinality. This makes HyperLogLog a powerful tool for efficient, large-scale counting tasks. Redis HyperLogLog provides an estimation with a standard error of approximately 0.81%, which is acceptable for most analytics and monitoring use cases.

Basic Commands Used in HyperLogLog in Redis:

- **PFADD**: Adds an element to the HyperLogLog, allowing for the approximation of the cardinality (number of unique elements) in a dataset
- **PFCOUNT**: Counts the approximate number of unique elements in the HyperLogLog, thus providing a memory-efficient way to estimate cardinality
- **PFMERGE**: Merges multiple HyperLogLogs into a single one, while combining the estimated unique elements from each to get a unified cardinality approximation

Geospatial Indexes

Redis provides powerful geospatial capabilities that **enable you to store, query, and perform operations based on geographical locations**. Using this data type, you can store coordinates (latitude and longitude) as members in a sorted set, while leveraging the efficient ordering and querying of data. With Redis's geospatial commands, you can perform operations such as finding nearby locations, calculating distances between two points, or retrieving elements within a specified radius, all while maintaining high performance.

These geospatial features are particularly useful in applications like mapping services, location-based recommendations, or ride-sharing platforms, where proximity and spatial relationships are key. Whether you are building a system to find the nearest stores, track vehicle locations, or calculate distances between points, Redis's geospatial support makes it easy to handle geographic data efficiently and at scale. With commands like GEOADD, GEOSEARCH, and GEODIST (**with GEORADIUS deprecated in Redis ≥ 6.2**), Redis allows you to build real-time, location-based applications with minimal overhead and maximum flexibility.

Basic Commands Used in Geospatial Indexes in Redis:

- **GEOADD:** Adds a geographic location (latitude and longitude) to a geospatial index and allows you to store locations associated with a specific key
- **GEOSEARCH:** Returns members within a specified radius or bounding box (optionally including distance/coordinates)

Streams

Streams are one of the more complex and versatile data types in Redis, specifically designed for **managing and processing real-time data flows.** A Redis stream functions as a log of messages or events, where each entry is assigned a unique ID and can contain multiple data fields. This makes streams ideal for building systems that require continuous data ingestion, such as messaging platforms, event-driven architectures, or real-time data pipelines. You can easily append data to the stream and consume it in real-time, which makes Redis streams highly suitable for tasks that demand low-latency processing.

In addition to basic stream functionalities, Redis streams offer advanced features such as consumer groups, which allow multiple consumers to process entries in parallel, improving throughput and scalability. This makes streams a powerful tool for handling large volumes of data and enabling efficient real-time processing. With commands like **XADD, XREAD, and XGROUP**, Redis streams provide a robust solution for managing complex data workflows, while ensuring efficient data distribution and processing across multiple clients or services.

Basic Commands Used in Streams in Redis:

- **XADD**: Adds an element (entry) to a stream, while allowing you to append data in a time-ordered sequence
- **XREAD**: Reads one or more entries from a stream, either blocking until new data is available or retrieving the latest entries
- **XRANGE**: Returns entries from a stream within a specified range, while providing a way to query data based on time or entry ID
- **XLEN**: Retrieves the length of the stream, while indicating the total number of entries stored in it

Summary

In this section, we explored several of the more advanced data types that Redis offers, including Bitmaps, Bitfields, HyperLogLog, Geospatial indexes, and Streams. Each of these data types serves a specific purpose and allows Redis to tackle complex tasks that go beyond the capabilities of its more basic data structures. For instance, Bitmaps and Bitfields are useful for efficiently managing and manipulating binary data, HyperLogLog excels at counting unique elements in massive datasets while conserving memory, and Geospatial indexes allow you to store and query location-based data with ease. Streams, on the other hand, are designed for handling real-time data, which makes them invaluable for building systems that require continuous data flow, such as messaging platforms or event-driven architectures.

By understanding the unique capabilities of these advanced data types and knowing when to apply them, you can unlock Redis's full potential in your projects. These tools enable you to manage large datasets, perform efficient operations, and handle real-time events with precision and speed. Leveraging Redis's advanced data structures allows you to solve complex problems more effectively, streamlining workflows and enhancing the performance and scalability of your applications.

Points to Remember

In this section, we will summarize the key takeaways from the chapter on Redis data structures and their uses. Here are the most important points you should keep in mind:

Five Core Data Structures

Redis provides five fundamental data types, each designed to handle specific data efficiently. These are mentioned as follows:

- **Strings:** Used for a wide range of applications, including caching, counters, and basic key-value storage
- **Sets:** Store unique values and are ideal for scenarios that require membership checks, such as tagging systems or managing unique IDs
- **Sorted Sets:** Maintain collections where each element is associated with a score, while ensuring that the data remains ordered. This makes them perfect for use cases like leaderboards or priority queues
- **Lists:** Useful for ordered collections, ideal for implementing queues, logs, and any use case where order matters, such as task processing or streaming data
- **Hashes:** Efficient for storing objects that contain multiple fields, like user profiles or configuration settings, while enabling quick access and modification of individual fields

Specific Commands for Each Data Type

Redis provides dedicated commands for interacting with each data structure:

- **Strings:** Commands like GET, SET, INCR, and APPEND allow for simple retrieval, storage, incrementing numeric values, and appending data to strings
- **Hashes:** Use commands such as HGET, HSET, HDEL, and HGETALL to interact with fields and values within a hash efficiently
- **Lists:** Commands like LPUSH, RPUSH, LPOP, and LRANGE help manage lists by pushing elements onto either end, popping elements, or retrieving ranges of list elements
- **Sets:** Utilize commands like SADD, SREM, SMEMBERS, and SINTER to add or remove elements, retrieve all members, or find intersections of sets
- **Sorted Sets:** Commands such as ZADD, ZRANK, ZRANGE, and ZREM allow for adding elements with scores, retrieving their rank, or fetching elements within a score range

Atomic Operations

Redis executes each individual command atomically, meaning each command either completes fully or does not happen at all. This ensures data integrity, even in high-concurrency environments where multiple clients are interacting with the same data simultaneously.

Memory Efficiency

It is crucial to choose the appropriate data structure to optimize memory usage. Each data type has its own strengths, so selecting the right one for your use case can lead to better memory management and improved performance.

Expiration Feature

Redis allows you to set an expiration time for keys, which makes it ideal for use cases like session management, caching with timeouts, and temporary data storage. This feature ensures that data can be automatically deleted after a specified period, while reducing memory consumption and maintaining system efficiency.

By understanding these key points, you will be well-equipped to make informed decisions about which Redis data structures to use in your applications and how to manage them effectively.

Conclusion

In this chapter, we took an in-depth look at the core data structures that make Redis such a versatile and powerful tool for data management. We explored essential data types such as Strings, Sets, Sorted Sets, Hashes, and Lists, where each is uniquely suited to different tasks. From simple key-value storage to handling ordered collections and creating efficient hash maps, we demonstrated how these data structures can be used effectively in practical, real-world scenarios. By understanding the strengths of each data type, you are now better equipped to make informed decisions on how to utilize Redis's offerings to meet your specific application needs.

Additionally, we explored Redis's more specialized data structures, including Bitmaps, Bitfields, HyperLogLog, Geospatial indexes, and Streams. These advanced data types address more complex use cases such as managing vast datasets, counting unique elements with minimal memory overhead, and processing real-time data streams. Understanding these advanced structures allows you to unlock even more potential from Redis, which enables you to build applications that handle a broad range of challenges like efficient counting, spatial indexing, and high-throughput event streaming.

Thus, by mastering the fundamentals and specialized data structures of Redis, you now have a solid foundation for leveraging its full capabilities in your applications. In the next chapter, we will move on to the practical side of things, while guiding you through the process of installing Redis on various operating systems. We will cover common installation challenges and provide solutions to ensure a smooth setup across different platforms and set the stage for you to start working with Redis in your development environment effectively.

Chapter 3

Getting Redis Up and Running on Various Platforms

Introduction

Welcome to a crucial chapter of our journey into Redis. In this chapter, we will walk through the complete process of installing and running Redis across various operating systems, including Linux, macOS, and Windows. Whether you are a developer working in a Linux environment, building applications on macOS, or deploying solutions on Windows, this chapter provides clear, platform-specific instructions to help you get started confidently. Each step is explained in a practical, straightforward manner, addressing common setup challenges and ensuring that Redis is installed, verified, and ready for use with minimal friction. By the end of this chapter, you will have a working Redis environment tailored to your operating system, laying a solid foundation for the hands-on chapters that follow.

However, we will not stop at installation. We will also show you how to verify that Redis is functioning correctly, helping you avoid any pitfalls right from the start. You will learn how to fine-tune Redis settings to ensure optimal performance as per your specific setup. And because technology might not always cooperate with you, we will guide you through troubleshooting common issues to equip you with solutions.

Our goal is to enhance your confidence as you work through this setup. By the end of this chapter, you will have Redis ready to go, prepared to handle the tasks required in subsequent chapters. We aim to make you less anxious about the setup and transform this experience from a daunting technical task into an empowering step toward exploring Redis's powerful features in the chapters to come. So, whether you are a complete beginner eager to dive in or an experienced user who is fine-tuning your environment, let us make sure your Redis journey begins on solid ground.

Structure

This chapter will cover the following topics:

- Installing Redis
    - Installing Redis on Linux
    - Installing Redis on CentOS
    - Installing Redis on Ubuntu
    - Installing Redis on macOS
    - Installing Redis on Windows
- Securing Redis

- Verifying Redis Installation
- Basic Configuration
- Troubleshooting Common Issues
- Key Points to Remember

Installing Redis

Redis is a versatile and high-performance in-memory data structure store. Its popularity spans various platforms like Ubuntu, Windows, and macOS. **However, the installation process is not one-size-fits-all** and requires specific steps tailored to each operating system. In this section, we will walk you through the process of installing Redis on your preferred platform, whether you are working on a local development project or setting up Redis on a server for production use.

Our instructions are crafted to be clear and approachable, even for those who might not be highly familiar with server installations. We have simplified complex steps and highlighted key areas to ensure you feel comfortable and confident throughout the installation process. From understanding package managers and dealing with system-specific configurations to managing permissions and verifying the installation, we will guide you every step of the way.

But our guide does not stop at installing Redis. We will also help you with essential post-installation configurations, including setting up Redis to run securely and efficiently. This involves optimizing settings for performance, addressing common security practices, and ensuring that Redis runs as expected every time your system starts up.

Additionally, we will cover troubleshooting tips to resolve any issues you might encounter along the way. Redis can sometimes be finicky depending on your system's settings. Therefore, it is important to know how to address potential conflicts or misconfigurations. By understanding these nuances, you will be better prepared to handle Redis smoothly and avoid any frustration down the road.

Platforms like Ubuntu, Windows, and macOS have their unique set of requirements and quirks. We will explain these differences in detail and show you how to adapt to them and ensure that Redis runs seamlessly on your chosen system. By the end of this section, you will not only have Redis installed, but also fully configured and optimized. This provides a strong foundation and prepares you to explore Redis's powerful features and capabilities in the chapters ahead.

Redis is more than just a database; it is a tool that can revolutionize the way you manage data in your applications. Let us get started with the installation, so that you can unlock the full potential of Redis and harness its speed and flexibility.

Here are the steps for installing Redis on various platforms:

Installing Redis on Linux

Installing Redis on a Linux-based system is generally straightforward, although the process may vary slightly depending on which Linux distribution you are using. In this section, we will walk you through the installation steps for two of the most widely used distributions: **Ubuntu and CentOS**. Each of these platforms comes with its unique characteristics and advantages, which makes them popular choices for different use cases.

Ubuntu is often preferred by developers due to its ease of use and simplicity. It has a user-friendly interface and extensive community support. Therefore, it is an excellent choice for development environments or for those who are newer to Linux. Installing Redis on Ubuntu is a seamless experience, thanks to its intuitive package management system and regular updates that keep things running smoothly.

On the other hand, **CentOS** is well-known for its stability and long-term support, making it a staple in enterprise environments. It is favored for production servers, where reliability and security are paramount. The process of setting up Redis on CentOS may be a bit more involved, but it is designed to deliver a robust and secure configuration suitable for demanding workloads.

In this guide, we will carefully explain how to install Redis on both platforms using their respective package management systems. We will cover key configuration options to ensure that Redis is optimized for performance and reliability and is tailored to your specific setup. Our instructions are detailed yet approachable and will help you avoid common pitfalls and troubleshoot any potential issues that may arise during installation.

By following our step-by-step guide, you will gain a solid understanding of how to get Redis up and running on your Linux system, whether you are working in a development or production environment. We will also provide insights into how to verify the installation and adjust settings to suit your needs, while ensuring that Redis can handle your data efficiently and securely.

By the end of this section, you will have a properly installed and configured Redis instance which is ready to support your projects whether you are building new applications or maintaining critical systems. So, let us dive in and set up Redis on your preferred Linux distribution, while paving the way for you to explore its full potential.

Checking the Operating System Name and Version

Before installing Redis, it is important to check your **operating system (OS) version** to ensure compatibility and follow the appropriate installation steps. You can do this by using the following command in the terminal:

```
cat /etc/os-release
```

The command will display the **OS name, version, and additional system information**. This helps you confirm your system details and ensures that you are following the correct installation instructions tailored to your specific Linux distribution.

Figure 3.1 displays the output of the **`cat /etc/os-release`** command executed on a **CentOS system**. This command provides essential information about the operating system, including its name, version, and metadata.

A typical output on a CentOS system looks like this:

```
NAME="CentOS Stream"
VERSION="9"
ID="centos"
ID_LIKE="rhel fedora"
VERSION_ID="9"
PLATFORM_ID="platform:el9"
PRETTY_NAME="CentOS Stream 9"
ANSI_COLOR="0;31"
LOGO="fedora-logo-icon"
CPE_NAME="cpe:/o:centos:centos:9"
HOME_URL="https://centos.org/"
BUG_REPORT_URL="https://issues.redhat.com/"
REDHAT_SUPPORT_PRODUCT="Red Hat Enterprise Linux 9"
REDHAT_SUPPORT_PRODUCT_VERSION="CentOS Stream"
```

Figure 3.1: *Output of the Command cat /etc/os-release on CentOS*

Figure 3.2 displays the output of the **`cat /etc/os-release`** command when it is **executed on an Ubuntu system**. This command is used to retrieve information about the operating system, such as the name, version, and other metadata.

A typical output on an Ubuntu system looks like this:

```
PRETTY_NAME="Ubuntu 22.04.5 LTS"
NAME="Ubuntu"
VERSION_ID="22.04"
VERSION="22.04.5 LTS (Jammy Jellyfish)"
VERSION_CODENAME=jammy
ID=ubuntu
ID_LIKE=debian
HOME_URL="https://www.ubuntu.com/"
SUPPORT_URL="https://help.ubuntu.com/"
BUG_REPORT_URL="https://bugs.launchpad.net/ubuntu/"
PRIVACY_POLICY_URL="https://www.ubuntu.com/legal/terms-and-policies/privacy-policy"
UBUNTU_CODENAME=jammy
```

Figure 3.2: *Output of the Command cat /etc/os-release on Ubuntu*

These outputs provide detailed information about the operating system, including the **name** (for example, "`CentOS Stream`" or "`Ubuntu 22.04.5 LTS`"), **version** (for example, "`9`" or "`22.04`"), and **related details** such as the platform and links to support resources. Understanding this information is crucial for installing and configuring Redis properly on your specific OS. Having the correct OS details ensures that you have followed the right steps for a successful and efficient setup.

Installing Redis on CentOS

Before diving into the step-by-step process of installing Redis on CentOS, it is helpful to understand something about the environment we are working with. CentOS is widely used in enterprise settings and is valued for its rock-solid stability and reliability. These features make it an excellent choice for running essential services like Redis, where consistency and long-term support are critical.

Fortunately, installing Redis on CentOS is a relatively straightforward process, made even easier by the **dnf package manager**, which simplifies software installation and management.**With dnf, you can efficiently handle package updates and dependencies**, while ensuring a smooth installation experience.

In this section, we will guide you through each step of the installation process. You will learn how to set up Redis and configure it properly to see that it runs seamlessly on your CentOS system. Our instructions are designed to be clear and manageable, even if you are not deeply familiar with CentOS. We will cover everything from installing necessary packages to configuring Redis for optimal performance and security.

By following our guide, you will be able to verify that Redis is running correctly and efficiently. We will also touch on important configuration options that will help you tailor Redis to meet your specific needs, whether you are setting up a development environment or preparing a production server.

By the end of this section, you will have a fully installed and configured Redis instance which is ready to handle data storage and caching tasks with speed and reliability. Your CentOS setup will be primed to take full advantage of Redis' powerful features and will set the stage for building scalable and efficient applications.

Note: *These steps also apply to RHEL, Rocky Linux, and AlmaLinux.*

To install Redis on a CentOS system, follow these steps:

1. **Update your CentOS system:** Before installing any package, it is important to update your system to ensure that all existing packages are up to date. This helps maintain system stability and security. Run the following command to update your system:

   ```
   sudo dnf update -y
   ```

2. **Install the Redis package:** Once your system is updated, you can proceed to install Redis using the following command:

   ```
   sudo dnf install redis -y
   ```

3. **Enable and start the Redis service:** After installing Redis, you need to enable it to ensure that it starts automatically after a reboot. Then, you can start the Redis service using the following commands:

   ```
   sudo systemctl enable redis
   sudo systemctl start redis
   ```

4. **Verify the status of the Redis service:** To ensure that Redis is running properly, check its status using the following command:

   ```
   sudo systemctl status redis
   ```

A typical output on a CentOS system with Redis running might look like this:

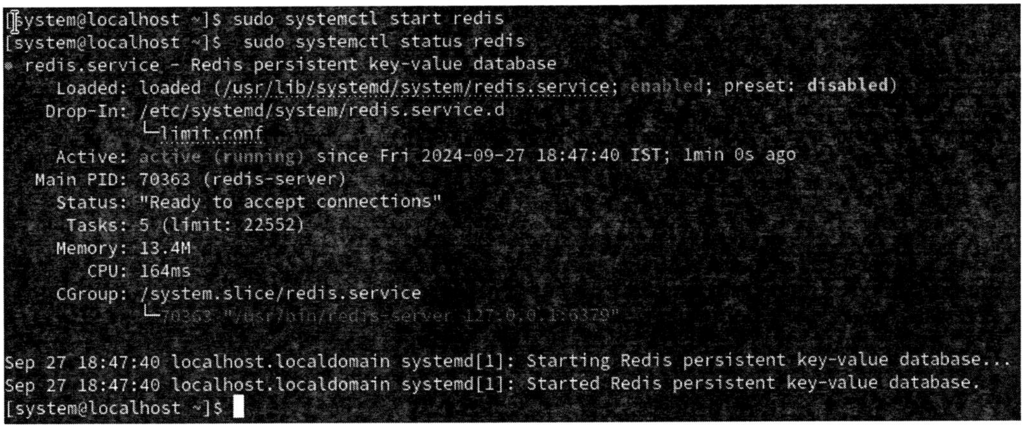

```
[system@localhost ~]$ sudo systemctl start redis
[system@localhost ~]$  sudo systemctl status redis
● redis.service - Redis persistent key-value database
     Loaded: loaded (/usr/lib/systemd/system/redis.service; enabled; preset: disabled)
    Drop-In: /etc/systemd/system/redis.service.d
             └─limit.conf
     Active: active (running) since Fri 2024-09-27 18:47:40 IST; 1min 0s ago
   Main PID: 70363 (redis-server)
     Status: "Ready to accept connections"
      Tasks: 5 (limit: 22552)
     Memory: 13.4M
        CPU: 164ms
     CGroup: /system.slice/redis.service
             └─70363 "/usr/bin/redis-server 127.0.0.1:6379"

Sep 27 18:47:40 localhost.localdomain systemd[1]: Starting Redis persistent key-value database...
Sep 27 18:47:40 localhost.localdomain systemd[1]: Started Redis persistent key-value database.
[system@localhost ~]$ 
```

***Figure 3.3**: Output of the Command sudo systemctl Status Redis on CentOS*

Figure 3.3 presents the output of the **`sudo systemctl status redis`** command on a CentOS system. This command provides the current status of the Redis service, including whether it is active, inactive, or encountering errors.

This output confirms that Redis is active and running, ready to accept connections. Seeing "active (running)" indicates that your Redis server is properly set up and functioning as expected.

Installing Redis on Ubuntu

Before diving into the step-by-step guide for installing Redis on Ubuntu, let us take a moment to understand why Ubuntu is such a popular choice among developers. Known for its simplicity, user-friendliness, and widespread community support, Ubuntu has become a preferred platform in development environments worldwide. One of the standout features of Ubuntu is its reliable **apt package management system**, which makes installing and managing software like Redis incredibly straightforward.

In this section, we will guide you through each step to ensure that Redis is installed, configured, and running smoothly on your Ubuntu system. Our instructions are designed to be clear and easy to follow, even if you are new to working with Ubuntu. We will cover everything from installing Redis using the apt package manager to configuring it for optimal performance and security.

By the end of this section, you will have Redis up and running on your Ubuntu machine, ready to support your development projects with speed and efficiency. You will be well-equipped to leverage Redis's powerful features, which will make your development workflow more robust and streamlined.

We will use the **APT package manager** to install Redis from the official Ubuntu repositories. This method ensures that you get a stable and well-tested version of Redis that integrates smoothly with your Ubuntu system.

1. **Begin by updating your local apt package cache to ensure that you have the latest information about available packages through the following command:**

    ```
    sudo apt update
    ```

2. **Next, install Redis. The following command will download and install Redis along with any necessary dependencies:**

    ```
    sudo apt install redis-server
    ```

3. **Before using Redis, it is important to make a crucial configuration change in the default configuration file to ensure optimal performance and security. To do this, access the `redis.conf` configuration file using your preferred text editor. You can use the following command:**

    ```
    sudo vim /etc/redis/redis.conf
    ```

    Inside the file, you can locate the supervised directive. This directive lets you specify an **`init`** system to manage Redis as a service, which offers you better control over its operation. **By default**, the supervised directive is set to **no**. Since Ubuntu uses the **`systemd init`** system, you should change this setting to **`systemd`**.

    Figure 3.4 highlights the default value of the supervised directive in the Redis configuration file (**`redis.conf`**). This directive determines how Redis interacts with process supervision systems such as **`systemd`**, **`upstart`**, or **`supervisord`**.

    ```
    # If you run Redis from upstart or systemd, Redis can interact with your
    # supervision tree. Options:
    #   supervised no      - no supervision interaction
    #   supervised upstart - signal upstart by putting Redis into SIGSTOP mode
    #                        requires "expect stop" in your upstart job config
    #   supervised systemd - signal systemd by writing READY=1 to $NOTIFY_SOCKET
    #   supervised auto    - detect upstart or systemd method based on
    #                        UPSTART_JOB or NOTIFY_SOCKET environment variables
    # Note: these supervision methods only signal "process is ready."
    #       They do not enable continuous pings back to your supervisor.
    supervised no
    ```

    Figure 3.4: *The Supervised Directive Default Value in the Redis Configuration File*

    Figure 3.5 illustrates a modified value of the **`supervised`** directive in the Redis configuration file (**`redis.conf`**). This directive is adjusted to enable Redis to integrate with a process supervision system, such as **`systemd`**, commonly used in production environments for enhanced reliability and process management.

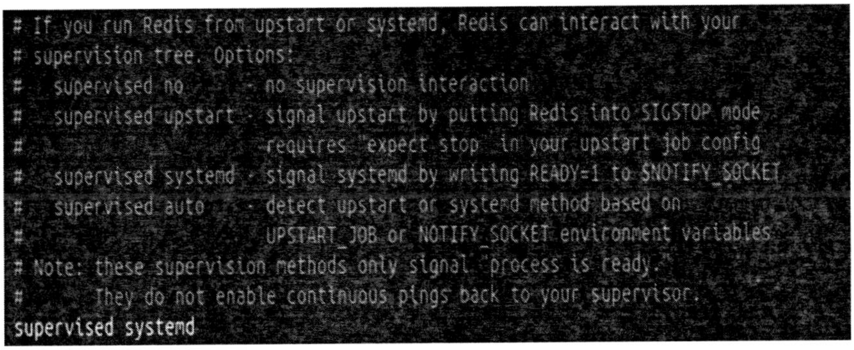

```
# If you run Redis from upstart or systemd, Redis can interact with your
# supervision tree. Options:
#   supervised no      - no supervision interaction
#   supervised upstart - signal upstart by putting Redis into SIGSTOP mode
#                        requires "expect stop" in your upstart job config
#   supervised systemd - signal systemd by writing READY=1 to $NOTIFY_SOCKET
#   supervised auto    - detect upstart or systemd method based on
#                        UPSTART_JOB or NOTIFY_SOCKET environment variables
# Note: these supervision methods only signal "process is ready."
#       They do not enable continuous pings back to your supervisor.
supervised systemd
```

Figure 3.5: *The Supervised Directive Changed Value in the Redis Configuration File*

That is the only change required for service supervision in this setup. Once you have made the adjustment, save and close the file.

Next, **restart the Redis service** to apply the changes you made to the configuration file using the following command:

```
sudo systemctl restart redis.service
```

This change ensures Redis benefits from the process management capabilities provided by the supervision system, while improving its operational robustness.

4. As with any newly installed software, it is crucial to verify that Redis is functioning correctly before proceeding with any further configuration changes. Ensuring that Redis is running smoothly from the start will save you time and prevent potential issues later on. In this section, we will explore several methods to confirm that Redis is operating as expected, including checking the service status and running basic commands to test its functionality.

```
sudo systemctl status redis
```

If Redis is running without any errors, this command will produce output similar to the following:

```
● redis-server.service - Advanced key-value store
     Loaded: loaded (/lib/systemd/system/redis-server.service; enabled; vendor preset: enabled)
     Active: active (running) since Thu 2024-10-03 14:44:04 IST; 1min 19s ago
       Docs: http://redis.io/documentation,
             man:redis-server(1)
   Main PID: 3932 (redis-server)
     Status: "Ready to accept connections"
      Tasks: 5 (limit: 4550)
     Memory: 2.9M
        CPU: 260ms
     CGroup: /system.slice/redis-server.service
             └─3932 "/usr/bin/redis-server 127.0.0.1:6379"
```

Figure 3.6: *Output of the Command sudo systemctl status redis on Ubuntu*

Figure 3.6 presents the output of the **`sudo systemctl status redis`** command executed on an Ubuntu system. This command provides the current status and detailed information about the Redis service.

Installing Redis on macOS

Setting up Redis on macOS is straightforward, especially when using **Homebrew**, which is a widely used and trusted **package manager for macOS**. In this section, we will guide you through each step of the installation process, while ensuring that Redis is installed correctly, properly configured, and running smoothly on your **Mac**. Whether you are a seasoned developer or just getting started, our step-by-step instructions are designed to make the setup as simple and stress-free as possible, which will allow you to quickly dive into Redis and take full advantage of its powerful features.

Homebrew provides a seamless and efficient way to manage the installation and updates of software, including Redis. It simplifies the process of keeping your software up-to-date and well-maintained, which ensures a hassle-free experience. With Homebrew, you can easily install Redis and be confident that your setup will work efficiently.

By following our guide, you will have Redis up and running in no time. The setup will be ready to support your development projects and optimize your workflow on macOS. We will also touch on some essential configuration options to ensure Redis performs optimally as per your development needs.

So, let us dive into the installation process together. By the end of this section, you will have a robust Redis setup on your Mac, which will be fully prepared to handle your caching and data management requirements with ease and efficiency.

To get Redis set up on your macOS system, follow these steps:

1. **Ensure that Homebrew is installed.**

   First, verify that Homebrew is installed on your system by running the following command in the terminal:

   ```
   brew --version
   ```

   > **Note:** If this command fails, you will need to install Homebrew. Visit **https://brew.sh/** and follow the installation instructions provided on the website.

2. **Install Redis via Homebrew.**

   Once Homebrew is set up, install Redis by running the following command in the terminal:

   ```
   brew install redis
   ```

3. **Test your Redis installation.**

   To test that Redis has been installed correctly, run the **`redis-server`** executable from the command line:

   ```
   redis-server
   ```

   If the installation is successful, you will see Redis startup logs displayed in the terminal that indicate if Redis is running in the foreground. To stop Redis, simply press *Ctrl-C*.

4. **Run Redis in the background with `launchd`**

   As an alternative to running Redis in the foreground, you can use **`launchd`** to start Redis in the background with the following command:

   ```
   brew services start redis
   ```

   This command starts Redis in the background and ensures that it will automatically restart each time you log in.

5. **Check the status of Redis.**

   To verify the status of a Redis instance managed by **`launchd`**, run the following command:

   ```
   brew services info redis
   ```

By following these steps, you can install Redis successfully and run it efficiently on your macOS system using Homebrew. This setup ensures that Redis is ready to support your development projects seamlessly.

Installing Redis on Windows

Setting up Redis on Windows **differs from the process on Linux or macOS**, as Redis was originally **designed to run on Unix-based systems**. Despite this, various tools and adaptations have made it possible to run Redis on Windows without sacrificing performance or functionality. In this section, we will guide you through the steps required to install and configure Redis on your Windows machine.

We will walk you through everything from downloading the appropriate Redis package for Windows to setting it up as a background service. Additionally, we will explore essential configuration options to optimize Redis based on your specific needs. This will include details on tuning memory settings, setting up authentication, and managing persistence options.

Hence, whether you plan to use Redis for development, testing, or simply exploring its features, our detailed instructions will ensure that you have a stable and efficient Redis instance running smoothly on your system. After following this guide, you will be prepared to leverage Redis' powerful data storage and caching capabilities that make it easier to build and test applications seamlessly in a Windows environment.

It is important to note that Redis is not officially supported on Windows. However, for development purposes, you can still install and run Redis effectively by following the steps outlined below. Let us dive into the installation process, and get Redis up and running on your Windows setup.

To install Redis on Windows, you will first need to enable **WSL2 (Windows Subsystem for Linux)**. **WSL2 allows you to run Linux binaries natively on Windows**, which provides a full Linux experience within your Windows environment. This method is essential for running Redis efficiently, as Redis was originally built for Unix-like systems.

System Requirements: To use WSL2, ensure that you are running Windows 10 version 2004 or higher, or Windows 11. If your system meets these requirements, you will be able to proceed with enabling and setting up WSL2.

Installing Linux on Windows with WSL

One of the most powerful features available to developers on a Windows machine is the ability to access both Windows and Linux environments simultaneously via the **Windows Subsystem for Linux (WSL)**. **WSL allows developers to install and run a full Linux distribution (such as Ubuntu, OpenSUSE, Kali Linux, Debian, or Arch Linux) directly on Windows**. This setup enables you to use Linux applications, utilities, and Bash command-line tools without modification, all while avoiding the overhead associated with traditional virtual machines or dual-boot configurations.

With WSL, developers can seamlessly switch between Windows and Linux-based tools, making it ideal for development workflows that require both environments. This integration provides the best of both worlds: the familiar Windows interface combined with the flexibility and power of Linux command-line tools.

The steps to enable and set up WSL are straightforward and ensure that you can run Linux distributions on your Windows system effectively. Let us now dive into the process of enabling WSL and setting up a Linux distribution on your Windows machine.

Prerequisites

To use the commands and features described below, you must be running **Windows 10 version 2004 and higher** (Build 19041 and higher) or **Windows 11**. Make sure your system is up-to-date to take full advantage of WSL2 and its capabilities.

1. To check the version of Windows in **PowerShell**, you can use the following command:

```
systeminfo | findstr /B /C:"OS Name" /B /C:"OS Version"
```

This command will provide information such as the OS name and version, allowing you to verify that your system meets the requirements for WSL2.

Figure 3.7 displays the filtered output of the **`systeminfo`** command using the **`findstr`** utility on a Windows system. This command is used to extract specific details about the operating system, such as its name and version.

A typical output might look like this:

```
PS C:\>
PS C:\> systeminfo | findstr /B /C:"OS Name" /B /C:"OS Version"
OS Name:                   Microsoft Windows 11 Home
OS Version:                10.0.22631 N/A Build 22631
PS C:\>
PS C:\> |
```

Figure 3.7: *Output of the Command systeminfo | findstr /B /C:"OS Name" /B /C:"OS Version"*

Install WSL Command

You can now install everything needed to run WSL with a single command. Open **PowerShell** or **Windows Command Prompt** in administrator mode. To do this, right-click on the PowerShell or Command Prompt icon and select **`"Run as administrator"`**. Once you are in the administrator mode, enter the following command:

```
wsl --install
```

Figure 3.8 demonstrates the output of the **`wsl --install`** command executed on a Windows system. This command is used to install the Windows Subsystem for Linux (WSL), which enables users to run a Linux environment directly within Windows.

```
Windows PowerShell

Installing: Windows Subsystem for Linux
Windows Subsystem for Linux has been installed.
Installing: Ubuntu
Ubuntu has been installed.
The requested operation is successful. Changes will not be effective until the system is rebooted.
PS C:\> |
```

Figure 3.8: *Output of the Command wsl --install*

This command will enable the features necessary to run WSL, and install the Ubuntu distribution of Linux. (This default distribution can be changed).

The **`--install`** command performs the following actions:

- Enables the optional WSL and Virtual Machine Platform components
- Downloads and installs the latest Linux kernel
- Sets WSL 2 as the default
- Downloads and installs the Ubuntu Linux distribution (a reboot may be required)

When you launch a newly installed Linux distribution for the first time, a console window will open and you will be asked to wait for files to de-compress and be stored on your machine. All future launches should take less than a second.

Change the Default Linux Distribution Installed

By default, the installed Linux distribution will be Ubuntu. This can be changed using the `-d` flag.

- To change the distribution installed, enter: `wsl --install -d <Distribution Name>`. Replace `<Distribution Name>` with the name of the distribution you would like to install.
- To see a list of available Linux distributions available for download through the online store, enter: `wsl --list --online` or `wsl -l -o`.
- To install additional Linux distributions after the initial install, you may also use the command: `wsl --install -d <Distribution Name>`.

Note: If the Linux distribution you want to use is not listed as available, you have the flexibility to import any Linux distribution using a TAR file. Alternatively, for distributions like Arch Linux, you can install them using an `.appx` file. Additionally, WSL supports the creation and use of custom Linux distributions, which offers you complete control over your Linux environment on Windows.

Setting Up Your Linux Username and Password

Once the process of installing your Linux distribution with WSL is complete, open the distribution (Ubuntu by default) using the Start menu. You will be asked to create a username and password for your Linux distribution.

- This username and password are specific to each separate Linux distribution that you install and has no bearing on your Windows user name.
- Please note that while entering the password, nothing will appear on the screen. This is called blind typing. You will not see what you are typing. This is completely normal.
- Once you create a username and password, the account will be your default user for the distribution and automatically sign in on launch.
- This account will be considered the Linux administrator, with the ability to run sudo (Super User Do) administrative commands.
- Each Linux distribution running on WSL has its own Linux user accounts and passwords. You will have to configure a Linux user account every time you add a distribution, reinstall, or reset.

  Figure 3.9 illustrates the output of the `wsl --install` command, a one-step process to enable the Windows Subsystem for Linux (WSL) and install a default Linux distribution. This command simplifies the installation of WSL on supported Windows systems.

```
Ubuntu
Installing, this may take a few minutes...
Please create a default UNIX user account. The username does not need to match your Windows username.
For more information visit: https://aka.ms/wslusers
Enter new UNIX username:
```

***Figure* 3.9:** *Output of the Command wsl --install*

Updating and Upgrading Packages

It is recommended to regularly update and upgrade your packages to ensure your system is secure and running the latest software. Use the preferred package manager for your Linux distribution. For **Ubuntu** or **Debian**, you can update and upgrade your packages with the following command:

```
sudo apt update && sudo apt upgrade
```

Installing Redis

Once you have Ubuntu running on Windows through WSL, you can install the recent stable version of Redis from the official packages.redis.io APT repository. Follow these steps to add the repository, update your package index, and install Redis:

1. **Add the GPG key for the Redis repository.**

   ```
   curl -fsSL https://packages.redis.io/gpg | sudo gpg --dearmor -o /usr/share/
   keyrings/redis-archive-keyring.gpg
   ```

   This command downloads and adds the GPG key to ensure the authenticity of the packages you are about to install.

2. **Add the Redis repository to your APT sources list.**

   ```
   echo "deb [signed-by=/usr/share/keyrings/redis-archive-keyring.gpg] https://
   packages.redis.io/deb $(lsb_release -cs) main" | sudo tee /etc/apt/sources.
   list.d/redis.list
   ```

   This step configures your system to use the official Redis APT repository, while making sure that you get the most recent updates and stable releases.

3. **Update the APT package index using the following command:**

   ```
   sudo apt-get update
   ```

4. **Install Redis using the following command:**

   ```
   sudo apt-get install redis
   ```

   This command installs Redis on your Ubuntu system.

   Lastly, start the Redis server using the following command:

   ```
   sudo service redis-server start
   ```

   This command launches the Redis server and allows you to begin using Redis on your WSL-enabled Ubuntu environment.You can now interact with Redis and verify that it is running properly.

   Note: *If systemd is enabled in WSL, you can also use sudo systemctl start redis-server.*

5. **Verify That Redis Is Running:**

   To ensure that Redis is running properly, check the status of the Redis server with the following command:

   ```
   sudo service redis-server status
   ```

   Figure 3.10 displays the output of the **`sudo service redis-server status`** command, which is used to check the status of the Redis server on systems that use the traditional service command for managing services.

```
● redis-server.service - Advanced key-value store
     Loaded: loaded (/usr/lib/systemd/system/redis-server.service; disabled; preset: enabled)
     Active: active (running) since Sun 2024-11-10 09:16:31 UTC; 42s ago
       Docs: http://redis.io/documentation,
             man:redis-server(1)
   Main PID: 2399 (redis-server)
     Status: "Ready to accept connections"
      Tasks: 6 (limit: 9339)
     Memory: 8.3M ()
     CGroup: /system.slice/redis-server.service
             └─2399 "/usr/bin/redis-server 127.0.0.1:6379"
```

Figure 3.10: *Output of the Command sudo service redis-server status*

Connect to Redis

Once Redis is running, you can test it by running **redis-cli**:

```
redis-cli
```

Test the connection with the **ping** command.

Figure 3.11 showcases the output of the ping command executed within the Redis command-line interface (**redis-cli**). This command is used to test the connection between the client and the Redis server.

```
127.0.0.1:6379> ping
PONG
127.0.0.1:6379> |
```

Figure 3.11: *Output of the Command ping inside redis-cli*

Securing Redis

After installing Redis, it is crucial to take steps to secure your instance to prevent unauthorized access and minimize potential vulnerabilities. By default, Redis is configured for simplicity and ease of use, which may not provide adequate protection in a production environment. In this section, we will outline key measures you can implement to strengthen Redis security and safeguard your data and system from unauthorized access or malicious attacks.

We will cover important topics such as setting a strong password, while binding Redis to specific network interfaces, and configuring your firewall for optimal protection. Following these instructions will help you create a more secure Redis environment, while ensuring that your instance is well-protected and maintaining performance and reliability.

Let us dive into these essential steps to enhance Redis security and keep your data safe.

1. **Edit the Redis configuration file:** Open the Redis configuration file using the following command. Depending on your system, the file may be located at **/etc/redis.conf** or **/etc/redis/redis.conf**:

   ```
   sudo vim /etc/redis.conf
   ```

   or

   ```
   sudo vim /etc/redis/redis.conf
   ```

2. **Set a strong password:** To secure Redis, you should set a password to prevent unauthorized access. Open the configuration file and look for the line that reads:

   ```
   requirepass YourStrongPasswordHere
   ```

   Note: For Redis 6 and above, ACL-based users are recommended over requirepass for fine-grained access control.

3. **Bind Redis to localhost:** To prevent external access and restrict Redis to only accept connections from the local machine, bind Redis to **localhost**. Ensure the following line is present and uncommented in the configuration file:

   ```
   bind 127.0.0.1
   ```

   If this line is commented out (with a # symbol at the beginning), remove the # to uncomment it. This setting ensures that Redis will only be accessible from the local server, which improves security by preventing external connections.

4. **Save the changes and restart the Redis service:** After making the changes, save the configuration file and restart the Redis service to apply the new settings. Use the following command:

   CentOS: `sudo systemctl restart redis`

   Ubuntu: `sudo systemctl restart redis.service`

   macOS (Homebrew): `brew services restart redis`

   Windows: `sc stop Redis && sc start Redis` (This applies only if you are using a native windows Redis build (not recommended), For WSL-based setups, manage Redis from the Linux environment.)

By following these steps, your Redis instance will be secured with a strong password and restricted to local access, which will significantly minimize the risk of unauthorized access and potential vulnerabilities.

Verifying Redis Installation

To ensure that Redis is functioning properly after installation, you can test it by connecting to the Redis server using **`redis-cli`, Redis's built-in command-line interface**. This tool allows you to interact directly with the Redis server, execute commands, and view responses in real time.

To begin, open your terminal and use the following command to connect to the Redis server:

```
redis-cli
```

In the prompt that follows, you can run simple commands like **`PING`** to check if the server responds. If everything is working correctly, Redis will return a "**`PONG`**" response, which indicates that the server is up and running. This straightforward test confirms that Redis is functioning properly on your system.

```
127.0.0.1:6379> ping
```

```
127.0.0.1:6379> ping
PONG
127.0.0.1:6379>
```

***Figure 3.12**: Output of the PING Command*

This output confirms that the connection to the Redis server is active and functioning properly. With the "**`PONG`**" response, you can be confident that Redis is up and ready to use.

Basic Configuration

Before diving into using Redis, it is important to configure it properly to ensure optimal performance, security, and reliability. Redis comes with a comprehensive configuration file, **`redis.conf`**, which allows you to customize various settings to suit your system's needs and your application's requirements.

In this section, we will explore the key aspects of Redis's basic configuration. This includes securing your Redis instance to prevent unauthorized access, managing memory efficiently to handle large datasets, enabling data persistence to safeguard against data loss, and optimizing performance to make the most of Redis's speed and capabilities.

By understanding and applying these configurations, you will be able to ensure that Redis is running smoothly and efficiently in any environment, whether you are using it for development purposes or deploying it in a high-stakes production setting.

1. **Configuring Redis Bind Address:** By default, Redis binds to **`127.0.0.1`**, which restricts access to the local machine only. You can modify this setting in the **`redis.conf`** file if you need to allow external connections. To do this, update the **`bind`** directive with your server's IP address. However, for enhanced security, it is recommended to keep Redis bound to **`localhost`** unless external access is absolutely necessary. This helps minimize the risk of unauthorized access.

   Figure 3.13 illustrates the **`bind`** directive in the Redis configuration file (**`redis.conf`**). This directive is used to specify the network interface(s) that Redis listens to for incoming connections.

   A typical configuration might look like this:

```
# ~~~ WARNING ~~~ If the computer running Redis is directly exposed to the
# internet, binding to all the interfaces is dangerous and will expose the
# instance to everybody on the internet. So by default we uncomment the
# following bind directive, that will force Redis to listen only on the
# IPv4 and IPv6 (if available) loopback interface addresses (this means Redis
# will only be able to accept client connections from the same host that it is
# running on).
#
# IF YOU ARE SURE YOU WANT YOUR INSTANCE TO LISTEN TO ALL THE INTERFACES
# JUST COMMENT OUT THE FOLLOWING LINE.
# ~~~~~~~~~~~~~~~~~~~~~~~~~~~~~~~~~~~~~~~~~~~~~~~~~~~~~~~~~~~~~~~~~~~~~~~~
bind 127.0.0.1 -::1
```

   Figure 3.13: *Redis Bind Address inside the Configuration File*

   The configuration directive **`bind 127.0.0.1 -::1`** in Redis specifies the network interfaces that Redis will listen to for incoming connections. Here is a simple breakdown:

   a. **127.0.0.1:** This is the loopback address for IPv4, which means Redis will only accept connections from the local machine. In other words, external devices or systems cannot connect to Redis when it is bound to this address. This helps in securing Redis, as it prevents outside access.

   b. **::1:** This is the loopback address for IPv6, serving the same purpose as 127.0.0.1 but for IPv6 connections. It allows Redis to listen to local connections over an IPv6 network.

   In simple terms, by using **`bind 127.0.0.1 -::1`**, Redis is configured to only accept connections from the local machine, both on IPv4 and IPv6. This is a common setup to restrict access to Redis and ensures that it is only accessible from the same server it is installed on, which enhances security by default.

2. **Setting a Redis Password:** By default, Redis does not require a password, which can be a security risk, especially in production environments. To enhance security, you can enable authentication by setting a password in the **`requirepass`** directive within the **`redis.conf`** file. Once configured, users have to authenticate with this password before they can access Redis commands, which provides an additional layer of protection.

   Figure 3.14 illustrates how to configure a password for Redis in the **`redis.conf`** file. Setting a password enhances the security of your Redis server by requiring authentication for client connections.

A typical configuration for enabling password protection might look like this:

```
# IMPORTANT NOTE: starting with Redis 6 "requirepass" is just a compatibility
# layer on top of the new ACL system. The option effect will be just setting
# the password for the default user. Clients will still authenticate using
# AUTH <password> as usually, or more explicitly with AUTH default <password>
# if they follow the new protocol: both will work.
#
# The requirepass is not compatable with aclfile option and the ACL LOAD
# command, these will cause requirepass to be ignored.
#
requirepass rootpassword
```

Figure 3.14: *Redis Password inside the Configuration File*

3. **Adjusting Redis Memory Usage:** Redis operates primarily in memory, making efficient memory management crucial for optimal performance and stability. You can use the **maxmemory** directive in the **redis.conf** file to set a limit on how much memory Redis is allowed to use. Hence, by configuring this cap, you can ensure that Redis does not consume excessive system resources. If it does otherwise, then it will impact the performance of other applications or lead to system instability.

   Setting an appropriate **maxmemory** value is especially important in production environments where resource management is a priority. Additionally, Redis provides various eviction policies that determine how data is handled once the memory limit is reached. This allows you to customize the behavior based on your application's needs.

   Figure 3.15 illustrates the use of the **maxmemory** directive in the Redis configuration file (**redis.conf**). This directive is used to limit the maximum memory Redis can use and ensures that the server does not consume all available system memory.

   A typical configuration might look like this:

```
############################## MEMORY MANAGEMENT ################################

# Set a memory usage limit to the specified amount of bytes.
# When the memory limit is reached Redis will try to remove keys
# according to the eviction policy selected (see maxmemory-policy).
#
# If Redis can't remove keys according to the policy, or if the policy is
# set to 'noeviction', Redis will start to reply with errors to commands
# that would use more memory, like SET, LPUSH, and so on, and will continue
# to reply to read-only commands like GET.
#
# This option is usually useful when using Redis as an LRU or LFU cache, or to
# set a hard memory limit for an instance (using the 'noeviction' policy).
#
# WARNING: If you have replicas attached to an instance with maxmemory on,
# the size of the output buffers needed to feed the replicas are subtracted
# from the used memory count, so that network problems / resyncs will
# not trigger a loop where keys are evicted, and in turn the output
# buffer of replicas is full with DELs of keys evicted triggering the deletion
# of more keys, and so forth until the database is completely emptied.
#
# In short... if you have replicas attached it is suggested that you set a lower
# limit for maxmemory so that there is some free RAM on the system for replica
# output buffers (but this is not needed if the policy is 'noeviction').
#
# maxmemory <bytes>
```

Figure 3.15: *Redis maxmemory Directive inside the Configuration File*

You can also configure eviction policies using the **maxmemory-policy** directive to control how Redis manages data when the memory limit is reached. These policies determine which keys are evicted to free up memory based on your chosen strategy. Here is a breakdown of the available options:

- **volatile-lru**: Evict keys using an approximated Least Recently Used (LRU) algorithm, but only keys that have an expiration set.
- **allkeys-lru**: Evict any key using an approximated LRU algorithm, regardless of whether it has an expiration set.
- **volatile-lfu**: Evict keys using an approximated Least Frequently Used (LFU) algorithm, but only keys with an expiration set.
- **allkeys-lfu**: Evict any key using an approximated LFU algorithm, regardless of whether it has an expiration set.
- **volatile-random**: Remove a random key that has an expiration set.
- **allkeys-random**: Remove a random key or any key in the dataset, regardless of expiration.
- **volatile-ttl**: Remove the key with the nearest expiration time (the one with the shortest remaining Time to Live, or TTL).
- **noeviction**: Do not evict any keys. Instead, return an error when the memory limit is reached and a write operation is attempted.

Choosing the right eviction policy is critical for ensuring that Redis behaves as expected under memory pressure. Your selection should align with your application's data retention requirements and performance goals.

Figure 3.16 highlights the **maxmemory-policy** directive in the Redis configuration file (**redis.conf**). This directive determines the behavior of Redis when the memory usage exceeds the limit defined by the **maxmemory** directive.

A typical configuration might look like this:

```
# LRU means Least Recently Used
# LFU means Least Frequently Used
#
# Both LRU, LFU and volatile-ttl are implemented using approximated
# randomized algorithms.
#
# Note: with any of the above policies, when there are no suitable keys for
# eviction, Redis will return an error on write operations that require
# more memory. These are usually commands that create new keys, add data or
# modify existing keys. A few examples are: SET, INCR, HSET, LPUSH, SUNIONSTORE,
# SORT (due to the STORE argument), and EXEC (if the transaction includes any
# command that requires memory).
#
# The default is:
#
# maxmemory-policy noeviction
```

Figure 3.16: *Redis maxmemory-policy Directive inside the Configuration File*

Memory Limits: maxmemory and Eviction-What Happens at the Limit

What maxmemory Does: Caps how much RAM Redis will use

What Happens When the Limit is Reached: Redis either refuses writes or evict keys, depending on the eviction policy.

- noeviction (default on many installs): Write commands that need more memory fail with "**`(error) OOM command not allowed when used memory > 'maxmemory'.`**" Reads still work.
- Eviction policies (allkeys-lru, allkeys-lfu, allkeys-random, volatile-*): Redis deletes keys to make space according to the policy and then accepts the write.

4. **Enabling Data Persistence:**

   Redis offers two options for data persistence: **RDB snapshots** and **AOF (Append Only File)**. Configuring these options allows you to control how and when data is saved to disk, which ensures data durability in case of a restart or system failure.

   - **RDB Snapshots**: RDB (Redis Database Backup) snapshots create point-in-time snapshots of your dataset at specified intervals. You can configure these intervals using the **`save`** directive in the **`redis.conf`** file. This approach provides a balance between performance and durability but may result in data loss if Redis crashes between snapshots.
   - **AOF (Append Only File)**: The AOF persistence method logs every write operation received by the server, appending these changes to a file. This method ensures a higher level of durability compared to RDB snapshots, as data can be reconstructed more accurately. You can enable AOF persistence by setting the **`appendonly`** directive to **yes** in the **`redis.conf`** file.

   Both options can be customized to fit your application's needs, and you can even use them together to achieve a more flexible persistence strategy. Carefully consider how often you need data saved and the performance impact, as these settings determine how frequently Redis writes data to disk.

   Figure 3.17 illustrates the **`appendonly`** directive in the Redis configuration file (**`redis.conf`**). This directive determines whether Redis enables **Append-Only File (AOF)** persistence, which logs every write operation to ensure durability.

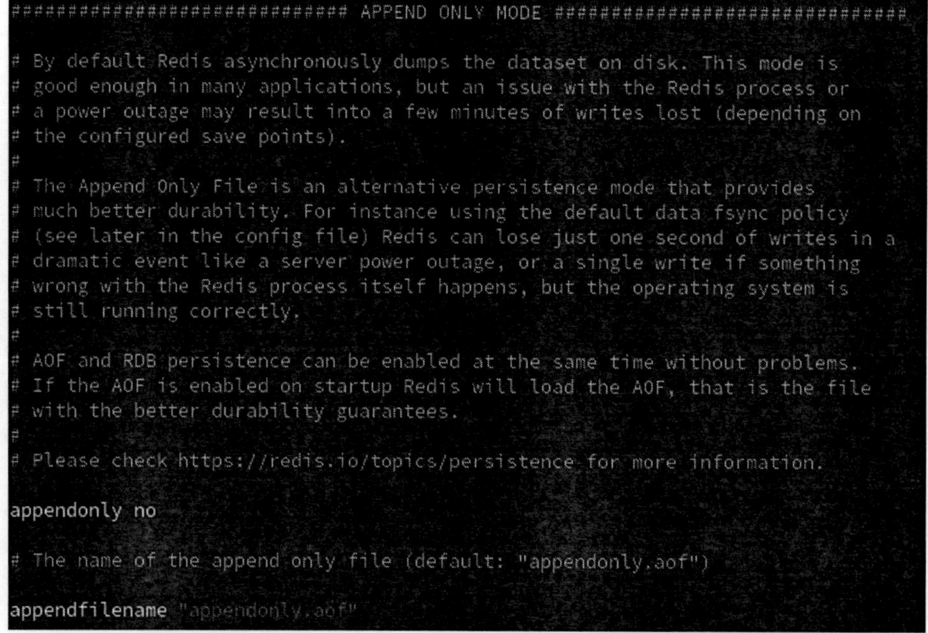

```
############################## APPEND ONLY MODE ###############################

# By default Redis asynchronously dumps the dataset on disk. This mode is
# good enough in many applications, but an issue with the Redis process or
# a power outage may result into a few minutes of writes lost (depending on
# the configured save points).
#
# The Append Only File is an alternative persistence mode that provides
# much better durability. For instance using the default data fsync policy
# (see later in the config file) Redis can lose just one second of writes in a
# dramatic event like a server power outage, or a single write if something
# wrong with the Redis process itself happens, but the operating system is
# still running correctly.
#
# AOF and RDB persistence can be enabled at the same time without problems.
# If the AOF is enabled on startup Redis will load the AOF, that is the file
# with the better durability guarantees.
#
# Please check https://redis.io/topics/persistence for more information.

appendonly no

# The name of the append only file (default: "appendonly.aof")

appendfilename "appendonly.aof"
```

Figure 3.17: *Redis appendonly Directive inside the Configuration File*

5. **Tuning Redis Performance:** For optimal performance, you can tweak several settings in **`redis.conf`** such as the number of databases (**`databases`** directive), the number of maximum clients (**`maxclients`**), and the **I/O thread** model. Tuning these configurations ensures Redis runs efficiently based on your application's demands.

   - In *Figure* 3.18, we will explore the number of databases directive within the Redis configuration file. This directive allows you to specify the number of databases that a Redis instance can support. By default, Redis provides 16 databases, which are indexed from 0 to 15.

     To configure this, you can adjust the **`databases`** directive in the **`redis.conf`** file as follows:

```
# Set the number of databases. The default database is DB 0, you can select
# a different one on a per-connection basis using SELECT <dbid> where
# dbid is a number between 0 and 'databases'-1
databases 16
```

Figure 3.18: *Redis Database Directive inside the Configuration File*

     This parameter can be modified to increase or decrease the number of databases based on your application requirements. Each database operates independently, but keep in mind that all databases share the same memory allocation. Therefore, increasing the number of databases may affect overall performance, especially in memory-constrained environments.

     For production environments, it is essential to carefully consider the number of databases required to balance memory usage and application architecture.

   - *Figure* 3.19 demonstrates the use of the **`maxclients`** directive within the Redis configuration file (**`redis.conf`**). This directive sets the maximum number of simultaneous client connections that a Redis instance can handle.

```
################################### CLIENTS ####################################

# Set the max number of connected clients at the same time. By default
# this limit is set to 10000 clients, however if the Redis server is not
# able to configure the process file limit to allow for the specified limit
# the max number of allowed clients is set to the current file limit
# minus 32 (as Redis reserves a few file descriptors for internal uses).
#
# Once the limit is reached Redis will close all the new connections sending
# an error 'max number of clients reached'.
#
# IMPORTANT: When Redis Cluster is used, the max number of connections is also
# shared with the cluster bus: every node in the cluster will use two
# connections, one incoming and another outgoing. It is important to size the
# limit accordingly in case of very large clusters.
#
# maxclients 10000
```

Figure 3.19: *Redis maxclients Directive inside the Configuration File*

This value determines the upper limit for client connections to the Redis server. If the limit is reached, additional clients attempting to connect will receive an error, which ensures the server's stability by preventing resource exhaustion.

Key Considerations for the `maxclients` Directive

- **System Limitations:** The maximum number of clients Redis can handle is also influenced by the system's file descriptor limits. Therefore, you must ensure that the operating system is configured to support the desired number of connections.

- **Performance:** Setting a very high value without sufficient system resources may degrade performance. Adjust this parameter based on workload and available resources.
- **Restart Requirement:** Changes to the **`maxclients`** directive require a Redis server restart for the new configuration to take effect.

Figure 3.20 showcases the **`io-threads`** directive within the Redis configuration file (**`redis.conf`**). This directive allows you to configure the number of I/O threads Redis uses for handling network requests. By default, Redis operates with a single-threaded event loop for network I/O. However, the io-threads directive enables multi-threaded I/O to improve performance in high-throughput scenarios.

A sample configuration in the **`redis.conf`** file might look like this:

```
################################ THREADED I/O #################################

# Redis is mostly single threaded, however there are certain threaded
# operations such as UNLINK, slow I/O accesses and other things that are
# performed on side threads.
#
# Now it is also possible to handle Redis clients socket reads and writes
# in different I/O threads. Since especially writing is so slow, normally
# Redis users use pipelining in order to speed up the Redis performances per
# core, and spawn multiple instances in order to scale more. Using I/O
# threads it is possible to easily speedup two times Redis without resorting
# to pipelining nor sharding of the instance.
#
# By default threading is disabled, we suggest enabling it only in machines
# that have at least 4 or more cores, leaving at least one spare core.
# Using more than 8 threads is unlikely to help much. We also recommend using
# threaded I/O only if you actually have performance problems, with Redis
# instances being able to use a quite big percentage of CPU time, otherwise
# there is no point in using this feature.
#
# So for instance if you have a four cores boxes, try to use 2 or 3 I/O
# threads, if you have a 8 cores, try to use 6 threads. In order to
# enable I/O threads use the following configuration directive:
#
# io-threads 4
```

Figure 3.20: *Redis io-threads Directive inside the Configuration File*

This example configures Redis to use four threads for handling I/O operations.

Key Points about the io-threads Directive

- **Use Case:** Multi-threaded I/O is beneficial when Redis is used for high-volume data streaming or when there are numerous simultaneous client connections.
- **Thread Count:** The number of I/O threads should be chosen based on the system's CPU cores and workload requirements. Using too many threads can lead to diminishing returns.
- **Thread Safety:** While I/O operations are multi-threaded, data manipulation operations (for example, GET, SET) remain single-threaded to ensure thread safety.
- **Default Setting:** The default value for io-threads is 1, meaning single-threaded operation.

Note: *Changes to the io-threads directive require restarting the Redis server for the new configuration to take effect. Careful tuning of this parameter can help optimize Redis performance in demanding environments.*

6. **Configuring Redis Logging:** Redis logs its activity, errors, and connections, which provides valuable insights into the server's performance and potential issues. You can adjust the verbosity and location of these logs by configuring the **`loglevel`** and **`logfile`** directives in the **`redis.conf`** file:

   - **`loglevel`**: This directive controls the level of detail in the logs. Options include **`debug, verbose, notice (default)`**, and **`warning`**. Increasing the verbosity can be helpful for troubleshooting, while lower verbosity is suitable for normal operation.
   - **`logfile`**: This directive specifies the location where Redis writes its logs. By default, logs are sent to the standard output, but you can set this to a specific file path to save logs in a designated location for easier monitoring and analysis.

   Properly configuring these settings can assist in troubleshooting issues and monitoring Redis behavior. This ensures that you have the necessary information to maintain and optimize your instance.

   Figure 3.21 showcases the **`logfile`** directive in the Redis configuration file (**`redis.conf`**). This directive specifies the file where Redis logs server activities, errors, and important events.

```
# Specify the server verbosity level.
# This can be one of:
# debug (a lot of information, useful for development/testing)
# verbose (many rarely useful info, but not a mess like the debug level)
# notice (moderately verbose, what you want in production probably)
# warning (only very important / critical messages are logged)
loglevel notice

# Specify the log file name. Also the empty string can be used to force
# Redis to log on the standard output. Note that if you use standard
# output for logging but daemonize, logs will be sent to /dev/null
logfile /var/log/redis/redis.log
```

Figure 3.21: *Redis logfile Directive inside the Configuration File*

7. **Adjusting TCP Keepalive:** The **`tcp-keepalive`** setting in Redis controls how often TCP keepalive packets are sent to clients to verify that the connection is still active. This setting is particularly important in environments with unstable or fluctuating network conditions, where long-term client connections might otherwise drop unexpectedly.

   Thus, by adjusting the **`tcp-keepalive`** value in the **`redis.conf`** file, you can help ensure that idle connections remain active and prevent disconnections caused by network timeouts. Setting a lower value can help maintain persistent connections more aggressively, while a higher value may reduce network traffic in more stable environments.

   Carefully tuning this setting based on your network conditions can improve the reliability of client connections to your Redis instance.

   Figure 3.22 demonstrates the **`tcp-keepalive`** directive in the Redis configuration file (**`redis.conf`**). This directive controls the TCP keepalive interval for connections to the Redis server, which ensures idle connections are monitored and terminated if necessary.

```
# TCP keepalive.
#
# If non-zero, use SO_KEEPALIVE to send TCP ACKs to clients in absence
# of communication. This is useful for two reasons:
#
# 1) Detect dead peers.
# 2) Force network equipment in the middle to consider the connection to be
#    alive.
#
# On Linux, the specified value (in seconds) is the period used to send ACKs.
# Note that to close the connection the double of the time is needed.
# On other kernels the period depends on the kernel configuration.
#
# A reasonable value for this option is 300 seconds, which is the new
# Redis default starting with Redis 3.2.1.
tcp-keepalive 300
```

Figure 3.22: *Redis tcp-keepalive Directive inside the Configuration File*

8. **Supervised Mode:** If you are running Redis under a service manager like **systemd** (on Linux) or a similar system, enabling **supervised mode** allows Redis to integrate seamlessly with your system's process manager. This setup provides enhanced monitoring and automatic restarting capabilities and makes Redis more robust and reliable in case of unexpected failures.

   To enable supervised mode, configure the **supervised** directive in the **redis.conf** file. Depending on your system, you can set this to **systemd**, **upstart**, or another supported service manager.

   Figure 3.23 demonstrates the **supervised** directive in the Redis configuration file (**redis.conf**). This directive configures how Redis interacts with process supervision systems like **systemd**, **upstart**, or **supervisord**.

```
# If you run Redis from upstart or systemd, Redis can interact with your
# supervision tree. Options:
#   supervised no      - no supervision interaction
#   supervised upstart - signal upstart by putting Redis into SIGSTOP mode
#                        requires "expect stop" in your upstart job config
#   supervised systemd - signal systemd by writing READY=1 to $NOTIFY_SOCKET
#                        on startup, and updating Redis status on a regular
#                        basis.
#   supervised auto    - detect upstart or systemd method based on
#                        UPSTART_JOB or NOTIFY_SOCKET environment variables
# Note: these supervision methods only signal "process is ready."
#       They do not enable continuous pings back to your supervisor.
#
# The default is "no". To run under upstart/systemd, you can simply uncomment
# the line below:
#
# supervised auto
```

Figure 3.23: *Redis supervised Directive inside the Configuration File*

Configuration Implications

- **bind + protected-mode**
  - **What It Does**: Controls who can connect

  - **If Mis-Set**: `Binding to 0.0.0.0` with `protected-mode no` (protected-mode set to no) exposes Redis to the internet and is therefore, risky. Keep protected-mode yes, bind to a private IP/VPC, and firewall it.
- `requirepass` **/ ACL Users**
  - **What It Does**: Enforces authentication
  - **If Missing**: Anyone who can reach Redis can run commands. Add a password/ACLs; clients must AUTH or fail.
- `appendonly` **yes (AOF) / save (RDB) /** `appendfsync`
  - **What It Does**: Controls durability
  - **If You Disable Persistence**: This is the fastest, but a crash can lose everything in RAM.
  - **If** `appendonly yes + appendfsync always`: Safest but slowest writes
  - **If** `appendfsync everysec` (common): May lose `~1s` (one second) of writes on crash, a good balance
  - **If Only save (RDB)**: Can lose changes since last snapshot
- `stop-writes-on-bgsave-error yes`
  - **What It Does**: Blocks new writes if Redis cannot persist (disk full, perms)
  - **If It Triggers**: Clients see write errors until the persistence issue is fixed; this prevents silent data loss.
- `timeout` **(Idle Client Timeout)**
  - **What It Does**: Disconnects idle clients automatically
  - **If Too Low**: Background workers or dashboards may get disconnected; if unset, idle clients linger and consume fds.
- `tcp-keepalive`
  - **What It Does**: Detects dead TCP connections
  - **If Too High**: Dead clients take longer to clean up; too low can drop flaky long-lived connections.
- `maxclients`
  - **What It Does**: Upper bound on concurrent connections
  - **If Hit**: New clients get "`max number of clients reached`."; increase limit or add pooling.
- `client-output-buffer-limit` **(For** `normal/pubsub/replica`**)**
  - **What It Does**: Caps per-client output buffers
  - **If Exceeded**: Redis disconnects that client to protect memory; often hits chatty Pub/Sub consumers or slow replicas.
- `slowlog-log-slower-than` **/** `slowlog-max-len`
  - **What It Does**: Records slow commands
  - **If Too Lax (Big Threshold)**: You might miss performance offenders; if it is too strict, it floods the log. Use 1–5 ms as a start.

- `notify-keyspace-events`
  - **What It Does**: Enables **`keyspace`** notifications
  - **If Enabled Widely**: It will result in extra CPU/traffic. You must turn it on only during required event classes (for example, **`Ex`** for expirations).

Troubleshooting Common Issues

While setting up and operating Redis, you may encounter various challenges. These issues can arise at different stages such as during installation, configuration, or regular use. Understanding how to troubleshoot these problems is essential for maintaining a smooth and efficient Redis environment. While it may be difficult to address every possible scenario without specific details, there are several common issues that often occur. Here is a list of typical problems and suggested solutions to help you quickly diagnose and resolve potential hurdles:

Redis Server Fails to Start

This could be due to the following reasons:

Incorrect Configuration File

Solution: Configuration errors are one of the most common reasons Redis fails to start. Redis validates its configuration file at startup, and any syntax errors or invalid directives will prevent the service from launching.

To troubleshoot, start Redis manually and observe the error output:

```
redis-server /etc/redis/redis.conf
```

In this example, replace **`/etc/redis/redis.conf`** with the actual path to your Redis configuration file. If there are syntax errors or invalid settings, Redis will display descriptive error messages indicating what needs to be corrected. Fix the reported issues and restart the Redis service.

Insufficient Permissions

Solution: If Redis fails to start due to insufficient permissions, it is likely that it does not have the necessary access rights to the configuration file, data directory, or other critical resources. To resolve this, make sure that Redis has the correct ownership and permissions for these files and directories. You can use the following commands to adjust permissions:

```
sudo chown redis:redis /etc/redis/redis.conf
sudo chown -R redis:redis /var/lib/redis
```

These commands assign the appropriate ownership (the **`redis`** user and group) to the Redis configuration file and the data directory (**`/var/lib/redis`**). Once you have updated the permissions, restart the Redis service to apply the changes.

Ensuring that Redis has the correct permissions will help prevent access-related issues and allow the server to function properly.

Conflicting Processes Using the Redis Port (Default: 6379)

Solution: If Redis fails to start because another process is using its default port (6379), it is likely that a different service is occupying the port. To troubleshoot, you can identify any processes using the Redis port with the following command:

```
sudo lsof -i :6379
```

This will list any processes using the Redis port. If another process is found, you can either stop that process or change the Redis port in the configuration file. To stop the conflicting process, use:

```
sudo kill <PID>
```

Replacing `<PID>` with the Process ID Listed in the Output

Alternatively, you can change Redis to use a different port by editing the Redis configuration file (**`/etc/redis/redis.conf`**) and modifying the port directive:

```
port 6380
```

After making changes, save them and restart the Redis service to apply the new configuration.

Masking

Solution: If Redis fails to start due to masking, it means that the Redis service has been intentionally masked, which prevents it from being started. Masking a service creates a symbolic link to **`/dev/null`** and makes it impossible to start the service until the mask is removed. To troubleshoot and resolve this, you can unmask the Redis service with the following command:

```
sudo systemctl unmask redis
```

After unmasking, try restarting the Redis service. Unmasking the service should allow Redis to start normally and resolve the issue.

Connection Refused When Accessing Redis

Cause: This issuc may occur if Redis is not running or if the server is bound only to **`localhost`**, preventing external connections. Additionally, firewall settings might be blocking access to the Redis port.

Solution: First, check if Redis is running via **`sudo systemctl`** status redis. If it is running but you are trying to connect remotely, check the bind directive in the **`redis.conf`** file to ensure Redis is bound to the correct IP address. Also, verify firewall settings that might be blocking access. By following these steps, you can resolve connection issues and ensure Redis is accessible whenever required.

Memory Limit Reached

Cause: Redis is an in-memory database and when the memory limit is reached, it may start rejecting new writes based on the configured **`maxmemory-policy`**. This situation can occur if Redis is using all the allocated memory, or if the server's memory resources are insufficient to support the current configuration.

Solution: If Redis is rejecting writes or becomes unstable due to memory pressure, it likely means that Redis is running out of available memory, either because the server's **`maxmemory`** setting is too high or because the system doesn't have enough free memory. To troubleshoot this, first check your system's available memory using the following command:

```
free -h
```

If the system is low on memory, you may need to free up resources or increase the available memory on your server. You can also adjust the **`maxmemory`** setting in the Redis configuration file (**`/etc/redis/redis.conf`**) to prevent Redis from using more memory than available. Open the **`config`** file and set an appropriate limit, for example:

```
maxmemory 512mb
```

After adjusting the configuration, restart Redis.

This should prevent memory overflow and ensure Redis starts properly by keeping its memory usage within the system's available limits.

Redis Crashing or High Latency

Cause: Redis may experience crashes or high latency due to heavy workloads, improper configurations, or insufficient system resources. These issues can significantly impact performance and reliability, especially under high traffic or when handling large datasets.

Solution: To address these issues, follow these steps:

1. **Monitor System Resources**: Check your CPU, memory, and disk I/O usage to ensure that your system can handle the current load. You can use tools like **`htop`**, **`top`**, or **`iostat`** to get a real-time overview of resource utilization.
2. **Adjust the Number of Allowed Connections**: If Redis is overwhelmed by too many client connections, consider lowering or adjusting the **`maxclients`** directive in the **`redis.conf`** file:

   ```
   maxclients 10000
   ```

   Set this value based on your server's capacity to manage simultaneous connections without affecting performance.
3. **Review and Adjust Memory Settings**: Ensure that your **`maxmemory`** setting is configured appropriately, so Redis does not use more memory than is available on your system. Align the **`maxmemory`** value with the available RAM to avoid performance degradation or crashes.
4. **Check Redis Logs for Errors**: Examine the Redis logs for any error messages or warnings that may provide clues about the root cause. The logs are typically located at **`/var/log/redis/redis-server.log`** or a similar path, depending on your system configuration. Address any issues highlighted in the logs.

   Thus, by monitoring your system and fine-tuning Redis configurations, you can reduce crashes and improve performance, while ensuring that Redis remains responsive even under heavy load.

Data Loss after Restart

Cause: Data loss after a Redis restart may occur if Redis is not configured with proper persistence settings. By default, Redis is an in-memory data store, and without enabling persistence, data can be lost when the server restarts or crashes. Redis may not have been configured with proper persistence settings (AOF or RDB).

Solution: To prevent data loss, ensure that you have enabled one or both of Redis's persistence mechanisms: **Append Only File (AOF)** and **RDB snapshots**. Here is how to configure these options:

1. **Enable Append Only File (AOF)**: AOF logs every write operation to ensure data durability. To enable AOF, open the **`redis.conf`** file and set the **`appendonly`** directive to **`yes, use the following command`**:

   ```
   appendonly yes
   ```

   You can also customize the AOF rewrite policies to control how frequently Redis creates backups and compacts the AOF file.

2. **Configure RDB Snapshots**: RDB creates point-in-time snapshots of your data at specified intervals. To enable RDB snapshots, configure the **`save`** directive in **`redis.conf`** as shown:
   a. **save 900 1 #** : Use this to save the dataset every 900 seconds (15 minutes) if at least 1 change is made.
   b. **save 300 10 #** : Use this to save every 300 seconds (5 minutes) if at least 10 changes are made.
   c. **save 60 10000 #** : Use this to save every 60 seconds if at least 10,000 changes are made.
3. **Combine AOF and RDB for Better Durability**: For a more robust setup, you can use both AOF and RDB persistence to balance performance and data safety. AOF ensures data durability with minimal loss, while RDB provides a quicker way to create snapshots.
4. **Test your persistence settings**: Regularly test your backup and recovery process to ensure data is saved as expected and that your setup aligns with your application's durability requirements.

   By enabling and properly configuring persistence, you can minimize the risk of data loss and ensure that Redis retains your data even after a restart.

Authentication Failures

Cause: If you have configured a password for Redis, you may encounter authentication errors when attempting to connect. These errors typically occur if the correct password is not provided or if there is a mismatch between the password set in the configuration and the one you are using.

Solution: Ensure you are providing the correct password with the auth command after connecting via **`redis-cli`**. Verify that the password set in the **`requirepass`** directive of the **`redis.conf`** file matches the one you are using.

Follow these steps to resolve authentication failures:

1. **Use the Correct Password**: After connecting to Redis using **`redis-cli`**, authenticate by using the **`AUTH`** command followed by the correct password: **`AUTH "YourPasswordHere"`**
2. **Verify the requirepass Directive**: Check the **`requirepass`** setting in the **`redis.conf`** file to ensure that the password is correctly configured:

   ```
   requirepass YourPasswordHere
   ```

   Make sure the password specified in the **`requirepass`** directive matches the one you are using to authenticate.
3. **Restart Redis if Necessary**: If you make any changes to the **`redis.conf`** file, restart the Redis service to apply the new settings.

Slow Redis Performance

Cause: Redis performance can degrade due to inefficient configuration, insufficient system resources, or suboptimal data management practices. Heavy workloads, large datasets, or poorly designed queries may also contribute to latency and slower response times.

Solution: To improve Redis performance, consider the following steps:

1. **Monitor Redis**: Use the following Redis monitoring commands to gain insights into the server's behavior and identify performance bottlenecks:

- `INFO`: Provides detailed information about the Redis server, including memory usage, keyspace statistics, and performance metrics. Use this command to pinpoint areas of concern.
- `MONITOR`: Displays real-time queries being executed on the server. This can help identify inefficient or high-latency commands that may be affecting performance.

2. **Optimize Configuration Settings**:
   - `maxmemory`: Set an appropriate memory limit to prevent Redis from consuming all available system RAM. This helps maintain system stability.
   - `maxclients`: Adjust the `maxclients` setting to control the number of simultaneous connections Redis can handle. Ensure that the value aligns with your server's capacity.
   - **Eviction Policies**: Choose a suitable eviction policy based on your use case (for example, `allkeys-lru` or `volatile-lfu`) to manage memory efficiently when the `maxmemory` limit is reached.
3. **Analyze Your Data Model**: If you have a large keyspace or complex data structures, consider optimizing your data model. Break down large keys into smaller, more manageable pieces, or use efficient data structures that suit your access patterns.
4. **Optimize Hardware Resources**: Ensure that your hardware is adequate for your workload. This includes having enough RAM and CPU power to support Redis operations, especially under high loads. Consider scaling up your server if necessary.
5. **Review Slow Queries**: Use the Redis Slow Log feature to identify and analyze slow commands. Optimize or restructure these queries to improve overall performance.

Redis Command Errors or Timeouts

Cause: Command errors or timeouts can occur due to high server load or network-related issues, such as latency or packet loss. These problems can impact the responsiveness of Redis, especially under heavy traffic or when network conditions are unstable.

Solution: To diagnose and resolve these issues, consider the following steps:

1. **Check for Network Issues**: Use network diagnostic tools, such as `ping`, `traceroute`, or `mtr` to identify latency or packet loss between the client and the Redis server. Address any network-related problems that may be causing delays or timeouts.
2. **Review Redis Logs**: Examine the Redis logs for signs of excessive load or errors that may be contributing to the problem. Logs can provide insight into resource bottlenecks such as memory exhaustion or an overwhelming number of client connections.
3. **Monitor Server Load**: Use system monitoring tools (like `htop` or `vmstat`) to check CPU, memory, and disk I/O usage. If Redis is under heavy load, consider optimizing your setup or distributing the load more efficiently.
4. **Scale Up your Redis Setup**: If your current resources are insufficient, consider scaling up by adding more RAM and CPU power, or even setting up a Redis cluster to distribute the load across multiple nodes.
5. **Optimize Redis Configuration**:
   a. **Memory Settings**: Adjust the `maxmemory` directive to ensure that Redis uses memory efficiently without exhausting system resources.

b. **Connection Settings**: Tweak **`maxclients`** to control the number of active connections Redis can handle, while ensuring that it matches your server's capacity.

c. **Eviction policies**: Implement an appropriate eviction policy to manage data in memory and prevent performance degradation.

By diagnosing network issues, monitoring system performance, and optimizing Redis settings, you can reduce command errors and timeouts to ensure a smoother and more reliable Redis experience.

Therefore, by understanding and addressing these common issues, you can ensure that your Redis instance operates smoothly and efficiently, while minimizing disruptions and maximizing performance. Troubleshooting Redis may seem challenging at times, but with the right tools, configuration adjustments, and monitoring, most problems can be quickly resolved. Keeping your Redis installation well-maintained and properly configured will help you avoid potential pitfalls, while ensuring a stable and reliable database environment for your applications.

Key Points to Remember

- **Redis Configuration File:** The Redis configuration file is typically located at **`/etc/redis/redis.conf`**. If it is not present at this location, the **locate** command can be used to identify its path:

  ```
  locate redis.conf
  ```

- If you have just installed **`locate`**, remember to update the database first by running:

  ```
  sudo updatedb
  ```

- **Searching in Redis Config File**: If you are using vim to check the Redis configuration file, you can search for specific settings by typing **`:/<setting_name>`** within the file. This will help you quickly navigate to the configuration option you are looking for.

- **Backup Configuration File**: Before making any changes to the Redis configuration file, create a backup. This allows you to easily compare settings or revert to the original configuration if necessary. Use the following command to create a backup:

  ```
  cp /etc/redis/redis.conf /etc/redis/redis_backup.conf
  ```

- **Making Configuration Changes**: Apply configuration changes one at a time and restart Redis after each modification. This way, if Redis fails to start, you will know which setting caused the issue and can revert it easily. Avoid making multiple changes at once, as it can complicate troubleshooting.

Conclusion

In this chapter, we have embarked on a comprehensive journey to set up Redis across various platforms, ensuring that no matter your operating system, you are equipped to get Redis up and running seamlessly. From installing Redis on Linux distributions like CentOS and Ubuntu, to macOS and Windows, we have covered step-by-step instructions tailored to each environment. Beyond installation, we delved into essential practices to secure your Redis instance, verify the installation, and perform basic configurations that lay the foundation for efficient and secure operation.

We also tackled common troubleshooting scenarios, empowering you with practical solutions to address challenges that might arise during setup. To reinforce your learning, key points were summarized to help you strengthen your recall of the critical aspects of Redis installation and configuration.

With Redis successfully set up and configured, you are now ready to explore the next chapter, "*Data Management in Redis with Popular Scripting Languages*." In the upcoming chapter, we will dive into how Redis integrates with scripting languages like Python, PHP, and shell scripts. You will learn how to perform powerful data management operations to leverage Redis in real-world applications.

Redis is more than just an in-memory data store; it is a versatile tool with limitless potential. Let us continue this exciting journey to unlock its full power!

CHAPTER 4

Data Management in Redis with Popular Scripting Languages

Introduction

In this chapter, you will learn how to interact with Redis and manage data using different scripting languages. Whether you are working with PHP, Python, Shell Script, or Lua, we will provide clear, step-by-step instructions to help you seamlessly integrate Redis into your applications. This chapter is designed to equip you with the essential knowledge and skills needed to harness the power of Redis in a variety of development environments.

We begin by covering the basics, such as establishing a connection to the Redis server using each language, and then move on to practical examples that demonstrate key data operations. You will learn how to insert new data into Redis, update existing data efficiently, and delete data when necessary. Additionally, we will explore techniques to handle more advanced scenarios, such as optimizing performance with pipelining and managing data persistence.

Throughout the chapter, our focus is on providing actionable and real-world examples that illustrate how Redis can be leveraged to solve common data management challenges. By the end of this chapter, you will have a solid understanding of how to use Redis with multiple scripting languages to efficiently store, modify, and manage your data. Hence, whether you are building web applications, automating scripts, or managing large datasets, you will be well-prepared to integrate Redis into your projects and maximize its potential.

Structure

This chapter will cover the following topics:

- Connecting to Redis
- Data Management
- Best Practices for Data Management in Redis

Connecting to Redis

Connecting to Redis is a crucial first step in harnessing the full potential of this versatile in-memory data store. Redis makes this process straightforward, whether you are working directly from the command line or through a programming language. At its core, **Redis provides a built-in command-line interface, `redis-cli`, which lets you interact with your Redis instance effortlessly**. Through **`redis-cli`**, you can quickly check the server status with a simple PING command, set and retrieve data, or perform other essential operations. It is a powerful tool for immediate feedback and debugging, which offers you a hands-on way to experience Redis in action.

While `redis-cli` is great for testing and simple tasks, most real-world applications require programmatic access to Redis. This is where connecting through programming languages becomes essential. In this chapter, we guide you through the process of integrating Redis with popular languages like **Python, PHP,** and **Shell Script**. Each language has dedicated libraries or extensions that are designed to make working with Redis both efficient and intuitive. For example, Python developers can take advantage of the `redis-py` client library, which provides a user-friendly API for managing connections and executing commands. PHP developers can use the `PhpRedis` extension to interact with Redis seamlessly, which further simplifies the process of incorporating Redis into web applications. Even for automation scripts, Shell Script users can send commands to Redis and retrieve responses, while streamlining various workflows.

We will walk through the steps for setting up these connections, from installing the necessary libraries or extensions to configuring your connection settings properly. Along the way, we will also discuss common pitfalls and how to handle connection errors gracefully. By the end of this section, you will have a clear understanding of how to connect to Redis, whether you are working directly from the command line or embedding Redis into your applications using different programming languages. This knowledge sets a strong foundation for managing and manipulating data effectively in your projects.

Connecting to Redis with redis-cli

The simplest way to connect to and interact with a Redis server is by using **redis-cli**, the built-in command-line interface provided by Redis. This tool is invaluable for developers who need to perform quick tests, run basic operations, or debug their Redis setup.

1. To connect to a local Redis server using redis-cli, open your terminal and type:

   ```
   redis-cli
   ```

   If Redis is running on the default port (**6379**), this command connects you to the server and presents you with a prompt where you can issue commands. For example, you can type:

   ```
   127.0.0.1:6379> PING
   ```

   You should receive the following response:

   ```
   PONG
   ```

   This simple command confirms that the Redis server is active and responding.

2. Connecting to a Remote Redis Server

   If your Redis server is running on a different host or a non-default port, you can specify the host and port when connecting:

   ```
   redis-cli -h <hostname> -p <port>
   ```

   Replace **<hostname>** with the IP address or domain name of the remote server and **<port>** with the port number. For example, to connect to a Redis server running on **192.168.1.100** and port **6380**, use the following command:

   ```
   redis-cli -h 192.168.1.100 -p 6380
   ```

Why Use `redis-cli`?

Using `redis-cli` is an excellent way to quickly test Redis commands, monitor server behavior, and gain hands-on experience with Redis. It is a **reliable tool for checking the status of your server, debugging issues, and experimenting with different data structures.**

While redis-cli is useful for direct interaction, most applications require Redis to be integrated programmatically. Redis can be seamlessly connected to various scripting languages, with each offering specific libraries or extensions to simplify this process. In this chapter, we dive into how to connect Redis to popular programming languages like Python, PHP, and Shell Script, along with practical examples to guide you through the setup.

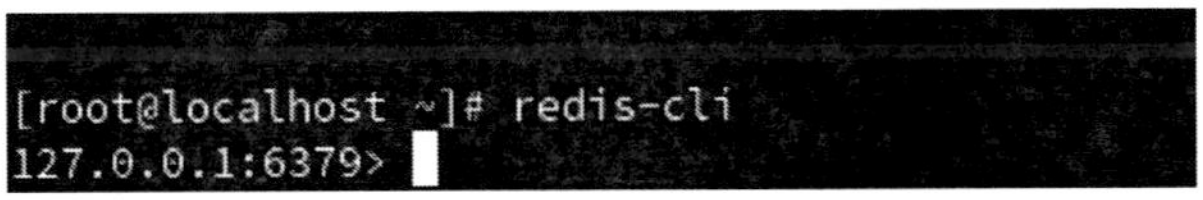

```
[root@localhost ~]# redis-cli
127.0.0.1:6379>
```

Figure 4.1: *Logging into Redis Using redis-cli*

Note: *If authentication is enabled, use redis-cli -a <password> or authenticate using* AUTH *after connecting.*

Connecting to Redis with a Shell Script

Using a shell script to connect and interact with Redis can be incredibly useful for automating tasks, setting up periodic data operations, or quickly running Redis commands from within a script. Shell Scripts provide a simple yet powerful way to execute Redis commands via **`redis-cli`**, which allows developers and system administrators to streamline their workflows.

To begin, you need to use **`redis-cli`** commands directly within your Shell Script. The following example demonstrates a basic Redis connection using a shell script:

```
#!/bin/bash
# Connect to Redis and test the connection with a PING command
response=$(redis-cli PING)
# Check the response from Redis
if [ "$response" = "PONG" ]; then
  echo "Connected to Redis successfully!"
else
  echo "Failed to connect to Redis. Please check if the Redis server is running."
fi
```

In this script, you will observe that:

- **The `redis-cli PING`** command sends a simple PING command to Redis. If Redis is running and accessible, it will respond with a PONG.
- The script captures the response and checks if it matches "**PONG**." If it does, it confirms a successful connection; otherwise, it provides an error message.

This basic script demonstrates how to establish a connection to Redis and verify that the server is running correctly.

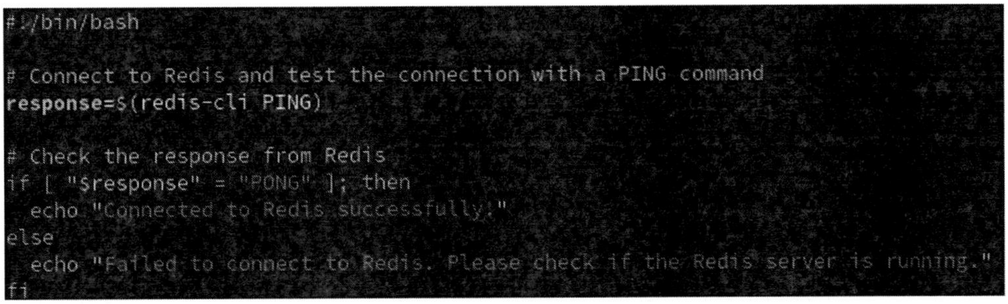

```
#!/bin/bash

# Connect to Redis and test the connection with a PING command
response=$(redis-cli PING)

# Check the response from Redis
if [ "$response" = "PONG" ]; then
  echo "Connected to Redis successfully!"
else
  echo "Failed to connect to Redis. Please check if the Redis server is running."
fi
```

Figure 4.2: *Shell Script to Connect and Test Redis Connection*

Figure 4.2 illustrates a shell script designed to connect to a Redis server and test the connection. The script sends a PING command to the Redis server and verifies the response to ensure that the server is running and accessible. This provides a simple and automated way to confirm the operational status of Redis.

```
[root@localhost ~]#
[root@localhost ~]# sh test_redis.sh
Connected to Redis successfully!
[root@localhost ~]#
[root@localhost ~]#
```

Figure 4.3: *Executing the Shell Script and Its Result*

Figure 4.3 demonstrates the execution of a shell script designed to connect to a Redis server and test its connectivity.

Connecting to a Remote Redis Server with redis-cli

If you need to connect to a Redis instance running on a different host or using a non-default port, you can specify these details using the following `redis-cli` command:

```
#!/bin/bash
# Shell script to connect to a remote Redis server and verify connectivity
response=$(redis-cli -h <hostname> -p <port> PING)
# Replace <hostname> with the IP address or domain name and <port> with the port number
if [ "$response" = "PONG" ]; then
  echo "Connected to Redis on <hostname> successfully!"
else
  echo "Failed to connect to Redis on <hostname>. Please check the server and port settings."
fi
```

Replace `<hostname>` with the IP address or domain name of the remote Redis server and `<port>` with the port number (**default is 6379**).

Using these simple scripts, you can establish connections to Redis and ensure that your scripts are ready to execute Redis commands in more complex operations covered in later chapters. This foundational understanding will enable you to automate tasks efficiently, and integrate Redis seamlessly into your workflows.

Connecting to Redis with PHP

Establishing a connection to Redis using PHP is straightforward and efficient, thanks to the popular `PhpRedis` extension. This extension provides a native interface for interacting with Redis and is widely used in PHP applications for caching, session management, and real-time data processing. To connect to Redis, first ensure that the `PhpRedis` extension is installed and enabled in your PHP environment.

Checking if `PhpRedis` is Installed in PHP

Before connecting to Redis using PHP, it is essential to verify that the `PhpRedis` extension is installed and enabled in your PHP environment. You can verify this in a couple of ways:

- **Using the `phpinfo()` Function**: Create a simple PHP script to display detailed information about your PHP configuration, including the following installed extensions:

```
<?php
phpinfo();
?>
```

Save this script as **info.php** and run it in your browser. Search for "**redis**" on the page. If PhpRedis is installed, you will see a section labeled "**redis**," confirming that the extension is enabled.

- **Using the `extension_loaded()` Function**: You can also use the **extension_loaded()** function in a PHP script to check if **PhpRedis** is installed, as shown here:

```
<?php
if (extension_loaded('redis')) {
    echo "PhpRedis is installed and enabled!";
} else {
    echo "PhpRedis is not installed.";
}
?>
```

Running this script will tell you whether the **PhpRedis** extension is available.

If **PhpRedis** is not installed, you may need to install it using your system's package manager or compile it manually, depending on your environment. This verification step is crucial before attempting to connect to Redis from PHP.

Installing PhpRedis

PhpRedis is a popular PHP extension used to interface with Redis servers. This section explains how to install it on different platforms:

1. **Installing PhpRedis on macOS**

   To install **PhpRedis** on macOS, you can use **Homebrew, as shown here**:

   a. **Install PHP (if not already installed)** using the following command:

   ```
   brew install php
   ```

   b. **Install `pecl` (if not already available)**. **Pecl** is a repository for PHP extensions, and it comes with most PHP installations. If you need to reinstall it, use the following command:

   ```
   brew install php-pear
   ```

   c. **Install PhpRedis using pecl by running the following command:**

   ```
   pecl install redis
   ```

   d. **Enable the Redis extension in your PHP configuration**.

   Open your **php.ini** file (you can find the path by running **php --ini**) and add: **extension =redis.so**

```
Configuration File (php.ini) Path: /opt/homebrew/etc/php/8.4
Loaded Configuration File:         /opt/homebrew/etc/php/8.4/php.ini
Scan for additional .ini files in: /opt/homebrew/etc/php/8.4/conf.d
Additional .ini files parsed:      /opt/homebrew/etc/php/8.4/conf.d/ext-opcache.ini
```

***Figure 4.4**: Output of the php --ini Command*

- **Restart your web server (if applicable).**

redis

Redis Support	enabled
Redis Version	6.1.0
Redis Sentinel Version	1.0
Available serializers	php, json

Figure 4.5*: Output of the Test PHP File with phpinfo() to Check if Redis is Installed*

Figure 4.5 showcases the output of a test PHP file that uses the **`phpinfo()`** function to display detailed information about the PHP configuration. The output includes a section for the Redis extension, which confirms whether Redis is installed and enabled. This figure serves as a visual representation to verify the successful integration of Redis with the PHP environment.

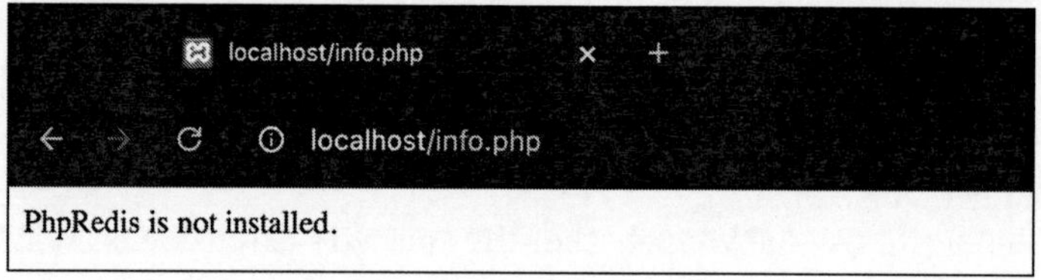

Figure 4.6*: Output of the info.php File Verifying the Redis Extension Installation*

2. **Installing PhpRedis on Ubuntu**

   To install **PhpRedis** on Ubuntu, use the following steps:

   - Update your package list using the following command:

     ```
     sudo apt-get update
     ```

   - Install PHP and the php-pear package (if they are not already installed) through:

     ```
     sudo apt-get install php php-pear php-dev
     ```

   - Install PhpRedis using pecl by running:

     ```
     sudo pecl install redis
     ```

     You may encounter a couple of errors, as shown here:

```
checking whether to enable msgpack serializer support... n
checking whether to enable lzf compression... n
checking use system liblzf... no
checking whether to enable Zstd compression... n
checking use system libzstd... yes
checking whether to enable lz4 compression... n
checking use system liblz4... yes
checking for hash includes... /usr/include/php/20210902
checking for json includes... /usr/include/php/20210902
checking for redis json support... enabled
checking for igbinary includes... configure: error: Cannot find igbinary.h
```

Figure 4.7*: Errors Encountered During Installation of PHPRedis Using pecl*

If you encounter an error related to the missing **`igbinary`** extension during the installation of PhpRedis, it can be resolved by installing the **`igbinary`** extension using PECL. The **`igbinary`** extension is often required as it provides efficient binary serialization, which is utilized by PHPRedis for optimal performance.

To solve this issue, execute the following command:

```
sudo pecl install igbinary
```

You may encounter the following error:

```
checking whether to enable igbinary serializer support... n
checking whether to enable msgpack serializer support... n
checking whether to enable lzf compression... n
checking use system liblzf... no
checking whether to enable Zstd compression... n
checking use system libzstd... yes
checking whether to enable lz4 compression... n
checking use system liblz4... y
checking for hash includes... /usr/include/php/20210902
checking for json includes... /usr/include/php/20210902
checking for redis json support... enabled
checking for igbinary includes... /usr/include/php/20210902
checking for redis igbinary support... enabled
checking for msgpack includes... configure: error: Cannot find php_msgpack.h
```

***Figure 4.8**: Error Encountered During Installation of igbinary*

If you encounter an error indicating the absence of the **msgpack** extension during **igbinary** or related installation, it can be resolved by installing the **msgpack** extension.

To resolve this issue, run the following command:

sudo pecl install msgpack

```
checking use system liblz4... y
checking for hash includes... /usr/include/php/20210902
checking for json includes... /usr/include/php/20210902
checking for redis json support... enabled
checking for igbinary includes... /usr/include/php/20210902
checking for redis igbinary support... enabled
checking for msgpack includes... /usr/include/php/20210902
checking for php msgpack version >= 2.0.3... yes
checking for pkg-config... /usr/bin/pkg-config
checking for liblz4 files in default path... not found
configure: error: Please reinstall the liblz4 distribution
```

***Figure 4.9**: Error Encountered During Installation of msgpack*

If you encounter errors related to missing dependencies, particularly the liblz4-dev library, during the installation of extensions such as **Msgpack** or other PHP modules. In that case, you can resolve this issue by installing the required library.

Use the following command to install **liblz4-dev**:

```
sudo apt-get install liblz4-dev
```

```
checking whether to enable lz4 compression... n
checking use system liblz4... y
checking for hash includes... /usr/include/php/20210902
checking for json includes... /usr/include/php/20210902
checking for redis json support... enabled
checking for igbinary includes... /usr/include/php/20210902
checking for redis igbinary support... enabled
checking for msgpack includes... /usr/include/php/20210902
checking for php msgpack version >= 2.0.3... yes
checking for pkg-config... /usr/bin/pkg-config
checking for liblz4 files in default path... found in /usr
checking for LZ4_compress in -llz4... yes
checking for libzstd files in default path... not found
configure: error: Please reinstall the libzstd distribution
```

***Figure 4.10**: Error Encountered During Installation of liblz4-dev*

If you encounter errors related to the **liblz4-dev** installation, it may be caused by missing dependencies, such as **libzstd-dev**. This library is often required alongside **liblz4-dev** for proper functionality in compression-related tasks.

To resolve the issue, use the following command:

```
sudo apt-get install libzstd-dev
```

```
install ok: channel://pecl.php.net/redis-6.1.0
configuration option "php_ini" is not set to php.ini location
You should add "extension=redis.so" to php.ini
```

***Figure 4.11:** Successful Installation of PHPRedis*

After following the necessary steps to install PHPRedis and resolving any encountered errors, a successful installation can be confirmed via the terminal output. Figure 4.11 illustrates the output indicating that PHPRedis has been installed correctly.

- **Enable the Redis extension**

  Add the following line to your **php.ini** file:

  (usually located at **/etc/php/<version>/cli/php.ini** or):

  extension=redis.so

- **Restart your web server.**

  For Apache:

  ```
  sudo systemctl restart apache2
  ```

  For Nginx:

  ```
  sudo systemctl restart nginx
  ```

3. **Install PhpRedis on CentOS.** To install **PHPRedis** on a CentOS system, follow these steps:

   a. Install PHP and development tools via:

   ```
   sudo yum install php php-pear php-devel
   ```

   b. Install PhpRedis using **pecl**:

   ```
   sudo pecl install redis
   ```

```
checking whether to enable msgpack serializer support... n
checking whether to enable lzf compression... n
checking use system liblzf... no
checking whether to enable Zstd compression... n
checking use system libzstd... yes
checking whether to enable lz4 compression... n
checking use system liblz4... y
checking for hash includes... /usr/include/php
checking for json includes... /usr/include/php
checking for redis json support... enabled
checking for igbinary includes... configure: error: Cannot find igbinary.h
```

***Figure 4.12:** Error Encountered During sudo pecl install redis*

When installing PHPRedis or other extensions that depend on **igbinary**, you might encounter the following error:

Cannot find igbinary.h

This error occurs when the **igbinary** extension is not installed or not properly configured on your system.

To resolve this error, install the **igbinary** extension using the **PECL** package manager, as shown here:

```
sudo pecl install igbinary
```

```
checking use system liblzf... no
checking whether to enable Zstd compression... n
checking use system libzstd... yes
checking whether to enable lz4 compression... n
checking use system liblz4... y
checking for hash includes... /usr/include/php
checking for json includes... /usr/include/php
checking for redis json support... enabled
checking for igbinary includes... /usr/include/php
checking for redis igbinary support... enabled
checking for msgpack includes... configure: error: Cannot find php_msgpack.h
```

Figure 4.13: *Error "Cannot find php_msgpack.h" Encountered During pecl install igbinary*

To resolve the error, install the **msgpack extension** and its development headers using the following command:

```
sudo pecl install msgpack
```

```
checking use system liblz4... y
checking for hash includes... /usr/include/php
checking for json includes... /usr/include/php
checking for redis json support... enabled
checking for igbinary includes... /usr/include/php
checking for redis igbinary support... enabled
checking for msgpack includes... /usr/include/php
checking for php msgpack version >= 2.0.3... yes
checking for pkg-config... /bin/pkg-config
checking for liblz4 files in default path... not found
configure: error: Please reinstall the liblz4 distribution
```

Figure 4.14: *Error "Please Reinstall the liblz4 Distribution" Encountered During pecl install msgpack*

This error typically indicates that the **liblz4** library or its development files are missing from your system.

Steps to Resolve

a. **Enable the EPEL Repository**

   Run the following command to enable EPEL:

   ```
   sudo yum install epel-release
   ```

b. **Install the lz4 Package**

   Install the lz4 package to provide the necessary runtime library through:

   ```
   sudo yum install lz4
   ```

c. **Install the lz4 Development Package**

   Install the lz4-devel package to provide the required development headers for Msgpack via:

   ```
   sudo yum install lz4-devel
   ```

d. **Retry the Msgpack Installation**

```
sudo pecl install msgpack
```

```
checking for hash includes... /usr/include/php
checking for json includes... /usr/include/php
checking for redis json support... enabled
checking for igbinary includes... /usr/include/php
checking for redis igbinary support... enabled
checking for msgpack includes... /usr/include/php
checking for php msgpack version >= 2.0.3... yes
checking for pkg-config... /bin/pkg-config
checking for liblz4 files in default path... found in /usr
checking for LZ4_compress in -llz4... yes
checking for libzstd files in default path... not found
configure: error: Please reinstall the libzstd distribution
```

Figure 4.15: *Error "Please Reinstall the libzstd Distribution" Encountered During pecl install msgpack*

If you encounter the error "**Please Reinstall the libzstd Distribution**" during the installation of Msgpack using PECL, it indicates that the **libzstd-devel** package, which contains development headers for the Zstandard compression library, is missing.

To resolve this issue, execute the following command:

```
sudo yum install libzstd-devel
```

```
Build process completed successfully
Installing '/usr/lib64/php/modules/redis.so'
install ok: channel://pecl.php.net/redis-6.1.0
configuration option "php_ini" is not set to php.ini location
You should add "extension=redis.so" to php.ini
```

Figure 4.16: *Successful Installation of PHPRedis*

After following the necessary steps to install **PHPRedis**, you can confirm the successful installation via the terminal output. *Figure* 4.16 illustrates the completion of the installation process.

- **Enable the Redis Extension**

  Add the following line to your php.ini file

  (usually found at **/etc/php.ini**):

  ```
  extension=redis.so
  ```

- **Restart your Web Server**

  For Apache:

  ```
  sudo systemctl restart httpd
  ```

  For Nginx:

  ```
  sudo systemctl restart nginx
  ```

4. **Installing PhpRedis on Windows**

   To install **PhpRedis** on Windows:

   a. **Download the PhpRedis DLL:** Visit the official PECL website and download the appropriate DLL file for your version of PHP and system architecture (x86 or x64).

b. **Move the DLL File:** Copy the downloaded `php_redis.dll` file to your PHP `ext` directory. This is typically located at:

`C:\xampp\php\ext\ (if using XAMPP)`

- **Enable the Redis Extension in php.ini:** Open your `php.ini` file (usually located in the PHP directory) and add the following line:

  `extension=php_redis.dll`

- **Restart your web server**: If you are using XAMPP, restart Apache from the XAMPP Control Panel.

  By following these steps, you can successfully install and enable **PhpRedis** on macOS, Ubuntu, CentOS, and Windows. This setup allows your PHP applications to interact with Redis seamlessly.

Here is a basic example of how to connect to a Redis server using PHP:

```
<?php
// Create a new Redis instance
$redis = new Redis();
// Connect to the Redis server
$redis->connect('127.0.0.1', 6379);
// Check if the connection is successful
if ($redis->ping()) {
    echo "Connected to Redis successfully!";
} else {
    echo "Failed to connect to Redis.";
}
?>
```

In this example:

- The Redis class is used to create a new instance of the Redis client.
- The connect method establishes a connection to the Redis server running on 127.0.0.1 (localhost) at port 6379.
- The `ping` method sends a simple **PING** command to check if the server is responsive. If the server responds with **PONG**, the connection is successful; otherwise, an error message is displayed.

This foundational setup allows you to establish a connection to Redis and sets the stage for more advanced data operations, which will be covered in later chapters.

Connecting to Redis with Python

Connecting to Redis using Python is made simple and efficient with the `redis-py` library, a popular and feature-rich Redis client for Python. To begin, you need to ensure that `redis-py` is installed in your Python environment. This can be done using `pip`, Python's package manager:

```
pip install redis
```

Once the library is installed, establishing a connection to your Redis server is straightforward. Here is a basic example of how to connect:

- Create a file named **test_python_redis.py** and add the following code:

```
import redis
# Create a Redis client instance
client = redis.Redis(host='localhost', port=6379, db=0)
# Test the connection by sending a PING command
if client.ping():
    print("Connected to Redis successfully!")
else:
    print("Failed to connect to Redis.")
```

Execute it using the following command:

```
python3 test_python_redis.py
```

The output should look like "Connected to Redis successfully!"

In this example:

- The **redis.Redis()** function creates a client instance to connect to the Redis server. By default, it connects to localhost on port 6379 and uses database 0.
- The **ping()** method sends a simple PING command to the Redis server to verify the connection. If the server responds with True, it confirms that the connection is active and Redis is ready to use.

This foundational setup allows you to connect to Redis effortlessly and lays the groundwork for performing various data operations, which we will explore in later chapters. Using Python and **redis-py**, you can build efficient and scalable applications that take full advantage of Redis's in-memory data management capabilities.

Note:

PIP: *pip is the default package installer for Python, which is widely used by developers to install and manage software packages written in the language. It stands for "Pip Installs Packages", and it provides a simple command-line interface to download libraries and dependencies from the Python Package Index (PyPI), which is a vast repository of Python software. With* **pip**, *you can easily add new functionality to your Python projects, upgrade existing packages, and manage dependencies efficiently. Whether you are setting up a new project or maintaining an existing one, pip is an essential tool for keeping your Python environment organized and up-to-date. Its ease of use and powerful features make it indispensable for anyone working with Python.*

pip is compatible with macOS, Ubuntu, CentOS, and Windows.

Overall, **pip** *is a cross-platform tool that works efficiently on all major operating systems, making it a vital utility for Python developers, regardless of their platform.*

Connecting to Redis with Lua

Connecting to Redis with Lua (Server-Side Lua Scripting)

Redis provides native support for Lua scripting executed directly inside the Redis server. This approach allows Lua scripts to run atomically, meaning no other commands are executed while the script is running. Server-side Lua scripting is commonly used for complex logic, conditional updates, counters, and multi-key operations that must execute as a single, uninterrupted unit.

Redis executes Lua scripts using the EVAL or EVALSHA commands. No external Lua interpreter or client library is required.

Executing Lua Scripts Using EVAL

You can execute Lua code directly from redis-cli using the **EVAL** command.

Syntax:

EVAL <lua-script> <numkeys> <key1> <key2> ... <arg1> <arg2> ...

Example: Lua Script Executed Inside Redis

Run the following command from the terminal:

```
redis-cli EVAL "return redis.call('PING')" 0
```

Output:

```
PONG
```

This confirms that the Lua script is executed **inside Redis** and can call Redis commands directly.

Server-side Lua scripting is ideal for:

- Atomic read-modify-write operations
- Business rules close to the data
- Preventing race conditions without transactions
- High-performance logic execution

Connecting to Redis with Lua (Client-Side Lua Using redis-lua)

In addition to server-side scripting, Lua can also be used as a client language to connect to Redis externally, similar to Python or PHP. This approach is useful when you want to write standalone Lua applications or scripts that interact with Redis.

To do this, you must use a Redis client library for Lua, such as redis-lua.

Prerequisites

- Lua installed on the system
- redis-lua client library available

Example: Connecting to Redis Using redis-lua (Client-Side)

- Create a file and name it **`test_lua_redis.lua`**. You can then use this code:

```
-- Import the redis library
local redis = require("redis")

-- Create a connection to the Redis server
    local client = redis.connect('127.0.0.1', 6379)

-- Test the connection by pinging the server
local pong = client:ping()

-- Handle the response appropriately
    if pong == "PONG" then
  print("Redis server response: PONG")
else
  print("Redis server response: " .. tostring(pong))
end
-- Close the connection
client:quit()
```

Execute it with the following command:

```
lua test_lua_redis.lua
```

This Lua script demonstrates how to connect to a Redis server using the **redis-lua** library, perform basic operations, and handle responses gracefully. It establishes a connection to the Redis server running on localhost (127.0.0.1) at port 6379, tests the connection with the PING command, and prints the server's response.

```
Redis server response: PONG
```

Figure 4.17: *Output of the Lua Script test_lua_redis.lua Execution*

Data Management

Redis is an incredibly powerful in-memory data store known for its speed and efficiency in handling data operations. When it comes to data management, Redis offers a flexible and robust platform that can be easily integrated with various scripting and programming languages. This section will explore how to perform essential data management operations in Redis using Shell Script, PHP, Python, and other popular languages. We will discuss how to efficiently insert, update, and delete data, automate tasks, and build scalable applications by leveraging Redis' capabilities.

Whether you are a developer looking to integrate Redis into your backend systems or a system administrator aiming to automate data workflows, our examples and best practices will guide you through managing data seamlessly. By the end of this section, you will have a comprehensive understanding of how to work with Redis across multiple languages, which will allow you to choose the right tools and techniques for your projects.

Data Management Operations Using Shell Script

Automating data management operations in Redis using Shell Script can greatly simplify repetitive tasks and streamline workflows. By leveraging the **redis-cli** command-line tool, you can perform a variety of data operations, such as adding, updating, and deleting data in Redis, all from within a script. This approach is particularly useful for system administrators and developers who need to manage data efficiently without manual intervention.

Example 1: Setting and Getting Data

Let us write a simple shell script that sets a key-value pair in Redis and then retrieves it. This will demonstrate basic Redis operations using a shell script. We will create a script named **test_redis_data.sh** and implement the following code:

```
#!/bin/bash
# Set a key-value pair in Redis
redis-cli SET mykey "Hello, Redis from Shell Script!"
echo "The key 'mykey' has been set with the value: 'Hello, Redis from Shell Script!'"
# Get the value of the key
value=$(redis-cli GET mykey)
echo "The value of 'mykey' is: $value"
```

Explanation:

- The **redis-cli SET** command sets a key named **mykey** with the value "Hello, Redis from Shell Script!".
- The **redis-cli GET** command retrieves the value of **mykey**, and the script uses the echo command to print the value to the terminal.

```
#!/bin/bash

# Set a key-value pair in Redis
redis-cli SET mykey "Hello, Redis from Shell Script!"
echo "The key 'mykey' has been set with the value: 'Hello, Redis from Shell Script!'"

# Get the value of the key
value=$(redis-cli GET mykey)
echo "The value of 'mykey' is: $value"
```

***Figure 4.18**: Shell Script test_redis_data.sh*

Figure 4.18 demonstrates a shell script named **`test_redis_data.sh`**. This script leverages the **`redis-cli`** command-line tool to perform a Redis SET operation.

```
[root@localhost ~]# sh test_redis_data.sh
OK
The key 'mykey' has been set with the value: 'Hello, Redis from Shell Script!'
The value of 'mykey' is: Hello, Redis from Shell Script!
[root@localhost ~]#
[root@localhost ~]#
[root@localhost ~]#
```

***Figure 4.19**: Execution of the Shell Script test_redis_data.sh and Its Output*

Figure 4.19 illustrates the execution of the **`test_redis_data.sh`** shell script and the corresponding output displayed in the terminal. This output confirms the successful interaction with a Redis database through the script.

Example 2: Updating Data

To update an existing key in Redis, you can use the **`SET`** command again with a new value. Let us create a shell script named **`test_redis_data_update.sh`** to demonstrate this:

```
#!/bin/bash
# Update the value of an existing key
redis-cli SET mykey "Updated value from Shell Script"
echo "The key 'mykey' has been updated with the new value: 'Updated value from Shell Script'"
# Verify the update
new_value=$(redis-cli GET mykey)
echo "The updated value of 'mykey' is: $new_value"
```

```
#!/bin/bash

# Update the value of an existing key
redis-cli SET mykey "Updated value from Shell Script"
echo "The key 'mykey' has been updated with the new value: 'Updated value from Shell Script'"

# Verify the update
new_value=$(redis-cli GET mykey)
echo "The updated value of 'mykey' is: $new_value"
```

***Figure 4.20**: Shell Script Using SET Command and redis-cli for Updating Data*

Figure 4.20 illustrates a shell script that demonstrates how to use the Redis SET command with **`redis-cli`** to update data in a Redis database. The script performs an update operation by setting a new value for an existing key, while showcasing Redis's ability to overwrite values with the same key.

```
[root@localhost ~]# sh test_redis_data_update.sh
OK
The key 'mykey' has been updated with the new value: 'Updated value from Shell Script'
The updated value of 'mykey' is: Updated value from Shell Script
[root@localhost ~]#
[root@localhost ~]#
[root@localhost ~]#
[root@localhost ~]#
[root@localhost ~]#
```

Figure 4.21: *Execution of Shell Script for Updating Data and Its Output*

Figure 4.21 illustrates a shell script that updates **mykey** with a new value and retrieves it to confirm that the update was successful.

Example 3: Deleting Data

To delete a key from Redis, you can use the **DEL** command. Let us create a shell script named **test_redis_data_delete.sh** to demonstrate this operation:

```
#!/bin/bash
# Delete a key from Redis
redis-cli DEL mykey
echo "The key 'mykey' has been deleted from Redis."
# Attempt to retrieve the deleted key
deleted_value=$(redis-cli GET mykey)
if [ -z "$deleted_value" ]; then
    echo "The key 'mykey' no longer exists in Redis."
else
    echo "The value of 'mykey' is: $deleted_value"
fi
```


```
#!/bin/bash

# Delete a key from Redis
redis-cli DEL mykey
echo "The key 'mykey' has been deleted from Redis."

# Attempt to retrieve the deleted key
deleted_value=$(redis-cli GET mykey)
if [ -z "$deleted_value" ]; then
    echo "The key 'mykey' no longer exists in Redis."
else
    echo "The value of 'mykey' is: $deleted_value"
fi
```


Figure 4.22: *Shell Script to Delete the Key from Redis*

Figure 4.22 illustrates a shell script designed to delete a specific key from a Redis database using the **redis-cli** command.

```
[root@localhost ~]# vim test_redis_data_delete.sh
[root@localhost ~]# sh test_redis_data_delete.sh
(integer) 1
The key 'mykey' has been deleted from Redis.
The key 'mykey' no longer exists in Redis.
```

Figure 4.23: *Output of Shell Script to Delete Key from Redis*

In *Figure* 4.23, the following behavior is observed:

- The **redis-cli** DEL command deletes **mykey** from Redis.

- The script then attempts to retrieve **mykey**. If the key has been successfully deleted, the script confirms that it no longer exists.

Combining Operations in a Script

You can also combine multiple operations in a single script to manage more complex data workflows. For instance, you can set multiple keys, retrieve them, and delete keys as needed. This is shown in the following example:

```
#!/bin/bash

# Set multiple keys
redis-cli SET key1 "Value 1"
redis-cli SET key2 "Value 2"
redis-cli SET key3 "Value 3"

echo "Keys 'key1', 'key2', and 'key3' have been set."

# Retrieve all values
value1=$(redis-cli GET key1)
value2=$(redis-cli GET key2)
value3=$(redis-cli GET key3)

echo "The value of 'key1' is: $value1"
echo "The value of 'key2' is: $value2"
echo "The value of 'key3' is: $value3"

# Delete all keys
redis-cli DEL key1 key2 key3

echo "Keys 'key1', 'key2', and 'key3' have been deleted."
```

In this example:

- This script demonstrates how to set, retrieve, and delete multiple keys in Redis using a shell script. It provides a complete flow for data management operations, while showcasing the simplicity and power of automating Redis tasks with scripts.

By using Shell Script for data management in Redis, you can automate routine operations, manage large datasets efficiently, and maintain a smooth workflow for your Redis-based applications. These examples provide a foundation for building more complex automation scripts tailored to your needs.

You can perform multiple Redis operations in a single script to manage more complex workflows, such as setting multiple keys, retrieving their values, and deleting keys as needed. Let us create a shell script named **test_redis_data_combine.sh** to demonstrate this workflow.

```
#!/bin/bash

# Set multiple keys
redis-cli SET key1 "Value 1"
redis-cli SET key2 "Value 2"
redis-cli SET key3 "Value 3"

echo "Keys 'key1', 'key2', and 'key3' have been set."

# Retrieve all values
value1=$(redis-cli GET key1)
value2=$(redis-cli GET key2)
value3=$(redis-cli GET key3)

echo "The value of 'key1' is: $value1"
echo "The value of 'key2' is: $value2"
echo "The value of 'key3' is: $value3"

# Delete all keys
redis-cli DEL key1 key2 key3

echo "Keys 'key1', 'key2', and 'key3' have been deleted."
```

Figure 4.24: *Shell Script Performing Multiple Redis Operations*

Figure 4.24 illustrates a shell script designed to execute multiple Redis operations in a single script.

```
[root@localhost ~]# sh test_redis_data_combine.sh
OK
OK
OK
Keys 'key1', 'key2', and 'key3' have been set.
The value of 'key1' is: Value 1
The value of 'key2' is: Value 2
The value of 'key3' is: Value 3
(integer) 3
Keys 'key1', 'key2', and 'key3' have been deleted.
```

Figure 4.25: *Output of Shell Script to Execute Multiple Redis Operations*

Figure 4.25 displays the terminal output generated by executing a shell script that performs multiple Redis operations. These operations include setting a key-value pair, retrieving the value, and finally deleting it.

Data Management Operations Using PHP

Using PHP to manage data in Redis is both powerful and intuitive, thanks to the **PhpRedis** extension. With PHP, you can seamlessly integrate Redis into your applications to handle caching, session management, and other real-time data operations. In this section, we will explore how to perform essential data management operations in Redis, such as setting, updating, and deleting keys, all while keeping it engaging and easy to follow.

Example 1: Setting and Retrieving Data

Redis provides a simple and efficient way to set and retrieve data using commands like **`SET`** and **`GET`**. Let us create a PHP script named **`test_redis.php`** to demonstrate how to perform these operations:

```
<?php
//connection
```

```
$redis = new Redis();
$redis->connect('127.0.0.1',6379);

// Set a key-value pair in Redis
$redis->set("greeting", "Hello, Redis from PHP!");
echo "The key 'greeting' has been set with the value: 'Hello, Redis from PHP!'<br>";
// Retrieve the value of the key
$value = $redis->get("greeting");
echo "The value of 'greeting' is: $value<br>";
?>
```

In this example:

- The **set()** method sets a key named greeting with the value "**Hello, Redis from PHP!**".
- The **get()** method retrieves the value of the greeting key and displays it.

This simple example shows how you can quickly store and access data in Redis, making it perfect for caching or fast data retrieval.

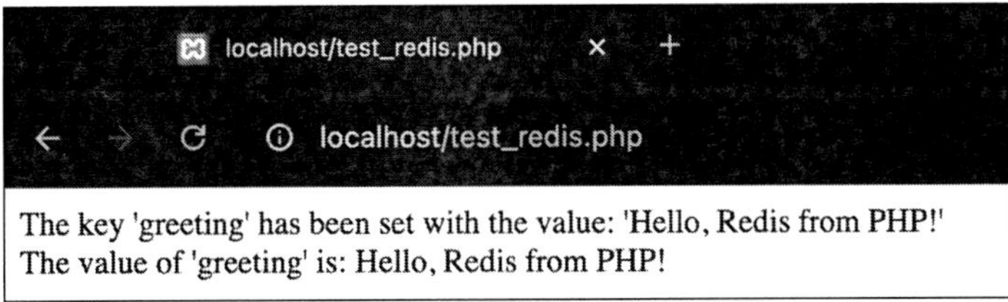

Figure 4.26: *Output of PHP Script to Set and Retrieve Data*

Example 2: Updating Data

Updating data in Redis with PHP is simple - you just set a new value for an existing key using the **SET** command. Let us create a PHP script named **test_redis_update.php** to demonstrate this process:

```
<?php
//connection
$redis = new Redis();
$redis->connect('127.0.0.1',6379);

// Update the value of an existing key
$redis->set("greeting", "Updated greeting from PHP!");

echo "The key 'greeting' has been updated with the new value: 'Updated greeting from
PHP!'<br>";

// Retrieve the updated value
$updatedValue = $redis->get("greeting");

echo "The updated value of 'greeting' is $updatedValue<br>";

?>
```

- **In this example:**
  - The **set()** method is used again to overwrite the value of the greeting.
  - The new value is then retrieved and displayed, showcasing how simple it is to update data in Redis.

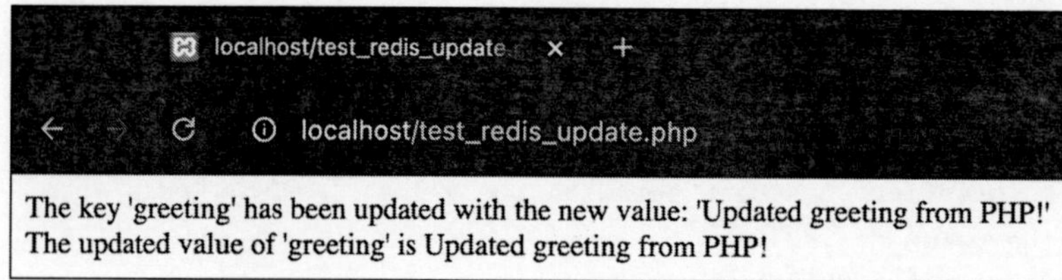

Figure 4.27: *Output of PHP Script to Update Data*

Figure 4.27 displays the output of a PHP script that updates data in a Redis database. The script uses the PHPRedis library to connect to the Redis server, modify the value of an existing key using the set method, and retrieve the updated value to confirm the operation.

Example 3: Deleting Data

Removing data from Redis is straightforward using the **`DEL`** command. Let us create a PHP script named **`test_redis_delete.php`** to demonstrate this process:

```
<?php

//connection
$redis = new Redis();
$redis->connect('127.0.0.1',6379);

// Delete a key from Redis
$redis->del("greeting");

echo "The key 'greeting' has been deleted from Redis.<br>";

// Attempt to retrieve the deleted key
$deletedValue = $redis->get("greeting");

if ($deletedValue === false) {
    echo "The key 'greeting' no longer exists in Redis.<br>";
} else {
    echo "The value of 'greeting' is: $deletedValue<br>";
}
?>
```

In this example:

- The **`del()`** method deletes the key **greeting**.
- The script then tries to retrieve the **greeting**, confirming that it no longer exists.

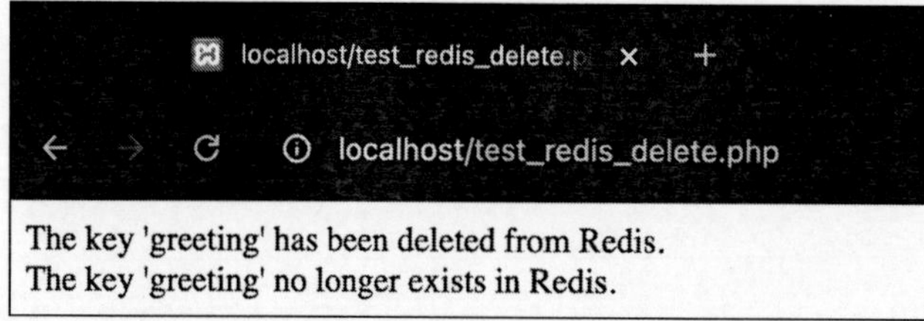

Figure 4.28: *Output of PHP Script to Delete a Redis Key*

Figure 4.28 displays the output of a PHP script that demonstrates the deletion of a key from a Redis database. The script utilizes the PHPRedis library to connect to the Redis server, delete a specified key using the del method, and confirm the deletion by checking the key's existence.

Example 4: Managing Multiple Keys

Let us take it a step further and work with multiple keys in Redis. In the following example, we will create a PHP script named **test_redis_multiplekeys.php** to demonstrate these operations:

```
<?php

//connection
$redis = new Redis();
$redis->connect('127.0.0.1',6379);

// Set multiple keys
$redis->set("user:1", "Alice");
$redis->set("user:2", "Bob");
$redis->set("user:3", "Charlie");

echo "Multiple keys have been set: 'user:1', 'user:2', 'user:3'<br>";

// Retrieve and display all values
echo "The value of 'user:1' is: ". $redis->get("user:1") . "<br>";
echo "The value of 'user:2' is: ". $redis->get("user:2") . "<br>";
echo "The value of 'user:3' is: ". $redis->get("user:3") . "<br>";

// Delete all keys
$redis->del("user:1", "user:2", "user:3");

echo "Keys 'user:1', 'user:2', and 'user:3' have been deleted.<br>";

?>
```

In this example:

- This example demonstrates how to set, retrieve, and delete multiple keys efficiently.
- It shows the power of PhpRedis when managing complex data structures in Redis, which makes it ideal for applications that require quick data access and manipulation.

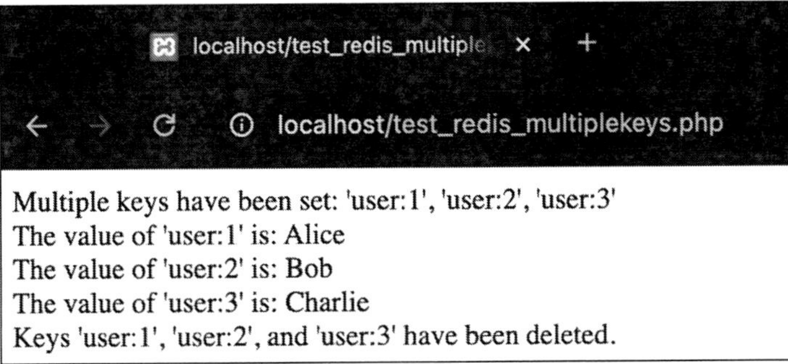

Figure 4.29: *Output of PHP Script to Set and Delete Multiple Keys*

Figure 4.29 illustrates the output of a PHP script that performs operations to set and delete multiple keys in a Redis database. The script leverages the PhpRedis library to connect to the Redis server, add multiple key-value pairs, delete specific keys, and confirm successful deletion.

By using PhpRedis for data management, you can integrate Redis into your PHP projects with ease, taking advantage of its speed and reliability. These examples illustrate the simplicity and effectiveness of using Redis for storing and manipulating data. In the upcoming chapters, we will explore more advanced Redis operations. Thus, whether you are building a caching mechanism, managing sessions, or handling real-time data, Redis and PHP make a formidable combination.

Data Management Operations Using Python

Python, with its simplicity and versatility, pairs exceptionally well with Redis for efficient data management. The **redis-py** library is a powerful and widely used tool that provides a straightforward interface for performing Redis operations. Whether you are working on caching, session management, or building real-time data applications, Python and Redis offer a reliable combination.

Example 1: Setting and Retrieving Data

Storing and retrieving data in Redis using Python is straightforward. Here is how you can set a key-value pair and then get the value in a Python script:

```
import redis

# Create a Redis client instance
client = redis.Redis(host='localhost', port=6379, db=0)

# Set a key-value pair in Redis
client.set("greeting", "Hello, Redis from Python!")
print("The key 'greeting' has been set with the value: 'Hello, Redis from Python!'")

# Retrieve the value of the key
value = client.get("greeting").decode("utf-8")
print(f"The value of 'greeting' is: {value}")
```

In this example:

- The **set()** method is used to store the key "**greeting**" with the value "**Hello, Redis from Python!**".
- The **get()** method retrieves the value, and **decode("utf-8")** converts the byte response returned by Redis into a readable string.


```
import redis

# Create a Redis client instance
client = redis.Redis(host='localhost', port=6379, db=0)

# Set a key-value pair in Redis
client.set("greeting", "Hello, Redis from Python!")
print("The key 'greeting' has been set with the value: 'Hello, Redis from Python!'")

# Retrieve the value of the key
value = client.get("greeting").decode("utf-8")
print(f"The value of 'greeting' is: {value}")
```


Figure 4.30: *Python Script to Set and Retrieve a Key-Value Pair in Redis*

Figure 4.30 demonstrates a Python script that connects to a Redis database, sets a key-value pair, retrieves the value of the key, and displays the result. This script utilizes the redis-py library to interact with the Redis server, which showcases the simplicity and effectiveness of Python when managing Redis operations.

```
The key 'greeting' has been set with the value: 'Hello, Redis from Python!'
The value of 'greeting' is: Hello, Redis from Python!
```

Figure 4.31: *Output of Python Script to Set and Retrieve a Key-Value Pair in Redis*

Figure 4.31 illustrates the output of a Python script designed to interact with a Redis database by setting a key-value pair and retrieving the value. This output confirms the successful execution of Redis operations using Python.

Example 2: Updating Data

Updating data in Redis with Python is as simple as setting a new value for an existing key and can be achieved via the following code:

```
import redis

# Create a Redis client instance
client = redis.Redis(host='localhost', port=6379, db=0)

# Update the value of an existing key
client.set("greeting", "Updated greeting from Python!")
print("The key 'greeting' has been updated with the new value: 'Updated greeting from Python!'")

# Verify the update
updated_value = client.get("greeting").decode("utf-8")
print(f"The updated value of 'greeting' is: {updated_value}")
```

In this example:

- The **`set()`** method updates the value of the key "**`greeting`**".
- The new value is retrieved and displayed to confirm the update.

```
import redis

# Create a Redis client instance
client = redis.Redis(host='localhost', port=6379, db=0)

# Update the value of an existing key
client.set("greeting", "Updated greeting from Python!")
print("The key 'greeting' has been updated with the new value: 'Updated greeting from Python!'")

# Verify the update
updated_value = client.get("greeting").decode("utf-8")
print(f"The updated value of 'greeting' is: {updated_value}")
```

Figure 4.32: *Python Script to Update the Value of an Existing Key in Redis*

Figure 4.32 presents a Python script that demonstrates how to update the value of an existing key in a Redis database.

```
The key 'greeting' has been updated with the new value: 'Updated greeting from Python!'
The updated value of 'greeting' is: Updated greeting from Python!
```

Figure 4.33: *Output of Python Script to Update the Value of an Existing Key in Redis*

Figure 4.33 displays the output generated by a Python script that updates the value of an existing key in a Redis database.

Example 3: Deleting Data

You can also delete a key from Redis when it is no longer needed using the following command:

```
import redis

# Create a Redis client instance
```

```
client = redis.Redis(host='localhost', port=6379, db=0)

# Delete a key from the Redis
client.delete("greeting")
print("The key 'greeting' has been deleted from Redis.")

# Attempt to retrieve the deleted key
deleted_value = client.get("greeting")
if deleted_value is None:
    print("The key 'greeting' no longer exists in Redis.")
else:
    print(f"The value of 'greeting' is: {deleted_value.decode('utf-8')}")
```

In this example:

- The **delete()** method removes the "greeting" key from Redis.
- The script checks if the key still exists and confirms that it has been deleted.

```
import redis

# Create a Redis client instance
client = redis.Redis(host='localhost', port=6379, db=0)

# Delete a key from Redis
client.delete("greeting")
print("The key 'greeting' has been deleted from Redis.")

# Attempt to retrieve the deleted key
deleted_value = client.get("greeting")
if deleted_value is None:
    print("The key 'greeting' no longer exists in Redis.")
else:
    print(f"The value of 'greeting' is: {deleted_value.decode('utf-8')}")
```

Figure 4.34: *Python Script to Delete an Existing Key in Redis*

Figure 4.34 presents a Python script demonstrating how to delete an existing key from a Redis database.

```
The key 'greeting' has been deleted from Redis.
The key 'greeting' no longer exists in Redis.
```

Figure 4.35: *Output of Python Script to Delete an Existing Key in Redis*

Figure 4.35 illustrates the output of a Python script designed to delete an existing key from a Redis database. The output confirms the successful execution of the deletion operation and verifies the absence of the key after the operation.

Example 4: Managing Multiple Keys

Python makes it easy to handle multiple keys in Redis, which allows for efficient data management. You can see how to manage these keys in the following example:

```
import redis

# Create a Redis client instance
client = redis.Redis(host='localhost', port=6379, db=0)

# Set multiple keys
```

```
client.set("user:1", "Alice")
client.set("user:2", "Bob")
client.set("user:3", "Charlie")
print("Keys 'user:1', 'user:2', and 'user:3' have been set.")

# Retrieve and display all values
print(f"The value of 'user:1' is: {client.get('user:1').decode('utf-8')}")
print(f"The value of 'user:2' is: {client.get('user:2').decode('utf-8')}")
print(f"The value of 'user:3' is: {client.get('user:3').decode('utf-8')}")

# Delete all keys
client.delete("user:1", "user:2", "user:3")
print("Keys 'user:1', 'user:2', and 'user:3' have been deleted.")
```

In this example:

- This example sets, retrieves, and deletes multiple keys while showing how easily Python and **`redis-py`** handle batch operations.

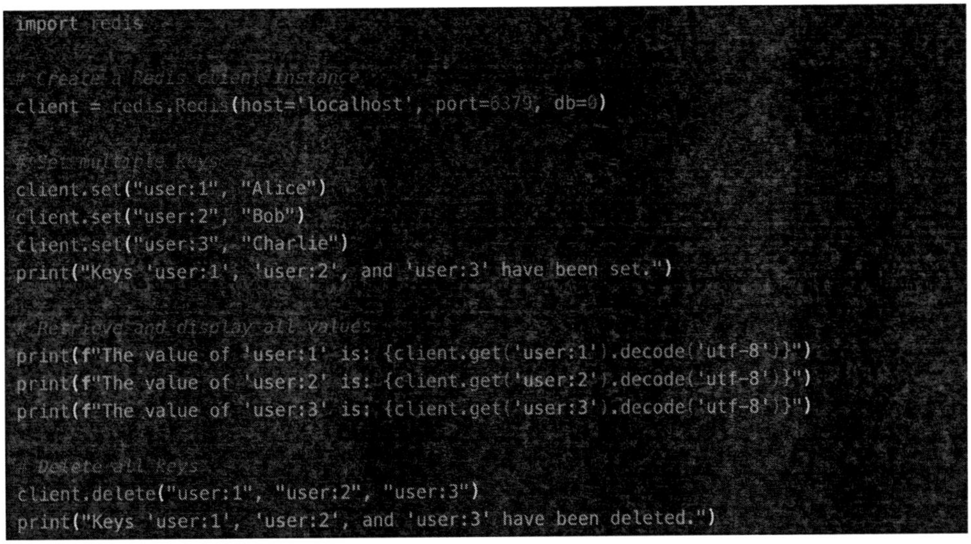

```
import redis

# Create a Redis client instance
client = redis.Redis(host='localhost', port=6379, db=0)

# Set multiple keys
client.set("user:1", "Alice")
client.set("user:2", "Bob")
client.set("user:3", "Charlie")
print("Keys 'user:1', 'user:2', and 'user:3' have been set.")

# Retrieve and display all values
print(f"The value of 'user:1' is: {client.get('user:1').decode('utf-8')}")
print(f"The value of 'user:2' is: {client.get('user:2').decode('utf-8')}")
print(f"The value of 'user:3' is: {client.get('user:3').decode('utf-8')}")

# Delete all keys
client.delete("user:1", "user:2", "user:3")
print("Keys 'user:1', 'user:2', and 'user:3' have been deleted.")
```

Figure 4.36: *Python Script to Set, Retrieve, and Delete Multiple Keys in Redis*

Figure 4.36 showcases a Python script designed to perform multiple operations on a Redis database. The script sets multiple key-value pairs, retrieves their values, and deletes the keys.

```
Keys 'user:1', 'user:2', and 'user:3' have been set.
The value of 'user:1' is: Alice
The value of 'user:2' is: Bob
The value of 'user:3' is: Charlie
Keys 'user:1', 'user:2', and 'user:3' have been deleted.
```

Figure 4.37: *Output of Python Script to Set, Retrieve, and Delete Multiple Keys in Redis*

Figure 4.37 illustrates the output of a Python script that performs operations to set, retrieve, and delete multiple keys in a Redis database.

By using Python for data management operations in Redis, you can automate tasks, optimize data handling, and build scalable applications with minimal effort. The **`redis-py`** library's intuitive API ensures that even complex data workflows remain efficient and easy to implement.

Data Management Operations Using Lua

Redis provides native support for executing Lua scripts directly within the Redis server. This capability enables efficient and **atomic execution** of multiple Redis commands as a single operation. Because the script runs entirely on the server, no other commands are processed while it is executing, which guarantees consistency and eliminates race conditions. Server-side Lua scripting is particularly useful for complex data management scenarios that require conditional logic, multi-step updates, or strict atomicity. Additionally, executing logic within Redis significantly reduces client-server round trips, resulting in improved performance and lower latency.

In this section, we will explore how to use Lua to manage data in Redis with practical examples.

Client-Side Data Management Using Lua (redis-lua Client Library)

In this approach, Lua is used as an external client language, similar to Python or PHP, to connect to Redis and perform data operations. The Lua script runs outside the Redis server and communicates with Redis over the network using a client library such as redis-lua.

Client-side Lua scripts:

- Use a Redis client library (for example, require("redis"))
- Explicitly create a connection to Redis using host and port
- Execute Redis commands over TCP
- Are **not executed inside Redis**
- Are **not atomic by default** (each command is a separate request)

Example 1: Setting and Getting Data

Lua scripts can be used to set and retrieve data in Redis using a simple client-side workflow. Here is a simple script that demonstrates this:

```
-- Import the Redis library
local redis = require("redis")

-- Create a connection to the Redis server
local client = redis.connect('127.0.0.1', 6379)

-- Set a key-value pair in Redis
local key = "mykey"
local value = "Hello, Redis from Lua!"
local set_result = client:set(key, value)
print("SET result:", set_result)

-- Get the value of the key from Redis
local get_result = client:get(key)
print("GET result:", get_result)
```

In this example:

- `redis.connect('127.0.0.1', 6379)` connects to the Redis server running on `127.0.0.1` (localhost) and port `6379`.
- `client:set(key, value)` sets the key `mykey` to the value `"Hello, Redis from Lua!"`. The result of the `SET` command is stored in `set_result` and printed.
- `client:get(key)` retrieves the value of `mykey`.
- The result of the `GET` command is stored in `get_result` and printed.

```
-- Import the Redis library
local redis = require("redis")

-- Create a connection to the Redis server
local client = redis.connect('127.0.0.1', 6379)

-- Set a key-value pair in Redis
local key = "mykey"
local value = "Hello, Redis from Lua!"
local set_result = client:set(key, value)
print("SET result:", set_result)

-- Get the value of the key from Redis
local get_result = client:get(key)
print("GET result:", get_result)
```

Figure 4.38: *Lua Script to Set and Retrieve a Key-Value Pair in Redis*

Figure 4.38 presents a Lua script designed to interact with a Redis database by setting and retrieving a key-value pair. The script establishes a connection to the Redis server and stores a key-value pair.

```
SET result:     true
GET result:     Hello, Redis from Lua!
```

Figure 4.39: *Output of Lua Script to Set and Retrieve a Key-Value Pair in Redis*

Figure 4.39 displays the terminal output generated by a Lua script that sets and retrieves a key-value pair in a Redis database. This output confirms the successful execution of Redis operations using Lua.

Example 2: Updating Data

You can use Lua scripts to update data in Redis, as shown in the following example:

```
-- Import the Redis library
local redis = require("redis")

-- Create a connection to the Redis server
local client = redis.connect('127.0.0.1', 6379)

-- Update the value of the key
print("Updating the value for 'mykey'...")
local update_result = client:set("mykey", "Updated value from Lua")
print("SET result:", update_result)

-- Retrieve and display the updated value
local updated_value = client:get("mykey")
print("Updated value for 'mykey':", updated_value)
```

In this example:

- The **`SET`** method is used to update the value of the key **`mykey`** to **`"Updated value from Lua"`**.
- The **`GET`** method fetches the updated value of the key to confirm the operation was successful.

```
-- Import the Redis library
local redis = require("redis")

-- Create a connection to the Redis server
local client = redis.connect('127.0.0.1', 6379)

-- Update the value of the key
print("Updating the value for 'mykey'...")
local update_result = client:set("mykey", "Updated value from Lua")
print("SET result:", update_result)

-- Retrieve and display the updated value
local updated_value = client:get("mykey")
print("Updated value for 'mykey':", updated_value)
```

Figure 4.40: *Lua Script to Update a Key in Redis*

Figure 4.40 presents a Lua script designed to update the value of an existing key in a Redis database.

```
Updating the value for 'mykey'...
SET result:     true
Updated value for 'mykey':      Updated value from Lua
```

Figure 4.41: *Output of Lua Script to Update a Key in Redis*

Figure 4.41 illustrates the terminal output generated by executing a Lua script designed to update a key's value in a Redis database. The output confirms the successful execution of the update operation and verifies the updated value in Redis.

Example 3: Deleting Data

You can also use Lua scripts to delete data from Redis, as shown here:

```
-- Import the Redis library
local redis = require("redis")

-- Create a connection to the Redis server
local client = redis.connect('127.0.0.1', 6379)

-- Delete the key
print("Deleting the key 'mykey' from Redis...")
local delete_result = client:del("mykey")
print("DEL result:", delete_result)

-- Check if the key still exists
local exists = client:exists("mykey")
if not exists then
    print("The key 'mykey' has been successfully deleted.")
else
    print("The key 'mykey' still exists.")
end
```

In this example:

- The **`DEL`** command is called within the Lua script to delete **`mykey`**.

- Using Lua for deletion operations can be useful when combined with other logic in a more complex script.

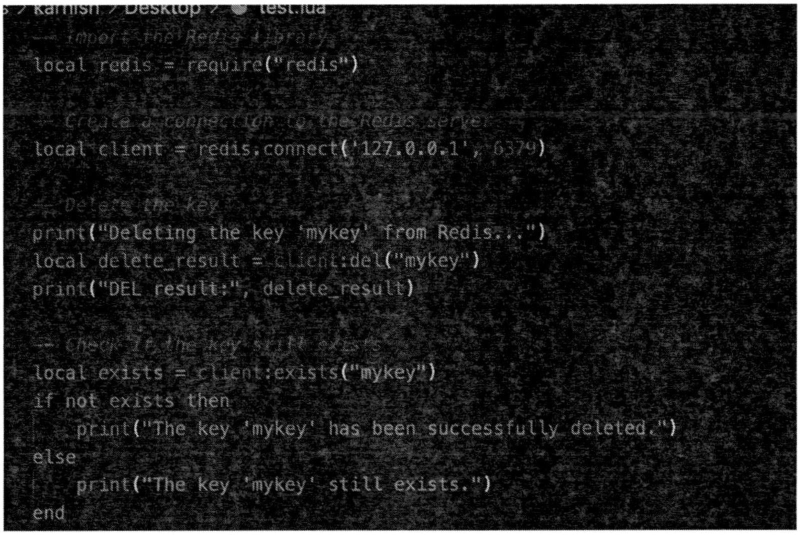

```
-- Import the Redis library
local redis = require("redis")

-- Create a connection to the Redis server
local client = redis.connect('127.0.0.1', 6379)

-- Delete the key
print("Deleting the key 'mykey' from Redis...")
local delete_result = client:del("mykey")
print("DEL result:", delete_result)

-- Check if the key still exists
local exists = client:exists("mykey")
if not exists then
    print("The key 'mykey' has been successfully deleted.")
else
    print("The key 'mykey' still exists.")
end
```

Figure 4.42: *Lua Script to Delete a Key in Redis*

Figure 4.42 presents a Lua script that demonstrates how to delete a key from a Redis database. The script establishes a connection to the Redis server, removes the specified key using the **DEL** command, and verifies the deletion by checking the existence of the key.

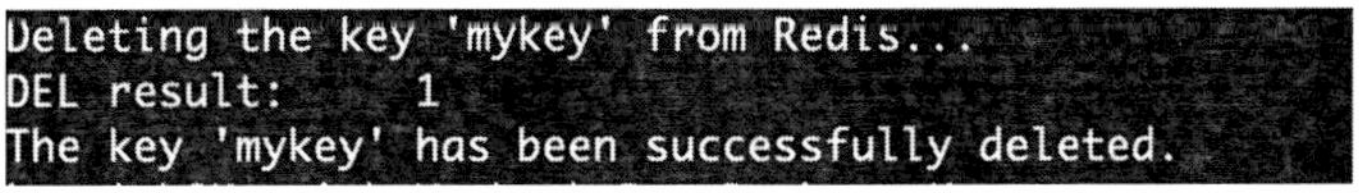

```
Deleting the key 'mykey' from Redis...
DEL result:     1
The key 'mykey' has been successfully deleted.
```

Figure 4.43: *Output of Lua Script to Delete a Key in Redis*

Figure 4.43 illustrates the terminal output generated by executing a Lua script designed to delete a key from a Redis database. The output confirms the successful execution of the deletion operation, and verifies whether the specified key still exists.

Example 4: Conditional Data Management

Lua scripts are great for adding conditional logic to your data operations. For instance, you can check if a key exists before performing an action, as shown here:

```
-- Lua script to check if a key exists and update its value if it does

-- Import the Redis library
local redis = require("redis")

-- Create a connection to the Redis server
local client = redis.connect('127.0.0.1', 6379)

-- Specify the key and the new value
local key = "mykey"
local new_value = "New value if key exists"

-- Check if the key exists
local exists = client:exists(key)
```

```
-- Update the value if the key exists
if exists then
    print("The key '" .. key .. "' exists. Updating its value...")
    local result = client:set(key, new_value)
    print("Update result:", result)
else
    print("The key '" .. key .. "' does not exist.")
end
```

In this example:

- The **`EXISTS`** command checks if **`mykey`** exists in Redis.
- If the key exists, the script updates its value to "**`New value if the key exists.`**"
- If the key does not exist, the script prints a message indicating that the key is missing, that is "**`Key does not exist.`**"

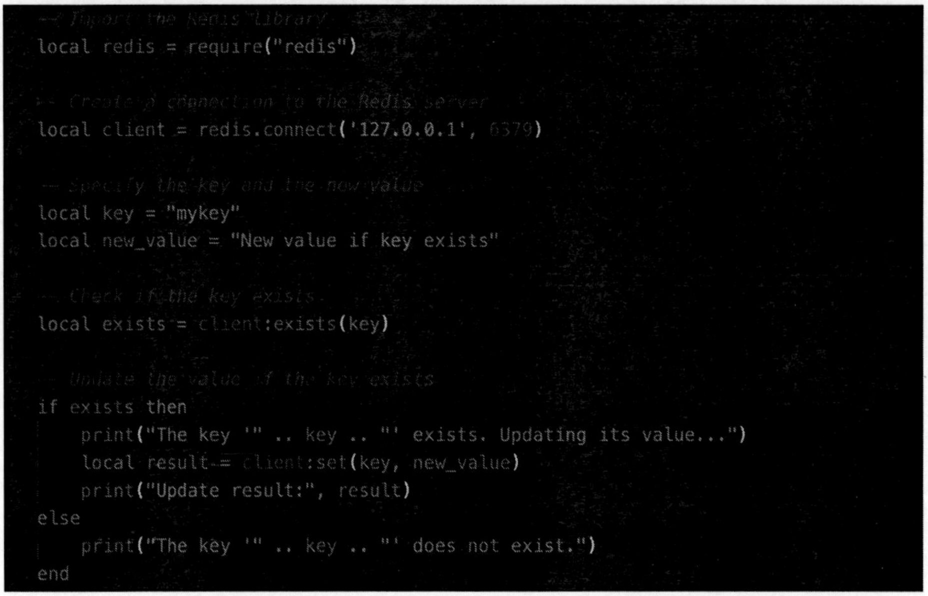

Figure 4.44: *Lua Script for Conditional Data Management*

Figure 4.44 showcases a Lua script designed to conditionally manage data in a Redis database. The script checks if a specific key exists and, if so, updates its value; otherwise, it provides a message indicating the key does not exist.

Figure 4.45: *Output of Lua Script for Conditional Data Management*

Figure 4.45 illustrates the terminal output generated by executing a Lua script designed for conditional data management in Redis. The script checks whether a specific key exists in the Redis database or not, updates its value if it exists, or informs the user if the key does not exist.

Example 5: Incrementing a Value

Lua scripts can be used to execute Redis commands that are inherently atomic, such as incrementing a value, which is shown here:

```
-- Import the Redis library
local redis = require("redis")

-- Create a connection to the Redis server
local client = redis.connect('127.0.0.1', 6379)

-- Specify the key and the increment value
local key = "counter"
local increment = 10

-- Increment the value in Redis
local new_value = client:incrby(key, increment)

-- Display the new value
print("The new value of '" .. key .. "' after incrementing by " .. increment .. " is: 
" .. new_value)
```

In this example:

- The **INCRBY** command increments the value of the **counter** by 10.
- The **INCRBY** command itself is atomic in Redis; however, when executed from client-side Lua, it is sent as a single command rather than a server-side Lua script.

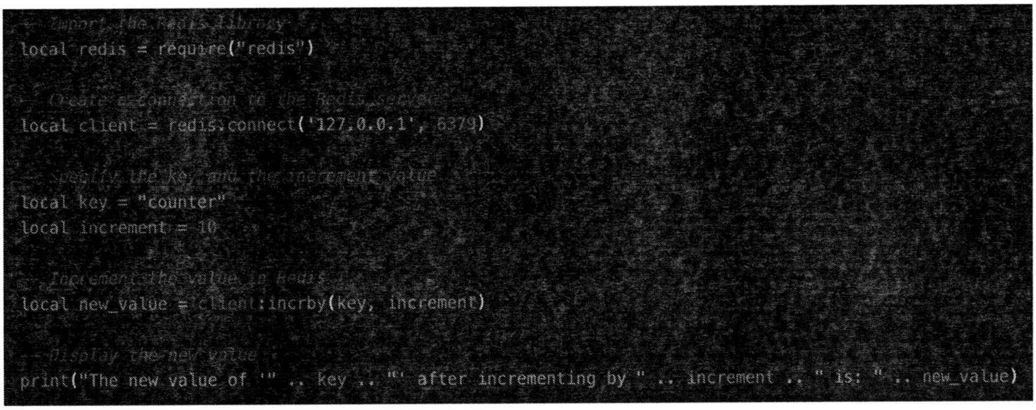

```
-- Import the Redis library
local redis = require("redis")

-- Create a connection to the Redis server
local client = redis.connect('127.0.0.1', 6379)

-- Specify the key and the increment value
local key = "counter"
local increment = 10

-- Increment the value in Redis
local new_value = client:incrby(key, increment)

-- Display the new value
print("The new value of '" .. key .. "' after incrementing by " .. increment .. " is: " .. new_value)
```


Figure 4.46: *Lua Script to Increment a Value in Redis*

Figure 4.46 presents a Lua script designed to increment the value of a specified key in a Redis database. The script connects to the Redis server, increments the value of the key using the **INCRBY** command, and displays the updated value.

```
The new value of 'counter' after incrementing by 10 is: 10
```

Figure 4.47: *Output of Lua Script to Increment a Value in Redis*

Figure 4.47 illustrates the terminal output generated by executing a Lua script to increment the value of a specified key in a Redis database. The output demonstrates the behavior of the script when the key does not exist (first-time increment).

Server-Side Data Management Using Lua (Redis EVAL)

Redis also provides native server-side Lua scripting, where Lua code is executed directly inside the Redis server using the EVAL or EVALSHA commands. In this model, Redis itself runs the Lua script as part of its execution engine.

Server-side Lua scripts:

- Do **not** use require("redis")
- Do **not** open network connections
- Use redis.call() or redis.pcall() to execute Redis commands
- Receive data via KEYS[] and ARGV[]
- Are executed **atomically**
- Block other Redis commands while running

A server-side Lua script is executed like this:

```
redis-cli EVAL "<lua-script>" <numkeys> <keys> <args>
```

Important: Server-side Lua scripts run entirely within Redis. Any Lua code that creates a Redis connection or imports a Redis client library is **not** server-side Lua.

Why Use Lua with Redis?

Using Lua for data management in Redis provides the following advantages:

- **Atomicity**: All commands within a Lua script are executed atomically, which means that no other commands can run between them. This is crucial for maintaining data consistency in complex operations.
- **Reduced Latency**: By bundling multiple operations into a single script, you can minimize the number of round-trips between the client and the Redis server, while significantly improving performance.
- **Conditional Logic**: Lua allows you to add logic to your scripts while enabling more sophisticated data management workflows.

By harnessing the power of Lua in Redis, you can perform efficient, atomic, and complex data operations, making your applications faster and more reliable. We will explore more advanced Lua scripting techniques in subsequent chapters, but these examples should give you a solid foundation to get started.

Best Practices for Data Management in Redis

Managing data efficiently in Redis is crucial to getting the most out of its high-performance capabilities while ensuring stability, reliability, and optimal resource usage. While Redis is known for its speed, poor data management practices can lead to issues such as memory exhaustion, data loss, or slow performance. Here are some best practices to guide you in effectively managing data in Redis that are presented in a relatable way, so that you can implement them confidently.

Choose the Right Data Structure for Your Use Case

Redis offers a variety of data structures: Strings, Lists, Sets, Hashes, Sorted Sets, Bitmaps, and more. Selecting the right one is essential to optimize performance and resource usage.

Example: If you need to store user profile information, using a **Hash** is more efficient than using multiple Strings because it keeps related data organized under a single key. For instance:

```
HSET user:1001 name "Alice" age "30" city "New York"
```

Using a Hash allows you to fetch all details in one command and reduces the number of keys you manage.

Tip: Take time to understand your data access patterns before deciding on a structure. Using Sorted Sets for leaderboards, Lists for message queues, or Sets for unique elements can greatly impact your Redis instance's efficiency.

Set Expiration Times for Volatile Data

For data that does not need to be stored permanently, use the **EXPIRE** command to set an expiration time. This ensures that old or unused data does not consume memory indefinitely.

Example: If you are storing session data, set it to expire after a certain period using the following command:

```
SET session:12345 "user_data" EX 3600  # Expires in 1 hour
```

By setting an expiration time, you prevent memory bloat and keep your data footprint manageable.

Tip: Use expiration wisely. For critical data that should never expire, avoid setting an **EXPIRE** unless you have a specific use case. Expired keys are automatically removed from memory and will make your Redis instance more efficient.

Monitor Memory Usage and Set a maxmemory Limit

Redis operates in memory, which means it is fast but also limited by the amount of RAM available on your server. Setting a **maxmemory** limit ensures that Redis does not consume all the system's resources, which could lead to performance degradation or crashes.

Here is an example configuration:

```
maxmemory 512mb  # Set a memory limit of 512 MB
maxmemory-policy allkeys-lru  # Use Least Recently Used (LRU) eviction policy
```

Setting a memory limit helps you manage resource consumption, while the eviction policy dictates how Redis will handle data when the memory limit is reached.

Tip: Monitor your memory usage regularly. Use the **INFO memory** command to get a snapshot of your current memory usage and adjust your settings as needed. An eviction policy like **allkeys-lru** ensures that less frequently used data is removed to make room for new data.

Leverage Persistent Storage for Critical Data

Redis offers two main persistence options: RDB snapshots and AOF (Append Only File). Use these to ensure that your data is not lost in case of a server failure.

- **RDB Snapshots:** Creates point-in-time snapshots of your data at regular intervals. This is useful for backups but may result in data loss between snapshots.
- **AOF (Append Only File):** Logs every write operation, while providing for more robust data durability.

  ```
  save 900 1  # Save a snapshot every 15 minutes if at least 1 change has
  occurred
  appendonly yes  # Enable AOF persistence
  ```

Tip: If data loss is unacceptable, use AOF with regular RDB snapshots. This hybrid approach balances durability and performance. However, remember that persistence comes with a performance cost, so fine-tune accordingly based on your application's needs.

Use Namespaces and Key Naming Conventions

Adopting a consistent key naming convention makes your Redis database easier to manage and avoids key collisions.

- **Example:** Use prefixes to categorize your keys:

```
SET user:1001:name "Alice"
SET user:1001:email "alice@example.com"
```

This approach organizes your data logically, which makes it easier to perform bulk operations using key patterns (for example, `user:*`).

> ***Tip***: Choose descriptive and meaningful prefixes. For example, **cache:** for cache data, **session:** for session data, and **queue:** for message queues. This helps other developers (or even your future self) quickly understand the purpose of each key.

Avoid Large Keys and Use Chunking When Necessary

Storing excessively large data in a single key can lead to performance issues and memory fragmentation. Instead, break down large data into smaller chunks when possible.

- **Example**: If you are storing a large log file, consider splitting it into smaller entries using Lists, as shown here:

```
RPUSH logs "entry1" "entry2" "entry3"
```

Using a List structure keeps your operations efficient, and reduces the risk of performance bottlenecks.

> ***Tip***: Always measure and monitor the impact of large keys. Use the **MEMORY USAGE** command to understand how much memory a key is consuming and optimize accordingly.

Be Mindful of Blocking Commands

Certain Redis commands, like **KEYS** and **FLUSHALL**, can block the server if used on a large dataset. Avoid these in production environments, or use safer alternatives.

- **Example**: Instead of using `KEYS user:*` to fetch all user-related keys, consider using **SCAN**, which is a non-blocking, incremental iterator. This is shown here:

```
SCAN 0 MATCH user:* COUNT 100
```

This approach ensures that your Redis server remains responsive, even when you are dealing with a large number of keys.

> ***Tip***: Plan for scalability. Use non-blocking commands and avoid patterns that could bring your server to a halt as your data grows.

By following these best practices, you can ensure that your Redis data management strategy is both efficient and robust. Redis is a powerful tool, and using it wisely will help you build scalable and high-performing applications that leverage the speed and reliability of in-memory data storage.

Conclusion

In this chapter, we explored how Redis integrates seamlessly with various scripting languages, empowering developers to perform efficient and versatile data management. From setting and retrieving simple key-value pairs to handling complex data structures, we saw how languages like Python, PHP, Lua, and Shell provide the tools to unlock Redis's potential. These scripting languages not only simplify operations but also enhance the ability to automate workflows, optimize performance, and meet the demands of dynamic applications.

By mastering these data management techniques, you have laid a solid foundation for leveraging Redis's speed and flexibility in real-world scenarios. Whether you are building a caching layer, a pub/sub system, or a session store, the knowledge from this chapter will enable you to integrate Redis effectively into your applications.

As we move to the next chapter, *Monitoring Redis for Optimal Performance*, we will shift our focus to maintaining a healthy Redis environment. Redis' performance is one of its key strengths, but to ensure it remains reliable and efficient, proper monitoring is essential. The next chapter will delve into the tools and techniques you need to track Redis's health, detect potential issues, and optimize its operation for the long haul. With the combination of effective data management and robust monitoring, you will be equipped to harness Redis's full potential and maintain its top-tier performance.

CHAPTER 5

Monitoring Redis for Optimal Performance - Part 1

Introduction

Redis is widely celebrated for its exceptional speed, reliability, and versatility. These qualities make it a foundational element in modern data-intensive applications. However, sustaining these advantages in production environments requires consistent and strategic monitoring. Proactive monitoring is not merely a safety net for when issues arise; it is a vital discipline that ensures Redis operates within optimal parameters, minimizes performance bottlenecks, and uses system resources efficiently. A well-monitored Redis instance helps avoid unforeseen downtime, improves responsiveness, and ultimately safeguards the user experience, especially under demanding workloads.

At the heart of Redis monitoring lies real-time visibility into the system's operational metrics such as memory consumption, command latency, throughput, and key expiration patterns. These metrics enable teams to detect anomalies, recognize trends, and take preventive action before minor inefficiencies grow into critical failures. For example, monitoring spikes in memory usage or increased command execution times can signal the need for configuration tuning or scaling resources. Thus, whether in development, staging, or production, monitoring allows engineers to make informed, data-driven decisions that align Redis's performance with business requirements. In this chapter, we will explore both **built-in tools like the `INFO` and `MONITOR` commands**, and **powerful third-party solutions** such as **RedisInsight**, **Prometheus**, and **Grafana**, to help you implement a robust monitoring strategy tailored for Redis at scale.

Structure

This chapter will cover the following topics:

- Built-In Redis Monitoring Tools
- Third-Party Monitoring Tools

Built-in Redis Monitoring Tools

Redis comes with a suite of built-in monitoring tools that provide detailed insights into the health and performance of your Redis instance. These tools are essential for understanding how Redis is operating under the hood and for identifying potential issues before they escalate. Hence, whether you are troubleshooting a sudden spike in latency or optimizing your instance for better resource utilization, Redis's built-in features offer invaluable support.

The INFO Command

The **INFO** command is one of the most comprehensive tools in Redis for retrieving server information and statistics. **It breaks down critical metrics into sections such as memory usage, CPU utilization, client connections, and much more**. Running the INFO command is as simple as typing:

```
redis-cli INFO
```

This will output detailed statistics grouped into categories such as Server, Clients, Memory, Persistence, and Replication. For instance, the Memory section will display metrics such as **used_memory** (how much memory Redis is using) and **maxmemory** (the maximum memory limit).

The **INFO** command in Redis is a powerful tool for obtaining detailed statistics and operational information about your Redis server. Using the **redis-cli INFO** command, you can view an extensive list of metrics and data grouped into various sections. Here is a breakdown of the categories of information it provides:

- **Server:** Displays information about the Redis server itself, such as the version, build ID, and operating system details
- **Clients:** Lists statistics about connected clients, including the number of client connections and their states
- **Memory:** Provides insights into memory usage, memory allocation details, and memory fragmentation
- **Persistence:** Shows the status of data persistence mechanisms, such as RDB snapshots and AOF (Append-Only File) logs
- **Stats:** Offers general statistics about Redis operations, including key hits, misses, and the number of commands processed
- **Replication:** Contains details about the replication setup, including primary-replica status and synchronization metrics
- **CPU:** Displays CPU usage statistics broken down by system and user-level processes
- **Modules:** Lists all loaded Redis modules along with their version and status
- **Errorstats:** Highlights error statistics to help identify potential issues or misconfigurations
- **Cluster:** Provides information specific to Redis Cluster configurations, such as node status and cluster health
- **Keyspace:** Displays details about the keyspace, such as the number of keys, expiration settings, and key distribution

Figure 5.1 displays the detailed output generated by the Redis info command. It provides a snapshot of your Redis instance's overall health by presenting the key metrics such as memory usage, uptime, CPU consumption, and other performance indicators.

```
# Server
redis_version:7.2.5
redis_git_sha1:00000000
redis_git_dirty:0
redis_build_id:bd81cd1340e80580
redis_mode:standalone
os:Darwin 23.4.0 arm64
arch_bits:64
monotonic_clock:POSIX clock_gettime
multiplexing_api:kqueue
atomicvar_api:c11-builtin
gcc_version:4.2.1
process_id:586
process_supervised:no
run_id:feb056bc5935890957e3bb0b793a1bc94f23b836
tcp_port:6379
server_time_usec:1734253179074673
uptime_in_seconds:1269795
uptime_in_days:14
hz:10
configured_hz:10
lru_clock:6199931
executable:/opt/homebrew/opt/redis/bin/redis-server
config_file:/opt/homebrew/etc/redis.conf
io_threads_active:0
listener0:name=tcp,bind=127.0.0.1,bind=::1,port=6379
```

Figure 5.1: *Part of the Output of the Redis Info Command*

Figures 5.2 *and* 5.3 represent Client and CPU Sections of the Redis **INFO** Command Output. These figures highlight key performance metrics from the Redis **info** command. *Figure* 5.2 focuses on the client section, detailing information about connected and blocked clients, while *Figure* 5.3 displays the CPU section, and provides insights into the server's processing efficiency.

```
# Clients
connected_clients:1
cluster_connections:0
maxclients:10000
client_recent_max_input_buffer:0
client_recent_max_output_buffer:0
blocked_clients:0
tracking_clients:0
clients_in_timeout_table:0
total_blocking_keys:0
total_blocking_keys_on_nokey:0
```

Figure 5.2: *Client Section in the Redis Info Command Output*

```
# CPU
used_cpu_sys:258.570828
used_cpu_user:120.604359
used_cpu_sys_children:0.030144
used_cpu_user_children:0.002587
```

Figure 5.3: *CPU Section in the Redis Info Command Output*

This information is invaluable for detecting memory leaks, adjusting memory policies, or scaling your infrastructure. You can also query specific sections by passing them as an argument to **INFO**, such as shown here:

```
redis-cli INFO memory
```

This focused query can help you pinpoint memory-related issues without being overwhelmed by unrelated data.

The MONITOR Command

In Redis, the **MONITOR** command is a **powerful utility designed for real-time debugging and diagnostics**. When executed, it streams every command received and processed by the Redis server in real-time. This can be incredibly useful for understanding the behavior of your application, identifying performance bottlenecks, or diagnosing unexpected issues.

The **MONITOR** command enables a connection to the Redis server to act as a passive observer. Once executed, the server continuously sends back a live feed of all incoming commands. Each entry in the output includes:

- **Timestamp**: Indicates the exact time the command was executed.
- **Client Information**: Provides details about the client that issued the command, such as the IP address and port number.
- **Command Details**: Shows the command itself, along with its arguments.

For real-time debugging, the **MONITOR** command is a powerful tool that streams every command processed by the Redis server. You can enable command monitoring by running:

```
redis-cli MONITOR
```

You can stop monitoring by closing the connection (**for example, using** *Ctrl+C* **in a terminal**).

Redis will display a live feed of all the commands being executed. For instance, look at the following image:

```
1738820428.141845 [0 127.0.0.1:64748] "set" "key" "value"
1738820430.447719 [0 127.0.0.1:64748] "get" "key"
1738820432.506471 [0 127.0.0.1:64748] "del" "key"
```

Figure 5.4: *Sample Output of the Redis Monitor Command*

Figure 5.4 displays sample output from the Redis MONITOR command, which provides a real-time stream of every command processed by the server. The output includes details such as timestamps, client information, and the executed commands, while offering valuable insights into the operations occurring on your Redis instance.

Important Considerations

- **Performance Overhead**: Since the **MONITOR** command streams all commands in real-time, it can impose significant performance overhead on a busy Redis server. Use it sparingly in production environments.
- **Single-Connection Limitation**: Only the client that issued the **MONITOR** command receives the command feed. If multiple clients need access, additional connections must be made.
- **Sensitive Data Exposure**: The **MONITOR** command reveals all commands, including those involving sensitive data. Be cautious about where and how you use it.

The **MONITOR** command is a crucial tool for any Redis developer or administrator, as it offers deep insights into the server's operation. However, its potential impact on performance and security highlights the need to use it judiciously, particularly in production environments.

Slow Log (SLOWLOG)

Performance bottlenecks are a frequent challenge in high-traffic Redis environments, where even small inefficiencies can escalate under heavy loads. **To address this, Redis provides the Slow Log (SLOWLOG) feature, which is a built-in tool designed to identify and analyze commands that take longer than expected to execute.**

The Slow Log is a diagnostic feature in Redis that captures and records details of commands that exceed a defined execution time threshold. This allows administrators to pinpoint performance issues caused by slow commands, such as inefficient queries, large data transfers, or high-latency operations.

Key Features of the Slow Log

- **Execution Time Threshold**: The Slow Log only records commands whose execution time exceeds a configurable threshold, while ensuring that routine commands do not clutter the log.
- **Command Capture**: Each Slow Log entry includes information such as:
  - The command and its arguments
  - The duration of execution in microseconds
  - The exact timestamp when the command was executed
  - The client ID and IP address that issued the command
- **Limited Storage**: Redis stores only the most recent Slow Log entries (defined by **`SLOWLOG MAXLEN`**), while ensuring that the log remains manageable in size.

How to Use the Slow Log

The **`SLOWLOG`** command provides several subcommands for interacting with the log such as the ones mentioned here:

- **View Slow Log Entries**

  To retrieve the Slow Log entries, use:

  ```
  redis-cli SLOWLOG GET [count]
  ```

  This command returns the specified number of entries (default is all). Each entry contains:
  - An ID for the log entry
  - The execution time in microseconds
  - The command and its arguments

Example output:

```
1) 1) (integer) 4
   2) (integer) 1738750909
   3) (integer) 10971
   4) 1) "INFO"
   5) "127.0.0.1:49338"
   6) ""
2) 1) (integer) 3
   2) (integer) 1738739386
   3) (integer) 11039
   4) 1) "INFO"
   5) "127.0.0.1:49338"
   6) ""
```

***Figure* 5.5:** *Sample Output of the Redis Slowlog Command*

Figure 5.5 presents a sample output from the Redis **`slowlog`** command. It details the logged information for commands that exceeded the specified execution time threshold, including timestamps, execution durations, and the commands themselves. This output is essential for diagnosing performance bottlenecks and optimizing your Redis setup.

- **Clear the Slow Log**

  To reset the Slow Log, clearing all its entries, use:

  ```
  redis-cli SLOWLOG RESET
  ```

  This does not affect the execution of commands but only clears the logged data.

- **Check Log Length**

  To find out how many Slow Log entries are currently stored, use:

  ```
  redis-cli SLOWLOG LEN
  ```

Configuring the Slow Log: The Slow Log behavior can be customized using the following configuration parameters:

- **`slowlog-log-slower-than`**

  Sets the execution time threshold (in microseconds) for commands to be logged. For example:

  ```
  CONFIG SET slowlog-log-slower-than 10000
  ```

  Setting this to 0 logs all commands, while -1 disables the Slow Log entirely.

- **`slowlog-max-len`**

  Defines the maximum number of Slow Log entries to retain. For example:

  ```
  CONFIG SET slowlog-max-len 128
  ```

Common Use Cases

- **Diagnosing Performance Bottlenecks**: Identify **`slow`** commands that may be contributing to latency in your application.
- **Optimizing Query Design**: Analyze frequently logged **`slow`** commands to optimize data structures and access patterns.
- **Monitoring High-Traffic Environments**: Detect potential issues caused by spikes in traffic or inefficient commands under heavy load.

Best Practices

- **Set a Meaningful Threshold**: Configure **`slowlog-log-slower-than`** to capture only genuinely slow commands, while reducing noise in the log.
- **Monitor Regularly**: Regularly review the Slow Log to proactively address performance issues before they impact users.
- **Pair with Other Tools**: Use the Slow Log in conjunction with other monitoring tools such as **`MONITOR`** and third-party solutions for a holistic view of Redis performance.

Limitations

While the Slow Log is a powerful tool, it is not a complete performance monitoring solution. **It does not capture metrics such as overall server load, memory usage, or network latency**. For a more comprehensive analysis, consider integrating the **Slow Log** with external monitoring systems.

The Slow Log is an indispensable feature for monitoring and improving the performance of Redis. By identifying slow commands and providing actionable insights, it enables administrators to maintain optimal performance in even the most demanding environments.

The CLIENT LIST Command

This command offers a real-time snapshot of all clients currently connected to the Redis server, including detailed information about their activities and states.

The **`CLIENT LIST`** command retrieves a list of all active client connections to the Redis server. Each connection (or client) is represented as a line of text, detailing various attributes such as the client's IP address, port, connection status, and the commands they are currently executing.

This command is particularly valuable for:

- Identifying misbehaving or problematic clients
- Diagnosing connection-related issues
- Monitoring client activity to ensure efficient resource utilization

Information Provided by `CLIENT LIST`

Each line of the **`CLIENT LIST`** output includes a wealth of information about a connected client. The key attributes are:

- **`id`**: A unique identifier for the client connection
- **`addr`**: The IP address and port of the client
- **`fd`**: The file descriptor used for the client's connection
- **`name`**: The name assigned to the client (if any). This can be set using the **`CLIENT SETNAME`** command
- **`age`**: The duration (in seconds) that the client has been connected
- **`idle`**: The number of seconds since the client last interacted with the server
- **`flags`**: The status of the client, represented by flags (for example, **`N`** for normal, **`S`** for slave/replica, **`M`** for master/primary)
- **`db`**: The currently selected database for the client
- **`sub`**: The number of active channel subscriptions (for Pub/Sub)
- **`psub`**: The number of active pattern subscriptions (for Pub/Sub)
- **`multi`**: Indicates whether the client is in a transaction
- **`qbuf`**: The query buffer size for the client
- **`cmd`**: The last command the client sent to the server

Here is an example of a CLIENT LIST output:

```
127.0.0.1:6379> client list
id=3 addr=127.0.0.1:49338 laddr=127.0.0.1:6379 fd=8 name= age=169642 idle=9 flags=N db=0 sub=0 psub=0 ssub=0 multi=-1 qbuf=0 qbuf-free=0 argv-mem=0 m
ulti-mem=0 rbs=1024 rbp=0 obl=0 oll=0 omem=0 tot-mem=1824 events=r cmd=slowlog|get user=default redir=-1 resp=2 lib-name=redis-py lib-ver=5.0.8
id=7 addr=127.0.0.1:64748 laddr=127.0.0.1:6379 fd=9 name= age=513 idle=7 flags=N db=0 sub=0 psub=0 ssub=0 multi=-1 qbuf=0 qbuf-free=0 argv-mem=0 mult
i-mem=0 rbs=1024 rbp=0 obl=0 oll=0 omem=0 tot-mem=1824 events=r cmd=del user=default redir=-1 resp=2 lib-name= lib-ver=
id=8 addr=127.0.0.1:64784 laddr=127.0.0.1:6379 fd=10 name= age=452 idle=7 flags=O db=0 sub=0 psub=0 ssub=0 multi=-1 qbuf=0 qbuf-free=0 argv-mem=0 mul
ti-mem=0 rbs=1024 rbp=0 obl=0 oll=0 omem=0 tot-mem=1824 events=r cmd=monitor user=default redir=-1 resp=2 lib-name= lib-ver=
id=11 addr=127.0.0.1:64877 laddr=127.0.0.1:6379 fd=11 name= age=43 idle=0 flags=N db=0 sub=0 psub=0 ssub=0 multi=-1 qbuf=26 qbuf-free=16864 argv-mem=
10 multi-mem=0 rbs=1024 rbp=0 obl=0 oll=0 omem=0 tot-mem=18730 events=r cmd=client|list user=default redir=-1 resp=2 lib-name= lib-ver=
```

Figure 5.6: *Part of the Output of the Redis Client List Command*

Figure 5.6 shows a segment of the output from the Redis client list command, while providing details about active client connections. It includes information such as client addresses, connection status, and other relevant metrics that help you monitor and manage client interactions with your Redis instance.

Key Use Cases for the `CLIENT LIST` Command

- **Identifying Misbehaving Clients:** By examining attributes such as **`cmd`** (the last executed command) and **`qbuf`** (query buffer size), administrators can detect clients that are consuming excessive resources or issuing inefficient commands.
- **Diagnosing Connection Issues:** The **`age`** and **`idle`** fields help pinpoint inactive or long-running connections, which can be indicators of stale clients or network issues.
- **Tracking Pub/Sub Activity:** The **`sub`** and **`psub`** fields allow administrators to monitor Pub/Sub subscriptions in real time, while providing insights into message distribution.
- **Analyzing Client Behavior:** By correlating the **`cmd`** field with specific client IDs or IP addresses, you can identify patterns in how clients are interacting with the Redis server.
- **Managing Resource Usage:** The **`CLIENT LIST`** command enables administrators to assess the load imposed by each client and take proactive measures, such as closing idle connections or rebalancing workloads.

Practical Scenarios

- **High Latency Investigation:** If Redis is experiencing latency issues, you can use CLIENT LIST to identify clients that are executing time-consuming commands or using large query buffers.
- **Security Audits:** By reviewing the **`addr`** and **`name`** fields, you can verify whether all connected clients are authorized and properly identified.
- **Pub/Sub Monitoring:** During Pub/Sub operations, the **`CLIENT LIST`** command helps ensure that clients are subscribing as expected and not overloading the server with unnecessary subscriptions.

Example Usage

To view the current list of connected clients, simply run:

```
redis-cli CLIENT LIST
```

This will output a list of all connected clients with their respective details.

For better readability and focused analysis, you can pair the **`CLIENT LIST`** command with tools or scripts to filter and parse its output. For example, using grep to filter clients by IP address in the following way:

```
redis-cli CLIENT LIST | grep 192.168.1.10
```

Limitations

- **Dynamic Nature**: The **`CLIENT LIST`** output is a real-time snapshot. Connections can open or close quickly, which make it challenging to capture transient clients.
- **Manual Interpretation**: While the data is rich, interpreting it requires familiarity with Redis and its attributes.

Best Practices

- Regularly monitor the **`CLIENT LIST`** output during high-traffic periods to ensure all connections are operating as expected.
- Combine **`CLIENT LIST`** with other monitoring tools such as **`MONITOR`** and **`INFO`** for a more comprehensive view of Redis activity.

- Use client names (`CLIENT SETNAME`) to make it easier to identify and group related connections in the CLIENT LIST output.

The `CLIENT LIST` command is a vital tool in the Redis administrator's arsenal. By providing detailed, real-time insights into connected clients, it enables effective monitoring, troubleshooting, and optimization of client-server interactions.

Combining Built-in Tools for Effective Monitoring

Redis's built-in monitoring tools are most powerful when used **together**, as they provide a **comprehensive view** of the system's performance. Each tool serves a unique purpose, but when combined, they help you quickly **identify and resolve potential issues** before they impact the Redis instance.

For example, suppose you notice an unexpected increase in memory usage. You can start by using the `INFO` command to get an **overview of Redis's memory metrics**, helping you detect any sudden spikes. To investigate further, the `MONITOR` command allows you to track **real-time Redis activity**, helping you pinpoint which commands are responsible for the increase. If you suspect certain operations are slowing down your system, the `SLOWLOG` command identifies **slow queries**, which will help you diagnose and optimize inefficient operations. Additionally, the `CLIENT LIST` command can show you **which clients are running these commands**, allowing you to track down specific users or applications causing the issue.

By integrating these tools into your daily monitoring routine, you can proactively **maintain a stable and efficient Redis environment**. These built-in tools provide a strong foundation for **diagnosing problems, optimizing performance, and ensuring that Redis runs smoothly**.

However, while Redis's built-in tools are powerful, they have certain limitations, such as a **lack of historical data analysis and graphical visualization**. To gain deeper insights and make monitoring even more efficient, you can combine them with **third-party monitoring solutions** that offer **real-time dashboards, alerts, and advanced analytics**. In the next section, we will explore some of these third-party tools, and how they can further enhance your Redis monitoring strategy.

Quick Command-Line Refresher (Before We Install)

Why This Matters: You will run a handful of commands to install and start the tools. If the terminal feels intimidating, this quick refresher will make the process straightforward.

Opening a Terminal

- **Windows:** Use **PowerShell** (`Start → type "PowerShell"`) or **Windows Terminal.**
- **macOS:** Open **Terminal** (`Applications → Utilities → Terminal`).
- **Linux (Ubuntu/CentOS):** Open **Terminal** from your applications menu.

Notes

- Lines that start with # are comments (explanations). Do not type them.
- Lines that start with $ just indicate a shell prompt. Type only what comes after $.

Paths and Spaces

- **File/folder names with spaces need quotes, like these:**

  `cd "C:\Program Files\Prometheus"` (Windows)

  `cd "/usr/local/bin"` (macOS/Linux)

If a command fails, do the following:

a. Read the error message; often it tells you exactly what is missing.

b. Try running the same command again; **typos are common**.
c. If permission is denied, try with **sudo** (on macOS/Linux).

Third-Party Monitoring Tools

While Redis offers built-in commands for real-time insights, third-party tools provide deeper visibility, rich visualizations, and powerful alerting mechanisms essential for managing Redis in production. In this section, we will explore two widely adopted tools: **RedisInsight, the official GUI from Redis Inc.** for real-time analysis and visual diagnostics, and other tools like **Prometheus and Grafana** that **deliver a scalable, customizable observability stack**. These tools significantly enhance operational efficiency and troubleshooting. We will provide detailed, OS-specific setup instructions for macOS, Ubuntu, CentOS, and Windows to help you seamlessly integrate Redis monitoring into your environment regardless of the platform.

RedisInsight

RedisInsight is a powerful graphical user interface (GUI) developed by Redis, Inc., which is designed to simplify the management, monitoring, and debugging of Redis instances. This versatile tool is compatible with various Redis deployments, including:

- Redis Open Source
- Redis Stack
- Redis Enterprise Software
- Redis Enterprise Cloud
- Amazon ElastiCache

RedisInsight can be used across all major operating systems, which makes it a universal solution for developers and administrators. The following are some of its key features that enhance the monitoring and management experience:

Key Features of RedisInsight

- **Intuitive Controls for Data Browsing and Filtering**
  - Easily browse through your Redis datasets.
  - You can filter and query data to find specific keys or patterns quickly.
- **Support for All Key-Value Data Types**
  - It provides full support for Redis data types, including lists, hashes, strings, sets, sorted sets, streams and JSON.
- **Built-In Monaco Editor**
  - It includes a powerful editor with syntax highlighting, developer shortcuts, and auto-completion.
  - It streamlines the process of writing and executing Redis commands directly within the tool.
- **Dark Mode and Accessibility Compliance**
  - It features a dark mode and an adjusted color palette designed to meet Web Content Accessibility Guidelines (WCAG) standards.
  - It enhances usability for users with visual impairments or those working in low-light environments.

- **Visualization and Analytics**
  - You can visualize memory usage, `keyspace` distribution, and other performance metrics.
  - It helps you gain insights into system health with detailed charts and reports.

Practical Use Case

Imagine you are managing a Redis instance that supports a high-traffic e-commerce application. Using `RedisInsight`, you can:

- Monitor memory usage in real-time to avoid exceeding configured limits
- Debug slow-running queries by identifying bottlenecks with the built-in editor and data filtering
- Generate visual reports on key usage patterns to optimize database schema and improve application performance

Thus, by providing these features, `RedisInsight` empowers teams to manage their Redis environments more efficiently, which reduces downtime and improves overall system reliability.

Installing RedisInsight on macOS

RedisInsight is a powerful GUI tool designed to simplify the management, monitoring, and debugging of Redis instances. Follow these steps below to install RedisInsight on macOS:

Step 1: Download the RedisInsight installer.

a. Visit the official RedisInsight download page and then navigate to the RedisInsight Downloads section.

b. Locate the **macOS** version of RedisInsight and click on `Download`.

Step 2: Install RedisInsight.

a. Once the `.dmg` file is downloaded, open it by double-clicking the file in your Downloads folder.

b. A window will appear prompting you to drag the RedisInsight application to the Applications folder. Drag and drop the icon accordingly.

c. After the transfer is complete, open the Applications folder and double-click on **RedisInsight** to launch the application.

Step 3: Grant Permissions (if required).

macOS may block the application from opening because it is downloaded from the internet. To resolve this:

a. Go to `System Preferences` > `Privacy & Security`.

b. Under the `General` tab, you will see a message about RedisInsight being blocked. Click `Open Anyway` to proceed.

Step 4: Connect RedisInsight to Your Redis Instance

a. Upon launching RedisInsight, you will be greeted with a connection screen.

b. Enter the details of your Redis instance, including:

   - **Host**: The IP address or hostname of your Redis server (for example, `localhost` if Redis is installed locally).
   - **Port**: The port number of your Redis instance (default is **6379**).

- **Password** (optional): The password for your Redis server, if authentication is enabled.
- Click on **Connect** to link **RedisInsight** to your Redis instance.

Figure 5.7 captures the moment when **RedisInsight** establishes a successful connection to a Redis server.

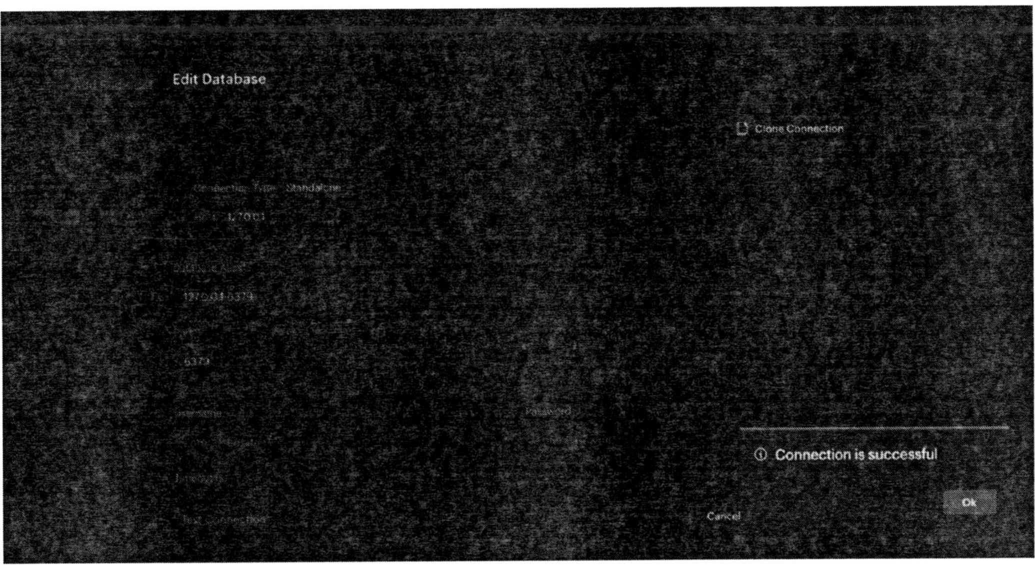

Figure 5.7: *Successful Connection of RedisInsight to Redis*

Figure 5.8 shows the **RedisInsight** dashboard once a successful connection to a Redis server has been established.

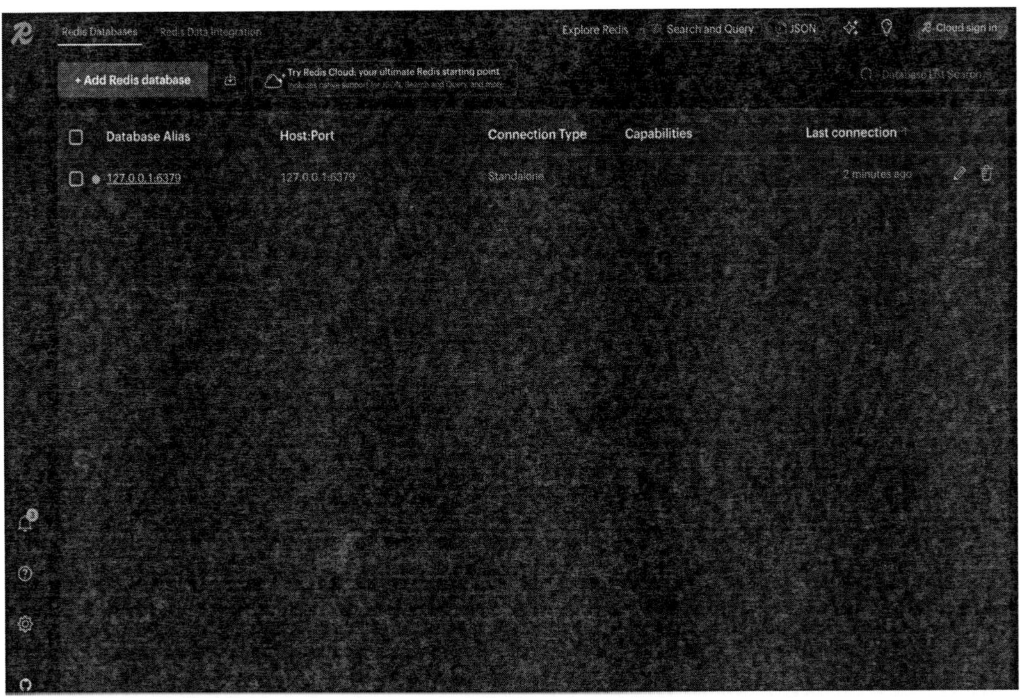

Figure 5.8: *RedisInsight Dashboard Displaying a Connected Redis Instance*

c. **Viewing Metrics:** Navigate to the "`Monitoring`" section to observe metrics such as:
   - Memory usage over time
   - Command execution latency
   - Keyspace statistics

Step 5: Verify Installation

Once connected, `RedisInsight` will display your Redis database, allowing you to browse data, monitor performance, and utilize its other features.

Tips for Optimizing `RedisInsight` on macOS

- Ensure your macOS system meets the minimum requirements for **`RedisInsight`**. This includes having sufficient memory and storage for smooth operation.
- Keep **`RedisInsight`** updated by checking for new versions regularly, as updates may include performance improvements and new features.

By following these steps, you will have **`RedisInsight`** installed and ready to manage your Redis instances effectively on macOS.

Installing RedisInsight on CentOS

`RedisInsight` can be installed using various methods; but for this guide, we will use **Docker to install `RedisInsight` on CentOS**. Docker is a popular containerization platform that simplifies deployment by packaging applications into lightweight, portable containers. This method is particularly useful for CentOS, as it ensures a quick and consistent setup.

If Docker is not already installed, you must first install it using the following steps:

Step 1: Set up the repository via this command here:

```
sudo dnf -y install dnf-plugins-core
sudo dnf config-manager --add-repo
https://download.docker.com/linux/centos/docker-ce.repo
```

Step 2: Install Docker Engine using this command:

```
sudo dnf install docker-ce docker-ce-cli containerd.io docker-buildx-plugin
docker-compose-plugin
```

If prompted to accept the GPG key, verify that the fingerprint matches **`060A 61C5 1B55 8A7F 742B 77AA C52F EB6B 621E 9F35`**. If it does, then accept it.

Step 3: Start Docker Engine via the following command:

```
sudo systemctl enable --now docker
```

This configures the Docker **`systemd`** service to start automatically when you boot your system. If you do not want Docker to start automatically, use **`sudo systemctl start docker`** instead.

Step 4: Verify that the installation is successful by running the hello-world image

```
sudo docker run hello-world
```

This command downloads a test image and runs it in a container. When the container runs, it prints a confirmation message and exits.

Figure 5.9 illustrates the successful execution of Docker's Hello World image within a container. It confirms that Docker is correctly installed and functioning, as proved by the expected output displayed from the container.

```
[root@localhost ~]# sudo docker run hello-world
Unable to find image 'hello-world:latest' locally

latest: Pulling from library/hello-world
478afc919002: Pull complete
Digest: sha256:5b3cc85e16e3058003c13b7821318369dad01dac3dbb877aac3c28182255c724
Status: Downloaded newer image for hello-world:latest

Hello from Docker!
This message shows that your installation appears to be working correctly.

To generate this message, Docker took the following steps:
 1. The Docker client contacted the Docker daemon.
 2. The Docker daemon pulled the "hello-world" image from the Docker Hub.
    (arm64v8)
 3. The Docker daemon created a new container from that image which runs the
    executable that produces the output you are currently reading.
 4. The Docker daemon streamed that output to the Docker client, which sent it
    to your terminal.

To try something more ambitious, you can run an Ubuntu container with:
 $ docker run -it ubuntu bash

Share images, automate workflows, and more with a free Docker ID:
 https://hub.docker.com/

For more examples and ideas, visit:
 https://docs.docker.com/get-started/
```

Figure 5.9: *Running the Hello World Docker Image in a Container*

Step 5: Install RedisInsight using Docker.

a. To install the Docker image of RedisInsight on CentOS, open your terminal and run the following command:

   `sudo docker pull redis/redisinsight:latest`

b. To start the container, use the following command:

   `sudo docker run -p 5540:5540 --name redisinsight redis/redisinsight:latest`

   Figure 5.10 displays the command-line instruction used to launch a container named "**`redisinsight`**". The snapshot highlights the specific syntax and parameters required to start the container, while ensuring that RedisInsight integrates seamlessly with your Redis environment.

```
[root@localhost ~]# sudo docker run -p 5540:5540 --name redisinsight redis/redisinsight:latest
Running docker-entry.sh
```

Figure 5.10: *Snapshot of the Command for Starting a Container Named Redisinsight*

This is what we see in the figure:

- **`sudo docker pull redis/redisinsight:latest`**: This command downloads the latest version of the RedisInsight Docker image from Docker Hub.

  `sudo docker run -p 5540:5540 --name redisinsight redis/redisinsight:latest:`

- **`-p 5540:5540`**: Maps the container's port 5540 to your host machine's port 5540, allowing you to access RedisInsight in your browser at **http://localhost:5540**.

- **`--name redisinsight`**: Assigns a name to the container for easier identification.

Step 6: Access RedisInsight

Once the container is running, open your web browser and navigate to **http://localhost:5540** to access the RedisInsight interface.

Figure 5.11 captures the RedisInsight dashboard as accessed through a web browser at **localhost:5540**. The interface confirms that the RedisInsight container is running successfully.

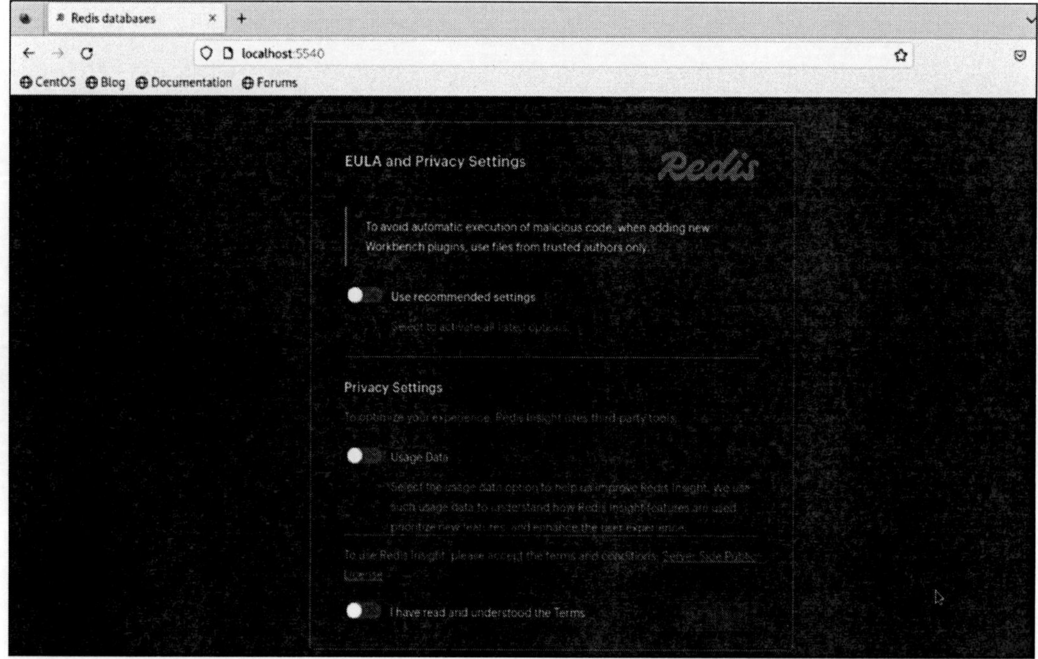

Figure 5.11: *RedisInsight Interface Hosted on Localhost:5540*

Figure 5.12 displays the RedisInsight dashboard when no Redis database is connected. The interface clearly indicates that there is no active connection, which will prompt the user to add and configure a Redis instance to begin monitoring its performance and metrics.

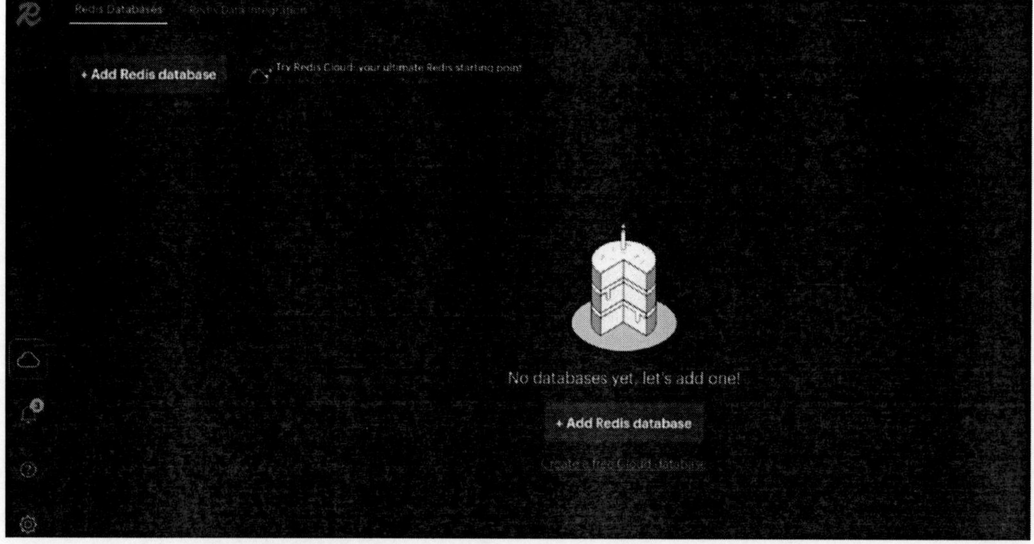

Figure 5.12: *RedisInsight Dashboard with No Connected Redis Database*

Figure 5.13 illustrates the process of integrating a Redis database into RedisInsight. It shows the interface where connection details are entered and enables the tool to begin monitoring and managing the connected Redis instance in real-time.

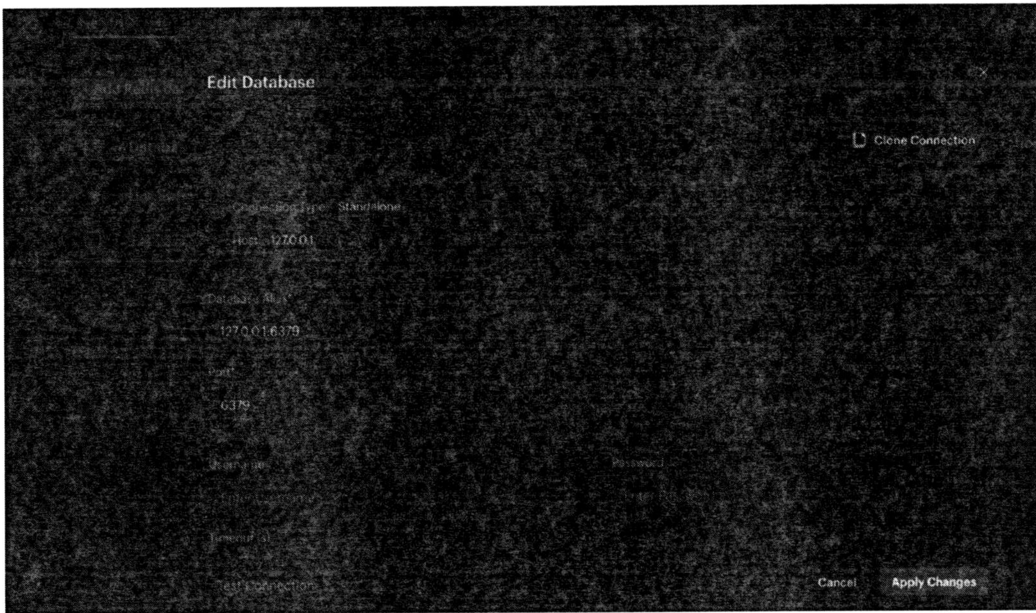

Figure 5.13: *Adding a Redis Database to RedisInsight*

Figure 5.14 demonstrates that RedisInsight has successfully established a connection with a Redis database.

Figure 5.14: *Successful Connection between RedisInsight and the Redis Database*

Installing RedisInsight on Ubuntu

In this section, we will demonstrate how to install RedisInsight on Ubuntu.

If you prefer to use Docker, RedisInsight can be installed and run as a Docker container via the following steps:

Step 1: Pull the RedisInsight Docker Image

a. Open a terminal on your Ubuntu system.

```
sudo docker pull redis/redisinsight:latest
```

Figure 5.15 displays the error output generated by a failed command to pull the RedisInsight Docker image, highlighting that Docker is not installed on the system.

```
root@ubuntu-QEMU-Virtual-Machine:~# sudo docker pull redis/redisinsight:latest
sudo: docker: command not found
root@ubuntu-QEMU-Virtual-Machine:~#
```

Figure 5.15: *Error Message When Attempting to Pull the RedisInsight Docker Image Without Docker Installed*

The **error serves as a reminder** that Docker must be properly set up before running RedisInsight in a containerized environment.

Step 2: If Docker is not already installed, first install docker

a. **Install using the apt repository:** Before you install Docker Engine for the first time on a new host machine, you need to set up the Docker apt repository. Afterwards, you can install and update Docker from the repository.

b. **Set up Docker's apt repository.**

Add Docker's official GPG key via the following command:

```
sudo apt-get update
sudo apt-get install ca-certificates curl
sudo install -m 0755 -d /etc/apt/keyrings
sudo curl -fsSL https://download.docker.com/linux/ubuntu/gpg -o /etc/apt/
keyrings/docker.asc
sudo chmod a+r /etc/apt/keyrings/docker.asc
# Add the repository to Apt sources:
echo \
  "deb [arch=$(dpkg --print-architecture) signed-by=/etc/apt/keyrings/docker.
asc] https://download.docker.com/linux/ubuntu \
  $(. /etc/os-release && echo "$VERSION_CODENAME") stable" | \
  sudo tee /etc/apt/sources.list.d/docker.list > /dev/null
sudo apt-get update
```

Step 3: Install the Docker packages.

a. **To install the latest version, run:**

```
sudo apt-get install docker-ce docker-ce-cli containerd.io docker-buildx-
plugin docker-compose-plugin
```

Step 4: Verify that the installation is successful by running the hello-world image, which is shown here:

```
sudo docker run hello-world
```

This command downloads a test image and runs it in a container. When the container runs, it prints a confirmation message and exits.

Figure 5.16 captures the successful execution of Docker's Hello World image on an Ubuntu system following the installation of Docker. The terminal output confirms that Docker is installed correctly and operating as expected, with the standard Hello World message indicating a successful setup.

```
root@ubuntu-QEMU-Virtual-Machine:~# sudo docker run hello-world
Unable to find image 'hello-world:latest' locally
latest: Pulling from library/hello-world
478afc919002: Pull complete
Digest: sha256:5b3cc85e16e3058003c13b7821318369dad01dac3dbb877aac3c28182255c724
Status: Downloaded newer image for hello-world:latest

Hello from Docker!
This message shows that your installation appears to be working correctly.

To generate this message, Docker took the following steps:
 1. The Docker client contacted the Docker daemon.
 2. The Docker daemon pulled the "hello-world" image from the Docker Hub.
    (arm64v8)
 3. The Docker daemon created a new container from that image which runs the
    executable that produces the output you are currently reading.
 4. The Docker daemon streamed that output to the Docker client, which sent it
    to your terminal.
```

Figure 5.16: *Running the Hello World Image After Docker Installation*

Step 5: Run RedisInsight Docker image.

a. If you want to persist your RedisInsight data, first attach the Docker volume to the /data path and then run the following command as shown in image:

```
root@ubuntu-QEMU-Virtual-Machine:~# docker run -d --name redisinsight -p 5540:5540 redis/redisinsight:latest -v redisinsight:/data
Unable to find image 'redis/redisinsight:latest' locally
latest: Pulling from redis/redisinsight
a258b2a6b59a: Pull complete
5b15dced3830: Pull complete
e1551dfea38b: Pull complete
d43745504edd: Pull complete
2bfe322d7c94: Pull complete
10407bdffe69: Pull complete
cbc9a9b1fa5f: Pull complete
4f4fb700ef54: Pull complete
8a992bd1db95: Pull complete
4730f9ae4272: Pull complete
e8a4b1fa8e4d: Pull complete
Digest: sha256:53618017b60bc825b5049d7f0bb40bc6bf5e551ae26a3b3dfc77f5af3733e812
Status: Downloaded newer image for redis/redisinsight:latest
d30aeff0fff787960a0b9f8d32a3370c2d139521ec102d2ccb00dced1927333a
```

Figure 5.17: *Pulling and Running the RedisInsight Image*

Figure 5.17 demonstrates the process of pulling the RedisInsight Docker image from the repository and launching it in a container.

Next, visit the link: **http://localhost:5540**.

Figure 5.18 confirms that RedisInsight has been successfully installed. Moreover, it shows that the application is now accessible through your web browser, which will allow you to easily monitor and manage your Redis environment online.

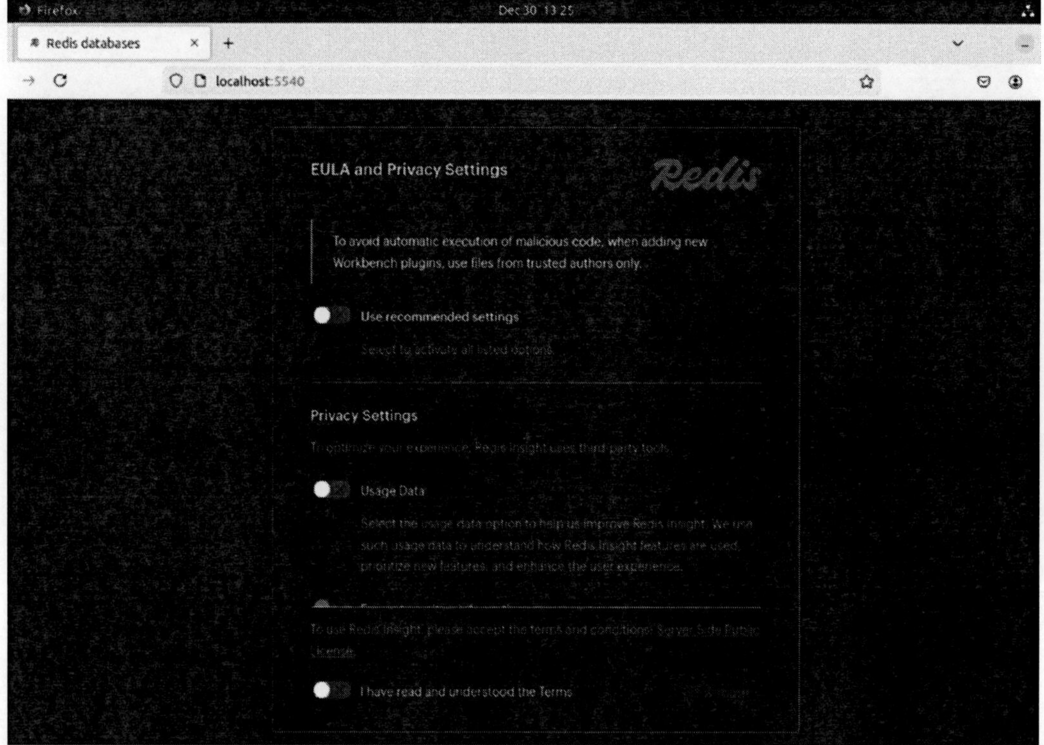

***Figure 5.18**: RedisInsight Successfully Installed and Accessible via Browser*

RedisInsight also provides a health check endpoint at **http://localhost:5540/api/health/** to monitor the health of the running container.

Figure 5.19 shows the health check endpoint in a web browser.

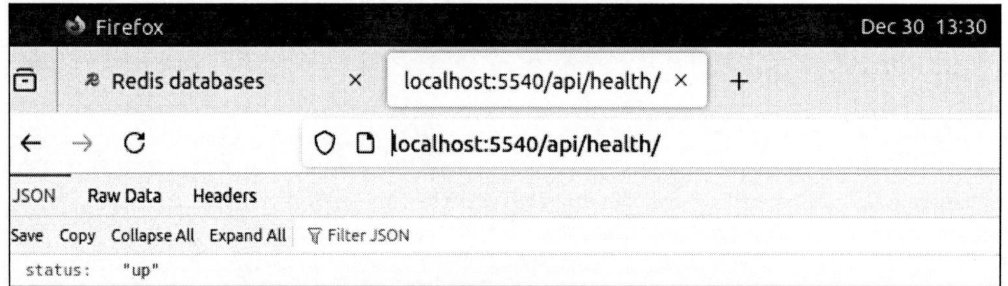

***Figure 5.19**: Health Check Endpoint Displayed in a Browser*

Figure 5.20 captures an error message displayed while attempting to add a Redis instance to **`RedisInsight`**. The error highlights issues with the connection or configuration, which signals that adjustments are needed to establish a successful integration between Redis and **`RedisInsight`**.

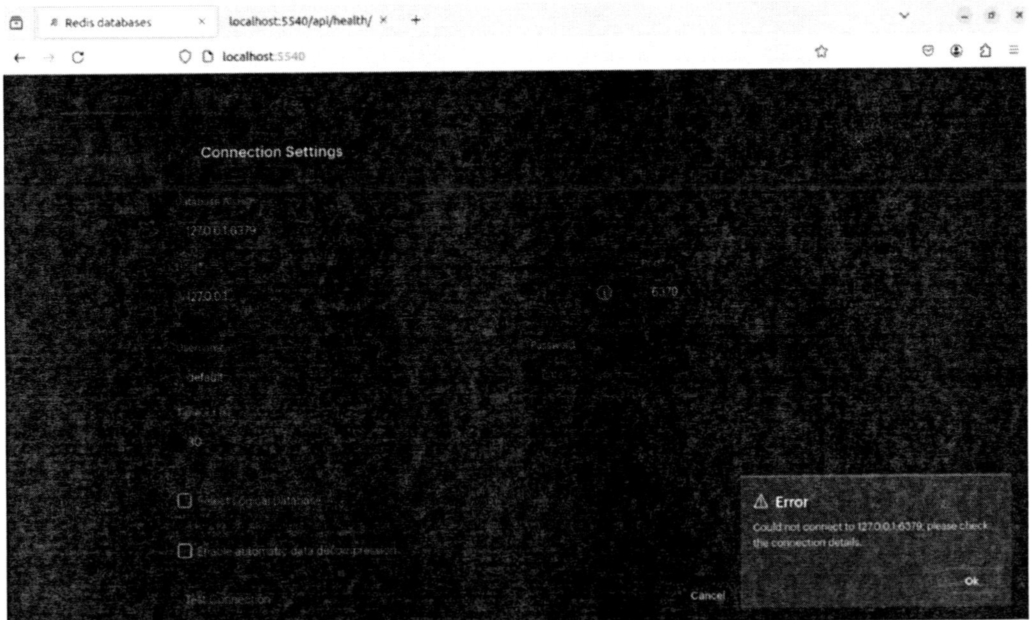

***Figure 5.20**: Error Encountered When Adding Redis to RedisInsight*

Note: *If you encounter a similar error, it might be because RedisInsight is running in a Docker container while the Redis server is installed on the host machine. The following solution should help resolve this issue:*

```
docker run --network=host  -d --name redisinsight -p 5540:5540 redis/
redisinsight:latest -v redisinsight:/data
```

We have used the **`--network=host`** flag. Not only does this resolve connectivity issues for Redis, but it also allows any service running on your localhost to be accessible within Docker containers. This flag bridges the gap between your Docker environment and the host network, while ensuring seamless communication with all your services.

Figure 5.21 captures the RedisInsight interface after the necessary configuration adjustments have been made. It confirms that RedisInsight now successfully connects to the Redis instance, while reflecting the effective use of the **`--network=host`** flag (or similar modifications) to bridge Docker and the host environment.

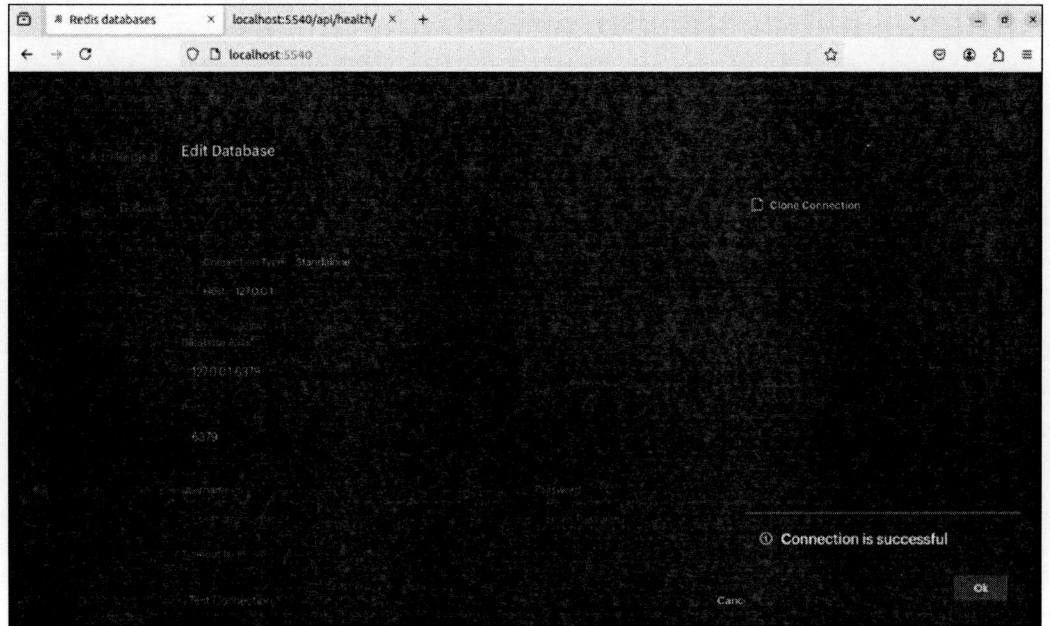

***Figure 5.21:** Successful Connection to Redis from RedisInsight after Applying Changes*

Installing RedisInsight on Windows

Setting up RedisInsight on a Windows system is a quick and straightforward process. In this section, we will walk you through the installation steps using the official installer provided by Redis. Whether you are using Windows 10 or Windows 11, the process is smooth and does not require any advanced configuration. Once installed, you will be able to connect to your Redis instance, and start working with your data right away.

Step 1: Download RedisInsight

a. Open your web browser and go to the official `RedisInsight` download page:

   https://redis.io/insight/

b. Click on the `Download` button and select the Windows version. Wait for the download to complete.

Step 2: Install RedisInsight

a. Locate the downloaded installer (`redisinsight-latest.exe`) in your Downloads folder.

b. Double-click on the installer to start the installation process.

c. Follow the on-screen installation instructions:

d. Choose the installation directory (default is usually fine).

e. Click Next and then Install to begin the installation.

f. Wait for the installation to complete.

g. Click Finish to close the installer.

Figure 5.22 captures the final stage of the RedisInsight installer on a Windows machine, confirming that the installation process is complete. The installer displays a success message, which indicates that RedisInsight has been properly set up and is now ready for use on your Windows system.

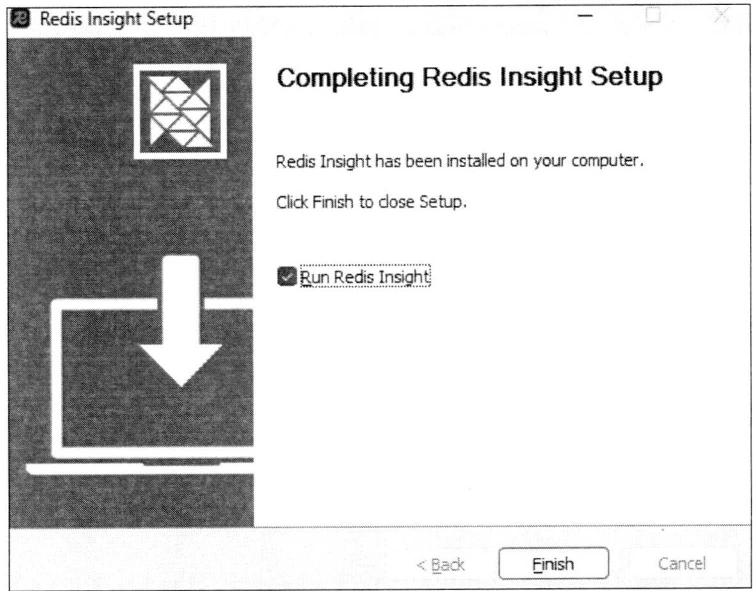

Figure 5.22: *Installer Completing Setup of RedisInsight on Windows*

Step 3: Launch `RedisInsight`

a. Open the **`Start`** Menu and search for **`RedisInsight`**.

b. Click on the **`RedisInsight`** application to launch it.

c. Once you open the application, you will see the **`RedisInsight`** dashboard.

Step 4: Connect to a Redis Server

a. Click on **`+ Add Redis Database`**.

b. Enter the following details:

- **Host**: **localhost (if Redis is running locally**) or the IP address of a remote Redis server
- **Port**: **6379 (default Redis port)**
- **Username and Password**: If Redis ACLs are enabled, enter the appropriate credentials.

c. Click on **`Connect`** to establish a connection.

In this section, we explored RedisInsight, a powerful graphical user interface (GUI) tool designed to make Redis database management and monitoring more intuitive. We discussed its standout features such as **real-time data visualization, performance insights, and query analysis**, which will help users gain a deeper understanding of their Redis instances. By providing a clear and interactive view of Redis data structures, RedisInsight makes it easier to identify performance bottlenecks, optimize queries, and efficiently manage large datasets.

For **developers and database administrators**, RedisInsight serves as a valuable tool, offering a streamlined way to **monitor, debug, and optimize Redis operations** without relying solely on command-line tools. Whether you are tracking keyspace metrics, analyzing slow queries, or visualizing data in a user-friendly manner, RedisInsight simplifies complex tasks, and enhances productivity.

As we move forward, we will continue to explore **other powerful monitoring tools and techniques** that further enhance Redis performance and usability. By leveraging the right tools, you can ensure a **more efficient, scalable, and well-optimized Redis environment**, which makes database management smoother and more effective.

Prometheus and Grafana

When you need more than just raw metrics like beautiful dashboards, historical trends, or automated alerts, **Prometheus and Grafana** become your go-to tools. **Prometheus** continuously pulls performance data from your Redis server, and **Grafana** helps you visualize that data in real-time charts and graphs. Together, they give you deep observability and help you catch issues before users even notice them.

In this section, we will guide you through setting up Prometheus and Grafana to monitor Redis on **macOS, Ubuntu, CentOS,** and **Windows** systems. You will learn how to install exporters, configure dashboards, and create useful alerts all with practical steps and screenshots so that monitoring Redis becomes second nature.

Introduction to Prometheus

Prometheus is an **open-source monitoring and alerting toolkit** widely used for tracking the performance and health of applications, services, and infrastructure. Originally developed at SoundCloud, Prometheus has grown to become one of the most popular monitoring tools, particularly in cloud-native and containerized environments.

Prometheus excels in collecting and storing metrics as time-series data, where each data point is identified by a timestamp, a metric name, and optional key-value pairs called labels. These metrics can range from system-level statistics such as CPU and memory usage to application-specific data such as request latency and error rates.

Key Features of Prometheus

- **Multi-Dimensional Data Model:** Prometheus uses labels to add metadata to metrics, which allows users to ask flexible and detailed queries. For example, you can monitor Redis memory usage for specific instances by applying filters on instance labels.
- **Powerful Query Language (PromQL):** PromQL allows users to perform complex queries on collected metrics, which facilitates detailed analysis and visualization. For instance, you can calculate Redis command execution rates or identify trends in key expiration events.
- **Built-in Alerting:** Prometheus includes an `Alertmanager` component for defining and managing alerts. This helps you stay proactive by notifying you of issues such as high memory usage or slow Redis command execution.
- **Scalability and Decoupling:** Prometheus operates as a standalone system with a pull-based metric collection model, which makes it suitable for distributed systems and scalable infrastructures.

Prometheus plays a vital role in monitoring Redis, as it can collect a wealth of metrics using the Redis Exporter. These metrics can then be visualized with tools such as Grafana, thereby enabling you to gain deep insights into your Redis instance's performance and reliability.

In essence, Prometheus empowers you to understand how Redis is performing, identify potential bottlenecks, and maintain a robust and efficient setup. Its integration with Redis and other components in your tech stack makes it an indispensable tool for modern system monitoring.

Introduction to Grafana

Grafana is an open-source data visualization and monitoring platform widely used for analyzing and displaying real-time metrics collected from various data sources. With its flexible dashboarding capabilities, Grafana has become a go-to tool for visualizing and understanding the performance of applications, systems, and services.

At its core, Grafana enables users to create interactive and dynamic dashboards that consolidate metrics from multiple sources into a single, cohesive view. These dashboards can display data as graphs, heatmaps, tables, and other visual formats, making it easier to interpret complex information.

Key Features of Grafana

- **Support for Multiple Data Sources:** Grafana integrates seamlessly with a variety of data sources such as Prometheus, Elasticsearch, InfluxDB, MySQL, and Redis. This flexibility allows users to aggregate and correlate data from different parts of their system in one place.
- **Customizable Dashboards:** Users can create highly customized dashboards with panels that suit their specific monitoring needs. For example, you can build a Redis-specific dashboard to monitor metrics such as memory usage, command rates, and latency.
- **Alerting and Notifications:** Grafana supports rule-based alerts, which can notify you of potential issues through email, Slack, PagerDuty, or other communication channels. This ensures that you stay informed about critical performance issues in real-time.
- **Interactive Querying:** Grafana provides an intuitive query editor for filtering and aggregating metrics. When connected to a Prometheus data source, users can leverage PromQL to analyze Redis metrics and visualize trends over time.
- **Extensibility Through Plugins:** Grafana offers a rich ecosystem of plugins for additional data sources, visualization types, and integrations. This extensibility makes Grafana adaptable to a wide range of monitoring and visualization scenarios.

Prometheus is an open-source monitoring and alerting toolkit, while Grafana provides powerful visualization dashboards. Together, they offer a robust solution for monitoring Redis performance.

Key Features of Prometheus and Grafana

- **Customizable Dashboards**: Grafana allows you to create visual dashboards tailored to Redis metrics.
- **Alerting**: Prometheus can trigger alerts when metrics exceed predefined thresholds.
- **Exporters**: The Redis Exporter (`redis_exporter`) bridges Redis and Prometheus by exporting Redis metrics.

Grafana and Redis

Grafana, when integrated with Prometheus, becomes a powerful solution for monitoring and visualizing the performance of your Redis instance. By leveraging the Redis Exporter, critical metrics from Redis can be ingested into Prometheus, where they are stored and queried. Grafana then takes these metrics and transforms them into interactive, customizable dashboards that provide a visual representation of Redis's operational health.

Grafana not only provides clear and intuitive visualizations but also offers advanced features such as threshold alerts, enabling you to set proactive notifications for critical Redis metrics. Its ability to correlate data across multiple systems further enhances its utility in diagnosing complex issues in distributed architectures.

In summary, Grafana transforms raw Redis metrics into actionable insights, which allows you to monitor and optimize your Redis instance effectively. Its seamless integration with Prometheus and its flexible, user-friendly dashboards make it an indispensable tool for maintaining Redis performance and reliability.

Before You Install: How `prometheus.yml` Works

Prometheus is driven by a single, **simple config file called `prometheus.yml`**. Think of it as Prometheus's checklist that includes questions like what to scrape, how often to scrape it, and what friendly names (labels) to attach so dashboards and queries are easy to build. You do not need to know every option just a few lines get you productive quickly.

What You Usually Set

- `global.scrape_interval`: How frequently Prometheus pulls metrics (every 15s is a practical default).
- `scrape_configs`: A list of jobs, where each tells Prometheus which targets (`host:port`) to scrape and optional labels

A Working Example

This example scrapes:

- **Redis Exporter** (Redis metrics) on **port 9121**
- **Node Exporter** (OS/VM host metrics) on **port 9100**

```
global:
  scrape_interval: 15s
  evaluation_interval: 15s

scrape_configs:
  - job_name: 'redis'
    static_configs:
      - targets: ['127.0.0.1:9121']
        labels:
          app: 'redis'

  - job_name: 'node'
    static_configs:
      - targets: ['127.0.0.1:9100']
        labels:
          role: 'demo-host'
```

The preceding configuration imply the following:

- **Global Section**: "Check metrics every 15 seconds." This cadence works well for most Redis setups.
- `job_name`: A human-friendly tag you will see in PromQL and Grafana (for example, `job="redis"`)
- `targets`: The endpoints Prometheus scrapes

  > **Note**: *Prometheus* ***scrapes the Redis exporter*** *(usually* ***`:9121`****), and not Redis itself (`:6379/:6380`).*

- `labels`: Extra tags (like **`app=redis, env=prod`**) that make filtering and dashboards easier.

Installing Prometheus and Grafana on macOS

To install Grafana on macOS using Homebrew, complete the following steps:

Step 1: Install Grafana

a. Open a terminal and run the following commands:

```
brew update
brew install grafana
```

b. The brew page downloads and untars the files into:

```
/usr/local/Cellar/grafana/[version] (Intel-based macOS)
/opt/homebrew/Cellar/grafana/[version] (Apple Silicon-based macOS)
```

c. To start Grafana, run the following command:

```
brew services start grafana
```

Step 2: Install Prometheus

```
brew install prometheus
brew services start prometheus
```

When Prometheus is running, its API becomes accessible on your local system. You can verify this by visiting **http://localhost:9090** in your web browser.

Figure 5.23 displays the Prometheus dashboard as accessed through a web browser on port 9090, which confirms that Prometheus is running properly.

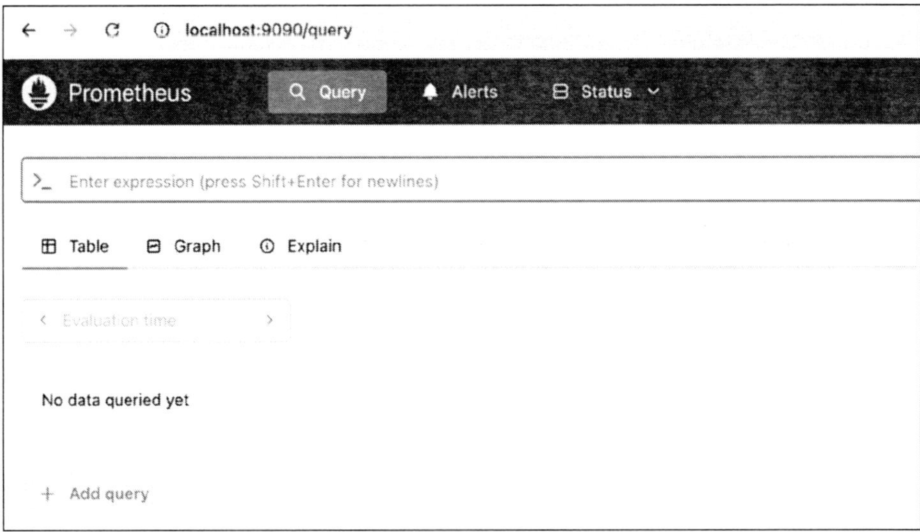

Figure 5.23: *Prometheus Running in a Web Browser on Port 9090*

Redis Exporter: The Redis Exporter (**`redis_exporter`**) bridges Redis and Prometheus by exporting Redis metrics.

Step 3: Install Redis Exporter

1. **Build and verify Redis Exporter locally using the following commands:**

```
git clone https://github.com/oliver006/redis_exporter.git
cd redis_exporter
```

```
go build .
./redis_exporter --version
```

2. **Run Redis Exporter with the following command:**

   ```
   ./redis_exporter
   ```

3. **Verify That Redis Exporter Is Running**

   Open a browser and navigate to:

   http://localhost:9121/metrics

4. **Configure Prometheus to Scrape Redis Exporter Metrics**

   Edit your Prometheus configuration file (for example, **`prometheus.yml`**) to include the Redis Exporter as a scrape target, as shown here:

   ```
   scrape_configs:
     - job_name: 'redis'
       static_configs:
         - targets: ['localhost:9121']
   ```

   Restart Prometheus to apply the changes through the following

   ```
   brew services restart prometheus
   ```

   Figure 5.24 displays the Prometheus dashboard with the Redis exporter successfully integrated. The exporter gathers key metrics from your Redis instance and makes them available for monitoring, while providing real-time insights into its performance directly within Prometheus.

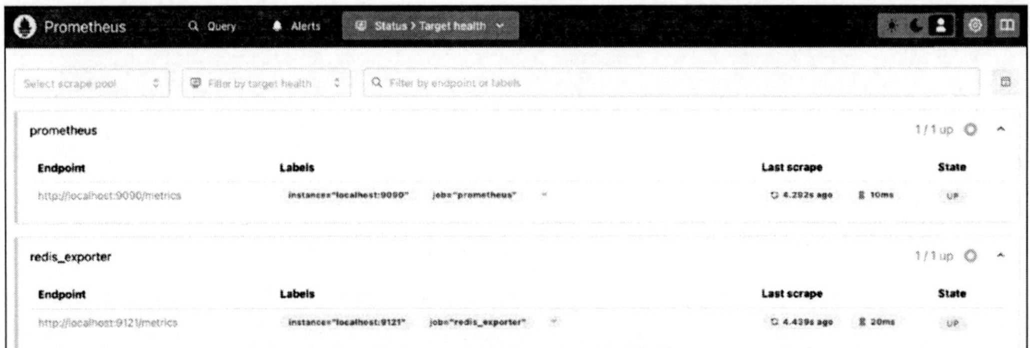

Figure 5.24: *Redis Exporter Added in Prometheus*

5. **Add Prometheus as a data source in Grafana, then import a Redis monitoring dashboard**
   Import a Redis monitoring dashboard. Grafana provides community dashboards designed for Redis Exporter metrics.

   a. Go to **`Dashboard → Import`**.

   b. Use the dashboard ID from the Grafana website (for example, **763 for Redis metrics**).

   Figure 5.25 showcases a Grafana dashboard specifically configured to monitor Redis. It presents a range of visualizations that display real-time metrics and offers a comprehensive overview of your Redis instance's health and activity.

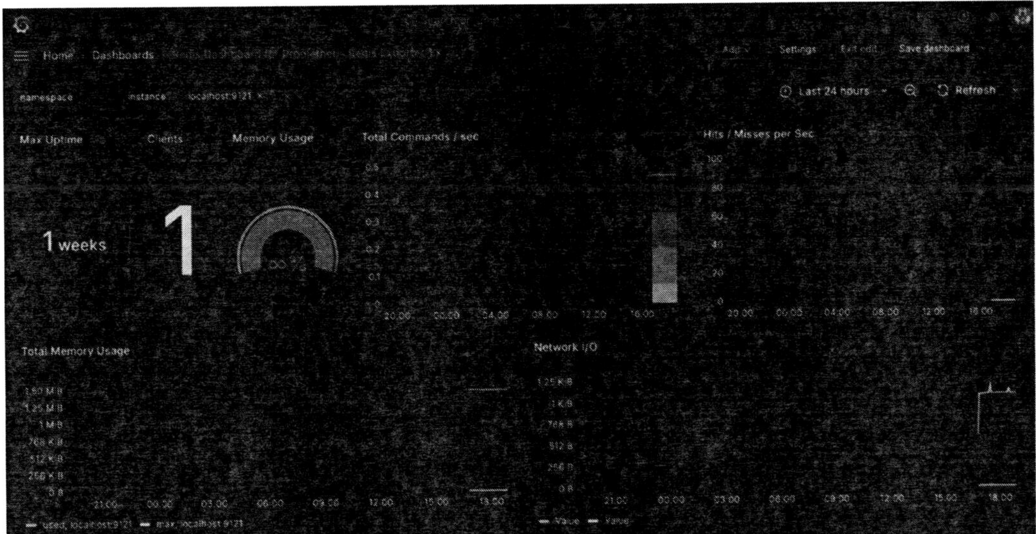

Figure 5.25: *Redis Monitoring Dashboard in Grafana*

Installing Prometheus and Grafana on Ubuntu

> **Note:** *To check if your system is "amd64" (which refers to the 64-bit x86 architecture) or another architecture such as ARM, you can use the command "***`uname -m`***" in your terminal; if the output is "x86_64", then you have an amd64 system; if it shows something else such as "aarch64", you are on an ARM architecture.*

Figure 5.26 shows the output of the **`uname -m`** command, which is used to determine the architecture of your system's CPU. The displayed result indicates whether your system is, for example, **`x86_64`** or **`arm64`**. This provides essential information for ensuring software compatibility and making informed configuration decisions.

```
root@OSUbuntu:~# uname -m
x86_64
root@OSUbuntu:~#
```

Figure 5.26: *Command uname -m to Check System Architecture*

To install Prometheus and Grafana on Ubuntu, follow these steps:

Installing Prometheus

Step 1: Update System Packages through the following command:

```
sudo apt update
```

Step 2: Create a System User for Prometheus via:

```
sudo groupadd --system prometheus
sudo useradd -s /sbin/nologin --system -g prometheus
```

Step 3: Create Directories for Prometheus via:

```
sudo mkdir /etc/prometheus
sudo mkdir /var/lib/prometheus
```

Step 4: Download Prometheus and Extract Files through:

```
wget https://github.com/prometheus/prometheus/releases/download/v2.43.0/
prometheus-2.43.0.linux-amd64.tar.gz
```

Note: *To download the latest version of Prometheus, visit the official download page at* ***https://prometheus.io/download/#prometheus*** *and select the appropriate version for your system.*

Step 5: Extract the contents of the downloaded file through:

```
tar vxf prometheus*.tar.gz
```

Step 6: Navigate to the Prometheus Directory via

```
cd prometheus*/
```

Step 7: Move the Binary Files and Set Owner through:

```
sudo mv prometheus /usr/local/bin
sudo mv promtool /usr/local/bin
sudo chown prometheus:prometheus /usr/local/bin/prometheus
sudo chown prometheus:prometheus /usr/local/bin/promtool
```

Step 8: Move the Configuration Files and Set Owner through these commands:

```
sudo mv consoles /etc/prometheus
sudo mv console_libraries /etc/prometheus
sudo mv prometheus.yml /etc/prometheus
```

Step 9: Give appropriate permissions via:

```
sudo chown prometheus:prometheus /etc/prometheus
sudo chown -R prometheus:prometheus /etc/prometheus/consoles
sudo chown -R prometheus:prometheus /etc/prometheus/console_libraries
sudo chown -R prometheus:prometheus /var/lib/prometheus
```

Note: *The* ***`prometheus.yml`*** *file serves as the primary configuration file for Prometheus, while defining scrape targets, alerting rules, and other essential settings.*

Step 10: Create Prometheus **`Systemd`** Service through:

```
sudo vim /etc/systemd/system/prometheus.service
```

Include these settings to the file, save, and exit via:

```
[Unit]
Description=Prometheus
Wants=network-online.target
After=network-online.target

[Service]
User=prometheus
Group=prometheus
Type=simple
ExecStart=/usr/local/bin/prometheus \
 --config.file /etc/prometheus/prometheus.yml \
 --storage.tsdb.path /var/lib/prometheus/ \
 --web.console.templates=/etc/prometheus/consoles \
 --web.console.libraries=/etc/prometheus/console_libraries

 [Install]
 WantedBy=multi-user.target
```

Step 11: Reload **`Systemd`** through:

```
sudo systemctl daemon-reload
```

Step 12: Start Prometheus service via these commands:

```
sudo systemctl enable prometheus
sudo systemctl start prometheus
```

Step 13: Check Prometheus status through this command:

```
sudo systemctl status prometheus
```

Figure 5.27 displays the result of running the **`sudo systemctl status prometheus`** command, which confirms that the Prometheus service is active and running. The output provides detailed status information and verifies the proper operation of your monitoring setup.

```
root@OSUbuntu:/home/ubuntu/prometheus-2.53.3.linux-amd64# sudo systemctl status prometheus
● prometheus.service - Prometheus
     Loaded: loaded (/etc/systemd/system/prometheus.service; enabled; vendor preset: enabled)
     Active: active (running) since Sat 2025-01-18 22:49:56 IST; 14s ago
   Main PID: 3957 (prometheus)
      Tasks: 7 (limit: 4581)
     Memory: 17.7M
     CGroup: /system.slice/prometheus.service
             └─3957 /usr/local/bin/prometheus --config.file /etc/prometheus/prometheus.yml --storage.tsdb.path /var/lib/prometheus/ --web.c
```

Figure 5.27: *Output of sudo systemctl status Prometheus Indicating Running State*

Step 14: Access Prometheus Web Interface via:

```
sudo ufw allow 9090/tcp
```

With Prometheus running successfully, you can access it via your web browser using **`http://localhost:9090`** or **`<ip_address>:9090`.**

Figure 5.28 displays the Prometheus dashboard in a web browser, confirming that Prometheus is running successfully.

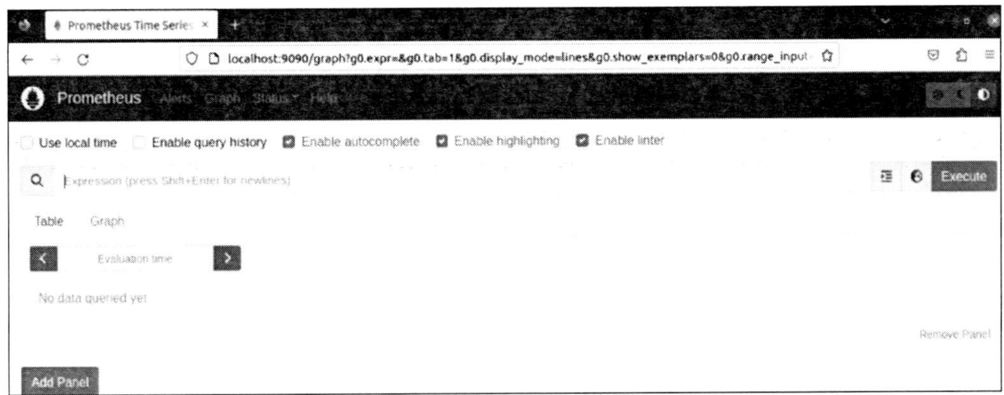

Figure 5.28: *Prometheus Running Successfully as Seen in a Web Browser*

Installing Grafana

1. **Add Grafana's Repository through:**

```
sudo apt-get install -y software-properties-common
sudo add-apt-repository "deb https://packages.grafana.com/oss/deb stable main"
wget -q -O - https://packages.grafana.com/gpg.key | sudo apt-key add -
```

2. **Install Grafana via:**

```
sudo apt update
sudo apt install grafana -y
```

3. **Start Grafana via:**

```
sudo systemctl start grafana-server
sudo systemctl enable grafana-server
```

4. **Check status through:**

```
sudo systemctl status grafana-server
```

Figure 5.29 shows the status of Grafana, confirming that the service is running in an active state. The displayed output indicates that Grafana is fully operational, which ensures that you can access and utilize its dashboard for monitoring purposes.

```
root@OSUbuntu:~# sudo systemctl status grafana-server
● grafana-server.service - Grafana instance
     Loaded: loaded (/lib/systemd/system/grafana-server.service; enabled; vendor preset: enabled)
     Active: active (running) since Tue 2025-01-21 18:00:30 IST; 38s ago
       Docs: http://docs.grafana.org
   Main PID: 137402 (grafana)
      Tasks: 12 (limit: 4581)
     Memory: 75.9M
     CGroup: /system.slice/grafana-server.service
             └─137402 /usr/share/grafana/bin/grafana server --config=/etc/grafana/grafana.ini --pidfile=/run/grafana/grafana-server.pid --p>
```

Figure 5.29: *Grafana Status in Active State*

5. **Open your browser and go to `http://<server-ip>:3000`.**

   Default Credentials

   - **`Username: admin`**
   - **`Password: admin`**

Figure 5.30 shows the Grafana dashboard as it appears in a web browser immediately following a fresh installation. The display confirms that Grafana is installed correctly and running and is ready to be configured for monitoring and data visualization.

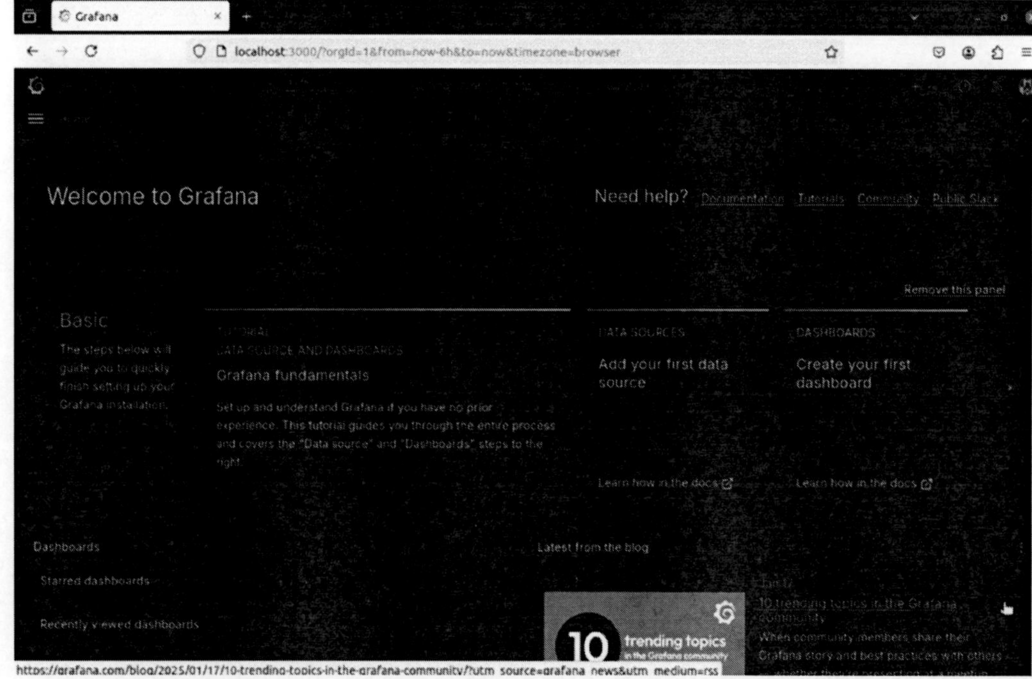

Figure 5.30: *Grafana Dashboard Displayed in a Web Browser after Fresh Installation*

Redis Exporter: This guide explains how to install Redis Exporter on Ubuntu, configure it with Prometheus, and visualize the metrics in Grafana.

Step 1: Install Redis Exporter on Ubuntu.

a. **Install Golang.** We need to build a binary from the redis exporter project, and we need a Golang environment. If you do not have Golang installed already, you can do it via:

```
sudo add-apt-repository ppa:longsleep/golang-backports
sudo apt update
sudo apt install golang-go
```

You should now be able to get the following response:

```
go version
```

b. **Redis Exporter.** Get the source code and build the binary, as shown:

```
git clone https://github.com/oliver006/redis_exporter.git
cd redis_exporter
go build .
```

c. **After building the binary, you should get a response when running this command:**

```
./redis_exporter --help
```

d. **Copy the binary via the following path:**

```
cp redis_exporter /usr/bin/
```

e. **Then create the systemd unit file through:**

```
/etc/systemd/system/redis_exporter.service:

[Unit]
Description=Redis Exporter
Wants=network-online.target
After=network-online.target

[Service]
User=root
Group=root
Type=simple
ExecStart=/usr/bin/redis_exporter \
    -web.listen-address ":9121" \
    -redis.addr "redis://ip.of.redis.server:6379" \
    -redis.password "your-strong-redis-password"

[Install]
WantedBy=multi-user.target
```

> **Note:** *In production, prefer environment variables or secrets managers instead of hardcoding Passwords.*

f. **Reload systemd via:**

```
systemctl daemon-reload
```

g. **Start the redis exporter through:**

```
systemctl restart redis_exporter
```

Now, you should be able to get redis metrics when you hit the redis exporter.

You can also go to the browser at: **http://127.0.0.1:9121/metrics** and check the raw metrics that are exposed by the exporter.

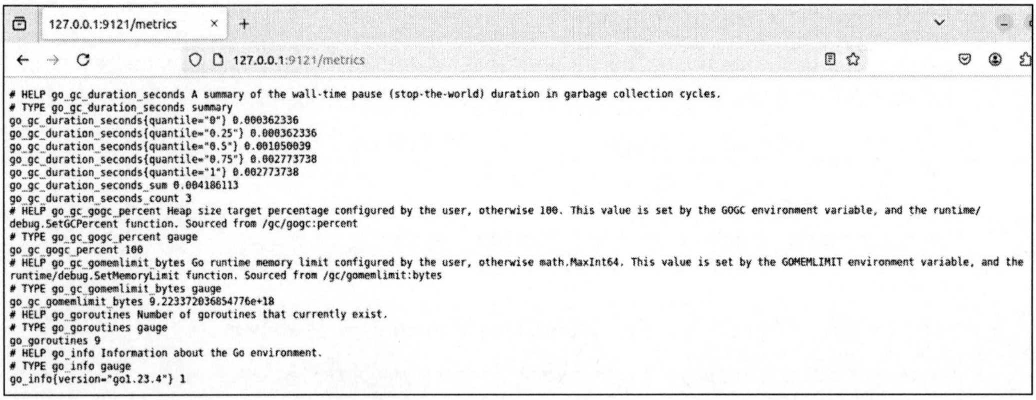

Figure 5.31: *Redis Exporter Displayed in a Browser, Confirming Proper Operation*

Configure Prometheus to Scrape Metrics:

1. Configure your **`prometheus.yml`** and add the target to scrape the redis exporter endpoint to write the time series data into Prometheus, as shown:

   ```
   scrape_configs:
     - job_name: redis_exporter
       static_configs:
       - targets: ['ip.of.redis.exporter:9121']
   ```

2. Restart Prometheus; if you have Docker, redeploy your stack or Prometheus container. For Prometheus as a service, you can use **`systemctl`** `restart prometheus` depending on your operating system distribution.

3. Add Prometheus as datasource and then import **dashboard ID 763**. After some time, you should see a dashboard.

Installing Prometheus and Grafana on centOS

Monitoring a Redis instance is crucial for ensuring optimal performance and identifying potential issues. Prometheus and Grafana provide a powerful combination for monitoring and visualization. This section will guide you through the installation and configuration of Prometheus and Grafana on a CentOS system.

Prerequisites

Before proceeding with the installation, ensure that your CentOS system is up to date and has the necessary dependencies installed through the following command:

```
sudo yum update -y
sudo yum install wget curl -y
```

Additionally, make sure the **firewall** is configured to allow the required ports, as shown:

```
sudo firewall-cmd --permanent --add-port=9090/tcp  # Prometheus
sudo firewall-cmd --permanent --add-port=3000/tcp  # Grafana
sudo firewall-cmd --reload
```

Step 1: Installing Prometheus

a. **Create a Prometheus User.** To improve security, create a dedicated system user for Prometheus through:

```
sudo useradd --no-create-home --shell /bin/false prometheus
```

b. **Download and Install Prometheus.** Download the latest Prometheus binary release from the official site through the following link:

```
wget https://github.com/prometheus/prometheus/releases/download/v3.2.1/
prometheus-3.2.1.linux-amd64.tar.gz

tar -xvzf prometheus-3.2.1.linux-amd64.tar.gz
```

c. **Move and Change the ownership to Prometheus user.**

```
sudo mv prometheus promtool /usr/local/bin/
sudo chown prometheus:prometheus /usr/local/bin/prometheus
sudo chown prometheus:prometheus /usr/local/bin/promtool
```

d. **Configurations should be added to the "/etc/prometheus/prometheus.yml".**

Create the `prometheus.yml` file via:

```
sudo vim /etc/prometheus/prometheus.yml
```

```
global:
       scrape_interval: 10s
scrape_configs:
       - job_name: 'prometheus_master'
         scrape_interval: 5s
         static_configs:
           - targets: ['localhost:9090']
```

Save and exit the file.

e. **Change the ownership of the file through:**

```
sudo chown prometheus:prometheus /etc/prometheus/prometheus.yml
```

f. **Configure the Prometheus Service file via:**

```
sudo vim /etc/systemd/system/prometheus.service
```

Copy the following content to the file:

```
[Unit]
Description=Prometheus
Wants=network-online.target
After=network-online.target
[Service]
User=prometheus
Group=prometheus
Type=simple
ExecStart=/usr/local/bin/prometheus \
--config.file /etc/prometheus/prometheus.yml \
--storage.tsdb.path /var/lib/prometheus/ \
--web.console.templates=/etc/prometheus/consoles \
--web.console.libraries=/etc/prometheus/console_libraries
[Install]
WantedBy=multi-user.target
```

Save and exit the file.

g. **Reload the systemd service via:**

```
sudo systemctl daemon-reload
```

h. **Start the Prometheus service through this command:**

```
sudo systemctl start prometheus
```

i. **Check service status through:**

```
sudo systemctl status prometheus
```

Figure 5.32 displays the status of the Prometheus monitoring service, which confirms that it is actively running. The output verifies that Prometheus is correctly installed, configured, and operational.

```
[root@localhost prometheus]# sudo systemctl status prometheus
● prometheus.service - Prometheus
     Loaded: loaded (/etc/systemd/system/prometheus.service; disabled; preset: disabled)
     Active: active (running) since Sat 2025-03-01 14:59:54 IST; 3s ago
   Main PID: 49978 (prometheus)
      Tasks: 13 (limit: 48252)
     Memory: 22.8M
        CPU: 95ms
```

Figure 5.32: *Output Showing Prometheus Status in Running State*

j. **Access Prometheus Web Interface.** Use the following URL to access UI:

http://localhost:9090/graph

You can see the following interface:

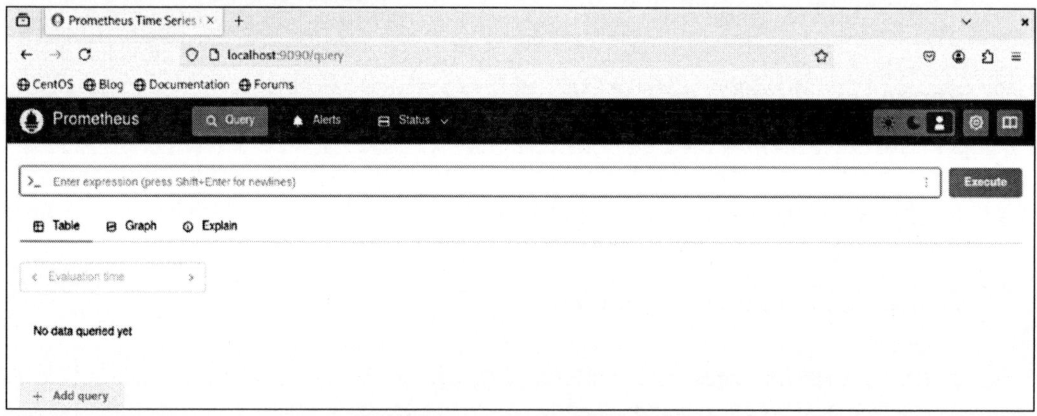

Figure 5.33: *Browser View of http://localhost:9090/*

Figure 5.33 showcases the **Prometheus web interface** accessed via a browser at **http://localhost:9090/**. The Prometheus UI allows users to query and visualize collected metrics, explore time-series data, and monitor system performance.

Step 2: Installing Grafana

a. **Install Grafana Repository.** Add the official Grafana repository through:

```
sudo tee /etc/yum.repos.d/grafana.repo <<EOF
[grafana]
name=Grafana
baseurl=https://packages.grafana.com/oss/rpm
```

```
repo_gpgcheck=1
enabled=1
gpgcheck=1
gpgkey=https://packages.grafana.com/gpg.key
EOF
```

b. **Install and Start Grafana via the following commands:**

```
sudo yum install -y grafana
sudo systemctl enable --now grafana-server
sudo systemctl status grafana-server
```

Figure 5.34 displays the status check output for the Grafana server, which confirms that it is actively running. The output verifies that Grafana is successfully installed and operational, which allows users to access its web-based visualization and monitoring features. A running state indicates that the service is functioning correctly and can be accessed via the configured web interface.

```
[root@localhost prometheus]# sudo systemctl status grafana-server
● grafana-server.service - Grafana instance
   Loaded: loaded (/usr/lib/systemd/system/grafana-server.service; enabled; preset: disabled)
   Active: active (running) since Sat 2025-03-01 15:49:03 IST; 10s ago
     Docs: http://docs.grafana.org
 Main PID: 51287 (grafana)
    Tasks: 17 (limit: 48252)
   Memory: 101.7M
      CPU: 2.667s
```

Figure 5.34: *Output of Status grafana-server in Running State*

c. **Access Grafana.** **`Grafana`** runs on port **3000**. Open a web browser and navigate to:

```
http://<server-ip>:3000
```

The default credentials are:

Username: **admin**

Password: **admin** (You will be prompted to change it upon first login)

Figure 5.35 showcases the **Grafana web interface**, which is accessible via a browser at **http://localhost:3000/**.

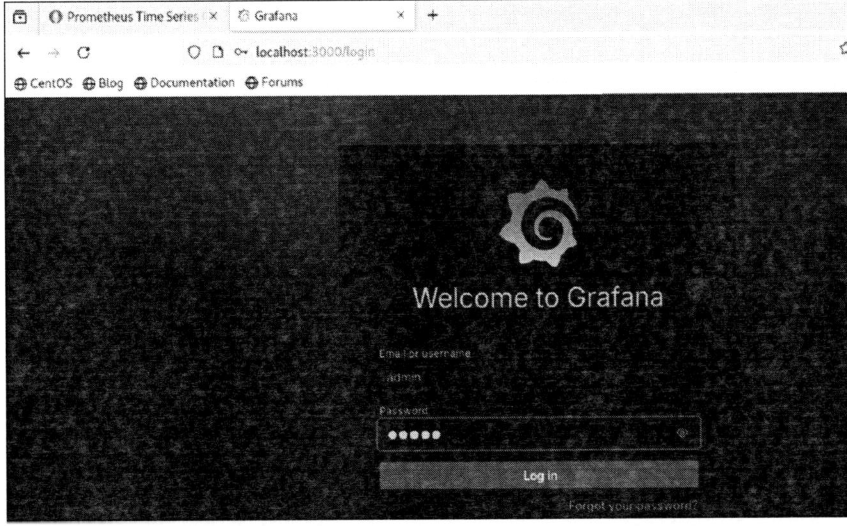

Figure 5.35: *GUI of Grafana Running on Port 3000*

Step 3: Adding Prometheus as a Data Source in Grafana consists of the following steps:

a. Log in to **`Grafana`**.

b. Click on **`Configuration`** > **`Data Sources`**.

c. Click **`Add data source`** and select **`Prometheus`**.

d. In the URL field, enter: **http://localhost:9090**

e. Click **`Save`** and **`Test`**.

Figure 5.36 illustrates the confirmation message displayed in Grafana after successfully adding Prometheus as a data source.

***Figure 5.36:** Successful Test after Adding Prometheus as a Data Source in Grafana*

Once Prometheus is configured, Grafana validates the connection to ensure proper data retrieval. A successful test indicates that Grafana can communicate with Prometheus, which allows users to create dashboards and visualize metrics.

Step 4: Configuring Prometheus to Monitor Redis.

a. Install Redis Exporter. Download and install Redis Exporter, which enables Prometheus to collect Redis metrics via the following link:

```
wget https://github.com/oliver006/redis_exporter/releases/download/v1.67.0/
redis_exporter-v1.67.0.linux-arm64.tar.gz
```

Extract and move the binary through:

```
tar -xvzf redis_exporter-linux-arm64.tar.gz
sudo mv redis_exporter /usr/local/bin/
```

Start Redis Exporter via:

```
cd /usr/local/bin/
./redis_exporter --redis.addr=redis://localhost:6379 &
```

b. Configure Prometheus to scrape Redis Metrics through:

```
Edit /etc/prometheus/prometheus.yml and add:
- job_name: 'redis'
  static_configs:
    - targets: ['localhost:9121']
```

Restart Prometheus via:

```
sudo systemctl restart prometheus
```

c. Add Redis Dashboard in Grafana through the following steps.

i. Log in to **`Grafana`**.

ii. Go to **`Dashboards > Import`**.

iii. Enter **`Dashboard ID 763`** (or another Redis dashboard ID from Grafana dashboards).

iv. Select Prometheus as the data source.

v. Click on **`Import`**.

Figure 5.37 demonstrates the process of importing a pre-configured Redis monitoring dashboard into Grafana using Dashboard ID 763.

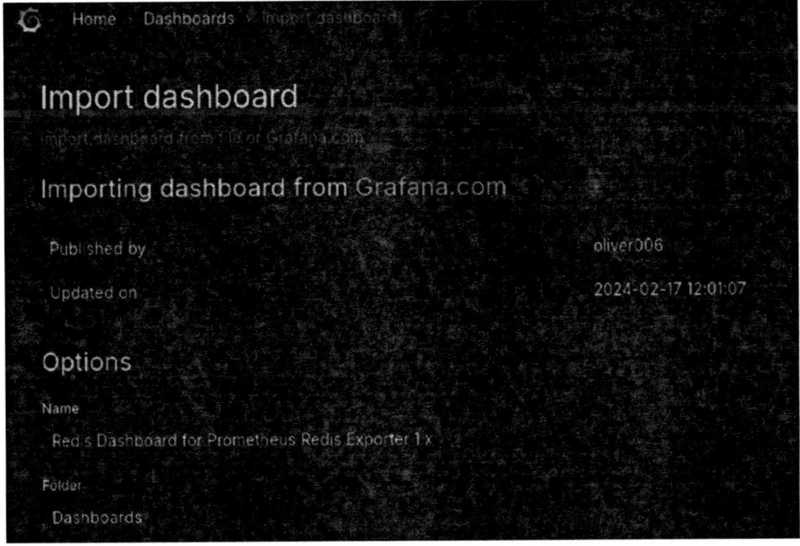

***Figure* 5.37**: *Importing Dashboard with ID 763 for Redis*

Grafana allows users to import dashboards from its official library or custom JSON files to quickly set up visualizations. **Dashboard 763** is specifically designed for monitoring Redis performance, while providing insights into key metrics such as memory usage, command rates, connected clients, and latency.

Installing Prometheus and Grafana on Windows

If you are working in a Windows environment and want to monitor your Redis setup using Prometheus and Grafana, you are in the right place. Both tools are fully compatible with Windows and can be installed manually with minimal setup. In this section, we will walk you through the complete installation process from downloading to launching both services on your local machine. This setup will allow you to scrape Redis metrics using Prometheus and visualize them in Grafana, while helping you gain real-time performance insights into your Redis instance.

Installing Prometheus

Step 1: Download Prometheus

a. Visit the official Prometheus website: **https://prometheus.io/download/**

b. Download the Windows binary (zip file) for Prometheus.

c. To extract files, unzip the downloaded file to a directory.

Step 2: Configure Prometheus

a. Navigate to the extracted folder and open `prometheus.yml` in a text editor.

b. Add a job configuration for Redis Exporter as shown:

```
scrape_configs:
  - job_name: 'redis'
    static_configs:
      - targets: ['localhost:9121']
```

Step 3: Run Prometheus

a. Open Command Prompt and navigate to the Prometheus folder via:

`cd C:\Prometheus` (adjust the path if Prometheus is extracted elsewhere)

```
prometheus.exe --config.file=prometheus.yml
```

Prometheus should now be running at **http://localhost:9090.**

Figure 5.38 shows the Prometheus dashboard accessed via a **web browser on port 9090**. The display confirms that the Prometheus service is actively running.

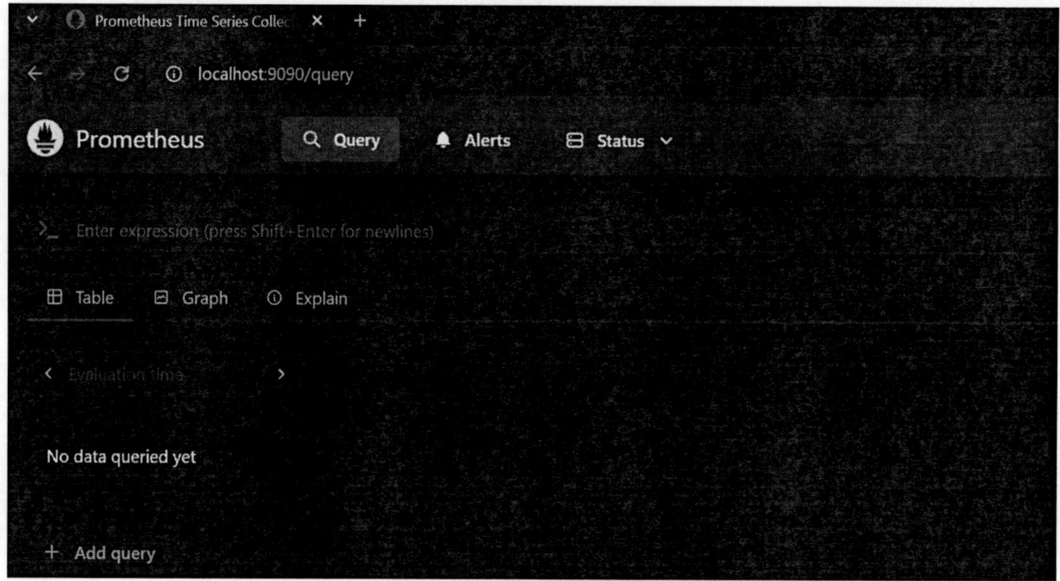

***Figure* 5.38:** *Prometheus Running on Port 9090 in a Web Browser*

Installing Redis Exporter:

Redis Exporter can be installed on Windows using WSL (Windows Subsystem for Linux). Redis Exporter is most stable on Linux-based environments. WSL provides a reliable workaround on Windows. The installation steps inside WSL are identical to those followed for Ubuntu. Therefore, once WSL is set up on your Windows system, refer to the section "Install Redis Exporter on Ubuntu" and execute the same commands within the WSL environment.

Installing Grafana

1. **Download Grafana.**

   Visit: **https://grafana.com/grafana/download**

2. **Start Grafana.**

   a. Run Grafana by opening **`grafana-server.exe`** from the installation directory (**C:\Program Files\GrafanaLabs\grafana\bin**).

   b. By default, it will run on http://localhost:3000.

3. **Login to Grafana.**

   a. Open a browser and go to http://localhost:3000.

   b. The default login credentials are as follows:

- `Username`: `admin`
- `Password`: `admin`

c. Change the password when prompted.

Connecting Grafana to Prometheus

1. **Add Prometheus as a data source through the following steps:**
   a. In Grafana, go to **`Settings → Data Sources → Add Data Source`**.
   b. Choose **`Prometheus`**.
   c. Set the URL to **http://localhost:9090**.
   d. Click on **Save and Test**.

Creating a Dashboard

1. Go to **`Dashboards → New Dashboard`**.
2. Import Dashboard - **The Redis Dashboard ID is 763**
3. Select **`Prometheus`** as the data source.
4. Click on **`Save`**.

Verifying the Setup

1. **Check Prometheus Targets:** Open **http://localhost:9090/targets** and ensure Redis Exporter is listed.
2. **Test Metrics in Grafana:** Open your Grafana dashboard and verify Redis metrics that are displayed.

Figure 5.39 shows the Prometheus web interface where the Redis Exporter has been configured to scrape metrics from a Redis instance. The interface highlights the setup details, which confirms that Prometheus is now actively collecting performance data from Redis for real-time monitoring and analysis.

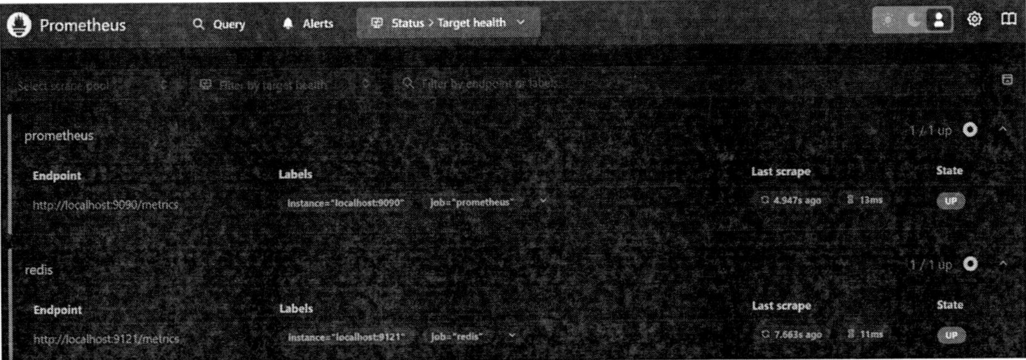

Figure 5.39: *Web Interface Displaying Redis Exporter Added in Prometheus for Scraping Redis Metrics*

Conclusion

So far, we have covered the essential aspects of monitoring Redis effectively. We began by exploring **Redis's built-in monitoring tools**, which offer quick and direct insights into key performance metrics such as memory usage, slow queries, and client activity. These tools provide a solid foundation for diagnosing issues and understanding Redis's real-time behavior.

However, while built-in tools are powerful, they have their limitations, especially when it comes to long-term monitoring, visualization, and alerting. That is where third-party monitoring solutions such as **RedisInsight**, **Prometheus**, and **Grafana** come in. These tools offer a richer monitoring experience with real-time dashboards, historical data analysis, and advanced performance tracking across different operating systems. With the right combination of built-in and third-party tools, you can maintain a well-optimized Redis instance, detect potential problems early, and make data-driven decisions to enhance overall performance.

But monitoring is not just about collecting data; it is about knowing how to use that data effectively. **In Part 2**, we will go deeper into choosing the right Redis monitoring tool based on your specific needs. We will also explore best practices for setting up alerts and notifications to ensure that you are always aware of performance issues before they escalate. Thus, by the end of this section, you will have a complete understanding of how to set up a proactive Redis monitoring strategy that keeps your database running smoothly.

Now, let us continue our journey into Redis monitoring with Part 2!

CHAPTER 6
Monitoring Redis for Optimal Performance - Part 2

Introduction

In the previous chapter, we explored various built-in Redis monitoring tools that provide insights into Redis performance and health, along with an overview of some widely used third-party monitoring solutions such as **RedisInsight**, **Prometheus**, and **Grafana**. These tools help in real-time monitoring, performance tuning, and visualization of the key Redis metrics.

However, Redis monitoring is a vast domain, and there are several other third-party tools that offer advanced capabilities, automation, and integrations for more comprehensive observability. In this chapter, we will continue our discussion by covering additional third-party monitoring solutions that can further enhance the monitoring, alerting, and troubleshooting of Redis instances in production environments.

In **Part 1**, we learned how to observe Redis metrics through dashboards, built-in commands, and basic health checks. In production, monitoring is not just about watching graphs; it is how you **prevent incidents**, **protect user experience**, and **control operational costs**. When Redis is healthy, everything feels snappy. When it is not, symptoms show up everywhere: rising API latencies, timeouts, unexpected *cache* misses, or stalled background jobs. Good monitoring turns those weak signals into **clear, early warnings** so that you can act before customers feel the pain.

Think of Redis as your application's fast lane. If memory is near the limit, eviction spikes, replicas start lagging, or persistence stalls, the "fast lane" slows down sometimes silently. That is why monitoring must go beyond pretty charts. You want **actionable signals**: which metric moved, how bad it is, and what to do next.

This chapter focuses on tools (**Datadog, ELK**) and practices that turn raw metrics into **operational confidence** with sensible defaults you can adopt right away.

By the end of this chapter, you will have a broader understanding of the available monitoring tools, and how to leverage them effectively to maintain optimal Redis performance.

Structure

In this chapter, we will cover the following topics:

- Datadog
- Elasticsearch, Logstash, Kibana (ELK) Stack
- Choosing a Redis Monitoring Tool

- Setting Up Alerts and Notifications
- Best Practices for Setting Up Redis Alerts

Datadog

Datadog is a **cloud-based monitoring and analytics platform** that provides comprehensive insights into the health and performance of your applications, services, and infrastructure. With its ability to collect and visualize metrics, logs, and traces in one unified interface, Datadog has become a popular choice for organizations seeking to maintain high levels of system reliability and performance.

For Redis users, Datadog offers specialized monitoring capabilities that allow you to track key Redis metrics, configure alerts, and analyze performance trends over time. Datadog integrates seamlessly with Redis, providing pre-built dashboards and support for custom configurations. By leveraging Datadog, you can gain a deep understanding of your Redis instance's behavior and ensure that it continues to operate optimally, even under heavy workloads.

Monitoring Redis with Datadog

Datadog simplifies Redis monitoring by collecting metrics from your Redis instance, and presenting them in easy-to-understand visualizations.

Registering for a Datadog Account

To monitor your Redis instance using Datadog, follow these steps to create a Datadog account:

1. **Visit Datadog's official website at https://www.datadoghq.com/**:

   Open your browser and navigate to the Datadog website.

2. **Sign Up for an Account:**

   Click on the "`Get Started for Free`" button on the homepage.

3. **Fill in the required details:**

   `Full Name`: *Enter your first and last name.*

   `Work Email`: *Provide a valid email address.*

   `Company Name`: *Enter the name of your organization.*

   `Phone Number`: *Enter your contact number.*

   `Password`: *Create a strong password.*

4. **Agree to the Terms:** Check the box to accept Datadog's terms and conditions.

5. **Start the Free Trial:** Click on "`Start Free Trial`" to proceed. Datadog offers a 14-day trial for its premium features.

6. **Verify Your Email:** Open the email sent to the address you provided, and click the verification link.

7. **Complete the Onboarding:** Log in to your account, and follow the guided setup to select your monitoring environment (for example, Redis, AWS, Docker, and so on).

Note: *If you need detailed guidance on installing the Datadog Agent to collect Redis metrics, the best place to start is the* ***official Datadog documentation****. Their website offers clear, step-by-step instructions tailored to different operating systems, including Linux, macOS, and Windows. To ensure a smooth installation process, visit the* ***Datadog Agent Installation Guide****, where you will find the exact steps tailored to your operating system and environment.*

Installing Datadog Agent on macOS

To connect Redis to Datadog, you need to install the Datadog Agent on your macOS system.

Step 1: Download the Datadog Agent

a. Log in to your Datadog account.

b. Navigate to the **Integrations** tab and select **Agents**.

c. Download the macOS version of the Datadog Agent.

Step 2: Execute the following command on your Mac terminal

```
DD_API_KEY=<YOUR_DATADOG_API_KEY> DD_SITE="<your_datadog_site>" bash -c "$(curl -L https://install.datadoghq.com/scripts/install_mac_os.sh)"
```

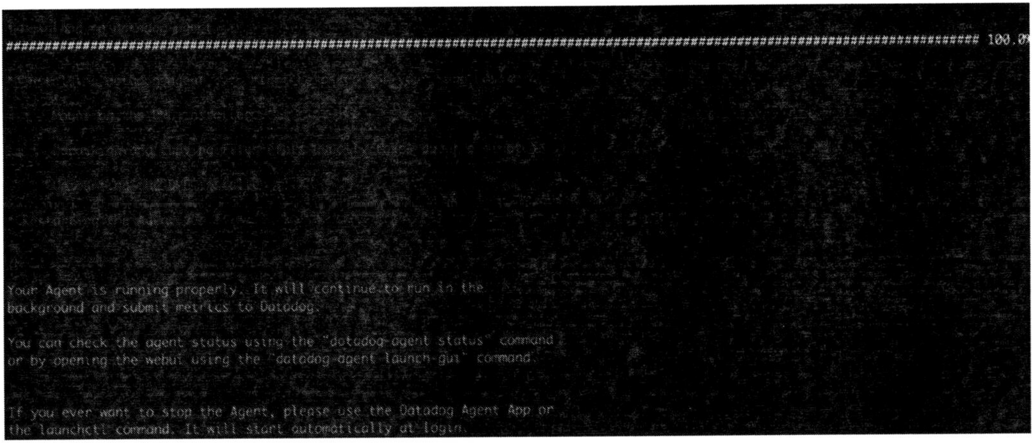

Figure 6.1: *Datadog Agent Downloaded, Installed, and Showing Running Status on macOS*

Figure 6.1 captures the Datadog Agent on a macOS system, illustrating that it has been successfully downloaded, installed, and is actively running. The displayed output confirms that the agent is operational, and ready to monitor system metrics.

Note: *Alternatively, you can download the DMG package and install it manually. This provides a straightforward installation process, especially for macOS users who prefer a graphical interface over a command-line setup.*

Step 3: Start the Datadog Agent

Once installed, start the Agent using the following command:

```
sudo datadog-agent start
```

Step 4: Verify the Installation

Confirm that the Agent is running:

```
datadog-agent status
```

Step 5: To launch the Datadog GUI, use the following command:

```
datadog-agent launch-gui
```

Step 6: Go to http://localhost:5002/ and verify if it is properly connected:

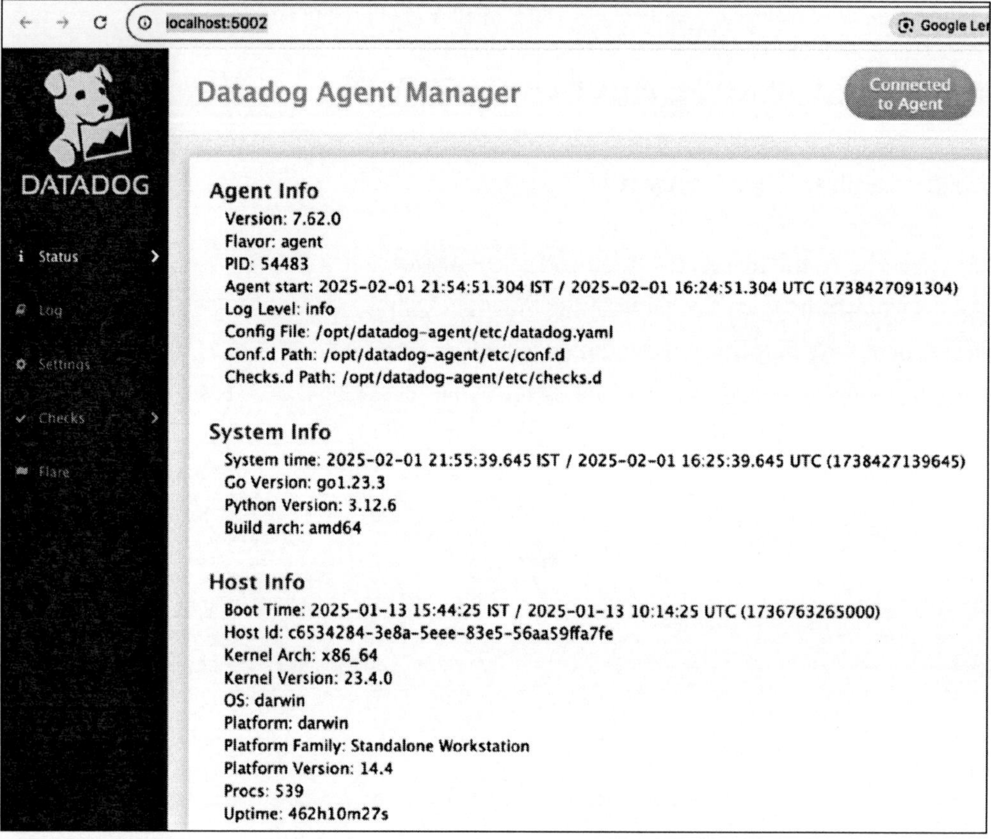

Figure 6.2: *Datadog GUI Running on Port 5002*

Figure 6.2 displays the **`Datadog Graphical User Interface`** as accessed via a web browser on port 5002. The interface confirms that Datadog is running properly.

Enable the Redis Integration

Step 1: Navigate to the Datadog configuration directory

```
/opt/datadog-agent/etc/conf.d/
```

In that directory, you will find a **`redisdb.d`** subdirectory, which contains a Redis configuration template named **`conf.yaml.example`** This file serves as a reference for configuring Redis monitoring settings, and can be customized based on your specific requirements.

Step 2: Edit the `conf.yaml.example` file, and save it as `conf.yaml`:

```
sudo cp conf.yaml.example conf.yaml
```

Step 3: Configure the Redis Integration

Modify the configuration file to point to your Redis instance:

```
    instances:
```

```
    - host: "127.0.0.1"   # Redis server host
      port: 6379          # Redis server port
      password: ""        # Redis password if enabled, leave empty otherwise
      db: 0               # Redis database number to monitor
```

Save and exit the file.

Step 4: Open the Datadog agent configuration file:

`~/.datadog-agent/datadog.yaml`

Step 5: Enable log collection

`logs_enabled` flag: Verify that **`logs_enabled: true`** is set in your **`datadog.yaml`** file

```
##################################
## Log collection Configuration ##
##################################

## @param logs_enabled - boolean - optional - default: false
## @env DD_LOGS_ENABLED - boolean - optional - default: false
## Enable Datadog Agent log collection by setting logs_enabled to true.
#
logs_enabled: true
```

Figure 6.3: *Setting logs_enabled to True in datadog.yaml*

Figure 6.3 displays the datadog.yaml configuration file with the **`logs_enabled`** parameter set to true. This change activates log collection, ensuring that the Datadog agent captures and monitors log data from your services effectively.

Step 6: Stop and start datadog agent

```
sudo datadog-agent stop
sudo datadog-agent start
```

Step 7: To verify that the Redis integration is working correctly, navigate to the GUI and go to `check_summary`. Look for the check named `redisdb`, which should display an "`OK`" status.

This confirms that the Redis monitoring setup is functioning properly. If you see any other status, such as "**`WARNING`**" or "**`CRITICAL`**," further investigation may be needed to resolve potential issues.

Figure 6.4: *Datadog Agent Showing RedisDB is Configured Properly*

Figure 6.4 displays the Datadog Agent's interface, confirming that RedisDB is correctly configured for monitoring. The dashboard indicates active integration, ensuring that metrics and logs from RedisDB are being effectively collected and analyzed for optimal performance monitoring.

Step 8: Verify Redis Metrics in Datadog

a. Log into your **`Datadog`** account.

b. Go to **`Integrations`** and search **`redis`**, and click **`Install Integration`**.

c. Go to **`Dashboard`** > **`Dashboardlists`**

d. Open the Redis dashboard to view metrics such as the following:

   - Memory usage
   - Command execution rates

- o Keyspace hits and misses
- o Connected clients

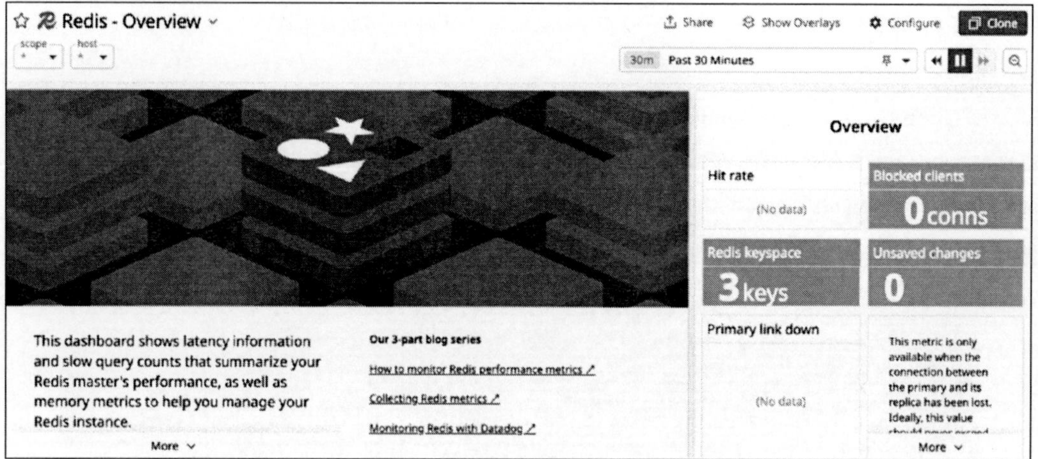

Figure 6.5: *Redis Dashboard Running in Datadog*

Figure 6.5 displays the Redis Dashboard within Datadog, showcasing real-time metrics and performance data from your Redis instance.

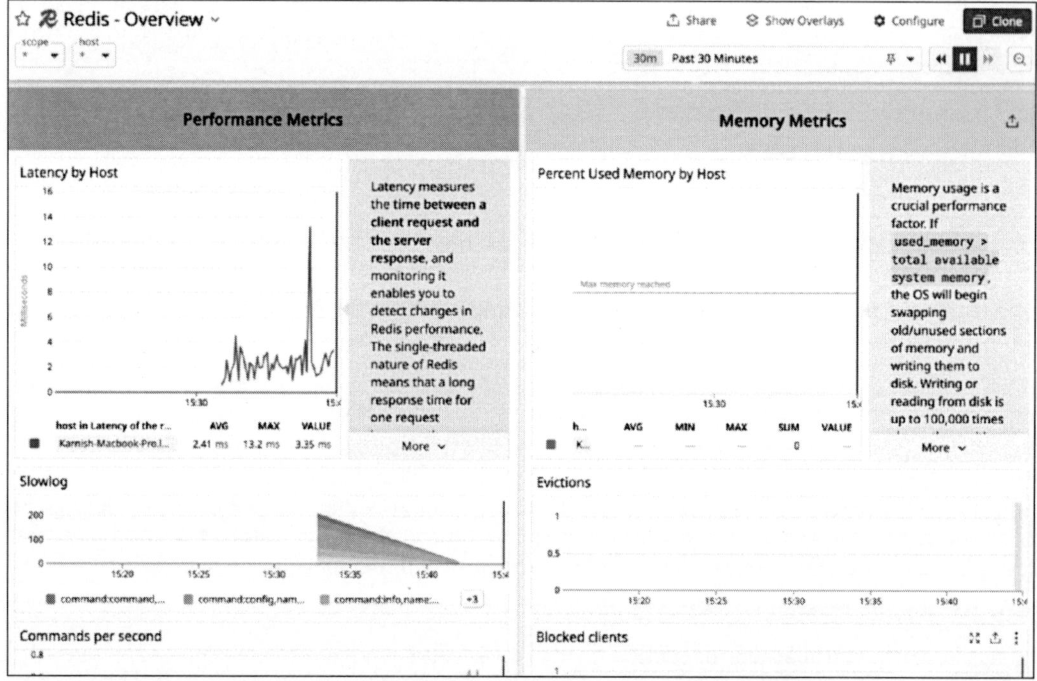

Figure 6.6: *Redis Dashboard Showing Performance and Memory Metrics*

Figure 6.6 displays a comprehensive Redis dashboard that highlights key performance indicators along with detailed memory metrics.

Installing Datadog Agent on Ubuntu

This section provides a step-by-step guide to installing the Datadog Agent on an Ubuntu system.

Step 1: Update system packages

Before installing the Datadog Agent, update the system package index to ensure that all dependencies are up to date:

```
sudo apt-get update
```

Step 2: Obtain a Datadog API key

To install the Datadog Agent, you need an API key, which is used to authenticate your agent with Datadog's platform.

a. Log in to your **Datadog** account on the **Datadog** website.

b. Navigate to **Integrations > APIs** and copy your API key.

```
DD_API_KEY=<YOUR_DATADOG_API_KEY> DD_SITE="<your_datadog_site>" bash -c "$(curl -L
https://install.datadoghq.com/scripts/install_script_agent7.sh)"
```

Note: The value of DD_SITE depends on the Datadog region you selected.

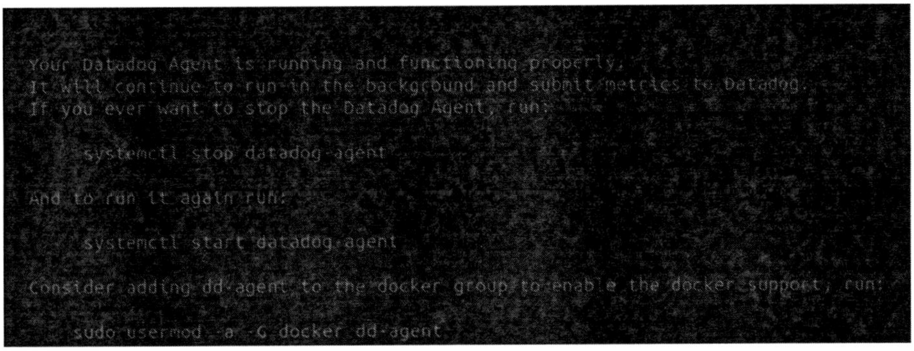

```
Your Datadog Agent is running and functioning properly.
It will continue to run in the background and submit metrics to Datadog.
If you ever want to stop the Datadog Agent, run:

    systemctl stop datadog-agent

And to run it again run:

    systemctl start datadog-agent

Consider adding dd-agent to the docker group to enable the docker support, run:

    sudo usermod -a -G docker dd-agent
```

Figure 6.7: *Datadog Agent Installed and Running Successfully on Ubuntu*

Figure 6.7 displays the Datadog Agent on an Ubuntu system, confirming that it has been successfully installed and is actively running.

Step 3: Verify the installation

After installation, check the status of the Datadog Agent to confirm it is running correctly:

```
sudo systemctl status datadog-agent
```

If the agent is running successfully, the output should indicate an **active** status.

```
● datadog-agent.service - Datadog Agent
     Loaded: loaded (/lib/systemd/system/datadog-agent.service; enabled; vendor preset: enabled)
     Active: active (running) since Sun 2025-02-02 15:59:49 IST; 1min 40s ago
   Main PID: 4062 (agent)
      Tasks: 13 (limit: 4549)
     Memory: 90.4M
        CPU: 3.824s
     CGroup: /system.slice/datadog-agent.service
             └─4062 /opt/datadog-agent/bin/agent/agent run -p /opt/datadog-agent/run/agent.pid
```

Figure 6.8: *Output of Datadog Agent Status in Running State*

Figure 6.8 displays the terminal output from running the **Datadog agent status** command. The output confirms that the agent is actively running and functioning correctly on the system.

Step 4: Enable the Datadog Agent to start on Boot

To ensure that the Datadog Agent starts automatically when the system reboots, enable the service:

```
sudo systemctl enable datadog-agent
```

Step 5: View Metrics in the Datadog Dashboard

a. Log in to your `Datadog` account.

b. Navigate to `Infrastructure` > `Hosts` to see your Ubuntu system listed.

c. Click on the host to view collected metrics, including CPU usage, memory utilization, disk activity, and network performance.

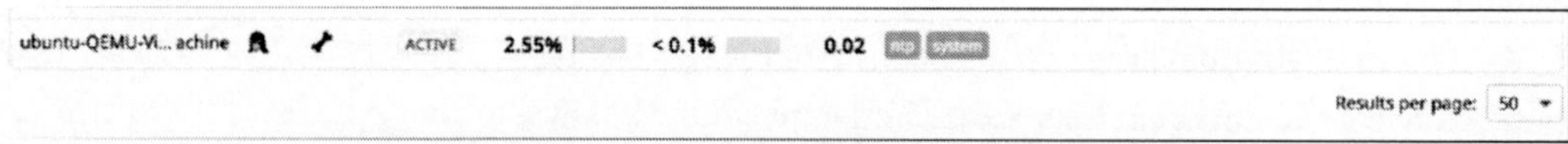

***Figure 6.9**: Ubuntu Machine Recognized as a Host in Datadog*

Figure 6.9 captures the Datadog host dashboard where an Ubuntu machine is listed among the monitored hosts. It confirms that DataDog has successfully detected the Ubuntu system, ensuring that its metrics are being collected and monitored in real-time.

Adding Local Redis Instance on Ubuntu to Datadog Monitoring

To monitor a Redis instance running on Ubuntu with **Datadog**, follow these steps to configure the Datadog Agent and integrate Redis monitoring.

Step 1: Ensure that Redis is Installed and Running

```
redis-cli ping
```

Expected output: `PONG`

Step 2: Ensure that Datadog Agent is Installed

```
sudo systemctl status datadog-agent
```

Step 3: Enable the Redis Integration in Datadog

Navigate to the Datadog Redis Integration Directory:

```
cd /etc/datadog-agent/conf.d/redisdb.d
```

Step 4: Copy the example configuration file and rename it:

```
sudo cp conf.yaml.example conf.yaml
```

Step 5: Open the conf.yaml file to configure the Redis instance:

```
sudo vim conf.yaml
```

Modify the file to look as follows:

```
instances:
      - host: "127.0.0.1"
        port: 6379
        password: ""    # Leave empty if Redis does not require authentication
        db: 0           # Default Redis database
```

Save the file (*CTRL+X*, **then** Y, **then** *Enter*).

Step 6: Restart the Datadog Agent

Apply the changes by restarting the Datadog Agent:

```
sudo systemctl restart datadog-agent
```

Step 7: Verify Redis Monitoring in Datadog

Run the following command to check if Datadog is collecting Redis metrics:

```
sudo datadog-agent status
```

Look for the **`redisdb`** integration section. If configured correctly, you should see Redis metrics being collected.

```
redisdb (7.0.0)
---------------
  Instance ID: redisdb:e43bb6bcd098d3d4 [OK]
  Configuration Source: file:/etc/datadog-agent/conf.d/redisdb.d/conf.yaml
  Total Runs: 3
  Metric Samples: Last Run: 48, Total: 144
  Events: Last Run: 0, Total: 0
  Service Checks: Last Run: 1, Total: 3
  Average Execution Time : 49ms
  Last Execution Date : 2025-02-02 16:39:41 IST / 2025-02-02 11:09:41 UTC (1738494581000)
  Last Successful Execution Date : 2025-02-02 16:39:41 IST / 2025-02-02 11:09:41 UTC (1738494581000)
  metadata:
    version.major: 6
    version.minor: 0
    version.patch: 16
    version.raw: 6.0.16
    version.scheme: semver
```

Figure 6.10: *RedisDB Integration Section in Datadog Agent Status*

Figure 6.10 displays the section of the Datadog agent status output that pertains to the RedisDB integration. It confirms that RedisDB is properly configured and integrated, ensuring that its metrics are being collected and monitored effectively by the DataDog agent.

Log in to your Datadog account and check whether the Redis dashboard is already installed. If not, install Redis from Integrations and then review the dashboard.

Installing Datadog Agent on CentOS

To effectively monitor a Redis server running on CentOS, it is important to have a reliable monitoring agent in place. The Datadog Agent helps collect system metrics, Redis-specific metrics, and logs, providing deeper visibility into server and database performance. In this section, we will walk through the step-by-step process of installing the Datadog Agent on a CentOS machine.

Step 1: Before installing the Datadog Agent, update the package index to ensure all dependencies are up to date:

```
sudo yum update -y
```

Step 2: Obtain a Datadog API key

To install the Datadog Agent, you need an API key, which is used to authenticate your agent with Datadog.

a. Log in to your **`Datadog`** account on the **`Datadog`** website.

b. Navigate to **`Integrations`** > **`APIs`** and copy your API key.

Step 3: Install the Datadog Agent

Run the following command, replacing **<YOUR_DATADOG_API_KEY>** with the API key obtained in

```
DD_API_KEY=<YOUR_DATADOG_API_KEY> DD_SITE="<your_datadog_site>" bash -c "$(curl -L
https://install.datadoghq.com/scripts/install_script_agent7.sh)"
```

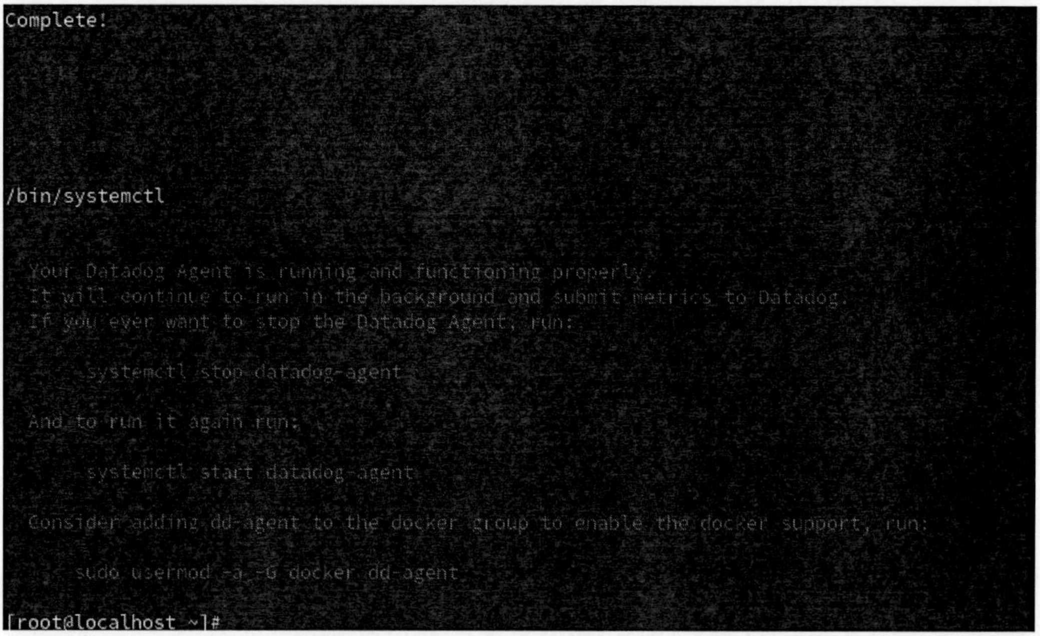

```
Complete!

/bin/systemctl

  Your Datadog Agent is running and functioning properly.
  It will continue to run in the background and submit metrics to Datadog.
  If you ever want to stop the Datadog Agent, run:

      systemctl stop datadog-agent

  And to run it again run:

      systemctl start datadog-agent

  Consider adding dd-agent to the docker group to enable the docker support, run:

     sudo usermod -a -G docker dd-agent

[root@localhost ~]#
```

Figure 6.11: *Datadog Agent Installed and Running*

Figure 6.11 displays the status output of the Datadog Agent, confirming that it is installed and actively running.

Step 4: Verify the installation

After installation, check the status of the Datadog Agent to confirm it is running correctly:

```
sudo systemctl status datadog-agent
```

If the agent is running successfully, the output should indicate an **`active`** status.

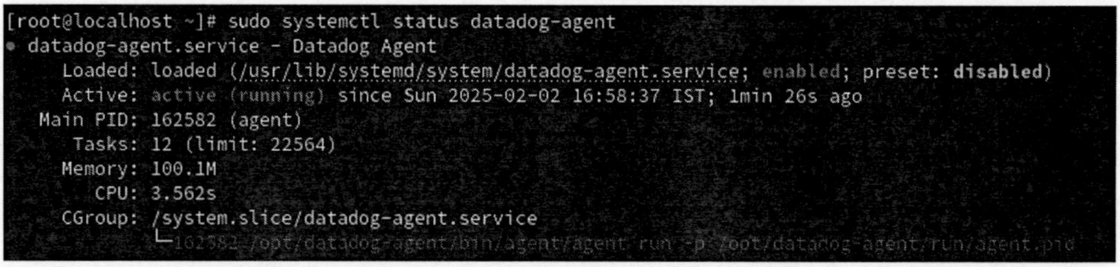

```
[root@localhost ~]# sudo systemctl status datadog-agent
● datadog-agent.service - Datadog Agent
     Loaded: loaded (/usr/lib/systemd/system/datadog-agent.service; enabled; preset: disabled)
     Active: active (running) since Sun 2025-02-02 16:58:37 IST; 1min 26s ago
   Main PID: 162582 (agent)
      Tasks: 12 (limit: 22564)
     Memory: 100.1M
        CPU: 3.562s
     CGroup: /system.slice/datadog-agent.service
             └─162582 /opt/datadog-agent/bin/agent/agent run -p /opt/datadog-agent/run/agent.pid
```

Figure 6.12: *Output of Datadog Agent Status Command Indicating Running State*

Figure 6.12 displays the terminal output from the datadog-agent status command, confirming that the agent is actively running. The output verifies that the Datadog Agent is properly configured and continuously monitoring system metrics.

Step 5: Enable the Datadog Agent to start on boot

To ensure that the Datadog Agent starts automatically when the system reboots, enable the service:

```
sudo systemctl enable datadog-agent
```

Step 6: View metrics in Datadog dashboard

a. Log in to your Datadog account.

b. Navigate to **`Infrastructure > Hosts`** to see your CentOS system listed.

c. Click on the host to view collected metrics, including CPU usage, memory utilization, disk activity, and network performance.

Connecting Datadog Agent Installed on CentOS to Redis

Step 1: Verify Redis is running:

```
redis-cli ping
```

Expected output: PONG

Step 2: Enable the Redis Integration in Datadog

Navigate to the Datadog Redis Integration Directory:

```
cd /etc/datadog-agent/conf.d/redisdb.d
```

Step 3: Copy the example configuration file and rename it:

```
sudo cp conf.yaml.example conf.yaml
```

Open the **`conf.yaml`** file to configure Redis monitoring:

```
sudo vim conf.yaml
```

Step 4: Modify the configuration file to point to the local Redis instance:

```
instances:
  - host: "127.0.0.1"
    port: 6379
    password: ""    # Leave empty if Redis does not require authentication
    db: 0           # Default Redis database
```

Step 5: Restart the Datadog Agent

```
sudo systemctl restart datadog-agent
```

Step 6: Verify Redis Metrics in Datadog

Check if Datadog is collecting Redis metrics by running:

```
sudo datadog-agent status
```

Look for the **`redisdb`** integration section. If configured correctly, you should see Redis metrics being collected.

```
redisdb (7.0.0)
---------------
  Instance ID: redisdb:e43bb6bcd098d3d4 [OK]
  Configuration Source: file:/etc/datadog-agent/conf.d/redisdb.d/conf.yaml
  Total Runs: 3
  Metric Samples: Last Run: 50, Total: 150
  Events: Last Run: 0, Total: 0
  Service Checks: Last Run: 1, Total: 3
  Average Execution Time : 83ms
  Last Execution Date : 2025-02-02 19:31:40 IST / 2025-02-02 14:01:40 UTC (1738504900000)
  Last Successful Execution Date : 2025-02-02 19:31:40 IST / 2025-02-02 14:01:40 UTC (1738504900000)
  metadata:
    version.major: 6
    version.minor: 2
    version.patch: 17
    version.raw: 6.2.17
    version.scheme: semver
```

Figure 6.13: *RedisDB Integration Section in the Output of the Datadog Agent Status Command*

Figure 6.13 displays the portion of the Datadog Agent status output that specifically details the RedisDB integration.

Step 7: View Redis Metrics in the Datadog Dashboard

a. Log in to your **Datadog account**.

b. Navigate to **`Infrastructure > Redis`**.

c. Select your **`CentOS`** Redis instance.

d. View metrics.

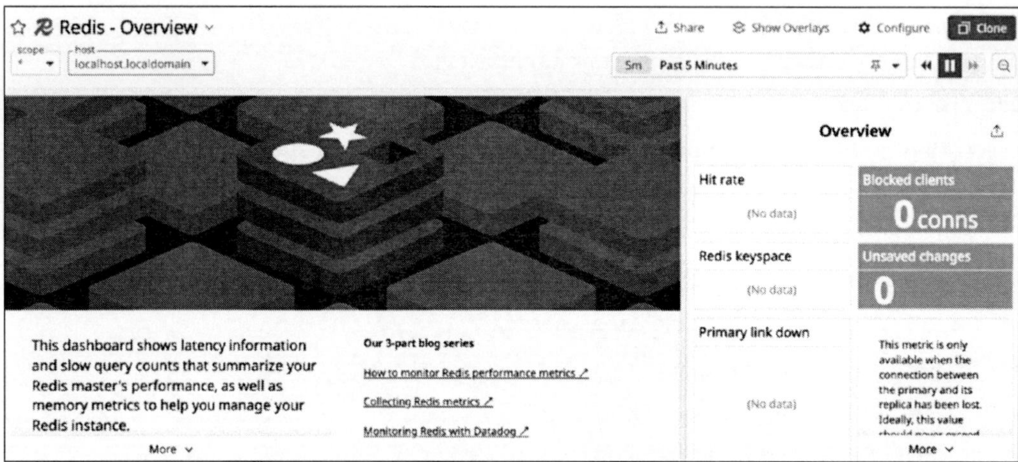

Figure 6.14: *Redis Dashboard in Datadog after Installation*

Figure 6.14 displays the part of the Redis dashboard within Datadog following its installation. The dashboard provides a comprehensive view of critical metrics.

Installing Datadog Agent on Windows

This step-by-step guide will walk you through installing and configuring the Datadog Agent on a Windows machine.

Step 1: Download the Datadog Agent for Windows

a. Open your web browser and go to the official Datadog Agent download page on the Datadog website.

b. Select **Windows** as the operating system.

c. Click the **Download Agent** button.

Step 2: Install the Datadog Agent

a. Locate the downloaded **Datadog Agent installer (.msi)** file and double-click it to begin the installation.

b. Follow the on-screen installation prompts:

   i. Accept the license agreement.

   ii. Choose an installation location (default is recommended).

   iii. Click **Next** to proceed.

Note: *You can also install the Datadog Agent using* ***PowerShell.***

Step 3: Enter your Datadog API key

a. When prompted, enter your **Datadog API Key** (found in your **Datadog** dashboard).

b. Click **Next** to continue.

Step 4: Configure Agent Services

a. Select the services you want to enable (for example, system metrics, logs, and network monitoring).

b. Choose **Enable logs collection** if you plan to monitor logs from your Windows machine.

c. Click **Install** to start the setup process.

Step 5: Verify the Datadog Agent Installation

Go to **http://localhost:5002/** and check.

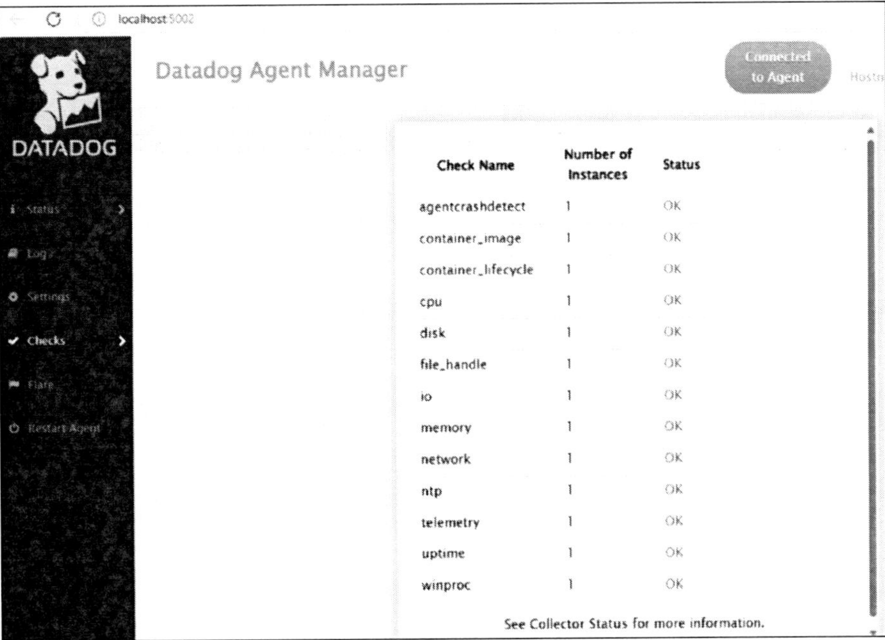

Figure 6.15: *Checks Section in Datadog Agent Manager in the Web Interface*

Figure 6.15 showcases the checks section within the **Datadog Agent Manager** on the web interface.

Adding Redis to Datadog monitoring on Windows

To monitor a Redis instance running on Windows using the Datadog Agent, follow these step-by-step instructions to configure Redis integration.

Step 1: Open the Redis Integration Configuration Directory

Navigate to the Datadog Redis integration directory:

```
cd "C:\ProgramData\Datadog\conf.d\redisdb.d"
```

Step 2: Enable the Redis integration

Copy the example configuration file and rename it:

```
copy conf.yaml.example conf.yaml
```

Step 3: Edit the configuration File

Open **`conf.yaml`** in a text editor (for example, Notepad++ or PowerShell ISE):

```
notepad conf.yaml
```

Modify the file to look like this:

```
instances:
  - host: "127.0.0.1"     # Redis server host
    port: 6379            # Redis server port
    password: ""          # Leave empty if no authentication is required
    db: 0                 # Default Redis database
```

Step 4: `Save` and `close` the file

Step 5: Restart the Datadog Agent

To apply the changes, restart the Datadog Agent:

```
net stop datadogagent
net start datadogagent
```

Note: *Alternatively, restart the agent via the Datadog Agent Manager.*

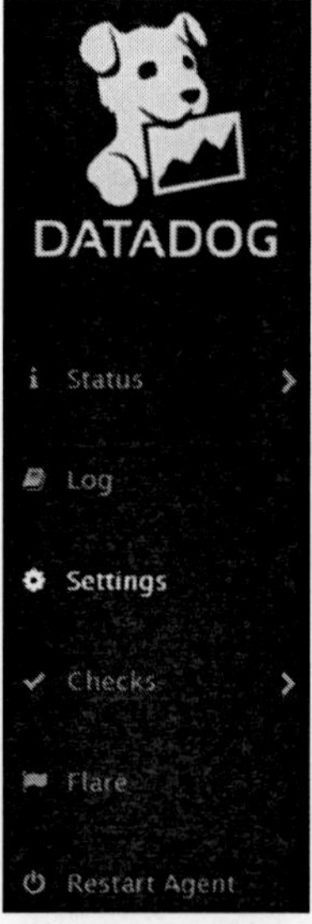

Figure 6.16: *Left Panel of Datadog Agent in the Web Interface*

Figure 6.16 displays the left panel of the Datadog Agent interface within the web portal. In addition to offering easy navigation to various sections, it also includes an option to restart the agent, providing a quick way to refresh or resolve issues with the agent's operation.

Step 6: View Redis metrics in the Datadog dashboard

Log in to Datadog at **https://app.datadoghq.com**.

a. Navigate to **`Infrastructure`** > **`Redis`**.
b. Select your Windows Redis instance.
c. View key metrics

Elasticsearch, Logstash, Kibana (ELK) Stack

Monitoring Redis effectively requires a comprehensive solution that can collect, analyze, and visualize logs and performance metrics in real-time. The **ELK** Stack - which consists of **Elasticsearch, Logstash, and Kibana** provides a powerful framework for Redis monitoring. It allows you to centralize Redis logs, analyze performance trends, and create interactive dashboards for better visibility into your Redis instance's health and activity.

This is where the **ELK Stack** comes into play:

- **Elasticsearch** stores and indexes Redis logs and metrics for fast and efficient searching.
- **Logstash** collects, processes, and ships Redis logs to Elasticsearch.
- **Kibana** provides a user-friendly interface for visualizing Redis performance data.

By using the **ELK Stack**, you can:

- **Aggregate logs from multiple Redis instances** in one centralized location.
- **Analyze slow commands and keyspace trends** over time.
- **Set up real-time alerts** for critical events such as high memory usage.
- **Create interactive dashboards** for better performance insights.

Note: *The ELK Stack has major differences between 7.x and 8.x. In this chapter, commands are shown for both versions where applicable.*

Installing ELK on macOS

Elasticsearch is the core storage and search engine of the ELK Stack.

Install Elasticsearch

1. **Download `Elasticsearch` from the official website**

   https://www.elastic.co/downloads/elasticsearch

2. **Choosing between macOS aarch64 and macOS x86_64**

   To determine if your macOS device uses the AArch (**ARM**) architecture, follow these steps:

   a. Click on the **`Apple`** menu and select **`About This Mac`**.
   b. In the overview, check the **`Chip`** or **`Processor`** section.
   c. If you see an entry such as **`M1`**, **`M2`**, or another Apple Silicon chip, your Mac is based on the **`AArch`** architecture.

3. **Unzip and run `elasticsearch`**

   ```
   cd ~/Downloads/elasticsearch-8.17.2/bin/
   ./elasticsearch
   ```

   Important: If you encounter the error message **"jdk cannot be opened because Apple cannot check it for malicious software"** you can resolve it using one of the following methods:

   a. **Allow the Application in Privacy and Security:** Navigate to your Mac's **`System Preferences`**, select **`Privacy and Security`**, and then allow the application to run.

   Figure 6.17: *Error Encountered while Starting the Elasticsearch Service*

   Figure 6.17 illustrates a common error that may occur when attempting to start Elasticsearch.

   b. **Remove the Quarantine Attribute:** Open Terminal and change to the directory containing the unzipped Elasticsearch folder where **`jdk.app`** is located. Then execute the following command:

   ```
   xattr -d com.apple.quarantine jdk.app
   ```

   This command removes the quarantine attribute, enabling the JDK to open without being blocked by macOS security checks.

4. Once **`Elasticsearch`** is successfully running, you may encounter the following message:

```
✅ Elasticsearch security features have been automatically configured!
✅ Authentication is enabled and cluster connections are encrypted.

ℹ️ Password for the elastic user (reset with `bin/elasticsearch-reset-password -u elastic`):
  zxPymeob2n13_ddMshrf

ℹ️ HTTP CA certificate SHA-256 fingerprint:
  cc2f12c7d8fb3179e6d4de7f93dc3be57dca4ff0dd46c9c644800c79c8c299e2

ℹ️ Configure Kibana to use this cluster:
• Run Kibana and click the configuration link in the terminal when Kibana starts.
• Copy the following enrollment token and paste it into Kibana in your browser (valid for the next 30 minutes):
  eyJ2ZXIiOiI4LjE0LjAiLCJhZHIiOlsiMTAuOTAuMTYuMjQ3OjkyMDAiXSwiZmdyIjoiY2MyZjEyYzdkOGZiMzE3OWU2ZDRkZTdmOTNkYzNiZTU3Z
GNhNGZmMGRkNDZjOWM2NDQ4MDBjNzljOGMyOTllMiIsImtleSI6InEwZm1aWlVCdGdJWDJ5ajV2b3RDOm1BWTNkYkNOUzJTamlEUGQzM213Y1EifQ==

ℹ️ Configure other nodes to join this cluster:
• On this node:
  - Create an enrollment token with `bin/elasticsearch-create-enrollment-token -s node`.
  - Uncomment the transport.host setting at the end of config/elasticsearch.yml.
  - Restart Elasticsearch.
• On other nodes:
  - Start Elasticsearch with `bin/elasticsearch --enrollment-token <token>`, using the enrollment token that you ge
nerated.
```

Figure 6.18: *Output after a Successful Run of Elasticsearch*

Figure 6.18 shows the terminal output confirming that Elasticsearch has started successfully. A successful startup is typically indicated by log messages such as "`started`" and the availability of the service on port **9200**. At this point, Elasticsearch is ready to accept HTTP requests, and begin indexing as well as storing data.

5. Please note this information, as it will be **helpful** for subsequent steps.
6. Verify installation by going to browser **http://localhost:9200/**

   If asked for a username and password, the username is elastic, and you can copy the password which is displayed in the preceding figure or reset the password with **`./elasticsearch-reset-password -u elastic`**.

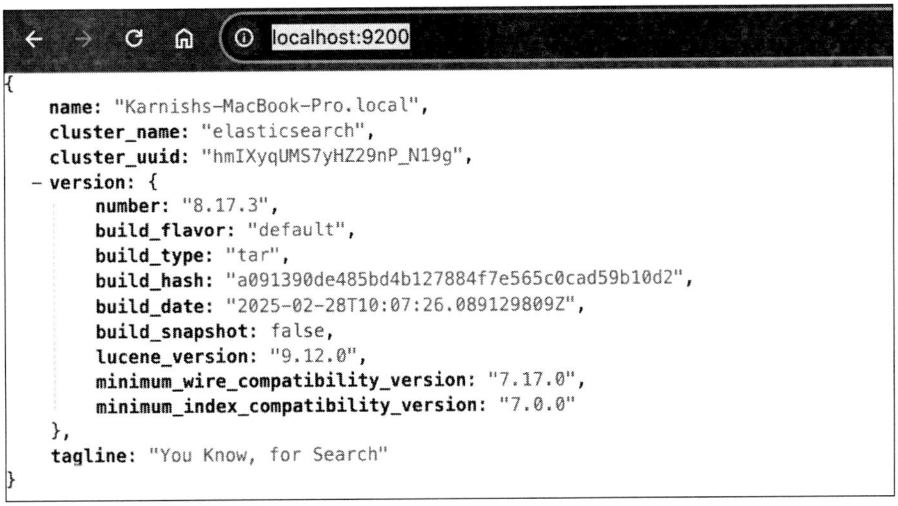

localhost:9200


```
{
  name: "Karnishs-MacBook-Pro.local",
  cluster_name: "elasticsearch",
  cluster_uuid: "hmIXyqUMS7yHZ29nP_N19g",
- version: {
    number: "8.17.3",
    build_flavor: "default",
    build_type: "tar",
    build_hash: "a091390de485bd4b127884f7e565c0cad59b10d2",
    build_date: "2025-02-28T10:07:26.089129809Z",
    build_snapshot: false,
    lucene_version: "9.12.0",
    minimum_wire_compatibility_version: "7.17.0",
    minimum_index_compatibility_version: "7.0.0"
  },
  tagline: "You Know, for Search"
}
```


Figure 6.19: *Output in the Browser When Accessing http://localhost:9200/*

Figure 6.19 displays the default JSON response returned by Elasticsearch when accessed through a web browser at **http://localhost:9200/**. The response includes key information such as the cluster name, node name, version number, and a tagline confirming that Elasticsearch is running and accessible.

Install Logstash

1. **Install Homebrew (if not already installed)**

   Homebrew is a package manager for macOS that simplifies software installation.

2. **Open the Terminal and run:**

   ```
   /bin/bash -c "$(curl -fsSL https://raw.githubusercontent.com/Homebrew/install/HEAD/install.sh)"
   ```

   ```
   export PATH=/opt/homebrew/bin:$PATH
   ```

3. **Once installed, verify by typing:**

   ```
   brew --version
   ```

4. **Add Elastic Homebrew Tap**

   To access the Elastic Stack packages, add the Elastic tap to Homebrew:

   ```
   brew tap elastic/tap
   ```

5. **Install Logstash**

   Now, **install Logstash using Homebrew:**

   ```
   brew install logstash
   ```

   This will download and install Logstash.

6. **After installation, you can verify Logstash by checking its version:**

   ```
   logstash --version
   ```

Install Kibana

In this section, we will cover how to install Kibana on a macOS system and configure it along with Logstash and Elasticsearch to collect and visualize data from Redis. This integration is ideal for real-time Redis log analysis, monitoring, and reporting through rich visual dashboards.

1. **Install Kibana using Homebrew**

   ```
   brew install elastic/tap/kibana-full
   ```

2. **Start Kibana**

   ```
   brew services start elastic/tap/kibana-full
   ```

   > **Note:** *By default, Kibana runs on port* **5601**.

3. **Access Kibana from the Browser**

   Open your browser and go to:

   http://localhost:5601

   You should see the Kibana dashboard.

   If you encounter issues as follows:

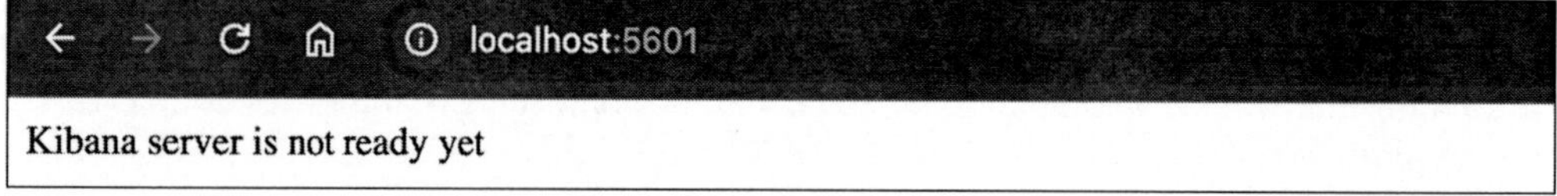

Figure 6.20: *Issue Encountered while Accessing Kibana through the Browser at http://localhost:5601*

Figure 6.20 shows the common error message, "*Kibana server is not ready yet*," which typically appears when Kibana is still initializing or encountering issues during startup.

Go to the elasticsearch config file and either disable **`xpack.security.enabled : False`**

or if enabled **specify username and password.**

```
elasticsearch.username = elastic
elasticsearch.password = your-password
```

Then restart **`Elasticsearch`**.

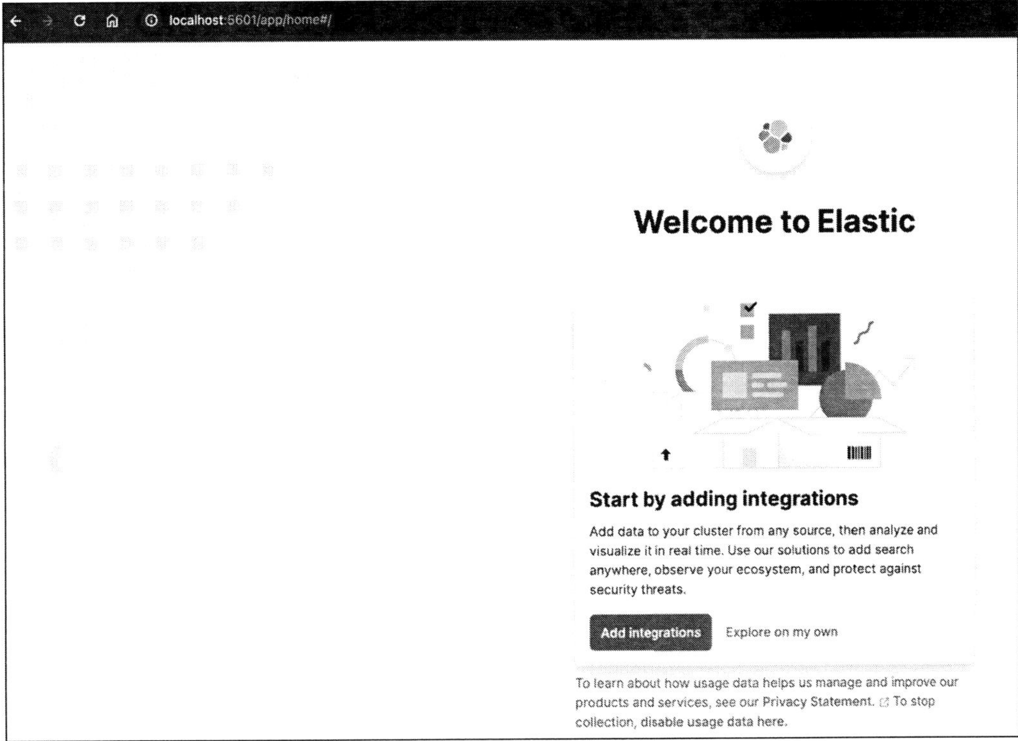

Figure 6.21: *Kibana Running Successfully on http://localhost:5601*

Figure 6.21 confirms that Kibana is up and running, accessible via the browser at http://localhost:5601. The user interface has loaded successfully, indicating that Kibana has connected to Elasticsearch, and is ready for use.

Connecting Redis to the ELK Stack

1. **Create a Logstash Configuration File**

   Create a new file named **`redis_to_elk.conf`**:

   ```
   vim redis_to_elk.conf
   ```

2. **Add the following configuration:**

   ```
   input {
     redis {
       host => "127.0.0.1"
       port => 6379
       data_type => "list"
       key => "logstash"
     }
   }

   output {
     elasticsearch {
       hosts => ["http://localhost:9200"]
       index => "redis-logs-%{+YYYY.MM.dd}"
     }
   ```

```
  stdout { codec => rubydebug }
}
```

3. **Push Sample Data into Redis**

   Use Redis CLI to push sample logs:

   ```
   redis-cli LPUSH logstash '{"message":"Redis to ELK test", "level":"info",
   "timestamp":"2025-03-23T10:00:00"}'
   ```

4. **Start Logstash with the `Config` File**

   ```
   logstash -f redis_to_elk.conf
   ```

   You should see the parsed data in the console output.

```
{
       "message" => "Redis to ELK test",
         "level" => "info",
     "timestamp" => "2025-03-23T10:00:00",
         "event" => {
        "original" => "{\"message\":\"Redis to ELK test\", \"level\":\"info\", \"timestamp\":\"2025-03-23T10:00:00\"}"
    },
      "@version" => "1",
    "@timestamp" => 2025-03-23T18:01:16.325033Z
}
```

Figure 6.22: *Redis Parsed Data Displayed in the Console after Starting Logstash*

Figure 6.22 shows the console output of Logstash after successfully reading and parsing data from Redis. The data is then displayed in a structured format using the rubydebug codec, which is useful for verifying that Logstash is correctly ingesting and interpreting data from the Redis list. This output confirms that the input and output pipeline between Redis and Logstash is functioning as expected.

5. **View Data in Kibana**
   a. Open Kibana in your browser (**http://localhost:5601**)
   b. Go to **`Management → Stack Management → Index Patterns`**
   c. Create a new index pattern: **`redis-logs-*`**
   d. Choose timestamp as the time field (if available)
   e. Go to **`Discover`** to view your Redis logs in real time

This setup is ideal for tracking Redis events, logs, or messages from applications that use Redis as a buffer or message queue.

Installing ELK on Ubuntu

Install the ELK Stack

Since the **ELK Stack** consists of three main components (**Elasticsearch, Logstash,** and **Kibana**), we need to install them one by one.

Step 1: Install Elasticsearch (Stores Redis Logs)

Elasticsearch is the heart of the ELK Stack, responsible for storing and indexing Redis logs for fast searching.

Elasticsearch is not available in Ubuntu's default repositories, so we need to add Elastic's package source manually. To ensure security, Elasticsearch packages are signed with a GPG key to prevent package spoofing.

To begin, import the Elasticsearch public GPG key using curl, and convert it into a format that APT can recognize:

```
curl -fsSL https://artifacts.elastic.co/GPG-KEY-elasticsearch | sudo gpg --dearmor -o
/usr/share/keyrings/elasticsearch-keyring.gpg
```

This key ensures that only **trusted Elasticsearch packages** are installed. Next, we will add the **Elastic package source list**, and proceed with the installation.

a. **Add the Elastic source list to the `sources.list.d` directory, where apt will search for new sources:**

   ```
   echo "deb signed-by=/usr/share/keyrings/elasticsearch-keyring.gpg] https://
   artifacts.elastic.co/packages/7.x/apt stable main" | sudo tee -a /etc/apt/
   sources.list.d/elastic-7.x.list
   ```

b. **Update your package lists so that APT will read the new Elastic source:**

   ```
   sudo apt update
   ```

c. **Then install Elasticsearch with this command:**

   ```
   sudo apt install elasticsearch
   ```

d. **Configuring Elasticsearch**

   ```
   sudo vim /etc/elasticsearch/elasticsearch.yml
   ```

e. **Set `network.host: localhost`**

```
#
# ---------------------------------- Network -----------------------------------
#
# By default Elasticsearch is only accessible on localhost. Set a different
# address here to expose this node on the network:
#
network.host: localhost
#
```

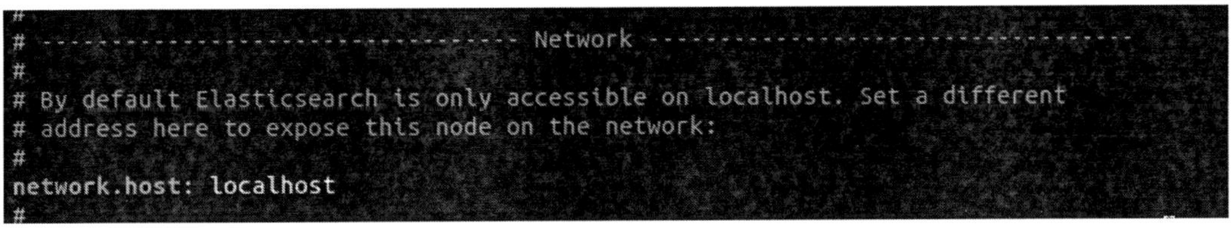

***Figure 6.23**: network.host Set to Localhost in elasticsearch.yml*

   Figure 6.23 illustrates the configuration of the **`network.host`** parameter in the **`elasticsearch.yml`** file, where it is set to localhost. This setting ensures that Elasticsearch only listens for connections from the local machine, enhancing security by preventing external access. It is useful for development and single-node setups where remote connections are not required.

f. **Start the Elasticsearch service with `systemctl`:**

   ```
   sudo systemctl start elasticsearch
   ```

   Check status with:

   ```
   sudo systemctl status elasticsearch
   ```

```
● elasticsearch.service - Elasticsearch
   Loaded: loaded (/lib/systemd/system/elasticsearch.service; disabled; vendor preset: enabled)
   Active: active (running) since Thu 2025-02-13 17:16:52 IST; 38s ago
     Docs: https://www.elastic.co
 Main PID: 7672 (java)
    Tasks: 87 (limit: 4549)
   Memory: 2.3G
      CPU: 23.769s
```

***Figure 6.24**: Output of Systemctl Status Elasticsearch Command*

Figure 6.24 shows the output of the **`systemctl status elasticsearch`** command, which is used to check the current status of the Elasticsearch service. The output provides important details such as whether the service is active (running), its process ID, memory usage, and so on. This command helps in verifying if Elasticsearch is properly running or troubleshooting issues, if the service fails to start.

g. **Run the following command to enable Elasticsearch to start up every time your server boots:**

```
sudo systemctl enable elasticsearch
```

h. **Test Elasticsearch**

```
curl -X GET 'http://localhost:9200'
```

```
{
  "name" : "ubuntu-QEMU-Virtual-Machine",
  "cluster_name" : "elasticsearch",
  "cluster_uuid" : "wahrdjsdRX6s1HoJSNn29w",
  "version" : {
    "number" : "7.17.27",
    "build_flavor" : "default",
    "build_type" : "deb",
    "build_hash" : "0f88dde84795b30ca0d2c0c4796643ec5938aeb5",
    "build_date" : "2025-01-09T14:09:01.578835424Z",
    "build_snapshot" : false,
    "lucene_version" : "8.11.3",
    "minimum_wire_compatibility_version" : "6.8.0",
    "minimum_index_compatibility_version" : "6.0.0-beta1"
  },
  "tagline" : "You Know, for Search"
}
```

Figure 6.25: *Output of curl -X GET 'http://localhost:9200'*

Figure 6.25 displays the response from Elasticsearch when sending a **`GET`** request to **http://localhost:9200**. The output confirms that Elasticsearch is running, and provides essential details such as the cluster name, node name, version information, and other metadata. This command is commonly used to verify a successful Elasticsearch installation, and check if the service is accessible.

Step 2: Install Logstash (Collects Redis Logs and Sends to Elasticsearch)

Logstash is responsible for collecting logs from Redis, processing them, and sending them to Elasticsearch.

a. **Download and install the Public Signing Key:**

```
wget -qO - https://artifacts.elastic.co/GPG-KEY-elasticsearch | sudo gpg
--dearmor -o /usr/share/keyrings/elastic-keyring.gpg
```

b. **You may need to install the `apt-transport-https` package on Debian before proceeding:**

```
sudo apt-get install apt-transport-https
```

c. **Save the repository definition to `/etc/apt/sources.list.d/elastic-8.x.list`:**

```
echo "deb [signed-by=/usr/share/keyrings/elastic-keyring.gpg] https://
artifacts.elastic.co/packages/8.x/apt stable main" | sudo tee -a /etc/apt/
sources.list.d/elastic-8.x.list
```

d. **Run `sudo apt-get update` and the repository is ready for use. You can install it with:**

```
sudo apt-get update
sudo apt-get install logstash
sudo systemctl status logstash
```

```
● logstash.service - logstash
     Loaded: loaded (/lib/systemd/system/logstash.service; disabled; vendor preset: enabled)
     Active: active (running) since Thu 2025-02-13 19:14:16 IST; 92ms ago
   Main PID: 33748 (java)
      Tasks: 7 (limit: 4549)
     Memory: 17.9M
        CPU: 100ms
```

Figure 6.26: *Output of Systemctl Status Logstash Command*

Figure 6.26 shows the output of the **`systemctl status logstash`** command, which provides the current status of the Logstash service. The output includes details such as whether Logstash is active (running), its process ID, memory usage, and so on. This command is useful for verifying that Logstash is running correctly and diagnosing any startup issues.

```
sudo systemctl enable logstash
```

Step 3: Install Kibana (Visualizes Redis Logs)

Kibana provides an easy-to-use web interface for viewing and analyzing Redis logs stored in Elasticsearch.

a. **Import the Elastic PGP key.** Download and install the public signing key:

```
wget -qO - https://artifacts.elastic.co/GPG-KEY-elasticsearch | sudo gpg
--dearmor -o /usr/share/keyrings/elasticsearch-keyring.gpg
```

b. **You may need to install the `apt-transport-https` package on Debian before proceeding:**

```
sudo apt-get install apt-transport-https
```

c. **Save the repository definition to `/etc/apt/sources.list.d/elastic-8.x.list`:**

```
echo "deb [signed-by=/usr/share/keyrings/elasticsearch-keyring.gpg] https://
artifacts.elastic.co/packages/8.x/apt stable main" | sudo tee /etc/apt/
sources.list.d/elastic-8.x.list\
```

d. **You can install the Kibana Debian package with:**

```
sudo apt-get update
sudo apt-get install kibana
```

e. **Start Kibana**

```
sudo systemctl start kibana
sudo systemctl enable kibana
sudo systemctl status kibana
```

```
● kibana.service - Kibana
     Loaded: loaded (/lib/systemd/system/kibana.service; enabled; vendor preset: enabled)
     Active: active (running) since Fri 2025-02-14 11:19:31 IST; 38s ago
       Docs: https://www.elastic.co
   Main PID: 132850 (node)
      Tasks: 11 (limit: 4549)
     Memory: 969.3M
        CPU: 20.571s
```

Figure 6.27: *Output of Systemctl Status Kibana Command Showing It in Running State*

Figure 6.27 displays the output of the **`systemctl status kibana`** command, confirming that the Kibana service is active (running).

f. **Open Kibana in a web browser**

http://localhost:5601

You should see the **`Kibana` dashboard.**

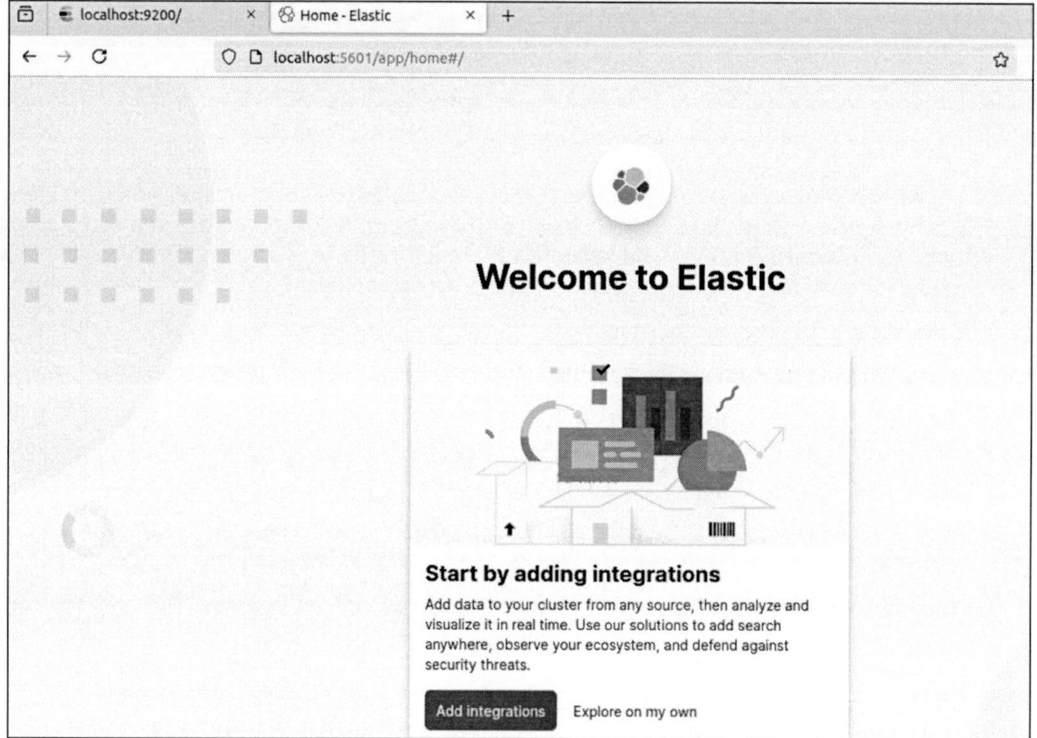

***Figure 6.28**: Kibana Dashboard on Opening http://localhost:5601*

Figure 6.28 shows that the **Kibana** dashboard when accessed via **http://localhost:5601** in a web browser. The dashboard provides a user-friendly interface for visualizing and analyzing data stored in Elasticsearch. From here, users can configure index patterns, explore logs, create dashboards, and set up monitoring alerts for Redis and other integrated services.

Step 4: Configure Logstash to Collect Redis Logs

Logstash needs to be configured to collect logs from Redis, process them, and send them to Elasticsearch.

a. **Open the Logstash configuration directory:**

```
cd /etc/logstash/conf.d/
```

b. **Create a new configuration file:**

```
sudo vim redis.conf
```

c. **Add the following configuration:**

```
input {
  redis {
    host => "127.0.0.1"
    port => 6379
```

```
      data_type => "list"
      key => "logstash"
    }
  }
  filter {
    json {
      source => "message"
    }
  }
  output {
    elasticsearch {
      hosts => ["http://localhost:9200"]
      index => "redis-logs-%{+YYYY.MM.dd}"
    }
    stdout { codec => rubydebug }
  }
```

```
input {
  redis {
    host => "127.0.0.1"
    port => 6379
    data_type => "list"
    key => "logstash"
  }
}

filter {
  json {
    source => "message"
  }
}


output {
  elasticsearch {
    hosts => ["http://localhost:9200"]
    index => "redis-logs-%{+YYYY.MM.dd}"
  }
  stdout { codec => rubydebug }
}
```

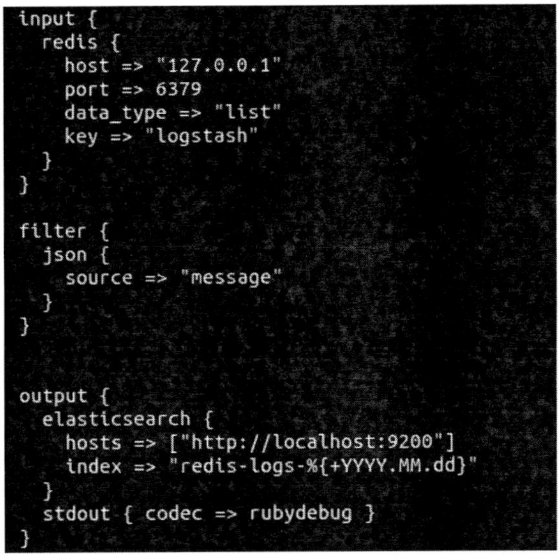

Figure 6.29: *Additions Made in redis.conf*

Figure 6.29 highlights the modifications made to the **`redis.conf`** file for configuring Redis.

d. **Save and exit the file.**

e. **Restart Logstash to apply changes:**

```
sudo systemctl restart logstash
```

Step 5: Configure Redis to Send Logs to Logstash

To monitor Redis logs, we need to make Redis send its logs to Logstash.

a. **Open the Redis configuration file:**

```
sudo vim /etc/redis/redis.conf
```

b. **Find the log configuration and change it:**

```
logfile ""
loglevel notice
```

c. **Enable Redis monitoring with:**

```
redis-cli MONITOR | tee /var/log/redis.log
```

d. **Save the changes and restart Redis:**

```
sudo systemctl restart redis
```

Logstash will now **read Redis logs** from disk, process them, and forward them to Elasticsearch.

Step 6: Verify Redis Logs in Kibana

Once everything is set up, we can check if Redis logs are being collected properly.

a. **Open Kibana in a browser:**

```
http://localhost:5601
```

b. **Go to Discover**

c. **Create an index pattern for Redis logs:**

Click on **`Management > Stack Management > Index Patterns`**.

Create a new index pattern with the name:

```
redis-logs-*
```

Click **`Next`** and save the index.

d. **You should now see real-time Redis logs flowing into Kibana.**

Step 7: Create Redis Monitoring Dashboards

To make Redis monitoring even easier, let us create visual dashboards in Kibana.

a. In Kibana, go to **`Dashboard`** and **click `Create Dashboard`.**

b. **Add the following key Redis metrics:**

```
Memory Usage (used_memory_human)
Keyspace Hits & Misses (keyspace_hits, keyspace_misses)
Command Execution Rates (total_commands_processed)
Slow Queries (slowlog_get 128)
```

c. **Save the dashboard, and monitor Redis visually.**

Final Thoughts

With the ELK Stack properly set up, you now have a complete Redis monitoring solution that collects logs, analyzes performance trends, and alerts you to issues before they impact your system.

- Elasticsearch stores Redis logs.
- Logstash collects and processes logs.
- Kibana visualizes Redis performance data.

Installing ELK on CentOS

This section provides a comprehensive, step-by-step guide to installing and configuring the ELK Stack on a CentOS system. It also demonstrates how to integrate Redis as a data source for monitoring purposes. By the end of this guide, you will have a fully functional ELK setup capable of collecting, indexing, and visualizing data from Redis. This integration is particularly useful for real-time log aggregation, performance monitoring, and gaining deeper insights into Redis operations through powerful visual dashboards.

1. **Install Java (OpenJDK)**

   ```
   sudo yum install -y java-11-openjdk-devel
   ```

2. **Verify the installation**

   ```
   java -version
   ```

3. **Add Elastic Stack Repository**

   ```
   sudo rpm --import https://artifacts.elastic.co/GPG-KEY-elasticsearch
   ```

   ```
   cat <<EOF | sudo tee /etc/yum.repos.d/elastic.repo
   [elastic-7.x]
   name=Elastic repository for 7.x packages
   baseurl=https://artifacts.elastic.co/packages/7.x/yum
   gpgcheck=1
   gpgkey=https://artifacts.elastic.co/GPG-KEY-elasticsearch
   enabled=1
   autorefresh=1
   type=rpm-md
   EOF
   ```

Step 1: Install Elasticsearch

```
sudo yum install -y elasticsearch
```

a. **Enable and start the service**

   ```
   sudo systemctl enable elasticsearch
   sudo systemctl start elasticsearch
   ```

b. **Check service status**

   ```
   curl -X GET "localhost:9200/"
   ```

```
[root@localhost root_user]# curl -X GET "localhost:9200/"
{
  "name" : "localhost.localdomain",
  "cluster_name" : "elasticsearch",
  "cluster_uuid" : "s1sXEww1TUe4oHjvZ3tKOw",
  "version" : {
    "number" : "7.17.28",
    "build_flavor" : "default",
    "build_type" : "rpm",
    "build_hash" : "139cb5a961d8de68b8e02c45cc47f5289a3623af",
    "build_date" : "2025-02-20T09:05:31.349013687Z",
    "build_snapshot" : false,
    "lucene_version" : "8.11.3",
    "minimum_wire_compatibility_version" : "6.8.0",
    "minimum_index_compatibility_version" : "6.0.0-beta1"
  },
  "tagline" : "You Know, for Search"
}
```

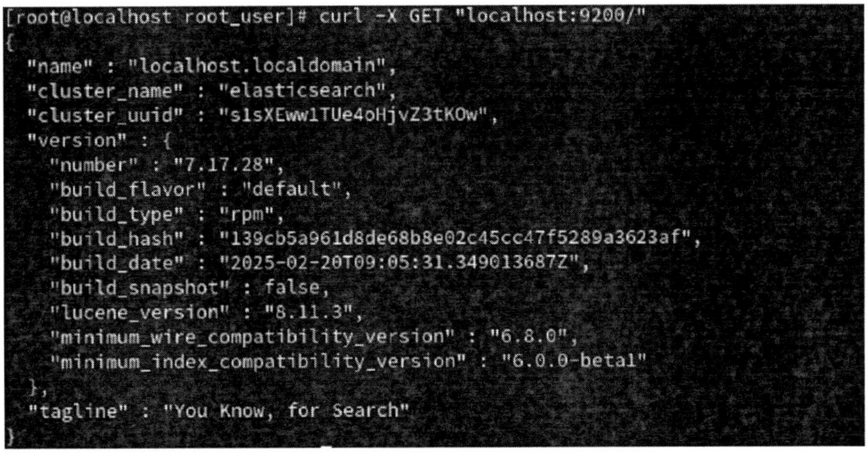

Figure 6.30: *Checking the Service Status Using curl localhost:9200*

Figure 6.30 shows the response from Elasticsearch when accessed via **`curl localhost:9200`**. This output confirms that Elasticsearch has been installed successfully, and is running on the local machine.

Alternatively, you can verify the service using a web browser.

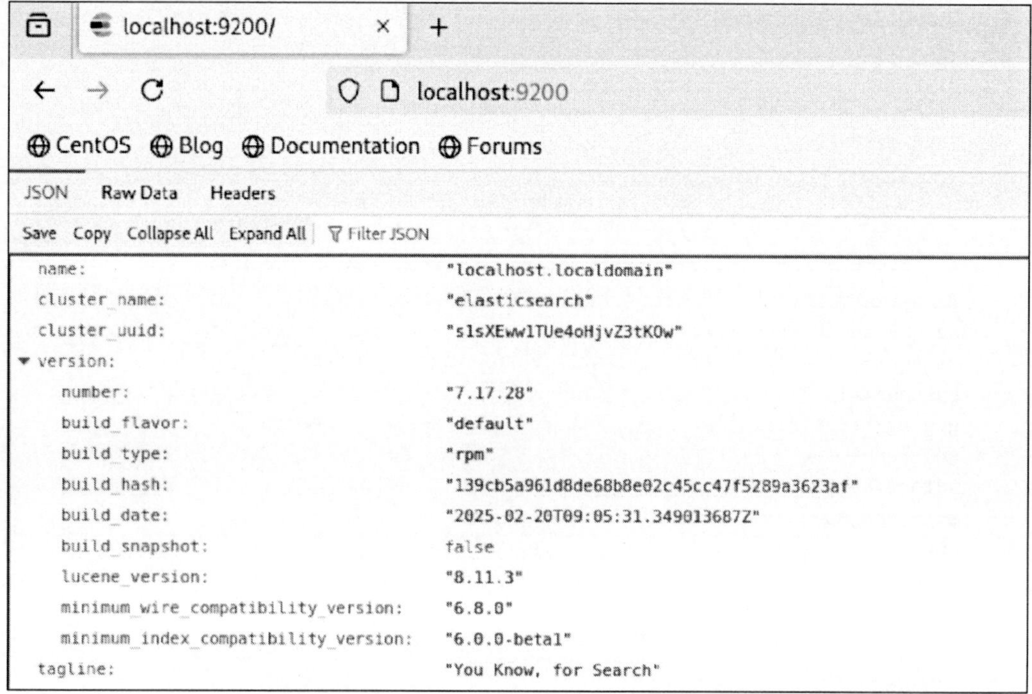

Figure 6.31: *Checking the Service Status on the Browser at localhost:9200*

Figure 6.31 displays the response received when accessing localhost:9200 through a web browser. A successful response indicates that the Elasticsearch service is up and running on the local system.

Step 2: Install Logstash

```
sudo yum install -y logstash
```

Logstash will be configured later to connect with Redis.

Step 3: Install Kibana

```
sudo yum install -y kibana
```

a. **Enable and start the Kibana service**

```
sudo systemctl enable kibana
sudo systemctl start kibana
```

b. **Kibana UI should be accessible at:**

http://<server-ip>:5601

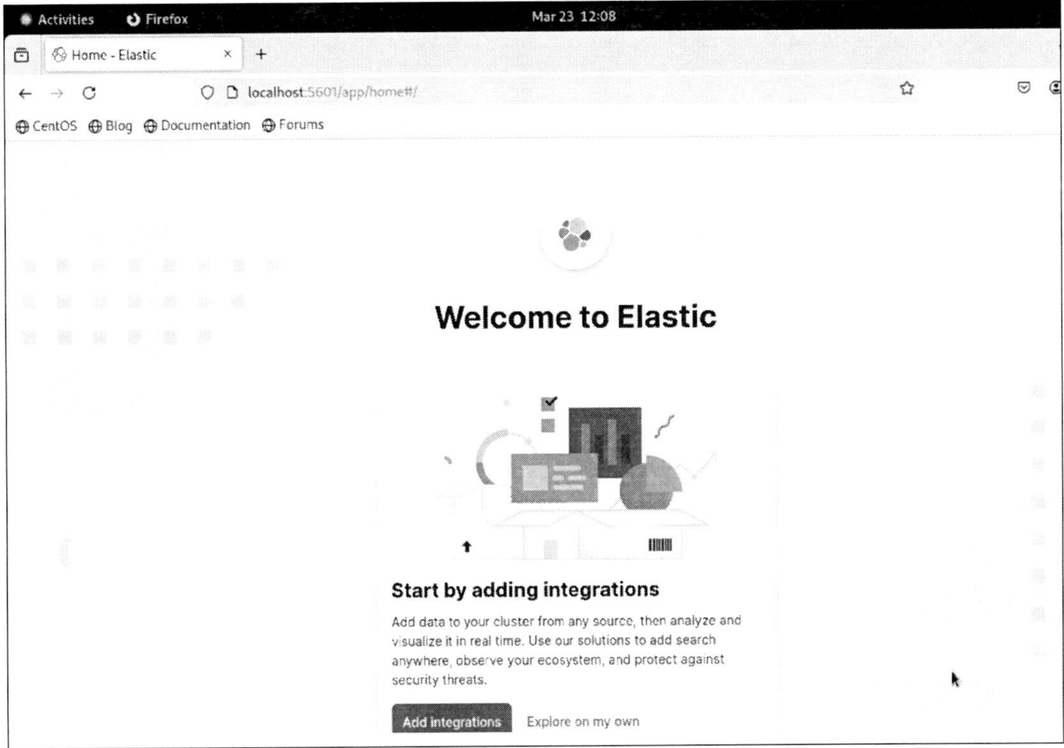

Figure 6.32: *Kibana UI Accessible in the Browser at localhost:5601*

Figure 6.32 shows that the Kibana web interface being accessed through a browser using localhost:5601. A successful load of the UI confirms that Kibana is properly installed and running.

Step 4: Configure Logstash to Read Data from Redis

Create a Logstash config file:

```
sudo vim /etc/logstash/conf.d/redis.conf

input {
  redis {
    host => "127.0.0.1"
    port => 6379
    data_type => "list"
    key => "logstash"  # Redis list key to read logs from
  }
}

output {
  elasticsearch {
    hosts => ["localhost:9200"]
    index => "redis-logs-%{+YYYY.MM.dd}"
  }

  stdout { codec => rubydebug }
}
```

This config reads logs from the Redis list named logstash and writes them to Elasticsearch.

Step 5: Test the Pipeline

Push some test data into Redis:

```
redis-cli LPUSH logstash '{"message":"Redis to ELK test log", "level":"info"}'
```

Step 6: Start Logstash

```
sudo systemctl start logstash
```

Step 7: Check if the data appears in Elasticsearch

```
curl -X GET "localhost:9200/redis-logs-*/_search?pretty"
```

Step 8: View in Kibana

a. Go to **`http://your_server_ip:5601`**
b. Navigate To **`Management → Stack Management → Index Patterns`**
c. Create a new index pattern: **`redis-logs-*`**
d. Select **`@timestamp`** or the relevant timestamp field
e. View logs in Discover

Summary

With the preceding setup:

- Redis acts as a buffer/data source.
- Logstash reads data from Redis and sends it to Elasticsearch.
- Kibana visualizes this data.

This is useful in systems where logs are pushed into Redis from various microservices or log shippers, and then pulled into ELK for analysis.

Installing ELK on Windows

Install JAVA

1. **Download Java (JDK)**
   a. Go to the Oracle JDK i.e. https://www.oracle.com/java/technologies/downloads/.
   b. Download **Oracle JDK 11 or later** (LTS recommended)
   c. Choose the **`Windows x64 Installer`** (**`.msi`**) or ZIP archive.
2. **Install Java**
   a. Using MSI Installer (Recommended).
   b. Double-click the downloaded .msi file.
   c. Follow the installation wizard steps:
   d. Accept the license agreement.
   e. Choose the installation path.
   f. Click Next and then Install.

   Wait for the installation to complete.

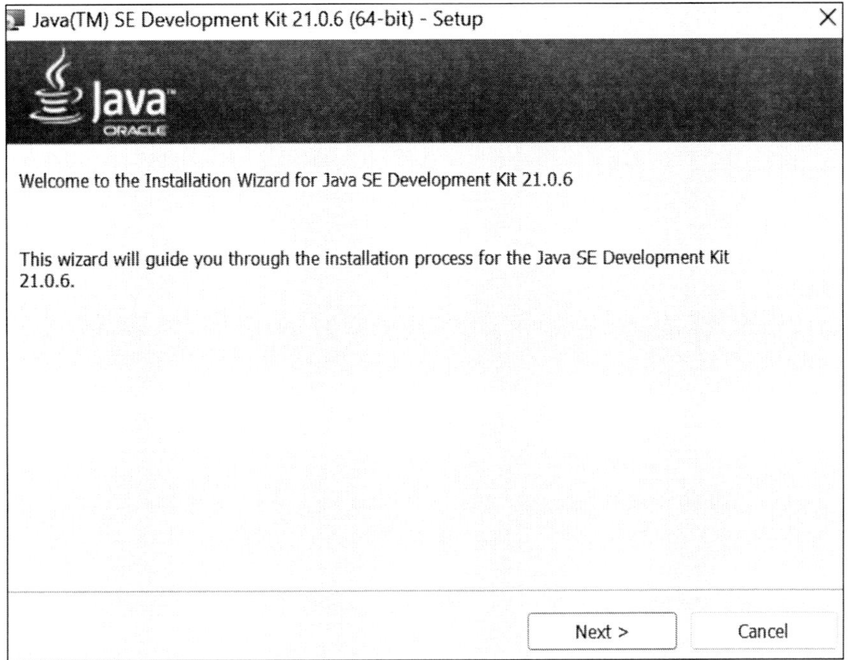

Figure 6.33: *MSI Installer – Java Installation Wizard*

Figure 6.33 displays the **MSI Installer** for Java, showing that the installation wizard is in progress. The wizard guides users through the setup process, allowing them to install Java on their system.

3. **Set Up the JAVA_HOME Environment Variable**
   a. Open **`Control Panel → System → Advanced system settings`**.
   b. Click **`Environment Variables`**.
   c. Under **`System variables`**, click **`New`** and enter:
      - **Variable Name:** `JAVA_HOME`
      - **Variable Value:** D:\Program Files\Java\jdk-21 (or your installation path)

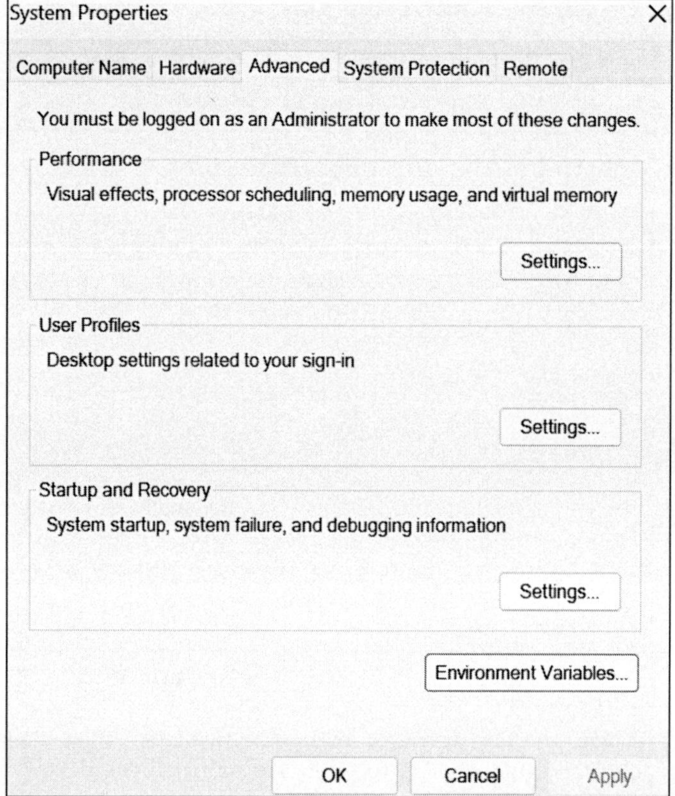

***Figure 6.34:** Setting Up the JAVA_HOME Environment Variable in System Properties*

Figure 6.34 illustrates the process of configuring the **`JAVA_HOME`** environment variable in **`System Properties`**. Setting this variable ensures that Java-based applications, such as Elasticsearch, can locate the Java installation directory correctly, enabling them to function properly.

System variables

Variable	Value
ComSpec	C:\Windows\system32\cmd.exe
DriverData	C:\Windows\System32\Drivers\DriverData
IGCCSVC_DB	AQAAANCMnd8BFdERjHoAwE/Cl+sBAAAA0TwpomnLT0amJm3...
NUMBER_OF_PROCESSORS	12
OS	Windows_NT
Path	C:\Program Files\Common Files\Oracle\Java\javapath;C:\Window...
PATHEXT	.COM;.EXE;.BAT;.CMD;.VBS;.VBE;.JS;.JSE;.WSF;.WSH;.MSC
PROCESSOR_ARCHITECTURE	AMD64

New... Edit... Delete

OK Cancel

***Figure 6.35:** Clicking "New" to Add a System Variable*

Figure 6.35 shows the process of adding a new system variable in the **`System Properties`** window.

```
New System Variable                                                    X

Variable name:      JAVA_HOME

Variable value:     C:\Program Files\Java\jdk-21

Browse Directory...     Browse File...                     OK      Cancel
```

Figure 6.36: *Adding the 'JAVA_HOME' Variable and Its Location*

Figure 6.36 illustrates the process of adding the **JAVA_HOME** environment variable in System Properties and specifying its installation path.

   d. Find the Path variable, click **Edit**, and add:

      `%JAVA_HOME%\bin`

   e. Click **OK** to save changes.

4. **Verify Java Installation**

   a. Open **Command Prompt** (*Win* + R, type **cmd**, press *Enter*).

      ```
      java -version
      ```

   b. If installed correctly, you should see the output as follows:

      ```
      java version "21.0.6" 2025-01-21 LTS
      Java(TM) SE Runtime Environment (build 21.0.6+8-LTS-188)
      Java HotSpot(TM) 64-Bit Server VM (build 21.0.6+8-LTS-188, mixed mode,
      sharing)
      ```

```
java version "21.0.6" 2025-01-21 LTS
Java(TM) SE Runtime Environment (build 21.0.6+8-LTS-188)
Java HotSpot(TM) 64-Bit Server VM (build 21.0.6+8-LTS-188, mixed mode, sharing)
```

Figure 6.37: *Output of java -version Command*

Figure 6.37 displays the output of the java **-version** command, which is used to check the installed Java version. This command confirms whether Java is properly installed and provides details such as the Java version, build number, and runtime environment, ensuring compatibility with applications such as Elasticsearch that depend on Java.

Java is now installed and ready to be used for the ELK setup.

Step 1: Install Elasticsearch

   a. **Download Elasticsearch from the official website:**

      https://www.elastic.co/downloads/elasticsearch

   b. **Extract the downloaded .zip file to a preferred location (for example, C:\elk\elasticsearch).**

   c. **Open a command prompt, navigate to the bin directory, and run:**

      ```
      elasticsearch.bat
      ```

```
PS C:\Program Files\elasticsearch-8.17.2\bin> .\elasticsearch.bat
warning: ignoring JAVA_HOME=C:\Program Files\Java\jdk-21; using bundled JDK
Could not create auto-configuration directory

ERROR: unable to create temporary keystore at [C:\Program Files\elasticsearch-8.17.2\config\elasticsearch.keystore.tmp],
 write permissions required for [C:\Program Files\elasticsearch-8.17.2\config] or run [elasticsearch-keystore upgrade],
with exit code 78
```

Figure 6.38: *Error Encountered Due to Write Permission Issues during Elasticsearch Execution*

Figure 6.38 displays an error message encountered while executing Elasticsearch, specifically related to write permissions. This issue typically occurs when Elasticsearch does not have the necessary access to write data to its required directories.

Note:

- *If you encounter an error related to write permissions (as shown in the figure), try the following solutions:*
    - **Run Elasticsearch as Administrator** *by right-clicking the command prompt and selecting* **Run as Administrator**.
    - **Change folder permissions** *to grant full control to your user account.*
    - *If Elasticsearch is installed in* `C:\Program Files`*, Windows may enforce strict permissions. Consider* **reinstalling Elasticsearch in a different directory***, such as* `C:\elk\elasticsearch`.
- *If, after installation, Elasticsearch prompts for a password when accessing* **port 9200***, disable security by modifying the* `elasticsearch.yml` *configuration file:*

```
xpack.security.enabled: false
xpack.security.enrollment.enabled: false
```

Note: The following settings apply to Elasticsearch 8.x. Security is enabled by default in 8.x. Disabling security is acceptable for local testing or learning environments only. In production, always configure authentication, TLS, and role-based access.

After making these changes, **restart Elasticsearch** for them to take effect.

d. **Verify Elasticsearch is running by visiting:**

`http://localhost:9200`

You should see a **JSON** response.

Step 2: Install Kibana

a. **Download Kibana from: https://www.elastic.co/downloads/kibana**

b. **Extract it to D:\elk\kibana or your desired location.**

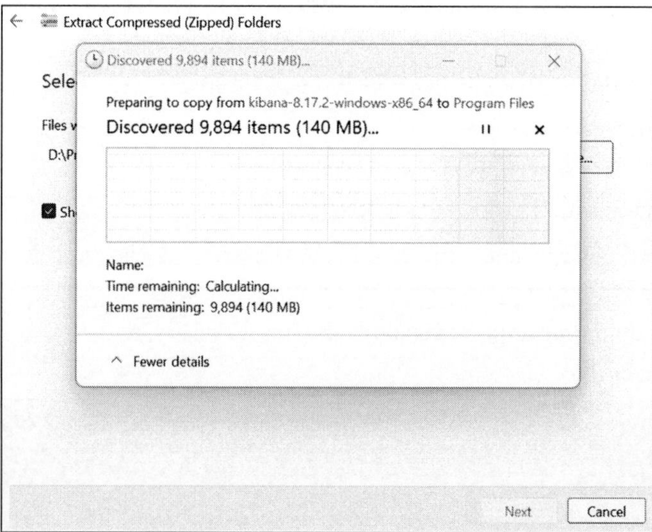

Figure 6.39: *Extracting the Kibana ZIP File*

Figure 6.39 illustrates the process of extracting the Kibana ZIP file to a specified location. This step is necessary for setting up Kibana, allowing it to be configured, and run for visualizing and analyzing Redis logs.

c. **Edit `kibana.yml` (inside the config folder) and set:**

```
server.port: 5601
elasticsearch.hosts: ["http://localhost:9200"]
```

d. **Start Kibana from the command prompt:**

```
kibana.bat
```

e. **Open Kibana in a browser:**

`http://localhost:5601`

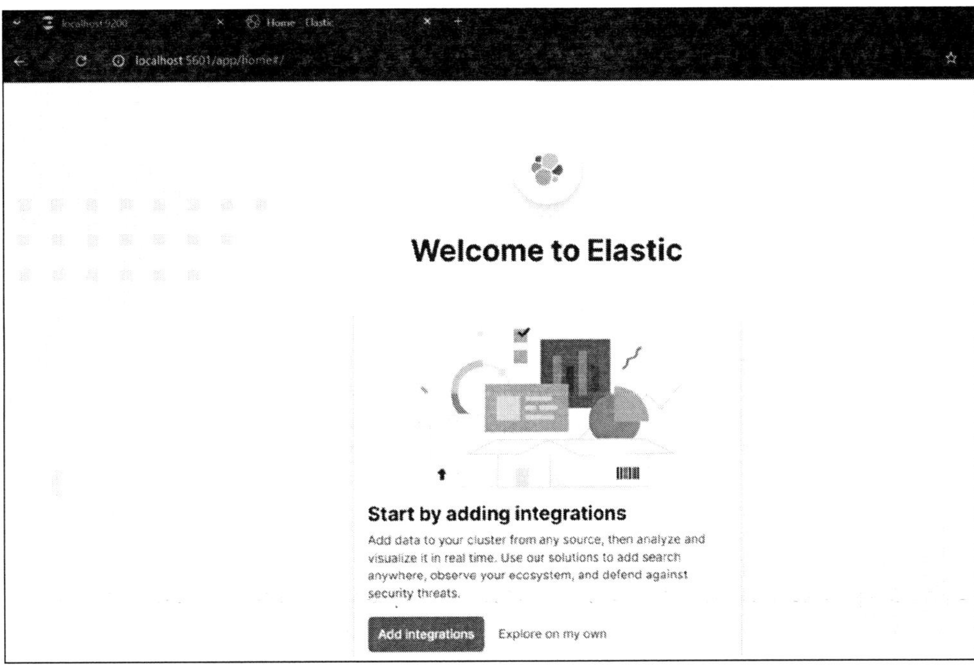

Figure 6.40: *Browser Displaying Kibana Dashboard Running on Port 5601*

Figure 6.40 shows the Kibana dashboard accessed through a web browser on port 5601. The interface confirms that Kibana is running successfully, and is ready to visualize and analyze log data, including Redis logs, for monitoring and troubleshooting purposes.

Step 3: Download and Install Logstash

a. **Download Logstash: https://www.elastic.co/downloads/logstash**

b. **Extract it to D:\elk\logstash**

c. Create a configuration file **`logstash.conf`** in the **config** folder:

```
input {
    redis {
        host => "localhost"
        port => 6379
        data_type => "list"
        key => "logstash"
```

```
        }
    }
    output {
        elasticsearch {
            hosts => ["http://localhost:9200"]
            index => "logs-%{+YYYY.MM.dd}"
        }
        stdout { codec => rubydebug }
    }
```

d. **Start Logstash with the config file:**

```
logstash.bat -f config/logstash.conf
```

e. **Enter `wcl` as root user**

```
wcl -u root
```

f. **`redis-cli` and execute the following command :**

```
RPUSH logstash '{"message":"Hello ELK","timestamp":"2025-02-19T12:00:00"}'
```

```
127.0.0.1:6379> RPUSH logstash '{"message":"Hello ELK","timestamp":"2025-02-19T12:00:00"}'
(integer) 1
127.0.0.1:6379>
127.0.0.1:6379> _
```

Figure 6.41: *Command Executed in Redis CLI to Test Redis Log Functionality*

Figure 6.41 shows a command run in the Redis Command Line Interface (CLI) to verify whether Redis logging is functioning as expected. The output helps confirm that Redis is properly capturing and storing log entries for monitoring and troubleshooting purposes.

g. **Verify the Setup**

   i. Check Logstash logs to see if it is receiving Redis data.

   ii. Open Kibana, go to **`Discover`**, and look for logs in the **`logs-* index`**.

   iii. You should see the test log from Redis.

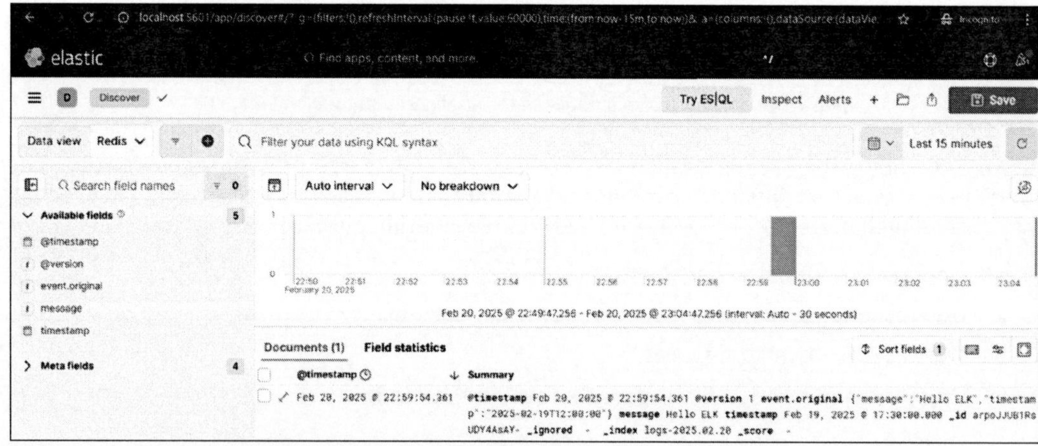

Figure 6.42: *Kibana Dashboard with Redis Log Sample*

Figure 6.42 displays a sample Kibana dashboard showcasing Redis logs. The dashboard helps in filtering, searching, and analyzing Redis-related events, allowing users to gain deeper insights into system activity, and troubleshoot potential issues effectively.

This setup ensures that ELK collects logs from Redis, processes them via Logstash, and visualizes them in Kibana.

Choosing a Redis Monitoring Tool

Selecting the right monitoring tool for Redis is crucial for ensuring that your database runs efficiently, identifying potential issues before they become critical, and fine-tuning its performance. With a wide array of monitoring options available, it is important to choose one that aligns with your specific requirements. The ideal tool for your needs will depend on factors such as the scale of your Redis deployment, how well it integrates with your existing infrastructure, and the level of insight you require into Redis's performance metrics. In the following sections, we will explore these considerations in greater detail to help you make an informed decision.

Important Metrics to Monitor for Optimal Performance

A good Redis monitoring tool should give you a clear picture of how your database is performing. At a minimum, it should track:

- **Memory Usage:** How much memory Redis is consuming, and whether you are approaching any limits.
- **Keyspace Hits and Misses:** How efficiently Redis is handling data lookups.
- **Command Execution Rates:** How frequently commands are being processed.
- **Latency and Response Time:** Whether Redis is responding quickly to requests.

If your workload is small, built-in tools such as the `INFO` command might be enough. But if you are running a high-traffic system, you will likely need a more advanced monitoring solution to keep up with performance trends over time.

Ease of Integration with Monitoring Tools

If you already use a monitoring system such as **Prometheus**, **Datadog**, or **New Relic**, choosing a tool that integrates seamlessly is a smart move.

- **Built-in Redis commands** such as `MONITOR` and `SLOWLOG` are easy to use but only provide real-time insights.
- **Prometheus + Grafana** is a great open-source option if you are comfortable setting up a monitoring stack.
- **Datadog** and **New Relic** offer cloud-based solutions that are easy to set up but come at a cost.

Your choice should depend on whether you prefer a **quick solution with limited insights** or a **fully managed monitoring system with detailed analytics**.

Importance of Alerts and Notifications in Monitoring

Proactive monitoring is crucial if you do not want to find out about issues after they have already caused downtime. A good monitoring tool should allow you to:

- Set alerts for **high memory usage, slow queries, or connection spikes**.
- Receive notifications via **Slack, email, or PagerDuty** when something goes wrong.
- Detect **anomalies in usage patterns** before they lead to bigger problems.

Datadog does a great job of automatically detecting unusual activity through built-in anomaly detection, while **Prometheus `Alertmanager`** lets you configure custom alerting rules.

Scaling Considerations for Monitoring Redis Deployments

If you are running a single Redis instance, you might not need a heavy-duty monitoring tool. But if you have **multiple instances** or **a distributed Redis setup**, you will want something that:

- Can monitor **multiple Redis nodes** simultaneously.
- Does not slow down Redis performance with excessive monitoring queries.
- Stores **historical data** to track trends over time.

Tools such as **Prometheus + Grafana** or **Datadog** can handle large-scale Redis deployments without affecting performance.

Importance of Visual Dashboards for Monitoring

Data is easier to understand when presented visually. If you want clear dashboards with **graphs, charts, and real-time statistics**, consider:

- **Grafana** (best for creating custom dashboards).
- **Datadog** (great pre-built dashboards for Redis).
- **Zabbix or New Relic** (enterprise-friendly monitoring tools).

If you just need raw numbers and logs, built-in Redis tools might be enough. But for **long-term performance tracking and easier troubleshooting**, a dashboard is a must-have.

Cost Considerations for Monitoring Solutions

Your budget plays a big role in deciding which tool to use. Some key things to consider:

- **Open-source options such as Prometheus and Grafana** are free but require setup and maintenance.
- **Cloud-based solutions such as Datadog and New Relic** charge based on usage but offer managed services.
- **Built-in Redis tools** are free and easy to use but limited in what they can track.

If you are running Redis in a production environment, **investing in a solid monitoring tool** is worth it to avoid downtime and performance issues.

Choosing the Right Monitoring Tool for Redis

There is no one-size-fits-all answer, but here is a general guide:

- **For quick, simple monitoring:** Use Redis's built-in tools (`INFO`, `MONITOR`, and `SLOWLOG`).
- **For detailed analytics and visualization:** Use **Prometheus + Grafana**.
- **For a fully managed, all-in-one solution:** Use **Datadog** or **New Relic**.

Thus, by choosing the right monitoring tool, you can **keep Redis running efficiently, prevent performance bottlenecks, and resolve issues proactively before they impact your application**.

Setting up Alerts and Notifications

Monitoring Redis is not just about collecting metrics, it is about acting on them before they become a problem. Imagine your Redis instance suddenly running out of memory, experiencing slow command execution, or losing replication sync. Without proper alerts, these issues could go unnoticed until they start affecting your application.

Setting up alerts and notifications ensures that you stay ahead of potential problems by receiving timely warnings when Redis performance deviates from expected behavior. Thus, whether you are using built-in Redis tools, third-party monitoring solutions such as Datadog, Prometheus, ELK Stack, or cloud-based monitoring services, configuring alerts properly can help you prevent downtime, improve performance, and optimize resource usage.

Key Metrics to Monitor in Redis

Before setting up alerts, it is important to decide **what to monitor**. Here are some of the **key Redis metrics** that can indicate potential issues:

- **Memory Usage (`used_memory`, `maxmemory`):** Prevents out-of-memory errors and unexpected evictions.
- **CPU Utilization (`used_cpu_sys`, `used_cpu_user`):** Ensures that Redis is not overloading your system.
- **Latency (`LATENCY LATEST`, `SLOWLOG GET`):** Detects slow queries and performance bottlenecks.
- **Key Expiration (`expired_keys`, `evicted_keys`):** Monitors key expiration and eviction rates.
- **Connected Clients (`connected_clients`):** Helps to identify excessive client connections or blocked requests.
- **Replication Lag (`master_link_status`, `slave_repl_offset`):** Ensures that replicas stay in sync with the primary instance.

Choosing an Alerting Tool

Since Redis does not have a built-in alerting system, setting up external monitoring tools is essential to ensure that you receive **real-time notifications** when Redis performance metrics cross critical thresholds. The good news is that Redis integrates seamlessly with various monitoring solutions, each catering to different needs. Let us explore some of the most popular tools you can use for alerting.

Prometheus + Alertmanager: Customizable and Self-Hosted Alerting

- If you prefer a self-hosted monitoring stack with complete control over your data, Prometheus combined with Alertmanager is an excellent choice.
- Prometheus continuously scrapes metrics from Redis, and stores them as time-series data.
- Alertmanager then processes these metrics, and triggers alerts based on predefined conditions.

Best for:

- Developers and DevOps teams who want custom alerting rules.
- Organizations looking for an open-source and self-hosted solution.
- Teams that want Grafana dashboards for better visualization of Redis metrics.

Example Use Case: You can set up an alert that triggers when Redis memory usage exceeds 80% for more than 2 minutes.

If the threshold is breached, `Alertmanager` can send a Slack message, email, or PagerDuty notification to your team.

Datadog: AI-Powered, Managed Alerting

If you are looking for a **fully managed** and easy-to-use alerting solution, **Datadog** is a great option.

- It comes with **pre-configured Redis dashboards** and **automatic anomaly detection** powered by AI.
- No complex setup - just install the **Datadog Agent** on your server, and Redis metrics will start flowing into your Datadog dashboard.
- Supports **multi-channel notifications**, including Slack, email, and webhook integrations.

Best for:

- Teams that want **plug-and-play Redis monitoring** without deep configuration.
- Businesses that prefer **AI-based anomaly detection,** instead of manually setting thresholds.
- Cloud-native applications and microservices running Redis at scale.

Example Use Case: If your **Redis replication lag increases** beyond a safe limit, Datadog will **automatically detect the anomaly** and **notify your team** before an outage occurs.

Elasticsearch + Kibana (ELK Stack): Log-Based Alerting

For teams that need **log-based monitoring** in addition to metrics, the **ELK Stack** is an excellent choice.

- **Logstash** collects Redis logs in real-time.
- **Elasticsearch** stores and indexes these logs, allowing for fast searching.
- **Kibana** provides a visual dashboard where you can track **slow queries, key evictions, and out-of-memory errors**.

Best for:

- Engineers who want **detailed logs and deeper insights** into Redis behavior.
- Teams managing **multiple Redis instances** and want **centralized log monitoring**.
- Businesses that need **historical log analysis** to detect patterns and recurring issues.

Example Use Case:

- Set up an **alert that triggers when Redis logs an "OOM command not allowed" error**, indicating that Redis has hit its memory limit.
- The system **sends an email alert** so that engineers can take immediate action to prevent failures.

Cloud Services: AWS CloudWatch, Google Cloud Monitoring, and Azure Monitor

- If you are running Redis in AWS, Google Cloud, or Azure, you can take advantage of built-in cloud monitoring services to track Redis health.
- AWS CloudWatch provides Redis monitoring metrics (if running on AWS ElastiCache).
- Google Cloud Monitoring (formerly Stackdriver) integrates with Cloud Memorystore for Redis.
- Azure Monitor can track Azure Cache for Redis performance and trigger alerts.

Best for:

- Teams using managed Redis services in the cloud (AWS ElastiCache, Google Cloud Memorystore, Azure Cache).
- Businesses that prefer using cloud-native monitoring tools, instead of setting up separate monitoring stacks.
- DevOps teams that want seamless integration with other cloud services.

Example Use Case: In AWS, you can set a CloudWatch alarm to notify you if Redis CPU usage exceeds 75% for 5 minutes.

The alert can trigger an AWS Lambda function that scales up the Redis instance automatically.

Which Alerting Tool Should You Choose?

- If you want full control and customization, go for Prometheus + Alertmanager.
- If you need AI-powered monitoring with minimal setup, Datadog is the best choice.
- If you need detailed Redis logs and historical log analysis, use ELK Stack (Elasticsearch + Kibana).
- If your Redis runs in AWS, Google Cloud, or Azure, leverage CloudWatch, Stackdriver, or Azure Monitor.

No matter which tool you choose, setting up alerts ensures that you stay ahead of Redis performance issues before they impact your application.

Best Practices for Setting Up Redis Alerts

Setting up alerts is crucial for keeping your Redis instance healthy, but too many alerts can become overwhelming. The key is to strike a balance - getting notified when something truly needs attention, without bombarding your team with unnecessary notifications. Here are some best practices to ensure that your alerts are useful, actionable, and effective.

Focus on What Really Matters (Avoid Alert Fatigue)

Not every small change in Redis metrics requires an alert. If you set up alerts for **every minor fluctuation**, your team will start **ignoring notifications**, and real problems could go unnoticed. Instead, focus on **critical performance indicators** such as:

- **Memory usage** (to prevent out-of-memory crashes)
- **High command execution time** (to detect slowdowns)
- **Replication lag** (to ensure data consistency)
- **Key eviction rates** (to prevent unexpected data loss)

By limiting alerts to **meaningful performance issues**, you ensure that when an alert goes off, it is worth investigating.

Use Multi-Level Alerts for Better Prioritization

Not every issue is urgent. Some problems require **immediate attention**, while others can wait a bit. To handle this, set **different alert thresholds**:

- **Warning Level (Yellow Alert):** Triggers when Redis **memory usage hits 70%** or when command execution time **starts increasing**. These alerts act as an **early warning** so that you can investigate before things get worse.

- **Critical Level (Red Alert)**: Triggers when Redis **memory usage exceeds 90%** or when query execution time **spikes beyond acceptable limits**. These alerts indicate that **immediate action is needed** to prevent downtime.

  By setting **tiered alerts**, your team can respond **efficiently** instead of treating every issue as an emergency.

Test Alerts Regularly to Ensure that They Work

An alert is useless if it **fails to trigger when needed** or **goes unnoticed**. That is why it is important to **test your alerts periodically**.

- **Trigger Test Alerts:** Simulate a Redis memory spike, and see if your alert system responds correctly.
- **Check Notification Channels**: Ensure that alerts reach the right people via Slack, email, or PagerDuty.
- **Fine-Tune Alert Sensitivity:** Adjust thresholds to reduce false alarms, while still catching real issues.

Think of your alerting system like a fire alarm you do not want it to go off for burnt toast, but you also do not want it to fail during a real fire.

Connect Alerts to Incident Management for Faster Resolution

Getting notified about an issue is just the first step - **how quickly your team responds makes all the difference**. Instead of relying on emails that might get missed, integrate alerts with **incident management tools** such as:

- **Slack or Microsoft Teams:** Send alerts directly to a team channel, so that engineers can discuss and act.
- **Webhook Integrations:** Connect alerts to automated scripts that **trigger failover mechanisms or scale resources** when needed.

Thus, by linking alerts to **response workflows**, you can **reduce downtime and resolve issues faster**.

Look for Trends, Not Just Spikes

A single performance spike does not always mean there is a problem. Redis workloads naturally fluctuate throughout the day - what matters is whether an issue is a part of a pattern.

Instead of setting alerts for momentary high CPU usage, track average CPU usage over 10 minutes, and set alerts based on sustained trends. This helps distinguish between temporary spikes, and growing problems that need fixing.

What Good Monitoring Looks Like?

- **It tells you a story, not just numbers.** “`Memory up → evictions up → latency up`” `is a narrative. Dashboards and alerts should help you see that chain quickly.`
- **It measures what users feel.** Track latency and error rate alongside Redis metrics (not instead of them).
- **It warns early and clearly.** A quiet alert at 70% memory is better than a blaring pager at

100% with OOM errors.

- **It is noise-resistant.** One alert should suggest one likely fix; avoid alert storms for the same root cause.
- **It is tied to action.** `Every alert should have a runbook hint: "If evictions spike → confirm` **`maxmemory-policy`**`, trim large keys, add TTLs, or scale."`

Conclusion

In this chapter, we explored how to effectively **monitor Redis for optimal performance**, dividing the discussion into two key parts based on the tools and techniques used.

In **Part 1**, we explored Redis's built-in monitoring commands and introduced third-party tools such as RedisInsight, Prometheus, and Grafana to establish a strong foundation for monitoring Redis performance.

In **Part 2**, we expanded our monitoring approach by integrating **Datadog and the ELK stack**, which provide deeper insights and log analysis capabilities. Datadog helped in **real-time alerting, advanced performance monitoring, and cloud integration**, making it suitable for large-scale deployments. Meanwhile, ELK provided a centralized logging system that allowed us to **analyze logs, detect anomalies, and troubleshoot performance bottlenecks efficiently**. We also discussed setting up **custom alerts and notifications** to proactively detect and resolve issues before they affect the system performance.

Thus, by leveraging these monitoring techniques, from **basic built-in commands to advanced third-party tools**, you can create a **comprehensive Redis monitoring strategy**. This ensures **better visibility, faster troubleshooting, proactive alerting, and overall system stability**, keeping your Redis environment optimized for high performance and reliability.

In the next chapter, "*Lua Scripting with Redis for Enhanced Functionality*" we will dive into how you can make Redis even smarter using Lua scripts. You will also learn how to write and run simple scripts, see real-world examples, and understand when and why scripting can give you a big advantage. By the end, you will be able to extend Redis's power in ways that regular commands alone cannot achieve.

CHAPTER 7
Lua Scripting with Redis for Enhanced Functionality

Introduction

Redis is known for its speed and efficiency, but sometimes, a single command is not enough to get the job done. Certain operations require multiple commands to be executed together, and if you send them one by one, it adds extra network overhead and can slow things down. This is where **Lua scripting** becomes a game-changer.

Lua is a lightweight, high-level scripting language designed for embedded use. Redis integrates Lua directly into its core, allowing you to write and execute custom scripts using the `EVAL` and `EVALSHA` commands. These scripts are **executed on the Redis server itself**, which offers several powerful advantages.

With Lua, you can write custom scripts that **run directly on the Redis server**, allowing multiple commands to be executed as a single unit. This not only reduces the back-and-forth communication between your application and Redis, but also ensures atomic execution, meaning all the commands in the script execute atomically, without interference from other clients. Lua scripting helps you streamline complex tasks, optimize performance, and even **enforce custom business logic right within Redis**.

In this chapter, we will start with the **basics of Lua scripting**, covering how to write and execute scripts in Redis. We will break it down step by step so that even if you are new to Lua, you can follow along easily. As we progress, we will explore **real-world use cases** where Lua can make a real difference, such as **implementing rate limiting, handling transactions efficiently, and reducing redundant data processing**.

By the end of this chapter, you will not only understand how Lua works in Redis but also how to use it to **enhance your applications, improve performance, and solve complex problems with ease**. Thus, whether you are optimizing an existing system or building a new one, Lua scripting will become a powerful tool in your Redis toolkit.

Structure

In this chapter, the following topics will be covered:

- Advanced Capabilities Unlocked by Lua Scripting
- Advanced Lua Script Operations in Redis
    - Recap: Basic Lua Script Format
    - Conditional Logic in Lua

- Working with Hashes: Conditional Field Update
- Using Loops for Batch Processing
- Rate Limiting Example Using Lua
- Return Types in Lua Scripts
- Pipelining vs. Lua Scripting
- Error Handling in Lua
- Caching Complex Computations

Advanced Capabilities Unlocked by Lua Scripting

Lua scripting in Redis unlocks a range of capabilities that go beyond what you can achieve with standard Redis commands or even transactions alone.

Here are some key enhancements provided by Lua scripts:

- **Atomic Multi-Command Operations:** Lua scripts allow you to execute a series of commands as a single atomic operation. This means you can combine several steps, such as reading, computing, and writing, without the risk of interference from other clients. While Redis transactions provide atomicity, they lack the ability to include conditional logic or flow control between commands.

  Note: Redis executes Lua scripts atomically because it is single-threaded. While a Lua script is running, Redis does not process any other client commands, ensuring uninterrupted and consistent execution.

- **Conditional Logic and Flow Control:** With Lua, you can incorporate complex business logic using conditionals (if/else) and loops. For instance, you can check a value and only update it if it meets a specific condition. This level of decision-making is not possible with standalone Redis commands.
- **Reduced Network Latency:** Hence, by bundling multiple commands into a single script, you eliminate the need for multiple round-trips between the client and the server. This can significantly enhance performance, especially in latency-sensitive applications.
- **Custom Computation and Aggregation:** Lua enables you to perform on-the-fly calculations, data transformations, or aggregations directly on the server. This means you can manipulate data or generate complex responses without having to retrieve all the raw data and process it on the client side.
- **Enhanced Error Handling:** Lua scripts allow you to include error-checking and handling mechanisms within the script itself. This helps in managing unexpected situations or invalid states more gracefully than a sequence of independent Redis commands.

In summary, Lua scripting in Redis is ideal for scenarios that require combining multiple operations, enforcing conditional updates, or executing custom logic in an atomic and efficient manner, capabilities that standard Redis commands or transactions alone cannot provide.

Advanced Lua Script Operations in Redis

Lua scripting in Redis is like having a tiny, efficient brain running directly inside your database. It allows you to write small programs that execute on the Redis server itself, eliminating the need for multiple round-trips between your application and the database. This can drastically improve performance, especially when you are dealing with complex operations that need to happen quickly and reliably.

While basic Lua scripting is great for simple tasks such as setting or retrieving a value or modifying a single key, Redis becomes even more powerful when you tap into its advanced scripting capabilities. With Lua, you can perform operations like conditional logic (for example, "only do this if that key exists"), iterate over lists or sets, run batch operations on multiple keys, and work with different data types all in one atomic, server-side execution. That means everything in the script runs as a single, isolated operation when executed as Redis server-side Lua, without interference from other clients.

In this section, we are going to dive deeper into these advanced Lua scripting techniques. You will see real-world examples and detailed explanations that will help you understand not just how to write these scripts but also when and why to use them. Thus, whether you are optimizing performance, implementing logic that cannot be easily done from the client side, or just want to reduce latency, advanced Lua scripting in Redis can be a game-changer!

Recap: Basic Lua Script Format

Let us write a Lua script that sets a key to a value, **only if the key does not already exist**. This is a classic use case where Lua scripting helps centralize logic in a single program. Atomic execution is achieved when the same logic is executed using Redis server-side Lua with EVAL, as shown later in this section.

Note: The following example demonstrates client-side Lua scripting using a Redis Lua client. This script runs outside Redis and is not executed atomically. Redis server-side Lua scripting using EVAL is covered immediately after this example.

Lua Script Logic (Client-Side Lua)

- **Create a file and name it `check_key.lua`.**
- **Copy the following code:**

```
-- Load the Redis client module
local redis = require "redis"

-- Connect to the Redis server (default: localhost:6379)
local client = redis.connect('127.0.0.1', 6379)

-- Define the key and value (these could come from user input or config)
local key = "mykey"
local value = "myvalue"

-- Check if the key exists
local exists = client:exists(key)

-- If it doesn't exist, set the key and print confirmation
if exists == false then
    local result = client:set(key, value)
    print("Key set successfully: " .. result)
else
    print("Key already exists")
end
```

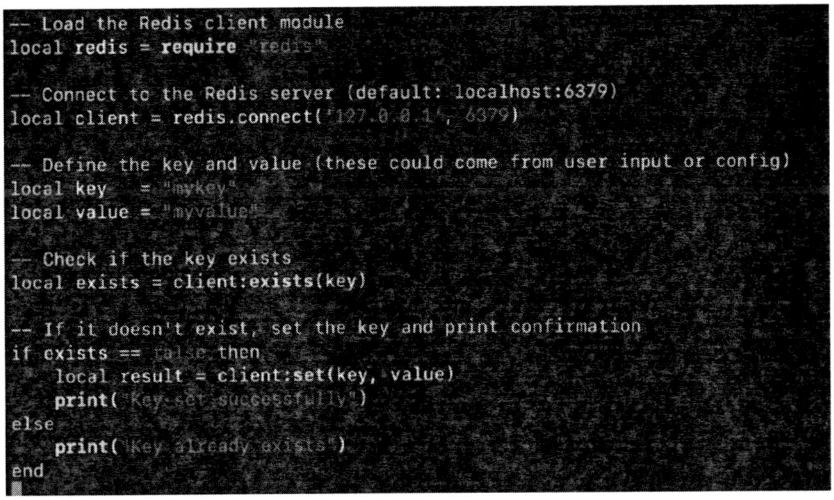

```
-- Load the Redis client module
local redis = require "redis"

-- Connect to the Redis server (default: localhost:6379)
local client = redis.connect('127.0.0.1', 6379)

-- Define the key and value (these could come from user input or config)
local key   = "mykey"
local value = "myvalue"

-- Check if the key exists
local exists = client:exists(key)

-- If it doesn't exist, set the key and print confirmation
if exists == false then
    local result = client:set(key, value)
    print("Key set successfully")
else
    print("Key already exists")
end
```

Figure 7.1: *Lua Script Which Sets a Value if the Key Does Not Exist*

Figure 7.1: The script checks if the key exists. If it does not, it sets the value. This ensures that the key is only set once, and avoids overwriting the existing data.

- **Execute the Lua Script**

  ```
  lua check_key.lua
  ```

```
Key already exists
```

Figure 7.2: *Output When Running the Lua Script check key.lua*

The output in *Figure* 7.2 shows that the key already exists in Redis, so the script skipped setting a new value and returned the message "**`Key already exists`**". This confirms that the conditional logic in the Lua script is working as intended.

What This Script Does?

- Connects to Redis.
- Checks if **`mykey`** exists.
- If not, sets **`mykey = "myvalue"`** and prints a confirmation.
- If it already exists, it prints "**`Key already exists`**".

How to Use It with Redis CLI (via `EVAL`)

```
EVAL "if redis.call('exists', KEYS[1]) == 0 then return redis.call('set', KEYS[1],
ARGV[1]) else return 'Key already exists' end" 1 mykey myvalue
```

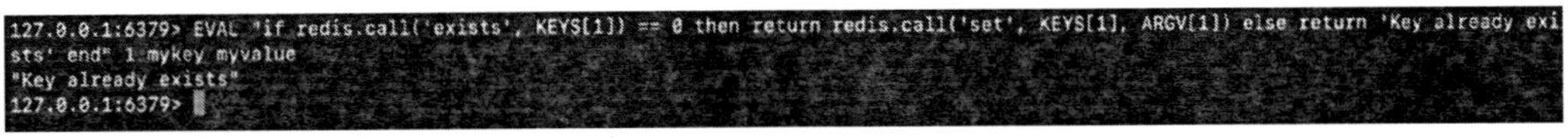

```
127.0.0.1:6379> EVAL "if redis.call('exists', KEYS[1]) == 0 then return redis.call('set', KEYS[1], ARGV[1]) else return 'Key already exi
sts' end" 1 mykey myvalue
"Key already exists"
127.0.0.1:6379>
```

Figure 7.3: *Redis CLI Using EVAL, Instead of a Lua Script*

Figure 7.3 shows that the Lua logic is being executed directly from the Redis CLI using the **`EVAL`** command. Instead of running a separate script file, the entire script is passed inline, allowing immediate execution of conditional logic within Redis.

Explanation of the `EVAL` Command:

- The first argument is the Lua script enclosed in double quotes.

- The number 1 tells Redis that you are passing 1 key (`mykey`).
- The key name `mykey` becomes `KEYS[1]` in the Lua script.
- The value `myvalue` becomes `ARGV[1]` in the Lua script.

Why This Matters?

In a typical application, if you wanted to implement this logic without scripting, you would need to:

1. Check if the key exists (`GET`)
2. If not, set the key (`SET`)

However, another client could change the key between these two operations, leading to race conditions. With Lua, the whole logic runs **atomically**, solving this problem.

Conditional Logic in Lua

Conditional logic is one of the most powerful aspects of using Lua scripting with Redis. It allows you to make decisions dynamically inside the script, based on the current state of Redis keys. With conditions, you can write scripts that check whether a key exists, compare values, update data based on certain rules, and avoid race conditions when executed as server-side Lua using EVAL, all in a single atomic operation.

Why Use Conditional Logic in Redis Lua Scripts?

Imagine you are building a login system, and want to store a user's session token only if they are not already logged in. Or maybe, you are caching the result of an expensive operation, and want to avoid overwriting an existing cache entry, unless it has expired. These are perfect examples of where conditional logic becomes essential.

Example Use Case: Setting a Key Only If It Does Not Exist, with Expiration

Let us write a Lua script that:

1. Checks if a session key already exists.
2. If not, it sets a new session token and sets an expiration time.
3. If it exists, it simply returns a message stating that the session is already active.

Client-Side Lua Script (Plain Lua Using redis-lua):

- **Create a file, and name it `session_check.lua`**
- **Copy the following code:**

```
-- Load Redis client
local redis = require "redis"

-- Connect to Redis
local client = redis.connect('127.0.0.1', 6379)

-- Define keys and values
local session_key = "session:user:123"
local session_token = "ABCDEFG123456"
local expiration = 3600  -- in seconds

-- Check if the session already exists
local exists = client:exists(session_key)

if exists == false then
    -- Set session token and expiration
    client:set(session_key, session_token)
```

```
        client:expire(session_key, expiration)
        print("New session started")
    else
        print("Session already active")
    end
```

```
-- Load Redis client
local redis = require "redis"

-- Connect to Redis
local client = redis.connect('127.0.0.1', 6379)

-- Define keys and values
local session_key = "session:user:123"
local session_token = "ABCDEFG123456"
local expiration = 3600  -- in seconds

-- Check if the session already exists
local exists = client:exists(session_key)

if exists == false then
    -- Set session token and expiration
    client:set(session_key, session_token)
    client:expire(session_key, expiration)
    print("New session started")
else
    print("Session already active")
end
```

***Figure 7.4**: Lua Script for Setting a Key if It Does Not Exist*

In *Figure* 7.4, this script demonstrates a basic conditional check using Lua. It verifies if a key exists in Redis, and if not, it sets the key with a specified value. This ensures that the existing data is not accidentally overwritten.

- **Run it with**

  `lua session_check.lua`

- **Expected Output**

  First Run:

  `"New session started"`

***Figure 7.5**: The Output Confirms a New Session was Started*

Second Run (within 1 hour):

`"Session already active."`

```
Session already active
```

***Figure 7.6**: The Output Confirms that the Existing Session is Already Active*

What the Script Does:

- Uses the Redis EXISTS command via the redis-lua client to check if the session key already exists.
- If it **does not exist**, it sets the key with the given session token and adds an expiration using **`EXPIRE`**.
- If it **`already exists`**, it returns a message indicating that the session is active.

How does this help?

Without Lua scripting, you would have to:

1. Check if the key exists (`GET` or `EXISTS`).
2. If it does not, then `SET` it and apply `EXPIRE`.

But this introduces a race condition. Between your `EXISTS` and `SET`, another client could modify the key. **Redis server-side Lua scripts (executed via EVAL) solve this by wrapping all the logic into one atomic operation.** Nothing else can modify the data between the checks and the writes.

How to Use It with Redis CLI (via `EVAL`)

```
EVAL "if redis.call(\"exists\", KEYS[1]) == 0 then redis.call(\"set\", KEYS[1],
ARGV[1]) redis.call(\"expire\", KEYS[1], tonumber(ARGV[2])) return \"New session
started\" else return \"Session already active\" end" 1 session:user:123
ABCDEFG123456 3600
```

```
127.0.0.1:6379> EVAL "if redis.call(\"exists\", KEYS[1]) == 0 then redis.call(\"set\", KEYS[1], ARGV[1]) redis.call
(\"expire\", KEYS[1], tonumber(ARGV[2])) return \"New session started\" else return \"Session already active\" end"
 1 session:user:123 ABCDEFG123456 3600
"Session already active"
```

***Figure** 7.7: Executing a Lua Script via Redis CLI Using EVAL*

In *Figure* 7.7, this output shows the result of running a Lua script using the `EVAL` command in the Redis CLI. Since the session key already exists, the script returns "**Session already active**", indicating that no new session was created. This demonstrates how conditional logic in Lua can help manage session states safely and atomically.

Working with Hashes: Conditional Field Update

Hashes in Redis are widely used for storing structured data such as user profiles, product records, or application settings. Often, you may want to update a specific field in a hash only if it already exists. This ensures that you do not accidentally insert a new field or overwrite data unintentionally.

Lua scripting provides an elegant way to implement this kind of conditional logic. Atomic execution is achieved when the script runs server-side using Redis EVAL, as shown later in this section. By using the `HEXISTS` command inside a Lua script, you can first check if a field exists within a hash, and then update it only if that condition is met.

This pattern is particularly useful when dealing with sensitive fields, audit data, or application logic, where new fields should be added only via explicit workflows.

Use Case: Update the "`status`" field in a user profile hash only if it already exists

Let us say you have a Redis hash that stores user information under the key user:1001. You want to update the status field to "`active`" only if the status field already exists. If it does not exist, the script should do nothing and return a custom message.

Let us write a client-side Lua script (using redis-lua) that:

1. Connects to Redis.
2. Checks if a specific field exists in a hash.
3. Updates the field only if it exists.
4. Prints the result.
    - **Create a file and name it `conditional_hash_update.lua`**

      `vim conditional_hash_update.lua`

- **Write the following in the script:**

```
-- Load the Redis client module
local redis = require "redis"

    -- Create a connection to Redis
local client = redis.connect('127.0.0.1', 6379)

-- Define the hash key and the field/value you want to update
local hash_key = "user:1001"
local field_name = "status"
local new_value = "active"
-- Check if the field exists in the hash
local exists = client:hexists(hash_key, field_name)
-- Conditional logic: update only if the field exists
if exists == 1 then
-- HEXISTS returns 1 if the field exists, otherwise 0
    client:hset(hash_key, field_name, new_value)
    print("Field updated")
else
    print("Field does not exist")
end
```

Figure 7.8: *Lua Script to Update a Field Only If It Exists in a Hash*

Figure 7.8: This script checks whether a specific field exists in a Redis hash using **`HEXISTS`**. If the field is present, it updates the value; otherwise, it skips the update. This ensures that only the existing fields are modified, preventing accidental creation of new fields in the hash.

- **Execute Lua Script**

```
lua conditional_hash_update.lua
```

```
Field does not exist
```

Figure 7.9: *Output of Lua Script Indicating "Field Does Not Exist"*

In *Figure* 7.9, The output confirms that the specified field was not found in the hash, so the script returned "**`Field does not exist`**", without performing any update. This behavior ensures safe and conditional updates, preventing unintended changes to the non-existent fields.

- **Let us populate the data and rerun the script:**

```
redis-cli HSET user:1001 name "Karnish Master" email "karnish.master@
testredis.com" status "inactive"
```

```
127.0.0.1:6379> HSET user:1001 name "Karnish Master" email "karnish.master@testredis.com" status "inactive"
(integer) 3
```

Figure 7.10: *Populating Hash Data Using HSET Command*

In *Figure* 7.10, this command uses HSET to populate a Redis hash with user information, including name, email, and status. It serves as the initial data setup for demonstrating Lua scripts that perform conditional updates on specific hash fields.

- **Then run the script to update the status field to "active"**

```
lua conditional_hash_update.lua
```

```
Field updated
```

Figure 7.11: *Output of Lua Script conditional_hash_update.lua*

Figure 7.11: The output displays the message **"Field updated"**, confirming that the specified field existed in the Redis hash and was successfully updated by the Lua script. This showcases how conditional logic in Lua ensures that only the existing fields are modified.

How to Use It with Redis CLI (via EVAL):

The following example shows how the same logic can be executed directly inside Redis using server-side Lua, ensuring atomic execution.

```
EVAL "if redis.call(\"hexists\", KEYS[1], ARGV[1]) == 1 then redis.call(\"hset\",
KEYS[1], ARGV[1], ARGV[2]) return \"Field updated\" else return \"Field does not
exist\" end" 1 user:1001 status active
```

Expected Output:

```
"Field updated"
```

Why Use This Approach:

- Ensures data safety by preventing unintended writes.
- Avoid inserting new fields unless explicitly allowed.
- Maintains atomicity and avoids race conditions when executed as a server-side Lua script using EVAL.
- Very useful in multi-user systems or concurrent applications.

Using Loops for Batch Processing

One of the powerful features of Lua scripting in Redis is the ability to use loops, which allow you to process multiple keys or values in a single script. Atomic execution is achieved when the same logic is executed server-side using Redis EVAL, as shown later in this section. This is incredibly useful for batch operations, such as deleting multiple keys, updating multiple fields, incrementing counters, or performing validations, all without multiple round-trips to the server.

Loops enable you to iterate through the **`KEYS`** or **`ARGV`** arrays and apply logic uniformly across a batch of items, making your scripts both efficient and concise.

Use Case: Delete Multiple Keys in a Single Operation

Imagine you have a set of temporary keys (like cache entries or session tokens) that need to be deleted in one go. Instead of issuing multiple **`DEL`** commands, you can pass all the keys to a Lua script and loop through them inside Redis.

How to Try This:

- **Set up some temporary keys:**

```
redis-cli set temp:1 "a"
redis-cli set temp:2 "b"
redis-cli set temp:3 "c"
```

Note: The following example demonstrates *client-side Lua scripting* using a Redis Lua client. This script runs outside Redis and is **not atomic**. A server-side atomic version using EVAL is shown afterward.

- **Create a file, and name it `batch_delete.lua`:**

```
vim batch_delete.lua
```

- **Copy the following code:**

```
-- Load the Redis client module
local redis = require "redis"

-- Connect to Redis server
local client = redis.connect('127.0.0.1', 6379)

-- Define a list of keys to delete
local keys = { "temp:1", "temp:2", "temp:3" }

-- Loop through keys and delete each
for i, key in ipairs(keys) do
    local deleted = client:del(key)
    print("Deleted:", key, "(Result:", deleted, ")")
end

print("All keys processed.")
```


```
-- Load the Redis client module
local redis = require "redis"

-- Connect to Redis server
local client = redis.connect('127.0.0.1', 6379)

-- Define a list of keys to delete
local keys = { "temp:1", "temp:2", "temp:3" }

-- Loop through keys and delete each
for i, key in ipairs(keys) do
    local deleted = client:del(key)
    print("Deleted:", key, "(Result:", deleted, ")")
end

print("All keys processed.")
```

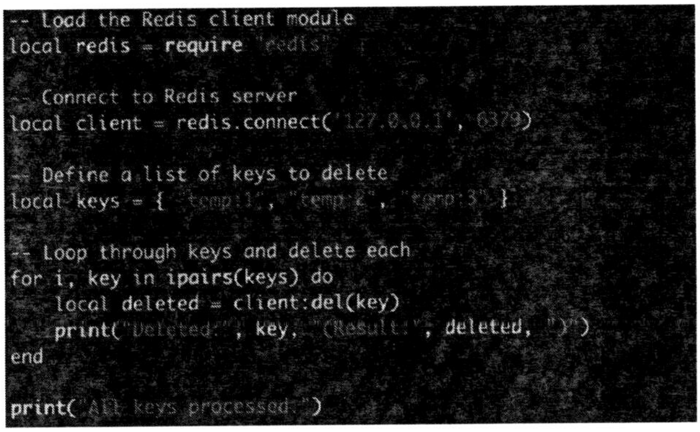

Figure 7.12: *Lua Script to Delete Multiple Keys in a Single Operation*

Figure 7.12: This Lua script uses a loop to iterate over a list of keys and delete each one using the **DEL** command. It performs batch deletions in a single script execution. Atomic execution is guaranteed when the same logic is executed server-side using EVAL, making it efficient and safe for batch cleanup tasks in Redis.

- **Save the script and run it:**

```
lua batch_delete.lua
```

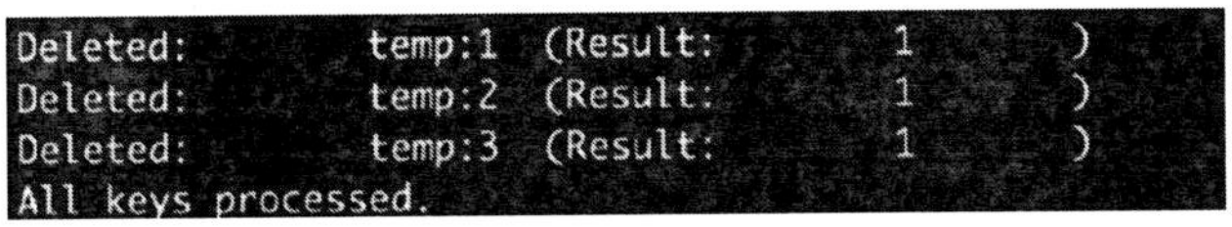

```
Deleted:        temp:1  (Result:        1       )
Deleted:        temp:2  (Result:        1       )
Deleted:        temp:3  (Result:        1       )
All keys processed.
```

Figure 7.13: *Output of Lua Script batch_delete.lua*

Figure 7.13: The output confirms that each specified key has been deleted successfully. The script processes the list of keys in a loop, and deletes them one by one, printing a confirmation for each. This demonstrates how Lua can be used for efficient batch key deletions in Redis.

- **How to Use It with Redis CLI (via EVAL):**

```
redis-cli EVAL "for i = 1, #KEYS do redis.call('del', KEYS[i]) end return 'All keys deleted'" 3 temp:1 temp:2 temp:3
```

```
"All keys deleted"
```

***Figure 7.14**: Output of Redis CLI via EVAL, Stating "All Keys Deleted"*

Figure 7.14: This output shows the result of executing a Lua script through the Redis CLI using the **`EVAL`** command. The script loops through multiple keys and deletes them in a single atomic operation. The message, **`"All keys deleted"`** confirms successful execution and cleanup.

Explanation:

- The Lua script uses a for loop: **`for i = 1, #KEYS do ... end`**
    - **`#KEYS`** gives the total number of keys passed.
    - **`KEYS[i]`** accesses each key in the loop.
- **`redis.call('del', KEYS[i])`** deletes each key.
- The script returns a confirmation string after deletion.

Why is this useful?

- **Atomicity**: The Redis-side Lua script runs as a single atomic operation; no other commands can interfere while it runs.
- **Efficiency**: One round trip, instead of multiple **`DEL`** commands from the client.
- **Scalability**: This pattern can be extended for batch updates, inserts, and checks, too.

Summary

Loops inside Redis Lua scripts make batch processing simple and powerful. Hence, whether you are cleaning up temporary keys, resetting user data, or processing multiple records at once, scripting loops allow you to perform complex multi-key operations efficiently. When executed as server-side Lua scripts using EVAL, these operations are also safe and atomic.

Rate Limiting Example Using Lua

Overview

Rate limiting is a critical technique for protecting your Redis-backed applications from abuse, whether it is excessive API calls, login attempts, or resource usage. With Lua scripting in Redis, you can implement a rate limiter. Atomic enforcement is achieved when the same logic is executed server-side using Redis EVAL, as shown later in this section.

One popular pattern is the **token bucket** or **fixed window** rate limiter, which allows a user to perform up to a certain number of actions within a specific time window.

Use Case: Allow a User to Make Up to 5 Requests Every 60 Seconds

Let us build a rate limiter using Lua that:

1. Tracks the number of requests a user has made.
2. Increments the counter each time a request is made.
3. Sets an expiration of 60 seconds (if not already set).
4. Allows the request only if the current count is below the defined limit.

Note: The following example demonstrates *client-side Lua scripting* using a Redis Lua client. This script runs outside Redis and is **not atomic**. A fully atomic server-side version using EVAL is shown later.

- **Create a file and name it `rate_limiter.lua`:**

```
vim rate_limiter.lua
```

- **Copy the following code into the script:**

```
-- Load Redis client
local redis = require "redis"

-- Connect to Redis
local client = redis.connect('127.0.0.1', 6379)

-- Define rate limiter config
local key = "rate:user:123"
local limit = 5
local window = 60

-- Get current count
local current = tonumber(client:get(key) or "0")

if current + 1 > limit then
    print("Rate limit exceeded. Please try again later.")
else
    client:incr(key)
    client:expire(key, window)
    print("Request allowed.")
end
```

Note: This example behaves like a sliding window limiter because the TTL is refreshed on each request.

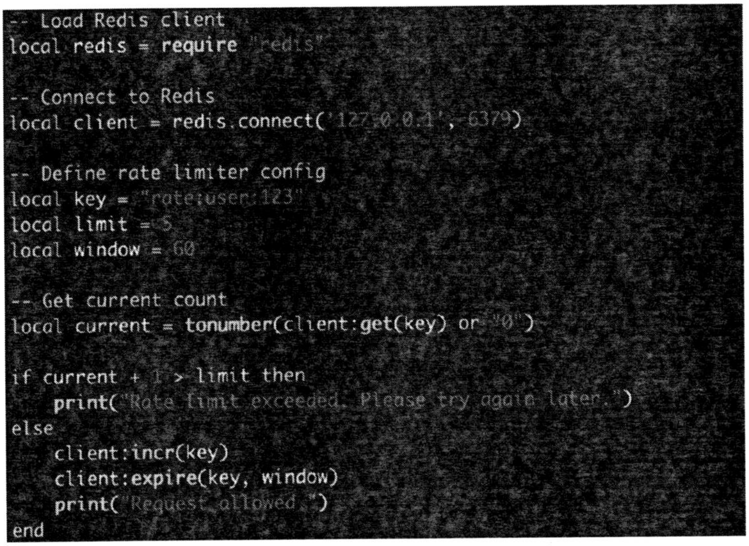

Figure 7.15: *Lua Script for Implementing a Rate Limiter*

Figure 7.15: This script defines a rate limit for user **123**, allowing a maximum of 5 requests within a 60-second window. It checks the request count stored in Redis under the key **rate:user:123**. If the user is within the limit, the count is incremented, and an expiration is set; otherwise, the script blocks the request, enforcing the rate limit policy.

- **Save it and run:**

  ```
  lua rate_limiter.lua
  ```

- **It allows you to increment the key five times (within 60 seconds) and then give your error message.**
- **Output when executed the first five times:**

```
Request allowed.
```

Figure 7.16: *Lua Script Output When Executed First 5 Times within 60 Seconds*

Figure 7.16: This output shows the result of executing the rate-limiting Lua script for the first five requests, within the defined 60-second window. Since the request count has not exceeded the set limit of 5, the script allows each request and returns **`"Request allowed"`** as confirmation.

- **Output when executed the sixth time:**

```
Rate limit exceeded. Please try again later.
```

Figure 7.17: *Lua Script Output When Executed the 6th Time within 60 Seconds*

Figure 7.17: This output shows the result of running the rate-limiting Lua script for the sixth time within the 60-second window. Since the predefined limit of five requests has already been reached, the script blocks further access and returns a message indicating that the rate limit has been exceeded.

- **How to Use It with Redis CLI (via `EVAL`):**

```
redis-cli EVAL "local key = KEYS[1] local limit = tonumber(ARGV[1]) local
ttl = tonumber(ARGV[2]) local current = tonumber(redis.call('get', key) or
'0') if current + 1 > limit then return 0 else redis.call('incr', key) redis.
call('expire', key, ttl) return 1 end" 1 rate:user:123 5 60
```

Explanation

a. **`KEYS[1]`** = The key that stores the request count (for example, rate:user:123).

b. **`ARGV[1]`** = Rate limit (for example, 5 requests).

c. **`ARGV[2]`** = Time window in seconds (for example, 60 seconds).

d. If the user exceeds the limit, return 0 (reject).

e. If within the limit, increment the counter, set TTL, and return 1 (allow).

- **Repeat the command up to 5 times, and you will continue to get 1. On the 6th attempt (within 60 seconds), you will get the following Output:**

  ```
  (integer) 0
  ```

  This means that the request was blocked due to the rate limit being reached.

Summary

This Lua-based rate limiter is ideal for real-time applications, APIs, login systems, or any use case where request limits are essential. Thus, by implementing the logic directly inside Redis using Lua scripting, you gain efficiency and simplicity. When executed server-side using Redis EVAL, the same logic also provides atomic enforcement.

In the next section, we will look at how to **return multiple values or structured data from Lua scripts to support more complex operations**.

Return Types in Lua Scripts

Overview

When writing Lua scripts in Redis, understanding **what your script returns** and how Redis interprets that return is just as important as the logic inside the script itself. Redis supports a variety of return types from Lua scripts, each of which maps to specific Redis response types.

This flexibility allows you to build powerful scripts that can return single values, collections, or even mixed results, depending on your use case.

Supported Return Types in Redis Lua Scripts

Lua Return Type	Redis Return Type	Example Return
`string`	Bulk String	`"ok"`
`number`	Integer	`42`
`boolean`	Integer (1) or Null Bulk Reply	`true → 1, false → nil`
`table (array)`	Multi-bulk reply	`["one", "two"]`
`nil`	Null Bulk Reply	`(nil)`

Table 7.1: *Mapping of Lua Return Types to Redis Return Types*

This table shows how different Lua return types are interpreted and returned by Redis when executing Lua scripts using the **`EVAL`** or **`EVALSHA`** commands.

Use Case: Return Multiple Key Values from a Lua Script

Let us say you want to get the values of multiple keys using a Lua script and return them as a list (array). You might do this to:

- Read multiple values atomically.
- Handle fallback logic if keys are missing.
- Simplify client-side processing.

Example: Pre-populate Keys

```
redis-cli SET user:1001:name "Karnish"
redis-cli SET user:1001:email "karnish@xyz.com"
```

- **Create a file and name it `return_values.lua`:**

  ```
  vim return_values.lua
  ```

- **Copy the following into this script:**

  ```
  local redis = require "redis"
  local client = redis.connect('127.0.0.1', 6379)

  -- Define the keys
  local key1 = "user:1001:name"
  local key2 = "user:1001:email"

  -- Fetch values
  local val1 = client:get(key1)
  local val2 = client:get(key2)

  -- Print values
  print("Name:", val1 or "nil")
  print("Email:", val2 or "nil")
  ```

```
local redis = require "redis"
local client = redis.connect('127.0.0.1', 6379)

-- Define the keys
local key1 = "user:1001:name"
local key2 = "user:1001:email"

-- Fetch values
local val1 = client:get(key1)
local val2 = client:get(key2)

-- Print values
print("Name:", val1 or "nil")
print("Email:", val2 or "nil")
```

Figure 7.18: *Lua Script for Returning Multiple Values*

Figure 7.18: This Lua script retrieves the **name** and **email** fields stored under separate Redis keys, and returns both values together. It demonstrates how multiple related pieces of data can be fetched and retrieved together in a single Lua execution. Atomic execution is achieved when the same logic is executed server-side using Redis EVAL, as shown below.

- **Run it with `Lua return_values.lua`:**

```
Name:   Karnish
Email:  karnish@xyz.com
```

Figure 7.19: *Output of Lua Script return_values.lua*

Figure 7.19: The output displays the retrieved values for `name` and `email` keys from Redis. The script executes both `GET` operations within Lua, and returns the results as a combined response, showing how multiple values can be fetched together in a single Lua execution. Atomic execution is achieved when the same logic is executed server-side using Redis EVAL, as shown below.

- **Using `EVAL` in `redis-cli`:**

```
redis-cli EVAL "local val1 = redis.call('get', KEYS[1]) local val2 = redis.
call('get', KEYS[2]) return {val1, val2}" 2 user:1001:name user:1001:email
```

Explanation

- **`KEYS[1] = user:1001:name`**
- **`KEYS[2] = user:1001:email`**
- **`val1`** and **`val2`** retrieve the values of these keys
- The script returns them as a **Lua table**, which Redis interprets as a **multi-bulk reply (array).**

Summary

Returning values in Lua scripts is simple but powerful. Hence, whether you return single strings, numbers, booleans, or arrays, Redis handles them gracefully and efficiently. This makes it easy to:

- Compose richer responses.
- Minimize round trips.
- Support atomic batch reads.

Understanding return types helps you write more expressive and efficient Lua scripts tailored to your application's needs.

Simulating Structured Data in Client-Side Lua

Overview

By default, when a Lua script returns a **table (array-like structure)**, Redis interprets it as a flat list (multi-bulk reply). However, in some scenarios, you may want to work with structured or grouped data, commonly represented as nested tables in Lua.

It is important to note that Redis does not support returning nested or associative Lua tables from server-side scripts. While Redis itself supports associative data through its Hash data structure, Lua scripts executed via EVAL or EVALSHA can only return flat, sequential tables to clients.

Use Case: Grouped Data for a User Profile

Let us say you want to fetch a user's basic info and activity metrics, and display them grouped by category using client-side Lua.

External Lua Script (for reference)

- **Create a file, and name it `nested_return.lua`:**

  ```
  vim nested_return.lua
  ```

- **Copy the following code into the above script and save:**

  ```
  local redis = require "redis"
  local client = redis.connect('127.0.0.1', 6379)

  local profile = {
      basic = {
          name = client:get("user:1001:name"),
          email = client:get("user:1001:email")
      },
      activity = {
          logins = client:get("user:1001:logins"),
          last_seen = client:get("user:1001:last_seen")
      }
  }

  -- Print formatted result
  print("User Profile:")
  for section, data in pairs(profile) do
      print(section .. ":")
      for key, value in pairs(data) do
          print("  " .. key .. " = " .. tostring(value))
      end
  end
  ```

```
local redis = require "redis"
local client = redis.connect('127.0.0.1', 6379)

local profile = {
    basic = {
        name = client:get("user:1001:name"),
        email = client:get("user:1001:email")
    },
    activity = {
        logins = client:get("user:1001:logins"),
        last_seen = client:get("user:1001:last_seen")
    }
}

-- Print formatted result
print("User Profile:")
for section, data in pairs(profile) do
    print(section .. ":")
    for key, value in pairs(data) do
        print("  " .. key .. " = " .. tostring(value))
    end
end
```

Figure 7.20: *Lua Script nested_return.lua for Returning Structured Data*

Figure 7.20: This script demonstrates how to simulate a nested structure in Lua by organizing Redis key values into grouped tables, for example, basic information like name and email, as well as activity details like login count and last seen date. Although Redis does not support true nested returns, this approach makes it easy to structure and interpret the data on the client side.

- **Populate additional data:**

  ```
  redis-cli SET user:1001:logins 120
  redis-cli SET user:1001:last_seen "2025-03-28"
  ```

- **Execute the LUA script and check:**

  ```
  lua nested_return.lua
  ```

```
User Profile:
activity:
  last_seen = 2025-03-28
  logins = 120
basic:
  name = Karnish
  email = karnish@xyz.com
```

Figure 7.21: *Output of Lua Script nested_return.lua*

Figure 7.21: The output displays grouped user data categorized into sections such as basic and activity. Each section contains relevant fields like name, email, login count, and last seen. This output illustrates how structured information can be simulated and printed in a readable format using Lua, even though Redis itself returns data in a flat structure.

Interpretation

- Redis does not support returning nested tables. In this example, structure is handled entirely within client-side Lua and printed for demonstration purposes.
- This makes it easy for client applications (Node.js, Python, PHP, and so on) to parse the data into structured JSON-like objects.

Summary

Redis does not natively support true nested tables in Lua script results, but you can simulate structure using key-value arrays and print structured output on the client side, keeping Redis interactions simple and predictable. This is especially useful when returning grouped results from a single script, reducing the need for multiple client-side parsing steps.

This approach is ideal for:

- User profile data
- Grouped analytics
- Dashboard-ready results
- API responses that expect structured output

Pipelining vs. Lua Scripting

Both **pipelining** and **Lua scripting** in Redis are techniques used to optimize performance and reduce latency, but they solve different problems and operate in fundamentally different ways. Understanding their strengths, limitations, and use cases will help you choose the right approach for various tasks in Redis.

What is Pipelining?

Pipelining is a technique where the client sends multiple commands to Redis in a single network request, without waiting for individual responses. The server processes them in order and returns the results back to the client in a batch.

This reduces the number of network round-trip requests and improves throughput, especially when executing a high number of independent commands.

Benefits of Pipelining:

- Reduces latency caused by the round-trip.
- Increases throughput for bulk operations.
- Ideal for independent, non-dependent operations.

Pipelining Example (Redis CLI simulation using MULTI)

While true pipelining is a client-side feature (used via libraries in Python, Node.js, and so on), you can simulate it like this:

```
redis-cli
> MULTI
> SET user:1:name "Karnish test"
> SET user:1:email "karnish@testingthis.com"
> INCR user:1:logins
> EXEC
```

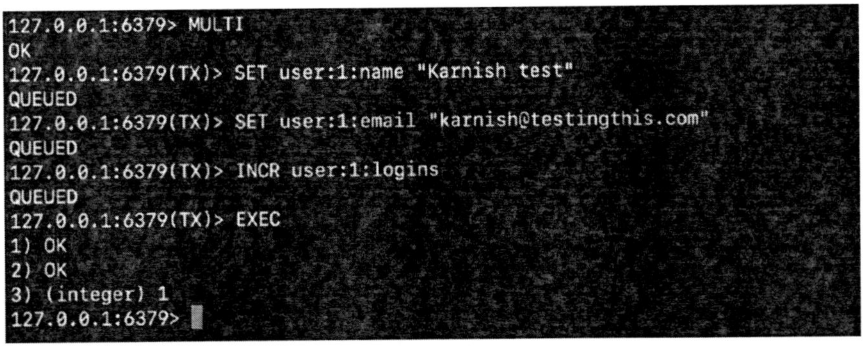

```
127.0.0.1:6379> MULTI
OK
127.0.0.1:6379(TX)> SET user:1:name "Karnish test"
QUEUED
127.0.0.1:6379(TX)> SET user:1:email "karnish@testingthis.com"
QUEUED
127.0.0.1:6379(TX)> INCR user:1:logins
QUEUED
127.0.0.1:6379(TX)> EXEC
1) OK
2) OK
3) (integer) 1
127.0.0.1:6379>
```

Figure 7.22: *Redis CLI Simulation Using MULTI for Pipelining*

Figure 7.22: This figure demonstrates the use of the **MULTI** command in the Redis CLI to simulate pipelining. Multiple commands are queued and then executed together using EXEC.

Note: This approach simulates batching using MULTI/EXEC transactions. It is not true pipelining, as commands are queued and executed atomically rather than being sent and processed in parallel.

In actual code (for example, Python), pipelining might look like this:

```
pipe = redis_client.pipeline()
pipe.set("user:1:name", "Karnish test")
pipe.set("user:1:email", "karnish@testingthis.com")
pipe.incr("user:1:logins")
responses = pipe.execute()
```

Each command is **independent** and does **not rely on previous ones** for execution.

Lua Scripting

Lua scripting in Redis allows you to write custom logic that is executed atomically on the server. This is useful when you need conditional execution, looping, or multiple dependent commands that must be run together, without interference from other clients.

Unlike pipelining, Lua ensures atomicity; the entire script is executed as a single, isolated operation.

Benefits of Lua Scripting:

- Ensures **atomic** execution.
- Allows **conditional logic**, loops, and branching.
- Useful for **dependent operations**, where one command's result affects the next.

Lua Scripting Example: Set key only if it does not already exist

```
redis-cli EVAL "if redis.call('exists', KEYS[1]) == 0 then redis.call('set', KEYS[1],
ARGV[1]) return 'Key set' else return 'Key exists' end" 1 user:1:name Karnish
```

```
"Key exists"
```

Figure 7.23: *Output of Redis CLI Using EVAL to Check If Key Exists, and Set It If Not Exists*

Figure 7.23: This output shows the result of executing a Lua script via **EVAL** that first checks whether a key exists using **EXISTS**. If the key is absent, it sets a new value; otherwise, it leaves the existing key untouched. The script then returns a confirmation message based on the key's presence, demonstrating atomic check-and-set logic in Redis.

This script:

- Checks if the key **user:1:name** exists.
- If not, set it to "**Karnish**".
- If it does, it does nothing and returns a message.

All of this happens **atomically**, and no other client can modify **user:1:name** during this execution.

Comparison Table

Feature	Pipelining	Lua Scripting
Reduces network latency	✅	✅
Atomic execution	✅ **Yes (MULTI/EXEC)**	✅ **(script runs as one transaction)**
Supports conditional logic	❌	✅
Supports loops	❌	✅
Server-side execution	❌ **(client-driven)**	✅
Good for bulk inserts	✔	✅
Good for dependent logic	❌	✅

Table 7.2: *Feature Comparison between Redis Pipelining and Lua Scripting*

Table 7.2: This table compares Redis pipelining and Lua scripting across key features such as atomicity, conditional logic, server-side execution, and suitability for different use cases.

When to Use What?

Scenario	Use Pipelining?	Use Lua Scripting?
You need to update 1000 keys with independent values.	✅	❌
You want to set a key only if it does not exist.	❌	✅
You need to increment a value and check if it exceeds a threshold in one step.	❌	✅
You want to reduce latency for independent reads.	✅	❌
You want to fetch and process multiple values as a group.	❌	✅

Table 7.3: *Choosing between Pipelining and Lua Scripting Based on Use Case*

Table 7.3: This table outlines common scenarios and indicates whether pipelining or Lua scripting is better suited for each, helping you to choose the right tool based on the operation's nature and requirements.

Real-World Analogy

- Pipelining is like submitting multiple forms at once to a counter. Each form is independent, and the clerk processes them in order.
- Lua scripting is like submitting a request with rules: "*If A is not present, then do B and C together*." The clerk reads the rules and performs the task without interruption.

Summary

- Use **pipelining** when you have **many independent commands** and want to reduce network latency.
- Use **Lua scripting** when you need **conditional logic, atomic operations, or complex server-side logic**.

Both are performance optimization tools, but they serve different purposes. Understanding their distinctions helps you build more efficient and reliable Redis-based systems.

Error Handling in Lua

Overview

Error handling is a crucial part of any scripting or programming environment, and Lua scripting within Redis is no exception. Although Redis Lua scripts are typically short and controlled, there can still be situations where things go wrong, such as operating on keys with the wrong data type, calling invalid Redis commands, or performing unsupported operations.

Redis provides a way to handle runtime Redis command errors inside Lua scripts using the **`pcall()` (protected call)** function. By wrapping potentially error-prone calls inside **`pcall()`**, you can prevent the script from aborting execution and instead return a controlled error response.

What is `pcall()`?

The **`pcall()`** function in Lua stands for "**protected call**." It runs a function call in protected mode and catches any error that might occur. Instead of halting execution with an error, it returns a status and result.

LUA Syntax:

```
local success, result = pcall(function()
    return redis.call("COMMAND", ...)
end)
```

- Success will be true if the operation succeeds, or false, if it fails.
- The result will contain the actual result or an error message.

Use Case: Gracefully Handling Errors When Accessing Keys

Let us write a script that tries to get a value from a key, and handles the case where an unexpected error might occur (for example, trying to use the wrong command or the wrong data type).

- **Set up the wrong type of key to simulate an error:**

  ```
  redis-cli HSET user:profile name "testdata" email "testdata@testdabc.com"
  ```

- **Create a file and name it `safe_get.lua`:**

  ```
  vim safe_get.lua
  ```

- **Copy the following code:**

  ```
  local redis = require "redis"
  local client = redis.connect('127.0.0.1', 6379)

  local key = "user:profile"

  local function safe_get()
      local ok, result = pcall(function()
          return client:get(key)
      end)

      if ok then
          print("Value:", result)
      else
          print("Error:", result)
      end
  end

  safe_get()
  ```

```
local redis = require "redis"
local client = redis.connect('127.0.0.1', 6379)

local key = "user:profile"

local function safe_get()
    local ok, result = pcall(function()
        return client:get(key)
    end)

    if ok then
        print("Value:", result)
    else
        print("Error:", result)
    end
end

safe_get()
```

Figure 7.24: *Lua Script safe_get.lua to Gracefully Handle Errors*

Figure 7.24: This script uses Lua's **`pcall()`** function to safely attempt a GET operation from Redis. If the key access is successful, it prints the value; if an error occurs, such as a type mismatch, it catches the error and returns a friendly message. This approach makes the client-side Lua script more robust and fault-tolerant by handling Redis command errors gracefully.

- **Now run the Lua script expecting a string:**

  `lua safe_get.lua`

```
Error: /opt/homebrew/share/lua/5.4/redis.lua:380: redis error: WRONGTYPE Operation against a key holding the wrong kind of value
```

Figure 7.25: *Output of Lua Script safe_get.lua*

Figure 7.25: The output shows the result of executing the **`safe_get.lua`** script. In this case, the script encountered a type-related error, such as attempting to GET a key holding a non-string data type, and handled it gracefully using **`pcall()`**. Instead of failing, it returned an error message, demonstrating how Lua can manage exceptions safely within Redis scripts.

- **Output:**

  `"Error: WRONGTYPE Operation against a key holding the wrong kind of value"`

  This shows how the script continues safely, instead of failing abruptly.

- **Lua Script with Error Handling (via EVAL in redis-cli):**

```
redis-cli EVAL "local success, result = pcall(function() return redis.
call('get', KEYS[1]) end) if success then return result else return 'Error: '
.. result end" 1 user:profile
```

Explanation:

- The script attempts to **`GET`** the value of **`user:profile`**.
- If the call succeeds, it returns the value.
- If it fails (for example, the key exists but is a hash, not a string), it catches the error and returns a message like:

  `"Error: WRONGTYPE Operation against a key holding the wrong kind of value."`

Use Cases for Error Handling in Redis Lua Scripts:

Situation	Example
Accessing a key with the wrong data type	Trying to GET a hash
Using an invalid Redis command	Typo or unsupported op
Unexpected nil values	Attempting math ops on nil
Operating on keys you expect to be set	Gracefully handling unexpected runtime errors

***Table 7.4:** Common Use Cases for Error Handling in Redis Lua Scripts*

Table 7.4: This table highlights situations where error handling is important within Lua scripts, along with examples of potential issues that can arise during script execution.

Summary

- Use **`pcall()`** in Lua scripts to catch and handle Redis command errors safely.
- This makes your Redis logic more robust and fault-tolerant, especially in complex systems.
- Even if something goes wrong, your script can fail gracefully and return meaningful information to your application or user.

Caching Complex Computations

Overview

One of Redis's most powerful use cases is caching, especially when it comes to computationally expensive operations. Thus, whether you are generating a report, rendering data-heavy dashboards, or fetching external API data, such operations can consume significant CPU or network resources.

Rather than executing these costly operations every time, you can compute the result once, cache it in Redis, and retrieve it quickly on subsequent requests. This pattern drastically improves performance, reduces load, and ensures a faster user experience.

Using **server-side Lua scripting with EVAL**, this caching logic can be performed atomically, avoiding race conditions where multiple clients might try to recompute the same result simultaneously.

Use Case: Cache a Computation Result Only if Not Already Present

Let us say you are calculating the total sales for a region, and the result does not change frequently. Instead of recalculating this every time, you can:

1. Check if the result is already cached.
2. If yes, return the cached value.
3. If not, cache the new value (provided from the application logic) and return it.

Try It Step by Step:

Step 1: No value yet in Redis

```
redis-cli DEL report:region:sales
```

Step 2: Run the Lua script

```
redis-cli EVAL "local value = redis.call('get', KEYS[1]) if not value then
redis.call('set', KEYS[1], ARGV[1]) return ARGV[1] else return value end" 1
report:region:sales 75820
```

Output:

```
"75820"
```

"75820"

***Figure 7.26**: Output of Lua Script Run with EVAL to Set a Value for Sales*

Figure 7.26: This output shows the result of a Lua script executed via the **EVAL** command, which checks if a sales key already exists in Redis. Since the key was not present, the script sets a new value and returns it. This demonstrates how Lua can be used to cache computed results only when needed, helping optimize performance and avoid redundant computations.

Step 3: Run it again (will return cached value):

```
redis-cli EVAL "local value = redis.call('get', KEYS[1]) if not value then
redis.call('set', KEYS[1], ARGV[1]) return ARGV[1] else return value end" 1
report:region:sales 90000
```

Output:

```
"75820"
```

> **Note:** *It does not store **90000** because a value already exists.*

Optional: Add Expiration for Freshness

You can modify the script to cache the value with a TTL (Time-to-Live):

```
redis-cli EVAL "local value = redis.call('get', KEYS[1]) if not value then redis.
call('set', KEYS[1], ARGV[1]) redis.call('expire', KEYS[1], tonumber(ARGV[2])) return
ARGV[1] else return value end" 1 report:region:sales 75820 300
```

- Adds a TTL of **300 seconds (5 minutes)**.
- Useful when your computation should be refreshed periodically.

Full External Lua Script

- **Create a file, and name it `cache_result.lua`:**

  ```
  vim cache_result.lua
  ```

- **Copy the following code into your script:**

  ```
  local redis = require "redis"
  local client = redis.connect('127.0.0.1', 6379)

  local key = "report:region:sales"
  local computed_value = "75820"

  -- Try to get the cached value
  local value = client:get(key)

  if not value then
      client:set(key, computed_value)
      print("Cached new value:", computed_value)
  else
      print("Using cached value:", value)
  end
  ```

```
local redis = require "redis"
local client = redis.connect("127.0.0.1", 6379)

local key = "report:region:sales"
local computed_value = "75820"

-- Try to get the cached value
local value = client:get(key)

if not value then
    client:set(key, computed_value)
    print("Cached new value:", computed_value)
else
    print("Using cached value:", value)
end
```

Figure 7.27: *Lua Script cache_result.lua for Caching Computed Results*

Figure 7.27: This script checks whether the key **report:region:sales** already exists in Redis. If it does not, the script sets a new computed value and caches it; if the key is already present, it returns the existing cached result. This pattern is ideal for caching expensive computations and reducing redundant processing by storing the result for future reuse.

Note: This client-side approach is not atomic; atomic behavior is achieved when the same logic is executed using Redis EVAL.

- **Execute the script:**

```
lua cache_result.lua
```

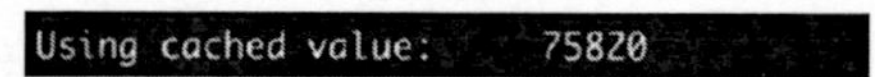

Figure 7.28: *Output of Lua Script cache_result.lua*

Figure 7.28: The output displays the cached value of the key `report:region:sales`, indicating that the script detected the key already exists in Redis. Instead of recalculating or overwriting the value, it returned the existing cached result. This behavior demonstrates the efficient use of Redis to serve previously computed data.

When to Use This Pattern?

Scenario	Benefit
Expensive SQL/reporting queries	Save compute time
API responses from external services	Reduce external calls
Processed image/video metadata	Avoid redundant processing
Dynamic dashboard or analytics widgets	Faster page load times
Backend rule engines or scoring functions	Consistent results

Table 7.5: *When to Use Lua Scripting for Caching and Computation Patterns*

Table 7.5: This table outlines scenarios where using Lua scripts (often with caching) is beneficial, along with the specific advantages each use case gains in terms of performance, reliability, or efficiency.

Advanced Example: Compute and Cache Total from Redis Hash Fields

Let us now build on the "Caching Complex Computations" concept with a version where the value is computed inside Redis itself using the existing keys, instead of being passed from the application.

This showcases real server-side computation and caching the result directly as one of the most powerful use cases for Lua scripting in Redis.

Use Case

Imagine a hash in Redis that tracks monthly sales for a region:

```
Key: sales:region:north
Fields: jan, feb, mar, apr, …
```

You want to:

1. Compute the total sum of all sales values stored in the hash.
2. Cache the total in a separate key.
3. Return the total (from cache if available, otherwise compute and cache it).

Step-by-Step Lua Script Logic:

Here is what we will do:

1. Check if the total is already cached.
2. If it is cached, return it.
3. If not:
    - Fetch all fields from the hash.
    - Sum the values.
    - Cache the result with an expiration (optional).
    - Return the total.

Redis CLI Version (Using `EVAL`):

```
redis-cli EVAL "
local cached = redis.call('get', KEYS[2])
if cached then
  return cached
else
  local fields = redis.call('hvals', KEYS[1])
  local sum = 0
  for i = 1, #fields do
    sum = sum + tonumber(fields[i])
  end
  redis.call('set', KEYS[2], sum)
  redis.call('expire', KEYS[2], tonumber(ARGV[1]))
  return sum
end
" 2 sales:region:north cache:region:north:total 300
```

Explanation:

- `KEYS[1]`: Source hash with monthly sales (**`sales:region:north`**)
- `KEYS[2]`: Destination key to store the cached total (**`cache:region:north:total`**)
- `ARGV[1]`: Expiration time in seconds (for example, 300 = 5 minutes)

Test the Script:

Step 1: Populate a hash:

```
redis-cli HSET sales:region:north jan 12000 feb 15800 mar 17500 apr 14000
```

Step 2: Run the script (first time = computes and caches):

```
redis-cli EVAL "
local cached = redis.call('get', KEYS[2])
if cached then
  return cached
else
  local fields = redis.call('hvals', KEYS[1])
  local sum = 0
  for i = 1, #fields do
    sum = sum + tonumber(fields[i])
  end
  redis.call('set', KEYS[2], sum)
  redis.call('expire', KEYS[2], tonumber(ARGV[1]))
  return sum
end
" 2 sales:region:north cache:region:north:total 300
```

Expected Output:

```
(integer) 59300
```

```
(integer) 59300
```

***Figure 7.29:** Output of Redis CLI Version Using EVAL for Computing and Caching Sales Total*

Figure 7.29: This output shows the result of executing a Lua script via the **EVAL** command in the Redis CLI.

Step 3: Run again (within TTL = returns cached value)

```
redis-cli GET cache:region:north:total
```

Output:

```
"59300"
```

External Lua Script Version:

- **Create a file and name it `compute_and_cache_sum.lua`:**

  ```
  vim compute_and_cache_sum.lua
  ```

- **Copy the following code into the newly created file:**

  ```
  local redis = require "redis"
  local client = redis.connect('127.0.0.1', 6379)

  local source_key = "sales:region:north"
  local cache_key = "cache:region:north:total"
  local ttl = 300  -- cache for 5 minutes

  -- Check if value is already cached
  local cached = client:get(cache_key)
  if cached then
    print("Using cached total:", cached)
  else
    local fields = client:hvals(source_key)
    local sum = 0
  ```

```
  for i = 1, #fields do
    sum = sum + tonumber(fields[i])
  end

  client:set(cache_key, sum)
  client:expire(cache_key, ttl)

  print("Computed and cached total:", sum)
end
```

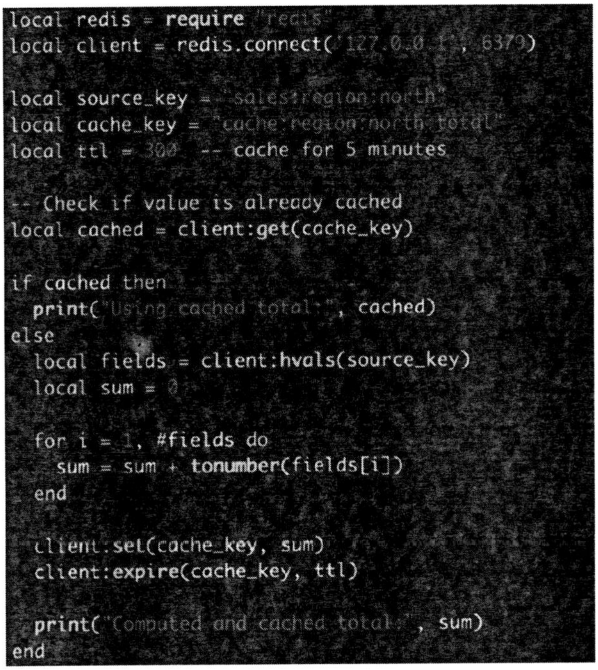

```
local redis = require 'redis'
local client = redis.connect('127.0.0.1', 6379)

local source_key = "sales:region:north"
local cache_key = "cache:region:north:total"
local ttl = 300  -- cache for 5 minutes

-- Check if value is already cached
local cached = client:get(cache_key)

if cached then
  print("Using cached total:", cached)
else
  local fields = client:hvals(source_key)
  local sum = 0

  for i = 1, #fields do
    sum = sum + tonumber(fields[i])
  end

  client:set(cache_key, sum)
  client:expire(cache_key, ttl)

  print("Computed and cached total:", sum)
end
```

***Figure 7.30**: Lua Script compute_and_cache_sum.lua for Summing and Caching Hash Data*

Figure 7.30: This script calculates the total of all monthly sales values stored in a Redis hash. If the total is already cached in a separate key, it returns the cached value directly. Otherwise, it computes the sum, caches the result, and then returns it. This technique improves performance by avoiding repeated aggregation and efficiently ensuring that the total is always fetched.

Summary

This advanced Lua scripting pattern allows you to:

- Perform computations **within Redis** using the existing key data.
- **Avoid redundant recalculations** by caching the result.
- Ensure the **correctness and atomicity of the logic when executed using Redis EVAL**, even under concurrent load.

This approach is ideal for:

- **Dashboards and analytics** (for example, cached KPIs)
- **Aggregated metrics** from real-time data
- **Snapshot caching** of rolling counters or batch values

Caching complex computations using Lua scripts in Redis provides:

- **Atomicity**: Avoids race conditions when multiple clients try to write simultaneously.
- **Performance**: It reduces the load on your backend or computation layer.
- **Simplicity**: It encapsulates the caching logic on the server in a single script.

Thus, whether you are dealing with heavy processing, slow APIs, or rarely changing data, this technique can dramatically improve your application's performance and responsiveness.

Conclusion

In this chapter, we took a deep dive into the world of **Lua scripting with Redis**, and hopefully, you have seen just how powerful and flexible it can be! Redis is already known for its speed and simplicity, but Lua scripting unlocks a whole new layer of functionality by letting you run logic right on the Redis server **close to the data, fast, and atomic**.

We started with the basics: how to write a Lua script, pass keys and arguments, and use the **EVAL** command. From there, we moved into more advanced use cases such as conditional updates, batch processing with loops, rate limiting, error handling, and even caching complex computations. Each of these examples showed how you can take what might normally require multiple round trips from the application and instead handle it all at once, **efficiently and safely, within a single script**.

We also explored how Lua handles return values, whether it is a simple string, a number, or a table of values, and how you can use these responses to make smarter decisions on the client side. Error handling with **pcall()** gave us the ability to safely manage unexpected situations, without crashing the whole script. By the time we reached caching logic and computed aggregations from Redis itself, it became clear just how much control Lua offers when it comes to shaping your application's behavior.

One of the biggest takeaways is this: **Lua scripts in Redis do not just perform operations; they let you think in logic**, the same way your application does, but do it right where your data lives. This brings major benefits, fewer race conditions, less back-and-forth between client and server, and faster execution for operations that would otherwise be complex or risky outside Redis.

Of course, Lua scripting is not always the answer. For simple commands, Redis is already great on its own. But when you need to bundle multiple steps into one atomic operation, or when you are looking to squeeze out every bit of performance and safety, **Lua is your go-to tool!**

As you continue exploring Redis, keep Lua in mind whenever you encounter a situation that requires smarter logic, tighter consistency, or just fewer moving parts. In the next chapters, we will cover how to safely use Lua scripts in production, manage and reuse them efficiently, and debug them when things go wrong, so that you can make the most out of this incredible feature that Redis has to offer.

CHAPTER 8

Mastering Redis Replication - Part 1

Introduction

When you first start working with Redis, it is often on a small scale, a single server, a few keys, blazing fast performance, and everything feels wonderfully simple. But as your application grows, and you start handling real users, real traffic, and real reliability expectations, things begin to change.

Imagine this: Your Redis instance goes down, and suddenly, sessions are lost, APIs start timing out, and dashboards stop loading. Or maybe, your app is so read-heavy that your single Redis server starts to feel the pressure. This is where Redis replication steps in, not just as a convenience, but as a **fundamental building block for scaling, performance, and fault tolerance**.

Terminology Note: Primary/Replica vs. Master/Slave

In earlier versions of Redis documentation and command outputs, replication roles were commonly referred to as **master** and **slave**. In more recent Redis versions and official documentation, these terms have been replaced with the more inclusive **primary** and **replica**, while preserving the same underlying replication model.

Throughout **this and subsequent chapters**, we primarily use the **primary/replica** terminology to align with modern Redis practices and current documentation. However, you may still encounter the terms **master** and **slave** in certain diagrams, command outputs, or examples where their usage helps reinforce conceptual understanding or reflects legacy environments.

Both sets of terms refer to the same replication roles:

- **Master → Primary**
- **Slave → Replica**

Please note that this naming difference does not affect Redis behavior in any way. The replication architecture, commands, configuration, and runtime behavior remain identical, regardless of the terminology used.

Structure

In this chapter, we will cover the following topics:

- Understanding Redis Replication
- How Redis Replication Works
- Setting up a Basic Primary-Replica Configuration
- Replication Configuration in `redis.conf`
- Verifying Replication Status
- Understanding the Replication Flow

Understanding Redis Replication

At its core, Redis replication allows one Redis server **(called the primary)** to be mirrored by **one or more replica servers** (sometimes referred to as "`slaves`" though Redis now prefers "`replicas`"). These replicas are exact copies of the primary; they automatically sync with it, and reflect any changes made.

In other words, when your application writes data to the primary, that **data is asynchronously propagated to the replicas** behind the scenes. This happens continuously and efficiently, without needing any manual intervention.

Why Use Replication?

Here are some real-world reasons why replication is a must-have in serious Redis deployments:

- **High Availability:** If the primary goes offline, one of the replicas can be promoted either manually or automatically using Redis Sentinel. This ensures that your application does not suffer downtime due to a single point of failure.
- **Read Scaling:** You can spread read traffic across multiple replicas. Instead of having one server handle thousands of reads per second, you can load and balance that traffic across replicas, reducing pressure on the primary.
- **Data Safety and Redundancy:** Replicas act as live backups. Even if something goes wrong on the primary, your data still lives on elsewhere, often just milliseconds behind.
- **Non-Disruptive Operations:** You can use replicas for background jobs, analytics, or slow queries that would otherwise bog down your main Redis instance. This separation keeps the user-facing parts of your app running smoothly.

Where Replication Fits in Redis Architecture

Redis replication is not a bolt-on feature; it is a foundational capability. It is the basis for:

- **Redis Sentinel**: which adds automated monitoring and failover
- **Redis Cluster**: which supports horizontal scaling with partitioned data
- **Disaster recovery and backup strategies**

In this chapter, you will learn how to set up replication from scratch, understand how it works under the hood, configure it properly for production, and use it in advanced scenarios such as failover, read scaling, and *caching computed results.*

How Redis Replication Works

Now that we understand why replication is essential, it is time to lift the hood and see how Redis actually performs it. While replication might feel like magic at first, '*write here, and it shows up there*', it is built on a clear and reliable mechanism that is both efficient and surprisingly elegant.

Redis replication is asynchronous by design, which means the primary does not wait for replicas to acknowledge the changes. This makes writes not only super-fast, but it also introduces some nuances like the possibility of replicas briefly falling behind. Let us walk through how it all works, step by step.

The Initial Handshake: Full Synchronization

When a new replica is connected to a primary, the process begins with a full synchronization. This is how Redis ensures that the replica gets a complete, accurate snapshot of the primary's current data.

Here is what happens:

1. **Connection Established:** The replica connects to the primary and sends the `PSYNC` command (or `SYNC` in older versions).
2. **Snapshot Created (RDB):** The primary takes a snapshot of the current dataset using the **RDB** (Redis Database) format. This is a binary representation of the entire keyspace at that moment.
3. **Data Transfer Begins:** While the snapshot is being transferred to the replica, the primary continues processing new writes from clients. But instead of losing them, it buffers these new commands in memory.
4. **Replica Loads Snapshot:** The replica receives and loads the snapshot into memory. After that, it replays the buffered write commands from the primary to bring itself fully up to date.
5. **Continuous Sync Begins:** Once the initial sync is complete, the primary sends every new write command to the replica in real time.

So, even if the replication process takes a few seconds or more, the replica does not miss any data changes during that window, thanks to Redis's clever buffering!

Continuous Replication

After the full `sync`, Redis enters the steady state of replication. At this point:

- Every new write operation (**`SET`, `HSET`, `INCR`, and so on**) that the primary receives is immediately forwarded to all connected replicas.
- This is done using a lightweight command stream over a persistent TCP connection.
- Redis does this efficiently, and with minimal overhead, which is why replication feels almost real-time.

It is important to note that **replication is still asynchronous**. So if a replica temporarily disconnects, it may lag slightly behind the primary.

What Happens When a Replica Disconnects?

Network failures happen. So, what does Redis do when a replica loses connection with the primary?

That depends on how long the replica was offline.

Scenario A: Short Disconnection → Partial Resynchronization

If the replica reconnects within a reasonable time window, and if the primary has retained enough command history in its replication backlog buffer, then Redis performs a partial resynchronization:

- The primary sends only the missing commands (based on replication offsets).
- No RDB snapshot is needed.
- The replica catches up quickly and efficiently.

Scenario B: Long Disconnection → Full Resynchronization

If too much time has passed, or if the primary has restarted and lost its backlog history, the replica must perform a full resync again, just like when it first connected.

What is the Replication Backlog?

Redis maintains a fixed-size circular buffer called the replication backlog. It stores recent write commands that were sent to replicas. This buffer:

- is used for partial resyncs.
- is defined by the **`repl-backlog-size`** setting (default: 1MB).
- should be tuned according to your write volume and expected network behavior.

If your replicas frequently disconnect and reconnect, a larger backlog can prevent costly full resyncs.

Important Terms to Understand

Term	Description
`master_link_status`	Shows whether the replica is connected to the primary.
`master_last_io_seconds_ago`	How long ago the replica received data from the primary.
`Offset`	The current replication offset. Used to determine synchronization progress.
`replid and second_replid`	Replication IDs. Used to uniquely identify the primary's data history.
`repl-backlog-size`	Size of the replication backlog. Critical for partial sync.

Table 8.1: *Key Replication Metrics and Their Meanings in Redis*

Real-Time Monitoring: `INFO` replication

From any Redis instance, you can run:

```
redis-cli INFO replication
```

Sample Output from a Standalone Redis Server:

```
role:master
connected_slaves:0
master_failover_state:no-failover
master_replid:ca8d37a343335f5aa09ba989134accc9fdf12053
master_replid2:0000000000000000000000000000000000000000
master_repl_offset:0
second_repl_offset:-1
repl_backlog_active:0
repl_backlog_size:1048576
repl_backlog_first_byte_offset:0
repl_backlog_histlen:0
```

Figure 8.1: *Output of INFO Replication Command Executed on a Standalone Redis Server*

Figure 8.1: This figure shows the result of running the **`INFO` replication** command on a standalone Redis instance. It confirms that the server is operating as a primary with no connected replicas, which is typical in non-replicated or single-node deployments.

Sample output on a replica:

```
role:slave # terminology retained in INFO output for backward compatibility
master_host:127.0.0.1
master_port:6379
master_link_status:up
master_last_io_seconds_ago:2
slave_repl_offset:124891
```

Sample output on a primary:

```
role:master # terminology retained in INFO output for backward compatibility
```

```
connected_slaves:1
slave0:ip=127.0.0.1,port=6380,state=online,offset=124891,lag=0
```

This gives you insight into the replication health and how in sync your replicas are.

NOTE: Redis INFO output uses legacy terminology such as slave/master for backward compatibility.

Asynchronous vs. "Synchronous-like" Replication in Redis

Asynchronous (default):

- **What it means:** The primary replies to the client before replicas have applied the write.
- **Why it is fast:** `No waiting on network/replicas` → **lowest latency**.
- **Trade-offs:** During failover, the **last few writes can be lost** if replicas have not received them (a.k.a. replication lag). Monitoring lag and backlog size is important.

"Synchronous-like" with WAIT:

- **What it means:** Redis does not offer true, fully synchronous replication, but you can ask the primary to **block until N replicas acknowledge** the write using WAIT.
- **Why it helps:** `Reduces the chance of losing the latest writes during failover` → **stronger durability**.
- **Trade-offs:** You are now **adding latency** and making writes sensitive to network hiccups or slow replicas.

Summary

Redis replication is lightweight, fast, and flexible. It begins with a full data sync, then keeps the replica up to date by streaming every change the primary receives. If a replica drops out, Redis does its best to catch it up using the replication backlog. With the right configuration, replication in Redis just works and forms the basis for high availability, horizontal scaling, and disaster recovery.

In the next section, we will walk through **how to set up Redis replication** yourself, using real instances and commands.

Setting Up a Basic Primary-Replica Configuration

Now that we understand how Redis replication works behind the scenes, let us get our hands dirty and actually set it up. Fortunately, Redis makes replication incredibly simple to configure, whether you are running everything on your local machine or across different servers.

In this section, we will walk through a **manual, two-node replication setup using two Redis instances running on different ports**. This is perfect for learning the basics and is commonly used for testing and development environments.

What You Will Need:

- Redis is installed on your system (version 5 or higher recommended)
- Terminal access
- Two available ports (we will use **`6379`** for the primary, and **`6380`** for the replica)

Step-by-Step Setup

Step 1: Redis Primary

Since we already have Redis running on port 6379, let us use it as the primary instance. This instance will handle all the writes and will be the source of truth for the replica.

Step 2: Start the Redis Replica

Now, in a new terminal window, start a second Redis instance on a different port. This will be the replica:

```
redis-server --port 6380
```

```
99020:C 24 Apr 2025 11:45:32.759 * oO0OoO0OoO0Oo Redis is starting oO0OoO0OoO0Oo
99020:C 24 Apr 2025 11:45:32.759 * Redis version=7.2.7, bits=64, commit=00000000, modified=0, pid=99020, just started
99020:C 24 Apr 2025 11:45:32.759 * Configuration loaded
99020:M 24 Apr 2025 11:45:32.759 * Increased maximum number of open files to 10032 (it was originally set to 2560).
99020:M 24 Apr 2025 11:45:32.759 * monotonic clock: POSIX clock_gettime

                Redis 7.2.7 (00000000/0) 64 bit

                Running in standalone mode
                Port: 6380
                PID: 99020

                      https://redis.io

99020:M 24 Apr 2025 11:45:32.760 # WARNING: The TCP backlog setting of 511 cannot be enforced because kern.ipc.somaxconn is s
et to the lower value of 128.
99020:M 24 Apr 2025 11:45:32.760 * Server initialized
99020:M 24 Apr 2025 11:45:32.760 * Ready to accept connections tcp
```

***Figure 8.2:** Output of Command "redis-server --port 6380"*

Figure 8.2: This figure displays the runtime information of the Redis server started on port 6380, including configuration details such as the Redis version, process ID, and network binding. It helps verify that the server is running independently and listening correctly.

You now have **two Redis servers running independently** on the same machine.

Step 3: Configure Replication via CLI

- **Connect to the second Redis instance (port 6380) using the CLI:**

  ```
  redis-cli -p 6380
  ```

- **Now make it a replica of the first Redis instance:**

  ```
  > REPLICAOF 127.0.0.1 6379
  ```

```
127.0.0.1:6380> REPLICAOF 127.0.0.1 6379
OK
127.0.0.1:6380>
```

***Figure 8.3:** Executing the REPLICAOF 127.0.0.1 6379 Command*

Figure 8.3: This figure illustrates the output of the `REPLICAOF 127.0.0.1 6379` command, which is used to convert the current Redis instance into a replica of the primary running on localhost at port `6379`. Once this command is executed, the replica begins synchronizing with the primary, receiving a full dataset snapshot followed by a continuous stream of write commands to stay in sync.

Once this command is issued, Redis on port **`6380`** will contact the primary at **`127.0.0.1:6379`**, perform a full sync, and then begin continuously replicating data.

Step 4: Verify that Replication is Working

Let us test it.

- **In the primary terminal (`redis-cli -p 6379`), run:**

  ```
  > SET user:1001 "Karnish"
  ```

- **Then, in the replica terminal (`redis-cli -p 6380`), run:**

  ```
  > GET user:1001
  ```

```
127.0.0.1:6380> GET user:1001
"Karnish"
```

Figure 8.4: *Executing the GET user:1001 Command*

Figure 8.4: This figure displays the output of the **`GET user:1001`** command executed on a Redis replica. The command retrieves the value associated with the key **`user:1001`**, confirming that the data has been successfully replicated from the primary to the replica. It demonstrates how read operations can be performed on replicas as part of a read-scaling strategy.

Congratulations, you have just set up your first Redis replication! Any data written to the primary will now automatically appear on the replica.

Step 5: Check the Role of Each Node

- **Execute the following command on the primary:**

  ```
  redis-cli INFO replication
  ```

```
# Replication
role:master
connected_slaves:1
slave0:ip=127.0.0.1,port=6380,state=online,offset=1282,lag=0
master_failover_state:no-failover
master_replid:69439cdedbbebb80bcd5d36f882fdce1fe840b26
master_replid2:0000000000000000000000000000000000000000
master_repl_offset:1282
second_repl_offset:-1
repl_backlog_active:1
repl_backlog_size:1048576
repl_backlog_first_byte_offset:1
repl_backlog_histlen:1282
```

Figure 8.5: *Output of the INFO Replication Command Executed on the Primary*

Figure 8.5: This figure shows the result of running the **INFO replication command** on the Redis primary node. The output confirms the server's role as primary, and provides details about connected replicas, including their IP addresses, ports, replication offsets, and link status. It helps to verify that replication is active, and the primary is successfully communicating with its replicas.

Execute the following command on the replica:

```
redis-cli -p 6380 INFO replication
```

```
# Replication
role:slave
master_host:127.0.0.1
master_port:6379
master_link_status:up
master_last_io_seconds_ago:9
master_sync_in_progress:0
slave_read_repl_offset:3032
slave_repl_offset:3032
slave_priority:100
slave_read_only:1
replica_announced:1
connected_slaves:0
master_failover_state:no-failover
master_replid:69439cdedbbebb80bcd5d36f882fdce1fe840b26
master_replid2:0000000000000000000000000000000000000000
master_repl_offset:3032
second_repl_offset:-1
repl_backlog_active:1
repl_backlog_size:1048576
repl_backlog_first_byte_offset:1
repl_backlog_histlen:3032
```

Figure 8.6: *Output of INFO Replication Command Executed on the Replica*

Figure 8.6: This figure displays the result of the INFO replication command executed on a Redis replica (formerly referred to as "`slave`"). The output confirms the server's role as a replica, identifies the primary it is connected to, and provides key replication metrics such as the master link status, replication offset, and lag. This information is essential for monitoring the health and synchronization status of the replica.

This confirms everything is working correctly.

Attempting Writes on the Replica

By default, Redis replicas are configured as read-only (replica-read-only yes), which means they reject write commands to maintain consistency.

Try running:

```
> SET user:1002 "test"
```

You will get an error like:

```
127.0.0.1:6380>  SET user:1002 "test"
(error) READONLY You can't write against a read only replica.
127.0.0.1:6380>
```

Figure 8.7: *Attempting to Write on a Replica Using the SET Command*

Figure 8.7: This figure shows the result of executing a **`SET`** command on a Redis replica. Since replicas are read-only by default, the write operation is rejected with an error message. This behavior reinforces Redis's replication model, where only the primary can accept write operations, ensuring consistency across the replication topology.

Note: *This is an expected behavior. All write operations must go through the primary.*

Disconnecting the Replica from the Primary

If you ever want to promote the replica back to a standalone primary (that is, break the replication link), run:

```
> REPLICAOF NO ONE
```

This stops replication and converts the replica into an independent primary.

Summary

Setting up basic replication in Redis is surprisingly simple:

- Start a **primary and a replica on different ports**.
- Use **`REPLICAOF`** to link the replica to the primary.
- **Verify replication** by writing to the primary and reading from the replica.
- Check the **`INFO` replication** output to monitor the link.

This setup gives you the foundation to start building high-availability systems, enable read-scaling, and prepare for more advanced scenarios such as Sentinel-based failover or geo-replicated setups.

In the next section, we will go one step further and see how to configure replication permanently by editing the **`redis.conf` file**, so that the setup persists across restarts.

Replication Configuration in redis.conf

In the previous section, we learned how to set up replication manually using the **`REPLICAOF`** command from the Redis CLI. While this method is perfect for testing or learning, it is not persistent, which means if you restart the replica, it will forget who its primary was.

In a real-world environment, you will want your replication configuration to survive restarts. This is where the **`redis.conf file`** comes in. Redis reads this configuration file when it starts, and you can use it to define replica behavior permanently.

Let us now walk through how to configure Redis replication using the **`redis.conf file`**, and explore other important settings that affect replication reliability and performance.

Where to Find redis.conf?

If you installed Redis using a package manager (like **`apt`**, **`brew`**, or **`yum`**), the configuration file is usually located in:

- **`/etc/redis/redis.conf (Linux)`**
- **`/usr/local/etc/redis.conf` (macOS with Homebrew)** or find with the following command:

  ```
  redis-cli INFO | grep config_file
  ```

- Or in your local directory if you downloaded Redis, and run it manually.

```
config_file:/opt/homebrew/etc/redis.conf
```

***Figure* 8.8:** *Locating the Redis Configuration File Using INFO | grep config_file*

Figure 8.8: This figure displays the output of the command **`INFO | grep config_file`**, which is used to extract the path of the Redis configuration file from the server's runtime information. This is a quick and effective way to identify the location of the **active `redis.conf file`**, especially useful for verifying or modifying server configurations in real-world deployments.

You can also copy and customize the default configuration:

```
cp redis.conf redis-6380.conf
```

Setting up the Replica in redis.conf

Let us assume that you are setting up a replica that should connect to a primary running on 127.0.0.1:6379.

Open the replica's configuration file **(`redis-6380.conf`)** and add or uncomment the following line:

```
replicaof 127.0.0.1 6379
```

and

```
port 6380
```

This tells Redis to automatically connect to the primary on startup.

Recommended Replication Settings

The following are some key options you can set in the **`redis.conf file`** to improve reliability and performance:

- **`replicaof <host> <port>`**

  ```
  replicaof 127.0.0.1 6379
  ```

  Defines which Redis server this node should replicate. This is equivalent to using **`REPLICAOF`** in CLI, but persistent across restarts.

- **`replica-read-only yes`**

  By default, Redis replicas are **read-only**. This prevents accidental writes, which is critical for maintaining data consistency. Keep this enabled unless you have a specific reason to allow writes on a replica (which is rare and risky).

- **`repl-diskless-sync yes`**

  This enables diskless replication, where the RDB snapshot is streamed directly over the network to the replica, without writing to disk. It is faster and avoids disk I/O overhead on the primary.

- **`repl-diskless-sync-delay 5`**

  This introduces a short delay (in seconds) before the RDB snapshot begins, allowing additional replicas to join and sync simultaneously. It improves efficiency when multiple replicas are starting up at the same time.

- **`repl-timeout 60`**

  Sets the timeout (in seconds) for communication between primary and replica. If no data is received from the primary during this time, the replica disconnects and retries. You can increase this in high-latency networks.

- **`min-replicas-to-write` and `min-replicas-max-lag`**

  These two settings help ensure that there is data safety in environments where you want the master to write only if enough replicas are in **`sync`**.

  Example:

  ```
  min-replicas-to-write 1
  min-replicas-max-lag 10
  ```

  This means the primary will only accept writes if at least 1 replica is connected, and has a lag of less than 10 seconds.

Starting Redis with a Custom Config

- **Now, once you have updated your config file, start the replica instance like this:**

  ```
  redis-server redis-6380.conf
  ```

  You can also check whether the replica is successfully connected to the master using:

  ```
  redis-cli -p 6380 INFO replication
  ```

  Look for:

  ```
  role:slave
  master_link_status:up
  ```

  That means your replica is connected and is replicating data!

```
# Replication
role:slave
master_host:127.0.0.1
master_port:6379
master_link_status:up
master_last_io_seconds_ago:6
master_sync_in_progress:0
slave_read_repl_offset:66382
slave_repl_offset:66382
slave_priority:100
slave_read_only:1
replica_announced:1
connected_slaves:0
master_failover_state:no-failover
master_replid:2a1d41ca82c54f7d2fb828d43d42a7081784b2c2
master_replid2:69439cdedbbebb80bcd5d36f882fdce1fe840b26
master_repl_offset:66382
second_repl_offset:66215
repl_backlog_active:1
repl_backlog_size:1048576
repl_backlog_first_byte_offset:66215
repl_backlog_histlen:168
```

Figure 8.9: *Output of the INFO Replication Command Executed on the Replica*

Figure 8.9: This figure presents the output of the **INFO** replication command executed on a Redis replica. The details confirm the node's role as a replica, and provide information about its connection to the master, including the master's host and port, synchronization status, and replication offset. This output is useful for monitoring replication health and ensuring that the replica is in sync with the primary.

Important Notes

- Do **not** use both **REPLICAOF** in CLI and **replicaof** in the **config** simultaneously, as they may conflict.
- Ensure that the primary's port/IP is accessible from the replica machine if you're running across different hosts.
- If you are using Docker or containers, make sure port bindings and hostnames are correctly configured.

Quick Command Reference Sheet

- **See current roles and links:**

  ```
  # Shows master/replica role, link status, offsets, connected replicas
  redis-cli INFO replication
  ```

- **Make a node follow a primary:**

```
# Point this node at a master (host:port)
redis-cli REPLICAOF 127.0.0.1 6379
```

- **Promote a replica to the primary:**

```
# Break replication link (use during manual failover)
redis-cli REPLICAOF NO ONE
```

- **Enforce read-only on replicas:**

```
# Confirm (should return 'replica-read-only' and 'yes')
redis-cli -p 6380 CONFIG GET replica-read-only

# Set explicitly if needed
redis-cli -p 6380 CONFIG SET replica-read-only yes
```

- **Watch live traffic (debug only):**

```
# Very verbose; use briefly and never in hot prod paths
redis-cli MONITOR
```

Summary

Configuring Redis replication through **`redis.conf`** ensures that your **setup is persistent, automatic,** and **production-ready**. You can define which primary to replicate, whether the replica is read-only, and how to handle syncing and disconnections.

With just a few lines in a config file, Redis handles the rest, making it one of the easiest distributed data replication setups you will ever use.

In the next section, we will learn how to **verify replication status**, monitor the health of your replication link, and diagnose any sync issues that might arise.

Verifying Replication Status

Once you have set up replication between a primary and one or more replicas, it is crucial to know how to verify that everything is working correctly. Redis provides simple but powerful commands to monitor and inspect the replication process in real time.

In this section, we will learn how to **check the role of a Redis node**, **confirm the health of the replication link**, and **understand important metrics** that help you troubleshoot issues quickly.

Using the `INFO` replication Command

The easiest way to check the replication status is by using the **`INFO replication`** command.

You can run it from the Redis CLI:

```
redis-cli -p 6379 INFO replication
```

Sample Output: On the Primary:

```
# Replication
role:master
connected_slaves:1
min_slaves_good_slaves:1
slave0:ip=127.0.0.1,port=6380,state=online,offset=69602,lag=0
master_failover_state:no-failover
master_replid:2a1d41ca82c54f7d2fb828d43d42a7081784b2c2
master_replid2:69439cdedbbebb80bcd5d36f882fdce1fe840b26
master_repl_offset:69602
second_repl_offset:66215
repl_backlog_active:1
repl_backlog_size:1048576
repl_backlog_first_byte_offset:66215
repl_backlog_histlen:3388
```

Figure 8.10: *Output of the INFO Replication Command Executed on the Primary*

Figure 8.10: This figure displays the output of the INFO replication command run on a Redis primary node. It confirms the server's role as master, and lists important replication details such as the number of connected replicas, their IP addresses and ports, current replication offsets, and the status of each replica link. This information is vital for verifying that replication is configured and functioning correctly in a multi-node Redis setup.

Key Fields Explained:

- `role`: Displays whether the instance is a primary or a replica (shown as master/slave in INFO output).
- `connected_slaves`: Number of replicas currently connected to the primary.
- **slave0**: Shows the replica's IP address, port, connection state, replication offset, and lag (delay).
- `master_replid`: A unique ID representing the primary's replication history.
- `master_repl_offset`: Current replication offset for the primary. It increases as new write operations occur.
- `repl_backlog_size`: Size of the replication backlog buffer (important for partial resynchronization).

Sample Output: On the Replica:

```
# Replication
role:slave
master_host:127.0.0.1
master_port:6379
master_link_status:up
master_last_io_seconds_ago:3
master_sync_in_progress:0
slave_read_repl_offset:69812
slave_repl_offset:69812
slave_priority:100
slave_read_only:1
replica_announced:1
connected_slaves:0
master_failover_state:no-failover
master_replid:2a1d41ca82c54f7d2fb828d43d42a7081784b2c2
master_replid2:69439cdedbbebb80bcd5d36f882fdce1fe840b26
master_repl_offset:69812
second_repl_offset:66215
repl_backlog_active:1
repl_backlog_size:1048576
repl_backlog_first_byte_offset:66215
repl_backlog_histlen:3598
```

Figure 8.11: *Key Fields Displayed in the Output of the INFO Replication Command*

Figure 8.11: This figure highlights the most important fields returned by the `INFO` replication command in Redis. These fields include the server's current replication role (master or replica), connected replicas, master replication offset, replication backlog size, and link status. Understanding these fields is essential for monitoring the health and synchronization status of a Redis replication setup.

Key Fields Explained:

- `role`: Should show slave (replica).
- `master_host and master_port`: IP address and port of the master that the replica is connected to.
- `master_link_status`: Should be up. If it is down, replication is broken.
- `master_last_io_seconds_ago`: Number of seconds since the last interaction with the primary. Lower numbers are better.
- `slave_repl_offset`: The offset of the replica's replication progress should be close to the primary's offset.
- `slave_read_only/replica_read_only`: Indicates if the replica is operating in read-only mode (recommended).

Quick Health Checklist

Here is a simple checklist you can use when checking replication health:

Check	Good Sign	Problem Sign
role on primary	master	Anything else
role on replica	slave	Anything else
`master_link_status`	up	down
`connected_slaves`	Correct number of replicas	Less than expected
`slave_repl_offset`	Close to master offset	Huge gap (lagging replica)
`master_last_io_seconds_ago`	Low number (0–5 seconds)	High number (>10 seconds)

Table 8.2: *Replication Health Checklist – What to Monitor and Why*

If any of these look off, it is a good idea to investigate further.

Why is Monitoring Important?

- Replication might silently break if the primary and replica lose connection.
- A replica that lags behind too much might trigger unnecessary full resynchronizations, causing system strain.
- In case of failover or Sentinel operations, **healthy replication links** ensure quick and smooth transitions.

Tip: *Always monitor your replication metrics proactively, especially in production environments.*

Troubleshooting Tips

Symptom: Replication lag creeping up

- What to check

```
redis-cli INFO replication | egrep 'role|master_link_status|master_last_io_
seconds_ago|.*repl_offset'

redis-cli INFO stats | egrep 'instantaneous_ops_per_sec|evicted_keys'

redis-cli SLOWLOG GET 10

redis-cli INFO persistence | egrep 'aof_rewrite_in_progress|rdb_bgsave_in_
progress'
```

- Likely causes (and fixes)

  ```
  Backlog too small → frequent full resyncs.
  Increase: repl-backlog-size 64mb (or higher).
  ```

  - Disk pressure during RDB/AOF rewrites.

    Use **`repl-diskless-sync yes`**; consider **no-appendfsync-on-rewrite `yes`**; move RDB/AOF to a faster disk.

  - Hot keys / slow commands.

    Fix app patterns; use **`SLOWLOG`** to spot offenders; consider pipelining/batching.

  - Evictions thrashing memory.

    Set maxmemory + sane policy (for example, **`allkeys-lru`**) or increase RAM.

Symptom: `master_link_status: down` (flapping link)

- What to check

  ```
  # On replica
  redis-cli INFO replication

  # OS/network
  ping <master_ip> -c 5
  traceroute <master_ip>   # or mtr
  ```

- Likely causes (and fixes)
  - Firewall / security group / SG rules.

    Allow TCP 6379 between master and replica (VPCs, NACLs, firewalls).

  - Unstable network / MTU mismatches.

    Align MTU; avoid jumbo frames if the path is not consistent.

  - Aggressive TCP keepalive.

    Set tcp-keepalive 300 in **redis.conf.**

Symptom: Replica keeps doing full resyncs

- What to check

  ```
  # Master's backlog & IDs
  redis-cli INFO replication | egrep 'run_id|repl_backlog_active|repl_backlog_
  size'
  ```

- Likely causes (and fixes)
  - Master restart or backlog expired.

    Increase **`repl-backlog-size`**; reduce churn; ensure master stability.

  - Replica is too slow to consume the stream.

    Check CPU/IO on replica; upgrade instance size or storage.

Summary

Verifying that your Redis replication is working is not just a one-time setup task; it is something you should feel comfortable doing regularly. A replication setup that looks perfect today can quietly drift into trouble tomorrow if you are not watching it carefully.

The good news is that Redis makes monitoring replication incredibly simple.

With a single command - **`INFO replication`**, you get a clear snapshot of how your primary and replicas are communicating. Are they connected? Is the data flowing smoothly? How far behind is the replica? These are the kinds of questions you can answer in seconds.

When checking replication health, always pay attention to key indicators like:

- Whether the **replica is properly linked** to the primary (`master_link_status: up`).
- How **fresh the connection** is (`master_last_io_seconds_ago`).
- Whether the **replication offsets** are close between primary and replica (indicating minimal lag).
- How many **connected replicas** does your primary see.

If something feels wrong, like a replica being disconnected, huge replication lag, or unusual timeouts, it is better to catch it early, rather than wait for it to become a system-wide issue.

Replication is not just about copying data; it is about maintaining trust that your system can handle failure gracefully, and still keep serving your users. And it all starts with **keeping an eye on these small but vital replication metrics.**

In the next section, we will go even deeper and break down the actual flow of replication - the life cycle of how a replica syncs with the primary, stays up to date, and what happens if things go wrong. Understanding this flow is key to mastering Redis replication truly and confidently.

Understanding the Replication Flow

Now that we know how to set up and monitor replication, let us dive deeper into what actually happens inside Redis when replication is running.

Understanding the replication flow will give you a huge advantage, not just for troubleshooting, but also for designing systems that are faster, safer, and more resilient.

Hence, let us walk through it step-by-step, just like Redis does under the hood.

Step 1: Initial Sync – How a Replica Joins the Primary

Whenever you connect a new replica to a primary, whether it is a fresh setup or after a restart, Redis must ensure that the replica has a complete and consistent copy of the primary's data.

Here is the complete sequence of steps Redis performs:

a. **Replica Sends `PSYNC` Command**

   The first thing that the replica does is send a **`PSYNC`** (Partial SYNC) command to the primary, asking:

   "Hey, can I just catch up from where I left off, or do I need the full dataset?"

Primary Decides:

- If the primary still **has recent changes saved in its replication backlog**, it will only send those missing updates, so that the replica can catch up.
- If not (for example, it has restarted, or the backlog expired), it falls back to **full synchronization**.

Step 2: Full Synchronization - The Big Transfer

If full `sync` is needed, here is what happens:

1. The primary **creates a new RDB snapshot**, a point-in-time image of the current dataset.
2. While the snapshot is being created, **Redis buffers new writes** in memory (so no changes are lost).
3. The snapshot (RDB file) is **sent over the network to the replica**.
4. The **replica loads the snapshot into memory**, replacing any old data.
5. Finally, the primary sends all the buffered write commands that happened while the snapshot was transferring. At this point, the replica is **perfectly up to date**.

Step 3: Ongoing Streaming Replication

Once the initial sync is done, the primary and replica maintain a **continuous live connection**.

- Every new write command (`SET`, `HSET`, `INCR`, and so on) that the primary processes is **immediately forwarded** to all connected replicas.
- This happens in **real time** over a persistent TCP connection.
- The replica applies these commands in the same order, keeping its dataset synchronized with the primary.

Important: *Replication is* ***asynchronous*** *- the master does not wait for the replica to confirm the receipt of commands. This keeps Redis ultra-fast but introduces tiny chances of replicas lagging slightly behind.*

Step 4: Handling Disconnections

No network is perfect. Disconnections happen, maybe the replica restarts, the network hiccups, or the master is temporarily overloaded.

What happens then?

`Scenario 1: Short Disconnection → Partial Resynchronization`

If the replica reconnects **quickly** and the master **still has the history** in its **replication backlog**, they can perform a **partial resync**:

- The replica says:

  "*I last received data at offset 980000. Can you send me everything after that?*"

- The master says:

  "*Sure, here is the missing part!*"

- No full RDB snapshot needed.
- Much faster recovery.

`Scenario 2: Long Disconnection → Full Resynchronization`

If the master no longer has the history the replica needs (maybe the backlog was overwritten, or the master restarted), Redis must perform a **full sync** again:

- Create a fresh RDB snapshot.
- Send it over.
- Apply buffered updates after the snapshot loads.

This is costlier and can cause brief delays; so ideally, you want to avoid it by **tuning the replication backlog** properly.

What is the Replication Backlog?

The replication backlog is a special memory buffer maintained by the Redis primary. It temporarily stores the most recent write commands that have been sent to replicas. Think of it as a short-term memory, keeping track of the latest changes so that replicas can quickly catch up if they momentarily lose connection.

This buffer is fixed in size and behaves in a circular manner. This means once the buffer is full, the oldest data is automatically overwritten by the newest data, ensuring that the master does not run out of memory trying to store too much history. The size of the replication backlog is controlled by the **`repl-backlog-size`** setting in the Redis configuration file. For example:

```
repl-backlog-size 1mb
```

This command sets the backlog size to **1 megabyte**.

```
# Set the replication backlog size. The backlog is a buffer that accumulates
# replica data when replicas are disconnected for some time, so that when a
# replica wants to reconnect again, often a full resync is not needed, but a
# partial resync is enough, just passing the portion of data the replica
# missed while disconnected.
#
# The bigger the replication backlog, the longer the replica can endure the
# disconnect and later be able to perform a partial resynchronization.
#
# The backlog is only allocated if there is at least one replica connected.
#
repl-backlog-size 1mb
```

***Figure 8.12:** repl-backlog-size Setting in the Redis Configuration File*

Figure 8.12: This figure shows the repl-backlog-size parameter as configured in the redis.conf file. This setting determines the size of the replication backlog buffer, which holds recent write commands for replicas. It plays a crucial role in enabling partial resynchronization when a replica reconnects after a brief disconnection. Properly sizing this buffer helps ensure smooth and efficient replication in high-traffic environments.

The replication backlog plays a crucial role during **short network interruptions**. If a replica disconnects from the master but reconnects before the backlog is overwritten, Redis can perform a **partial resynchronization**, instead of a full synchronization. This greatly reduces the time and resources needed to get the replica back in sync.

In simple terms, the replication backlog helps Redis handle small network hiccups gracefully, without making replicas start from scratch every time they reconnect.

Why the Replication Backlog Matters?

The replication backlog is essential during **brief network interruptions** between the master and its replicas. Here is how it helps:

Imagine this scenario:

- A replica temporarily disconnects from the master, maybe, due to a network glitch lasting a few seconds.
- During this time, the master continues receiving and processing new write commands.
- Thanks to the replication backlog, the master retains those recent write operations.
- When the replica reconnects - **if it happens quickly enough**, before the backlog is overwritten, Redis can perform a **partial resynchronization**.
- The replica simply applies the missing operations from the backlog, instead of doing a full data resync from scratch.

This process saves a lot of time and network bandwidth. Without the replication backlog, even a tiny disconnection could force a full data transfer from master to replica, leading to unnecessary load and delays.

The replication backlog is a smart mechanism that allows Redis replicas to recover quickly from short disconnections. By maintaining a rolling buffer of recent changes, Redis ensures high availability, faster recovery, and efficient synchronization across distributed environments.

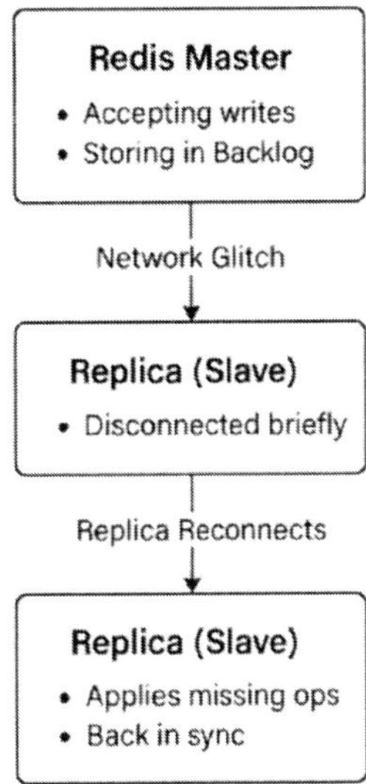

***Figure 8.13:** Replication Break Scenario Caused by a Network Glitch*

Figure 8.13: This figure illustrates a scenario where Redis replication is interrupted due to a temporary network glitch between the master and replica. As a result, the replica loses connection to the master and enters a disconnected state. If the network is restored quickly and the backlog buffer on the master is still intact, a partial resynchronization may occur. Otherwise, a full resynchronization is triggered, depending on the duration and buffer size.

> **Note:** *If you have high write volumes or slow networks, increase the backlog size to reduce full resyncs!*

Real-World Example: What Happens During Replication

Suppose you have:

- A Redis master on port 6379
- A replica on port 6380

1. **You run:**

   ```
   redis-cli -p 6380
   > REPLICAOF 127.0.0.1 6379
   ```

2. **Master takes an RDB snapshot and sends it to the replica.**
3. **You set a key while syncing:**

   ```
   redis-cli -p 6379
   > SET user:1005 "user_replication"
   ```

4. **The master buffers the `SET` command and sends it to the replica after the snapshot loads.**

Now the replica knows everything the master knows.

Key Metrics You Can Monitor during Replication:

Metric	What It Tells You
`master_link_status`	If the replica is connected to the primary
`master_last_io_seconds_ago`	Time since the last communication
`slave_repl_offset`	Replication progress on the replica
`master_repl_offset`	Replication progress on primary
`connected_slaves` **(on master)**	Number of active replicas

Table 8.3: *Key Metrics to Monitor for Assessing Redis Replication Health*

Check these regularly (on replica) using:

```
redis-cli INFO replication
```

```
# Replication
role:slave
master_host:127.0.0.1
master_port:6379
master_link_status:up
master_last_io_seconds_ago:3
master_sync_in_progress:0
slave_read_repl_offset:87130
slave_repl_offset:87130
slave_priority:100
slave_read_only:1
replica_announced:1
connected_slaves:0
master_failover_state:no-failover
master_replid:2a1d41ca82c54f7d2fb828d43d42a7081784b2c2
master_replid2:69439cdedbbebb80bcd5d36f882fdce1fe840b26
master_repl_offset:87130
second_repl_offset:66215
repl_backlog_active:1
repl_backlog_size:1048576
repl_backlog_first_byte_offset:66215
repl_backlog_histlen:20916
```

Figure 8.14: *Checking Key Replication Metrics on the Primary*

Figure 8.14: This figure demonstrates how to review important replication-related metrics on a Redis primary node using the INFO replication command. Key fields such as **`connected_replicas`**, **`master_repl_offset`**, and **`repl_backlog_active`** provide insights into the current replication status, backlog activity, and synchronization progress. Monitoring these metrics helps ensure that connected replicas are in sync and that the replication pipeline is functioning correctly.

```
# Replication
role:master
connected_slaves:1
min_slaves_good_slaves:1
slave0:ip=127.0.0.1,port=6380,state=online,offset=87480,lag=1
master_failover_state:no-failover
master_replid:2a1d41ca82c54f7d2fb828d43d42a7081784b2c2
master_replid2:69439cdedbbebb80bcd5d36f882fdce1fe840b26
master_repl_offset:87480
second_repl_offset:66215
repl_backlog_active:1
repl_backlog_size:1048576
repl_backlog_first_byte_offset:66215
repl_backlog_histlen:21266
```

Figure 8.15: *Checking Key Replication Metrics on the Replica*

Figure 8.15: This figure displays key replication-related metrics obtained by running the INFO replication command on a Redis replica. Fields such as **`master_host`**, **`master_link_status`**, **`master_last_io_seconds_ago`**, and **`slave_repl_offset`** provide critical information about the replica's connection to the master and its synchronization status. These metrics are necessary for diagnosing replication lag, connectivity issues, and the overall replica health.

Summary

Redis replication follows a smooth and predictable flow designed to ensure high availability:

- A replica first connects to the master and requests synchronization.
- The master then decides whether a full synchronization or a partial synchronization is needed, based on the situation.
- During a full sync, a snapshot of the dataset is transferred, followed by the replaying of any buffered commands.
- After synchronization, the master continuously streams new commands to keep the replica updated in real time.
- If a replica disconnects, Redis intelligently handles it - using the replication backlog for quick recovery whenever possible, or falling back to a full sync, if needed.

Understanding this replication flow is essential for designing Redis architectures that are resilient, efficient, and fault-tolerant.

In the next section, we will dive into failover scenarios, exploring what happens when a master node goes down, and how Redis can recover quickly and safely to maintain high availability.

Handling Failover Scenarios

Until now, we have explored how Redis replication operates smoothly under normal conditions.

However, in real-world systems, failures are inevitable - machines can crash, networks can go down, and primary nodes may unexpectedly go offline.

Handling failover - the process of responding to a Redis primary failure - is one of the most important aspects of mastering Redis replication.

In this section, we will walk through the failover process step-by-step, using real-world examples to understand how Redis helps you manage failures gracefully and maintain system stability.

What Happens When the Primary Fails?

Imagine that your Redis primary suddenly goes offline.

Here is what immediately happens:

- Replicas notice the disconnection **(they realize that they cannot talk to the primary anymore).**
- Replication status becomes `master_link_status: down`.
- New writes cannot happen as your application cannot write to the primary anymore.
- Replicas continue to serve reads (if your app is smart enough to query replicas).
- No automatic promotion happens by default. **Redis replicas do not magically become primary, unless you configure tools like Sentinel** (which we will discuss later).

In short: Redis replication alone does not provide automatic failover or leader election.

You must intervene manually, unless you are using Redis Sentinel or Redis Cluster.

Manual Failover: Promoting a Replica to Primary

Let us say your primary on **port 6379** crashes. You have a healthy replica running on **port 6380**.

You can promote the replica manually by running:

```
redis-cli -p 6380
```

```
> REPLICAOF NO ONE
```

This command tells the replica:

"You are no longer following any primary and will accept writes independently."

- After this, the server on **`6380`** accepts **write operations**.
- It behaves like a **normal, standalone primary**.

You can now point your application to this new primary!

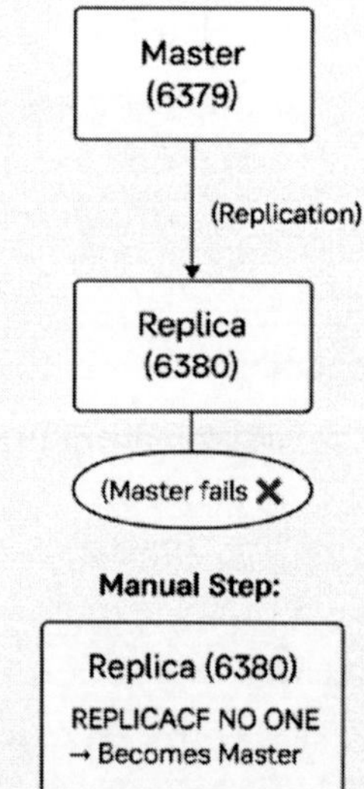

Figure 8.16: *Failover Flow Diagram – Promoting the Replica after Master Failure*

Figure 8.16: This figure illustrates a manual failover scenario in Redis where the master node fails, and a replica is promoted to master by executing the **`REPLICAOF NO ONE`** command. The flow shows the sequence: the master becomes unavailable, the replica is disconnected, and then the replica is manually promoted to take over the master role. This approach is useful in environments without Redis Sentinel or automated failover mechanisms.

Manual Failover: Step-by-Step

Let us go through a real scenario:

Step 1: The primary is running

```
redis-server --port 6379
```

Replica is running and replicating:

```
redis-server --port 6380
redis-cli -p 6380
> REPLICAOF 127.0.0.1 6379
```

Step 2: Simulate Primary Failure

```
Kill the master manually (simulate a crash):
kill $(lsof -t -i:6379)
```

(Or simply stop the Redis process)

Step 3: Verify Replica Status

Connect to replica:

```
redis-cli -p 6380
> INFO replication
You will see:
role:slave
master_link_status:down
```

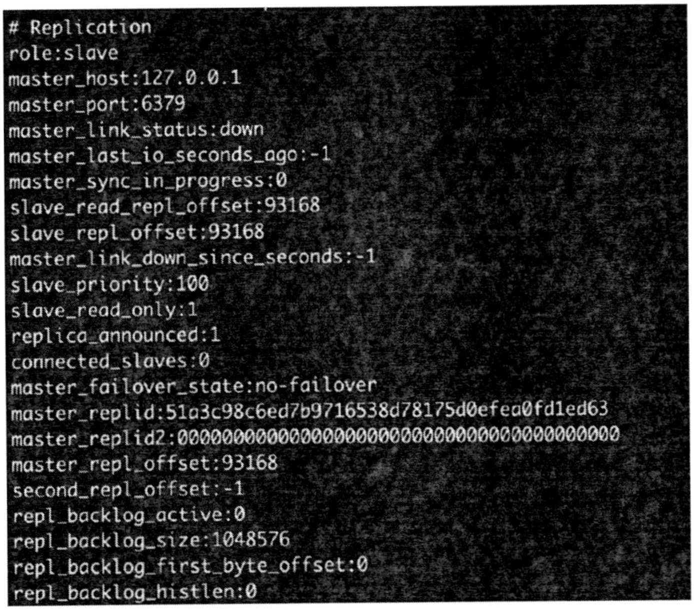

```
# Replication
role:slave
master_host:127.0.0.1
master_port:6379
master_link_status:down
master_last_io_seconds_ago:-1
master_sync_in_progress:0
slave_read_repl_offset:93168
slave_repl_offset:93168
master_link_down_since_seconds:-1
slave_priority:100
slave_read_only:1
replica_announced:1
connected_slaves:0
master_failover_state:no-failover
master_replid:51a3c98c6ed7b9716538d78175d0efea0fd1ed63
master_replid2:0000000000000000000000000000000000000000
master_repl_offset:93168
second_repl_offset:-1
repl_backlog_active:0
repl_backlog_size:1048576
repl_backlog_first_byte_offset:0
repl_backlog_histlen:0
```

Figure 8.17: *Replication State on the Replica after Master Failure Using INFO Replication*

Figure 8.17: This figure shows the output of the INFO replication command on a Redis replica after the original master has failed. The output reflects the disconnected state, where fields such as **`master_link_status`** show down, and replication metrics may pause or reset. This helps in identifying that the replica has lost contact with its master, a critical observation before initiating failover or promoting the replica manually.

Replica knows the primary is unreachable.

Step 4: Promote Replica to Primary

Still inside the replica's CLI:

```
> REPLICAOF NO ONE
```

Now check `INFO replication` again:

```
role:master
```

Replica is now a primary. You can now perform writes to 6380.

```
127.0.0.1:6380>  REPLICAOF NO ONE
OK
127.0.0.1:6380> INFO replication
# Replication
role:master
connected_slaves:0
master_failover_state:no-failover
master_replid:500afdc4e32a3f6c0dd9673a261613a59ab8e0d1
master_replid2:51a3c98c6ed7b9716538d78175d0efea0fd1ed63
master_repl_offset:93168
second_repl_offset:93169
repl_backlog_active:0
repl_backlog_size:1048576
repl_backlog_first_byte_offset:0
repl_backlog_histlen:0
```

Figure 8.18: *Replication State on the Replica after Executing* REPLICAOF NO ONE

Figure 8.18: This figure displays the output of the **`INFO`** replication command on a Redis replica after executing the **`REPLICAOF NO ONE`** command. The output confirms that the replica has been promoted to the primary, with its role now shown as master, and no connected replicas listed. This transition marks the completion of a manual failover, allowing the promoted instance to independently accept write operations.

Important Things to Remember during Manual Failover

- Once a replica becomes a primary, it **stops following** its old master permanently (unless you reconfigure it later).
- If the original primary comes back online, it will not automatically know about this change.
- You need to manually reconfigure the old primary to **become a replica**, if needed.

Example: After the primary restarts, tell the old primary to follow the new primary (**`6380`**):

```
redis-cli -p 6379
> REPLICAOF 127.0.0.1 6380
```

This way, the system can heal properly.

```
127.0.0.1:6379> REPLICAOF 127.0.0.1 6380
OK
127.0.0.1:6379> INFO replication
# Replication
role:slave
master_host:127.0.0.1
master_port:6380
master_link_status:up
master_last_io_seconds_ago:1
master_sync_in_progress:0
slave_read_repl_offset:93182
slave_repl_offset:93182
slave_priority:100
slave_read_only:1
replica_announced:1
connected_slaves:0
master_failover_state:no-failover
master_replid:01c585269f08f1f5dee46ac77f6b82dae1db5465
master_replid2:0000000000000000000000000000000000000000
master_repl_offset:93182
second_repl_offset:-1
repl_backlog_active:1
repl_backlog_size:1048576
repl_backlog_first_byte_offset:93183
repl_backlog_histlen:0
127.0.0.1:6379>
```

Figure 8.19*: Replication State on the Former Master after Executing* REPLICAOF 127.0.0.1 6380

Figure 8.19: This figure shows the output of the **INFO** replication command on a Redis primary node, after it has been reconfigured to become a replica of another Redis instance (at 127.0.0.1:6380) using the **REPLICAOF** command. The output confirms that the server's role has changed to slave (replica), and displays details such as the new primary's address, link status, and synchronization progress. This step is often a part of re-establishing replication in a failover recovery process.

Problem with Manual Failover

While manual failover gives you control, it also means:

- Someone must **notice** the failure.
- Someone must **act** quickly to promote a replica.
- Your app must **switch connections** to the new master.

If you do not automate this, there will always be **downtime** during failure, which might not be acceptable for high-traffic, critical applications.

That is why tools like **Redis Sentinel** exist, as they automate this entire failover process, without human intervention. (We will cover Sentinel in the next section.)

Summary

Handling failover manually in Redis is possible and relatively straightforward:

- Replicas detect if a primary is unavailable.
- You can promote a replica to primary using **REPLICAOF NO ONE**.
- You need to manually reconfigure your system to recognize the new primary.

However, in production systems, **automatic failover** is essential for minimizing downtime, and that is where Redis Sentinel shines.

Quick Reference: Core Replication Commands

- `redis-cli INFO replication`: Check whether a node is primary or replica, and see link status and offsets.
- `redis-cli REPLICAOF 127.0.0.1 6379`: Make the current node start following the primary at 127.0.0.1:6379.
- `redis-cli REPLICAOF NO ONE`: Stop following the primary and promote this node to a standalone primary.
- `redis-cli CONFIG GET replica-read-only` / `CONFIG SET replica-read-only yes`: View or enforce read-only mode on replicas to avoid accidental writes.
- `redis-cli WAIT 1 200`: Ask the primary to wait until at least 1 replica has acknowledged the last write (up to 200 ms), useful for extra safety on critical data.

Conclusion

In this first part of our deep dive into Redis replication, we explored the fundamental building blocks that power Redis's ability to scale out reads, and enhance data redundancy. We began by understanding how Redis replication works - a primary-replica model that is simple in design yet highly effective in ensuring that the data is propagated across nodes.

We then walked through the steps of setting up a basic primary-replica configuration, highlighting just how easy it is to get started with replication using either redis.conf or runtime configuration. This was followed by a closer look at the key configuration parameters, giving you control over how replication behaves in your environment, from persistence settings to read-only access on replicas.

Next, we examined how to verify replication status using built-in Redis commands like INFO replication, and learned to interpret crucial metrics such as `role`, `master_link_status`, and `slave_repl_offset`. These checks form the backbone of replication monitoring and give early signals if something goes wrong.

Finally, we gained a high-level view of the replication flow from full synchronization during replica startup to partial resynchronization using the replication backlog, equipping you with a conceptual foundation to understand how Redis handles both normal operation and reconnect scenarios.

As you move forward, this knowledge will prepare you for more advanced topics such as replica promotion, failover handling, and troubleshooting common issues, which we will cover in Part 2 of this chapter.

Redis replication may seem simple on the surface, but as we have seen, it offers powerful capabilities when used correctly. Thus, with a solid grasp of the essentials, you are now ready to build highly available and read-scalable Redis architectures with confidence!

CHAPTER 9

Mastering Redis Replication - Part 2

Introduction

In Part 1, we covered the foundational aspects of Redis replication, including how it works, how to set up a basic master-replica configuration, and configure replication settings in **redis.conf**, verify replication status, and understand the replication flow. In Part 2, we will take a deeper dive into more advanced and practical topics that are essential for running Redis in production environments. This includes using Redis Sentinel for automatic failover, strategies for read scaling with replicas, identifying and resolving common replication issues, and applying advanced tips as well as best practices to ensure a robust and high-performing Redis setup.

Terminology Note for This Chapter: Master/Slave vs. Primary/Replica

While Redis documentation has largely transitioned to the more inclusive **primary/replica** terminology, Redis Sentinel internally continues to use the **master/slave** terms in its configuration, logs, commands, and runtime outputs.

Because this chapter focuses heavily on **Redis Sentinel**, we will primarily use the **master/slave** terminology to align with:

- Sentinel configuration files (for example, sentinel monitor)
- Sentinel log messages
- INFO and Sentinel command outputs
- Real-world troubleshooting and production scenarios

This choice is intentional and aims to make it easier for you to:

- Follow Sentinel behavior step by step
- Match explanations with actual Sentinel outputs
- Avoid confusion when working with live systems

Please note that these terms refer to the same replication roles:

- **Master = Primary**
- **Slave = Replica**

The underlying replication model, behavior, and commands remain exactly the same regardless of the terminology used.

Structure

In this chapter, we will cover the following topics:

- Using Redis Sentinel for Automatic Failover

- Setting up Redis Sentinel
- Testing Automatic Failover
- Read Scaling with Replicas
- Common Issues and Troubleshooting
- Advanced Tips and Best Practices

Using Redis Sentinel for Automatic Failover

We have already explored **how manual failover works** - where, in the event of a master node failure, an administrator steps in to promote one of the replicas to master, manually updates client configurations, and hopes the system returns to a stable state. While this approach may be acceptable in controlled or development environments, it poses significant risks in real-world production systems. In high-availability environments where uptime and reliability are critical, relying on a human to detect the failure, assess the situation, and take corrective action introduces unacceptable delays. Even a few minutes of downtime can lead to lost revenue, degraded user experience, and cascading failures across dependent services. For truly resilient Redis deployments, failover needs to be **automated, fast, and reliable,** and that is where **Redis Sentinel** comes into play.

In fact, **Redis Sentinel** serves as an intelligent watchdog for your Redis infrastructure, constantly monitoring both master and replica nodes to ensure high availability. It operates independently and tirelessly, detecting failures in real time. When a master node becomes unreachable, Sentinel steps in to coordinate an automated failover process. It elects and promotes one of the available replicas to become the new master, updates other replicas to follow the newly promoted node, and broadcasts the change to the system. **This entire sequence happens without any human intervention**, drastically reducing recovery time and ensuring that client applications can quickly reconnect and resume operations. Redis Sentinel is a critical component for building resilient, self-healing Redis deployments in production environments. It is a critical component for achieving **high availability in Redis deployments**.

In the next section, we will explore Redis Sentinel in detail, step-by-step, to understand how it ensures seamless failover, and keeps your Redis environment resilient.

What is Redis Sentinel?

Redis Sentinel is a **built-in tool** that provides:

Feature	Purpose
Monitoring	Checking if masters and replicas are alive.
Notification	Alerting clients or systems when something changes.
Automatic Failover	Promoting replicas if the master goes down.
Service Discovery	Helping clients find the current master dynamically.

Table 9.1: *Overview of Redis Sentinel Features*

Table 9.1 provides a quick overview of Redis Sentinel's key features and their roles in maintaining a healthy Redis environment.

Think of **Redis Sentinel as a smart and vigilant guardian**, constantly watching over your Redis servers 24/7 to ensure everything runs smoothly, and to step in immediately when something goes wrong.

How Sentinel Works:

- You run multiple Sentinel instances **(best practice is at least three for quorum)**.
- Each Sentinel monitors the Redis master and replicas.
- If the master goes down, they vote to confirm the failure.
- Once a majority agrees, they:
    - Elect a replica to become the new master (primary).
    - Reconfigure remaining replicas to follow the new master.
    - Inform clients (or the application) that the master has changed.

Result: Failover happens automatically. No human action is needed.

Figure 9.1 shows a setup with three Sentinel instances monitoring a Redis master and its replicas. If the master fails, the Sentinels vote to confirm the failure, promote a replica to master, and reconfigure the remaining replicas automatically, ensuring high availability.

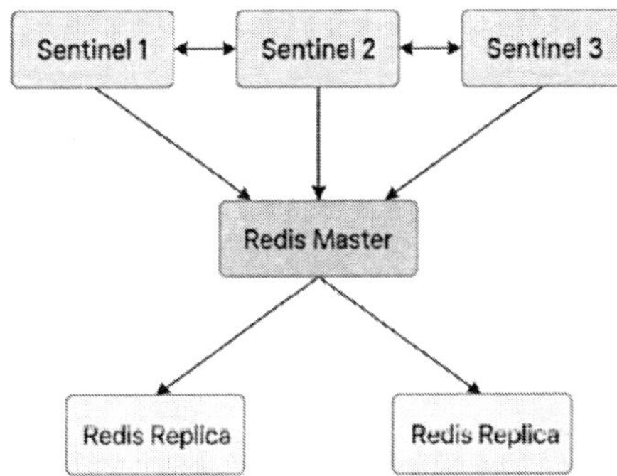

***Figure* 9.1:** *High Availability Setup with Three Redis Sentinel Instances*

If the Master fails:

- Sentinels detect it.
- Elect a new master from the replicas.
- Update all replicas to follow the new master.

Setting up Redis Sentinel

Let us set it up practically.

Step 1: Set up Redis Master and Replicas

You should already have:

- Redis master (primary) on **`port 6379.`**
- Redis replica on **`port 6380.`**

(If not, quickly set them up using `REPLICAOF`).

Step 2: Configure a Sentinel

Create a simple Sentinel configuration file, for example, **`sentinel.conf`**:

```
port 26379
sentinel monitor mymaster 127.0.0.1 6379 2
```

```
sentinel down-after-milliseconds mymaster 5000
sentinel failover-timeout mymaster 10000
sentinel parallel-syncs mymaster 1
```

Figure 9.2 displays a sample Sentinel configuration where the Sentinel runs on port 26379 and monitors the master at 127.0.0.1:6379. It sets a quorum of 2, specifies a 5-second failure detection window, a 10-second failover timeout, and allows one replica to sync at a time.

```
port 26379
sentinel monitor mymaster 127.0.0.1 6379 2
sentinel down-after-milliseconds mymaster 5000
sentinel failover-timeout mymaster 10000
sentinel parallel-syncs mymaster 1
```

Figure 9.2: *Configuring a Redis Sentinel Instance*

What do these settings mean:

- **`port 26379`:** The default Sentinel port.
- **`sentinel monitor mymaster 127.0.0.1 6379 2`:** Monitor master (primary) **`127.0.0.1:6379`** with a quorum of 2 Sentinels (at least 2 must agree that the master is down).
- **`down-after-milliseconds 5000`:** If Sentinel cannot talk to the master for 5 seconds, it considers subjectively down.
- **`failover-timeout 10000`:** Timeout for the entire failover operation.
- **`parallel-syncs 1`:** Number of replicas to resync with the new master simultaneously.

Step 3: Start the Sentinel

Run the Sentinel:

```
redis-server sentinel.conf --sentinel
```

You will see logs such as:

```
+monitor master mymaster 127.0.0.1 6379 quorum 2
```

Figure 9.3 shows Sentinel logs confirming that monitoring has started for the master named mymaster at 127.0.0.1:6379 with a quorum of 2, indicating that the Sentinel is active and watching the master's status.

```
72778:X 28 Apr 2025 19:55:42.396 * Sentinel new configuration saved on disk
72778:X 28 Apr 2025 19:55:42.396 * Sentinel ID is bc300ca833e6727289792e01f30870056d826df0
72778:X 28 Apr 2025 19:55:42.396 # +monitor master mymaster 127.0.0.1 6379 quorum 2
72778:X 28 Apr 2025 19:55:42.396 * +slave slave 127.0.0.1:6380 127.0.0.1 6380 @ mymaster 127.0.0.1 6379
72778:X 28 Apr 2025 19:55:42.399 * Sentinel new configuration saved on disk
```

Figure 9.3: *Verifying Sentinel Logs after Startup*

Now, Sentinel is watching your master!

Step 4: Add More Sentinels (Best Practice)

Ideally, **run at least 3 Sentinels** for real production setups.

Each one will have a similar config but different ports (for example, **`26379, 26380, 26381,` and so on**).

Start them similarly:

- Create **two more sentinel config files** with the same configuration as earlier, just change the port number:

  `vim sentinel-26380.conf (Will use port 26380)`

- Add the following:

```
port 26380
sentinel monitor mymaster 127.0.0.1 6379 2
sentinel down-after-milliseconds mymaster 5000
sentinel failover-timeout mymaster 10000
sentinel parallel-syncs mymaster 1
```

Figure 9.4 shows the configuration of a second Sentinel running on port 26380. It monitors the same master (mymaster at **127.0.0.1:6379**) with a quorum of 2, the same failure detection and failover settings, ensuring redundancy and participation in failover decisions.

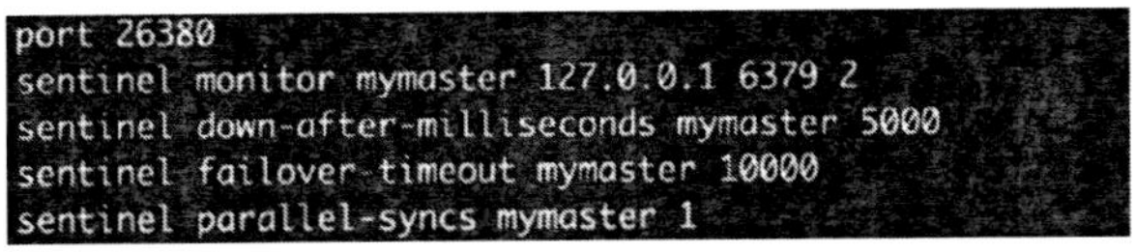

```
port 26380
sentinel monitor mymaster 127.0.0.1 6379 2
sentinel down-after-milliseconds mymaster 5000
sentinel failover-timeout mymaster 10000
sentinel parallel-syncs mymaster 1
```

Figure 9.4: *Configuring an Additional Redis Sentinel Instance*

```
vim sentinel-26381.conf (Will use port 26381)
```

- Add the following code:

```
port 26381
sentinel monitor mymaster 127.0.0.1 6379 2
sentinel down-after-milliseconds mymaster 5000
sentinel failover-timeout mymaster 10000
sentinel parallel-syncs mymaster 1
```

Figure 9.5 shows the configuration for a third Sentinel running on port 26381. Like the previous Sentinels, it monitors the master at 127.0.0.1:6379 with a quorum of 2, ensuring reliable consensus during failover decisions.

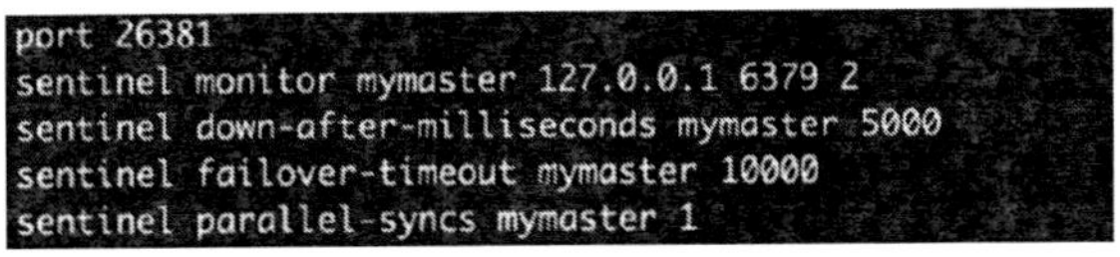

```
port 26381
sentinel monitor mymaster 127.0.0.1 6379 2
sentinel down-after-milliseconds mymaster 5000
sentinel failover-timeout mymaster 10000
sentinel parallel-syncs mymaster 1
```

Figure 9.5: *Configuring a Third Redis Sentinel Instance*

- Execute the following code:

```
redis-server sentinel-26380.conf --sentinel
redis-server sentinel-26381.conf --sentinel
```

With **three Sentinels**, they can **vote on failures** and elect new masters safely.

Key Sentinel Settings to Remember

Redis Sentinel has a few configuration options that look technical, but each one answers a very simple question.

```
sentinel monitor mymaster 127.0.0.1 6379 2
sentinel down-after-milliseconds mymaster 5000
sentinel failover-timeout mymaster 10000
sentinel parallel-syncs mymaster 1
```

Here is what they really mean:

- **`sentinel monitor mymaster 127.0.0.1 6379 2`**: "*Watch the master at 127.0.0.1:6379 and consider it 'officially down' only if* ***at least 2 Sentinels*** *agree.*"

  The last number is the **quorum** (how many Sentinels must agree before failover happens).

- **`down-after-milliseconds mymaster 5000`**: "*If this master does not respond for 5 seconds, treat it as possibly down.*"

  Smaller values = faster reaction, but more risk of false alarms. 5–10 seconds is a reasonable starting point.

- **`failover-timeout mymaster 10000`**: "*Give the failover process (choosing and promoting a replica) up to 10 seconds to complete.*"

  It also affects how often Sentinels retry if something goes wrong.

- **`parallel-syncs mymaster 1`**: "*After promoting a new master, let only 1 replica sync at a time.*"

  This avoids overloading the new master with too many full syncs in parallel.

If these settings feel advanced, you can start with values like the ones above, and adjust later once as you see how your system behaves in testing.

Testing Automatic Failover

Now, let us simulate a master (primary) crash!

1. **Kill the primary Redis:**

   ```
   kill $(lsof -t -i:6379)
   ```

2. **Watch Sentinel logs.**

   You will see something like:

```
53420:X 04 May 2025 19:20:24.113 # +sdown master mymaster 127.0.0.1 6379
53420:X 04 May 2025 19:20:24.212 * Sentinel new configuration saved on disk
53420:X 04 May 2025 19:20:24.212 # +new-epoch 27
53420:X 04 May 2025 19:20:24.218 * Sentinel new configuration saved on disk
53420:X 04 May 2025 19:20:24.218 # +vote-for-leader bc300ca833e6727289792e01f30870056d826df0 27
53420:X 04 May 2025 19:20:24.218 # +odown master mymaster 127.0.0.1 6379 #quorum 2/2
53420:X 04 May 2025 19:20:24.218 * Next failover delay: I will not start a failover before Sun May  4 19:20:45 2025
53420:X 04 May 2025 19:20:25.292 # +config-update-from sentinel bc300ca833e6727289792e01f30870056d826df0 127.0.0.1 26379 @ mymaster 127.0.0.1 6379
53420:X 04 May 2025 19:20:25.292 # +switch-master mymaster 127.0.0.1 6379 127.0.0.1 6380
53420:X 04 May 2025 19:20:25.292 * +slave slave 127.0.0.1:6379 127.0.0.1 6379 @ mymaster 127.0.0.1 6380
53420:X 04 May 2025 19:20:25.300 * Sentinel new configuration saved on disk
53420:X 04 May 2025 19:20:30.320 # +sdown slave 127.0.0.1:6379 127.0.0.1 6379 @ mymaster 127.0.0.1 6380
```

Figure 9.6: *Sentinel Logs during Automatic Failover*

   Figure 9.6 captures Sentinel logs during a failover event, where the Sentinel detects that the master is down, and automatically promotes the replica running on port 6380 to become the new master.

   Sentinel promoted the replica (**6380**) to master automatically!

   No manual steps. No downtime (except maybe a few seconds).

3. **Check the replication information, and verify the changes on both the master and replica nodes.**

   On node 6380 :

```
127.0.0.1:6380> info REPLICATION
# Replication
role:master
connected_slaves:1
slave0:ip=127.0.0.1,port=6379,state=online,offset=387216,lag=1
master_failover_state:no-failover
master_replid:39c619354f85eeeb143a74d5c6f11d2533406007
master_replid2:0000000000000000000000000000000000000000
master_repl_offset:387216
second_repl_offset:-1
repl_backlog_active:1
repl_backlog_size:1048576
repl_backlog_first_byte_offset:375365
repl_backlog_histlen:11852
```

Figure 9.7: *Verifying Replication Status Using INFO Replication on the Promoted Master*

Figure 9.7 shows the output of the **`INFO replication`** command on the former replica (**`port 6380`**), now promoted to master after automatic failover. The output confirms its new role as **master,** and shows one connected replica.

On node 6379:

```
127.0.0.1:6379> info REPLICATION
# Replication
role:slave
master_host:127.0.0.1
master_port:6380
master_link_status:up
master_last_io_seconds_ago:1
master_sync_in_progress:0
slave_read_repl_offset:377426
slave_repl_offset:377426
slave_priority:100
slave_read_only:1
replica_announced:1
connected_slaves:0
master_failover_state:no-failover
master_replid:39c619354f85eeeb143a74d5c6f11d2533406007
master_replid2:0000000000000000000000000000000000000000
master_repl_offset:377426
second_repl_offset:-1
repl_backlog_active:1
repl_backlog_size:1048576
repl_backlog_first_byte_offset:376580
repl_backlog_histlen:847
```

Figure 9.8: *Verifying Replication Status Using INFO Replication on the New Replica*

Figure 9.8 displays the **`INFO replication` output** from a replica now connected to the newly promoted master (previously replica 6380). It confirms the **replica (slave) role** and shows a healthy connection to the new master, indicating successful reconfiguration after failover.

Important Sentinel Notes:

- Sentinels themselves **do not store data.** They only manage servers.
- Your **application must support** connecting to Sentinel to discover the new master.
- **Always use odd numbers of Sentinels (3, 5, and so on) to avoid tie votes.**
- Sentinels can notify your app using Pub/Sub or client libraries that support auto-reconnects.

Summary

Redis Sentinel makes your Redis deployment **truly highly available** by:

- Monitoring master and replicas continuously.
- Detecting failures automatically.
- Promoting a new master, if needed, without human intervention.
- Helping clients find the current master.

While setting up Sentinels might feel like extra work initially, it pays off by **saving your system from downtime** when failures inevitably happen.

In the next section, we will explore how **read scaling with replicas** can supercharge your Redis performance - distributing the load smartly, without touching the master at all!

Read Scaling with Replicas

Up to this point, we have focused on using Redis replication to achieve high availability and support automatic failover. But replication offers another major advantage: It enables **horizontal scaling of read operations**, without putting additional load on the master.

Think of it this way: The master (primary) is already responsible for handling all write operations, such as session updates, counter increments, and leaderboard inserts. If it also has to serve a high volume of read traffic, such as API lookups or dashboard metrics, it can quickly become a bottleneck.

This is where replicas prove their value. By redirecting read-heavy workloads to replica nodes, you can offload the master and significantly improve the overall performance and responsiveness of your Redis setup.

In the next section, we will explore how read scaling with Redis replicas works in practice and how you can implement it effectively in your applications.

What is Read Scaling?

Read scaling is the practice of **distributing read queries** across multiple servers, instead of sending all requests to a single Redis master.

Here is how it works with Redis:

- All **writes** go to the master.
- All **replicas** stay up-to-date by receiving the master's updates.
- You can **send read commands (`GET`, `HGET`, `LRANGE`, and so on)** to any replica to reduce pressure on the master.

It is like cloning your master into extra workers, without paying the cost of write replication delays (since Redis handles that for you).

Visual Example

The following *Figure* 9.9 illustrates a read-scaling setup where all write operations are directed to the Redis master, while read operations are distributed across multiple replicas (slaves). This approach reduces load on the master and improves the overall read throughput.

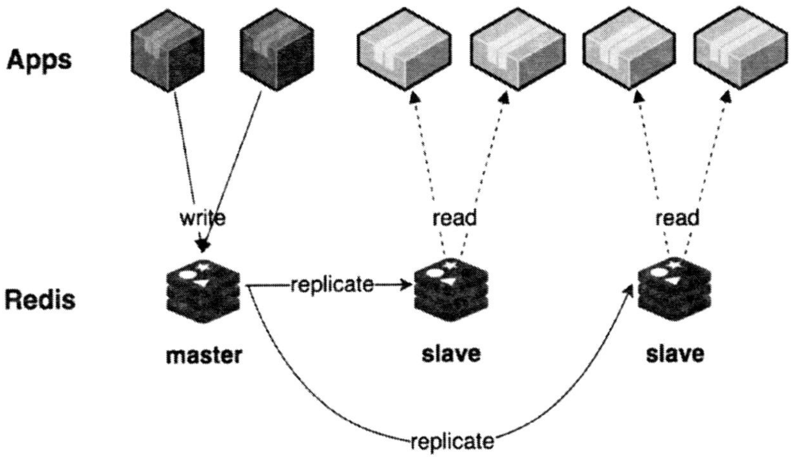

***Figure 9.9**: Read Scaling with Redis Replication*

Using Read Scaling

Consider using replicas for reads if:

- You have **high read-to-write ratios** (for example, 10 reads per write).
- Your master is seeing **CPU/memory spikes** under load.
- Your app performs **frequent lookups**, especially on large datasets.
- You want to build **read-heavy dashboards** or **public APIs**, without slowing down the main Redis instance.

Using Replicas for Reads

By default, Redis replicas are **read-only**, which is great as it ensures consistency and safety.

Step 1: Verify Read-Only Mode on Replica

```
redis-cli -p 6380 CONFIG GET replica-read-only
```

The following *Figure* 9.10 shows the use of the **`CONFIG GET replica-read-only`** command on port 6380 to confirm that the replica is operating in read-only mode, ensuring that it does not accept write operations, and maintains data consistency with the master.

```
1) "replica-read-only"
2) "yes"
```

***Figure 9.10**: Verifying Read-Only Mode on Redis Replica*

You are good to go.

Step 2: Send Read Queries to Replica

Let us assume:

- Master: **`6379`**
- Replica: **`6380`**

 # Write to the master

```
redis-cli -p 6379 SET user:1:name "replication_test"
```

 # Read from the replica

```
redis-cli -p 6380 GET user:1:name
```

Tip: Use Load Balancers or Smart Clients

In **production**, you do not manually switch ports.

You use:

- A load balancer (such as HAProxy or nginx) to distribute reads across replicas.
- Or a smart Redis client (such as **`ioredis`**, **`Jedis`**, **`Lettuce`**, and so on) that:
  - o Writes to the master
  - o Reads from replicas

This helps you automate read-routing efficiently.

Caveats to Keep in Mind

Replication is Asynchronous

- Writes on the master may take a few milliseconds to reach replicas.
- So, reads from a replica might return slightly stale data.
- This is usually fine for dashboards, analytics, or product views.
- But for real-time validation or session updates, always use the master.

Real-World Use Cases

Here are some real-world examples where read scaling with replicas helps:

Use Case	Why It Works Well
Mobile app config fetches	Frequent reads, rare updates
Product catalog pages	Heavy traffic, infrequent changes
Dashboard visualizations	Can tolerate eventual consistency
API caching	Great for GET-heavy public endpoints
Geo-distributed reads	Place replicas closer to users

Table 9.2: *Real-World Use Cases for Read Scaling with Replicas*

Table 9.2 highlights real-world scenarios where this approach proves especially effective, along with explanations of why it works well in each case.

Quick Checklist of Best Practices:

- Use replicas for read-heavy workloads.
- Keep **`replica-read-only yes`** to avoid accidental writes.
- Monitor replication lag with **`INFO replication`**.
- Use smart clients or load balancers to route traffic.
- Do not expect real-time updates, and plan for eventual consistency.

Summary

Redis replication not only provides high availability but also enables powerful read scaling. By offloading read traffic to replicas, you keep the master optimized for writes, improving the overall system performance and stability.

While replicas offer near real-time data, they are not exact clones. When used effectively, they help your applications handle heavy loads and maintain responsiveness under pressure.

Common Issues and Troubleshooting

While Redis replication is generally reliable and easy to set up, real-world systems, especially those operating under heavy load or unstable network conditions, can still experience issues.

Understanding the potential pitfalls, recognizing early warning signs, and knowing how to troubleshoot effectively are vital skills for maintaining a healthy Redis replication environment.

In this section, we will walk through the most common replication challenges, provide practical troubleshooting techniques, share real-world examples, and offer tips to prevent these issues from occurring in the first place.

Common Problems in Redis Replication

Replica Disconnection (`master_link_status: down`)

When you run **`INFO replication`** on a replica, you see:

```
master_link_status: down
```

The following *Figure* 9.11 shows the output of the **`INFO replication`** command on a replica, where the **`master_link_status: down`** indicates that the replica has lost connection to the master.

```
127.0.0.1:6380> info REPLICATION
# Replication
role:slave
master_host:127.0.0.1
master_port:6379
master_link_status:down
```

***Figure* 9.11:** *Checking master_link_status on a Redis Replica*

What does it mean: The replica has lost its connection to the master.

Possible causes:

- Network issues between the master and the replica.
- The master Redis process crashed or was restarted.
- Firewall rules are blocking ports.
- The master is under heavy load, dropping connections.

How to troubleshoot:

- Check if the master Redis process is still running.
- Verify firewall and network settings.
- Restart the replica if needed to re-establish the link:

```
redis-cli -p 6380
> REPLICAOF 127.0.0.1 6379
```

Full Resynchronization Happening too Often

Your replicas keep doing full syncs, and Redis performance drops when this happens.

What does it mean:

Partial resynchronization is failing, so replicas are forced to reload the entire dataset.

Possible causes:

- The replication backlog (**`repl-backlog-size`**) is too small.
- Replicas disconnect for too long, losing backlog history.
- The master restarts, losing backlog memory.

How to troubleshoot:

- Increase the backlog size in **`redis.conf`**:

  ```
  repl-backlog-size 10mb
  ```

  The following *Figure* 9.12 displays the default repl-backlog-size configuration set to 1 megabyte. This buffer stores the recent write commands to allow partial resynchronization with replicas in case of temporary disconnections, helping to avoid costly full syncs.

```
# Set the replication backlog size. The backlog is a buffer that accumulates
# replica data when replicas are disconnected for some time, so that when a
# replica wants to reconnect again, often a full resync is not needed, but a
# partial resync is enough, just passing the portion of data the replica
# missed while disconnected.
#
# The bigger the replication backlog, the longer the replica can endure the
# disconnect and later be able to perform a partial resynchronization.
#
# The backlog is only allocated if there is at least one replica connected.
#
repl-backlog-size 1mb
```

***Figure* 9.12:** *Configuring repl-backlog-size in redis.conf*

- Ensure that replicas reconnect quickly after short disconnections.
- Monitor network stability between the master and the replicas.

High Replica Lag

Replication is active, but replicas are falling significantly behind the master.

```
master_link_status: up
slave_repl_offset much lower than master_repl_offset
```

What does it mean:

The replica cannot keep up with the write traffic being sent by the master.

Possible causes:

- The replica hardware (CPU/disk) is underpowered.
- The master is handling too many writes too quickly.
- Network bottlenecks.

How to troubleshoot:

- Monitor the **`master_last_io_seconds_ago`** field to measure lag.

- Scale your Redis architecture (more replicas or bigger hardware).
- Use replication diskless sync to improve replica speed.

Writes Accidentally Hitting Replicas

Applications accidentally send **SET, DEL, or INCR** commands to replicas.

What does it mean:

Replicas are read-only by default, but if this protection is disabled, you could corrupt the data.

Possible causes:

- The client library is misconfigured or unaware of node roles.
- Application logic treats replicas and masters the same.
- The load balancer is distributing writes to all nodes.
- DNS or service discovery points to a replica.
- Writes are made during failover before promotion completes.
- Manual writes are done on a replica during testing.

How to troubleshoot:

- Ensure that **replica-read-only yes** is set in your **redis.conf**.

  The following *Figure* 9.13 shows the **replica-read-only yes** directive in the Redis configuration file, which ensures that replicas operate in read-only mode and do not accept any write commands, preserving replication integrity.

```
# You can configure a replica instance to accept writes or not. Writing against
# a replica instance may be useful to store some ephemeral data (because data
# written on a replica will be easily deleted after resync with the master) but
# may also cause problems if clients are writing to it because of a
# misconfiguration.
#
# Since Redis 2.6 by default replicas are read-only.
#
# Note: read only replicas are not designed to be exposed to untrusted clients
# on the internet. It's just a protection layer against misuse of the instance.
# Still a read only replica exports by default all the administrative commands
# such as CONFIG, DEBUG, and so forth. To a limited extent you can improve
# security of read only replicas using 'rename-command' to shadow all the
# administrative / dangerous commands.
replica-read-only yes
```

***Figure* 9.13:** *Verifying replica-read-only setting in redis.conf*

- Always configure your clients to **write to the master only**.
- Add strict routing at the application layer to separate reads and writes.

Split-Brain Problems after Master Recovery

After a master crash and replica promotion, the old master comes back online, **still thinking it is the master**, causing two conflicting masters.

What does it mean:

Without Sentinel or manual intervention, the old master does not know that a failover has happened.

Possible causes:

- No external system to reconfigure the old master as a replica.

- Manual failover was done, but the old master was not reconfigured.
- The old master restarted without clearing its role state.
- Network partition isolated the original master during promotion.

How to troubleshoot:

- When the old master comes back, reconfigure it immediately:

  ```
  redis-cli -p 6379
  > REPLICAOF 127.0.0.1 6380
  ```

  (Assuming `6380` was promoted to the master.)
- Use Sentinel to manage masters automatically and prevent split-brain issues.

Note: *Sentinel greatly reduces split-brain scenarios, but correct quorum placement and network design are still critical.*

Memory Exhaustion on the Replica

The replica process crashes or is killed by the OS (for example, `OOM Killer` in Linux). You might also see replication failing or Redis restarting repeatedly.

What does it mean:

Replication is memory-intensive, especially during full synchronization. If your replica does not have enough RAM to hold:

- The **RDB snapshot**
- The **live dataset**
- Plus extra memory for **buffering commands**

Possible causes:

- The replica has **less memory than the master**.
- The **dataset size grew** unexpectedly.
- You are doing **frequent full syncs** (for example, reconnects) that spike memory usage.

How to troubleshoot:

- Check logs for **Out of Memory (OOM)** errors.
- Make sure that the **replica has at least as much RAM** as the master.
- Monitor memory usage with:

  ```
  redis-cli -p 6380 INFO memory
  ```

  The following *Figure* 9.14 shows the output of the **`INFO memory`** command run on a replica (**`port 6380`**), providing details such as used memory, peak usage, fragmentation ratio, and allocator statistics useful for monitoring memory health and diagnosing issues such as memory exhaustion.

```
# Memory
used_memory:1203056
used_memory_human:1.15M
used_memory_rss:5046272
used_memory_rss_human:4.81M
used_memory_peak:1203056
used_memory_peak_human:1.15M
used_memory_peak_perc:101.30%
used_memory_overhead:1100780
used_memory_startup:1098736
used_memory_dataset:102276
used_memory_dataset_perc:98.04%
allocator_allocated:1168256
allocator_active:5014528
allocator_resident:5014528
total_system_memory:19327352832
total_system_memory_human:18.00G
used_memory_lua:31744
used_memory_vm_eval:31744
used_memory_lua_human:31.00K
used_memory_scripts_eval:0
number_of_cached_scripts:0
number_of_functions:0
number_of_libraries:0
used_memory_vm_functions:32768
used_memory_vm_total:64512
used_memory_vm_total_human:63.00K
used_memory_functions:216
used_memory_scripts:216
used_memory_scripts_human:216B
maxmemory:0
maxmemory_human:0B
maxmemory_policy:noeviction
```

Figure 9.14: *Checking Memory Usage on Replica Using INFO Memory*

- Consider reviewing diskless replication settings based on memory constraints:

  `repl-diskless-sync no`

  The following *Figure* 9.15 shows the repl-diskless-sync parameter set to **yes** in the Redis configuration file. Enabling this setting allows Redis to stream the RDB snapshot directly to replicas during full synchronization, improving performance by avoiding the disk I/O.

```
# Replication SYNC strategy: disk or socket.
#
# New replicas and reconnecting replicas that are not able to continue the
# replication process just receiving differences, need to do what is called a
# "full synchronization". An RDB file is transmitted from the master to the
# replicas.
#
# The transmission can happen in two different ways:
#
# 1) Disk-backed: The Redis master creates a new process that writes the RDB
#                 file on disk. Later the file is transferred by the parent
#                 process to the replicas incrementally.
# 2) Diskless: The Redis master creates a new process that directly writes the
#              RDB file to replica sockets, without touching the disk at all.
#
# With disk-backed replication, while the RDB file is generated, more replicas
# can be queued and served with the RDB file as soon as the current child
# producing the RDB file finishes its work. With diskless replication instead
# once the transfer starts, new replicas arriving will be queued and a new
# transfer will start when the current one terminates.
#
# When diskless replication is used, the master waits a configurable amount of
# time (in seconds) before starting the transfer in the hope that multiple
# replicas will arrive and the transfer can be parallelized.
#
# With slow disks and fast (large bandwidth) networks, diskless replication
# works better.
repl-diskless-sync yes
```

Figure 9.15: *repl-diskless-sync Setting in redis.conf*

`repl-diskless-sync yes/no` in Redis

The `repl-diskless-sync` setting in Redis controls **how the master sends data to replicas during a full synchronization.** By default, when a replica connects and requests a full sync, the master generates an RDB (Redis Database Dump) file and saves it to the disk. Then it reads it back to stream the data to the replica.

When you set:

```
repl-diskless-sync yes
```

Redis **bypasses the disk completely** and **streams the RDB snapshot directly to the replica over the network**. This is known as **diskless replication**.

The Need for Using Diskless Replication:

- **Faster sync:** Avoids writing to and reading from disk, reducing latency during full synchronization.
- **Reduced I/O load:** Eliminates unnecessary disk I/O, which is valuable on systems with heavy disk usage.
- **Better for ephemeral environments:** Useful when the server does not have persistent storage or when replication speed is a priority.

Considerations:

- Diskless replication is efficient but can be **memory-intensive**, as the RDB snapshot must be fully held in memory during the streaming process.
- If the replication process fails mid-way, the master **cannot reuse a pre-saved RDB file** and must regenerate the snapshot for the next attempt.

In summary, **`repl-diskless-sync yes`** helps optimize replication performance by streaming data directly from memory to replicas, making replication **faster and more resource-efficient**, especially in setups where high throughput and minimal disk I/O are important.

In disk-based replication (**`repl-diskless-sync no`**, which is the default), Redis writes the RDB snapshot to disk and then reads it back to send to the replicas. This reduces the memory footprint because the snapshot is temporarily stored on disk, not fully held in memory.

Frequent Evictions on the Replica

You notice that keys are being evicted (deleted automatically) from the replica, even though you did not explicitly delete them.

What does it mean:

Redis is an in-memory database. If memory is full and eviction is enabled (like **`maxmemory-policy allkeys-lru`**), Redis starts evicting keys to free up space.

In replication, this can be dangerous because:

- The master keeps a full dataset.
- The replica starts evicting keys when it is out of the RAM, causing it to diverge from the master!

Possible causes:

- Replica has less memory than the master.
- Eviction policy (for example, **`allkeys-lru`**) is enabled on the replica.
- Memory usage is not monitored or capped properly.

- Background processes on the replica consume additional RAM.

How to troubleshoot:

- Run:

```
redis-cli -p 6380 INFO stats
```

The following *Figure* 9.16 displays the **evicted_keys** field in the output of the **INFO stats** command on a replica (port 6380). A non-zero value indicates that Redis has evicted keys due to memory pressure, which may lead to data inconsistencies if not properly handled in replication scenarios.

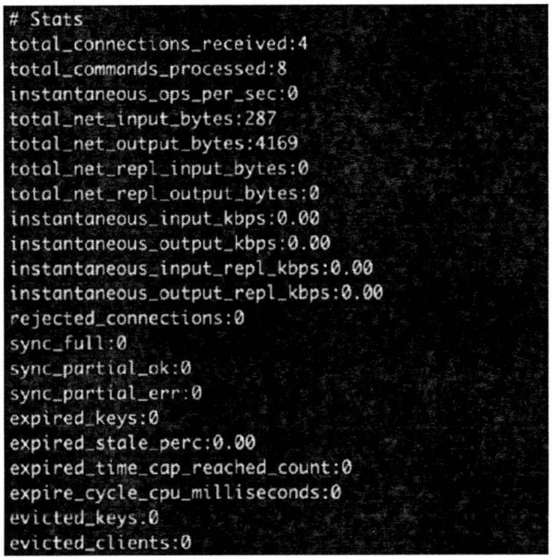

```
# Stats
total_connections_received:4
total_commands_processed:8
instantaneous_ops_per_sec:0
total_net_input_bytes:287
total_net_output_bytes:4169
total_net_repl_input_bytes:0
total_net_repl_output_bytes:0
instantaneous_input_kbps:0.00
instantaneous_output_kbps:0.00
instantaneous_input_repl_kbps:0.00
instantaneous_output_repl_kbps:0.00
rejected_connections:0
sync_full:0
sync_partial_ok:0
sync_partial_err:0
expired_keys:0
expired_stale_perc:0.00
expired_time_cap_reached_count:0
expire_cycle_cpu_milliseconds:0
evicted_keys:0
evicted_clients:0
```

Figure 9.16: *Observing evicted_keys in Replica Using INFO stats*

Look for the **evicted_keys** field.

- Ensure that your replica has the same (or more) RAM as the master.
- Check your eviction policy:

```
redis-cli CONFIG GET maxmemory-policy
```

The following *Figure* 9.17 shows the maxmemory-policy setting in the Redis configuration file. This parameter controls how Redis behaves when it reaches its memory limit, for example, whether it evicts keys and decides which keys to evict. Proper configuration is essential to avoid unintended data loss, especially on replicas.

```
# MAXMEMORY POLICY: how Redis will select what to remove when maxmemory
# is reached. You can select one from the following behaviors:
#
# volatile-lru -> Evict using approximated LRU, only keys with an expire set.
# allkeys-lru -> Evict any key using approximated LRU.
# volatile-lfu -> Evict using approximated LFU, only keys with an expire set.
# allkeys-lfu -> Evict any key using approximated LFU.
# volatile-random -> Remove a random key having an expire set.
# allkeys-random -> Remove a random key, any key.
# volatile-ttl -> Remove the key with the nearest expire time (minor TTL)
# noeviction -> Don't evict anything, just return an error on write operations.
#
# LRU means Least Recently Used
# LFU means Least Frequently Used
#
# Both LRU, LFU and volatile-ttl are implemented using approximated
# randomized algorithms.
#
# Note: with any of the above policies, when there are no suitable keys for
# eviction, Redis will return an error on write operations that require
# more memory. These are usually commands that create new keys, add data or
# modify existing keys. A few examples are: SET, INCR, HSET, LPUSH, SUNIONSTORE,
# SORT (due to the STORE argument), and EXEC (if the transaction includes any
# command that requires memory).
#
# The default is:
#
# maxmemory-policy noeviction
```

Figure 9.17: *Verifying maxmemory-policy in redis.conf*

- Set a **safe `policy`** on replicas, for example:

  `maxmemory-policy noeviction`

This way, if you hit the limit, Redis will **reject writes**, instead of silently evicting the data.

Replica Not Starting Because of Wrong Permissions

When starting the replica, you see errors such as:

`Can't save in RDB format: Permission denied`

Or the replica fails to write files.

What does it mean:

The Redis process **lacks permission** to write snapshot files (RDB) or append-only files (AOF).

Possible causes:

- The Redis user does not have write access to the data directory.
- Ownership of Redis files or folders is incorrect.
- The file system is mounted as read-only.
- Misconfigured **`dir`** path in **`redis.conf`**.

How to troubleshoot:

- Make sure Redis is running as the correct user (e.g., **`redis`**).
- Fix directory permissions:

  ```
  chown redis:redis /var/lib/redis
  chmod 700 /var/lib/redis
  ```

Check the path set in **`redis.conf`** for **`dir`** and **`dbfilename`**.

Replication Traffic Overloading the Network

During replication (especially full sync), the **network gets saturated**, and other services slow down or time out.

What does it mean:

The master is pushing **large datasets** across the network. This can happen if:

- Your dataset is **big**.
- You have multiple replicas syncing **at the same time**.
- You are on a **narrow or busy network**.

Possible causes:

- The dataset size is too large for the current network capacity.
- Multiple replicas are syncing simultaneously.
- Network bandwidth is limited or already under heavy use.
- Frequent replica restarts trigger repeated full syncs.

How to troubleshoot:

- Use `repl-diskless-sync-delay` to **stagger syncs**:

  ```
  repl-diskless-sync-delay 5
  ```

Figure 9.18 shows the **`repl-diskless-sync-delay`** parameter set in the Redis configuration file. This setting introduces a delay (in seconds) before the diskless replication starts, allowing multiple replicas to join the sync session and share the same RDB stream, optimizing network and resource usage during full synchronization.

```
# When diskless replication is enabled, it is possible to configure the delay
# the server waits in order to spawn the child that transfers the RDB via socket
# to the replicas.
#
# This is important since once the transfer starts, it is not possible to serve
# new replicas arriving, that will be queued for the next RDB transfer, so the
# server waits a delay in order to let more replicas arrive.
#
# The delay is specified in seconds, and by default is 5 seconds. To disable
# it entirely just set it to 0 seconds and the transfer will start ASAP.
repl-diskless-sync-delay 5
```

Figure 9.18: *Configuring repl-diskless-sync-delay in redis.conf*

This lets multiple replicas **join the sync session** and **download the snapshot once**, reducing duplication.

- If using cloud, **place replicas near the master** (same availability zone).
- Monitor bandwidth usage with system tools (for example, **`iftop`**, **`nload`**, and so on).

Security Misconfigurations (Replication Open to the World)

Unauthorized systems can **connect to your Redis server**, potentially reading sensitive data or hijacking replication.

What does it mean:

Redis replication **exposes a TCP port**, and unless you have secured Redis, anyone who knows your IP:port can connect.

Possible causes:

- Redis is bound to `0.0.0.0` or a public IP without restrictions.
- No authentication (`requirepass` or `masterauth`) is configured.
- Firewall or network security group rules are too permissive.
- Redis is exposed directly to the internet.

How to troubleshoot:

- Always **bind Redis to localhost** or trusted IPs:

```
bind 127.0.0.1 192.168.1.10
```

- Require authentication:

```
requirepass your-strong-password
masterauth your-strong-password
```

- Use firewalls (for example, `ufw`, `iptables`) to **restrict access.**

Expanded Troubleshooting Summary

Here is a more complete view of common Redis replication challenges:

Problem	How to Handle
Replica disconnects	Check network/firewall; restart replica.
Full resyncs are too frequent	Increase backlog; stabilize connections.
High replica lag	Upgrade hardware, balance load, and diskless sync.
Writes hitting replicas	Enforce replica-read-only yes; review app logic.
Split-brain after failover	Reattach the old primary to the new primary.
Memory exhaustion	Match replica memory to master; enable repl-diskless-sync.
Frequent evictions	Adjust eviction policy; increase RAM.
Permission errors	Fix file ownership and directory permissions.
Network overload	Use repl-diskless-sync-delay; collocate nodes.
Security risks	Bind to trusted IPs, require passwords; firewall Redis ports.

Table 9.3: *Common Redis Replication Issues and How to Handle Them*

Table 9.3 summarizes common problems that can occur in a Redis replication setup, and provides actionable solutions for resolving or preventing them.

Final Thoughts

Replication is a fantastic feature, but it comes with real-world challenges. By **understanding the full lifecycle of replication** and **watching out for these common pitfalls**, you can build Redis systems that are not only fast and scalable but also **resilient and secure.**

Advanced Tips and Best Practices

By now, you must have learned how Redis replication works, how to set it up, monitor it, and troubleshoot the common issues. That is already a solid foundation, but as your system scales and your needs become more demanding, fine-tuning your replication setup becomes essential.

In this section, we will explore advanced tips, tricks, and best practices that real-world engineers use to keep their Redis environments fast, reliable, and future-proof.

- **Enable Diskless Replication for Faster Syncs**

  By default, Redis creates an RDB snapshot on disk and then streams it to replicas during full sync. This can cause:

  - Disk I/O bottlenecks
  - Delays, especially on large datasets

  Better option: Enable diskless replication to stream the RDB snapshot directly from memory.

  How to enable:

  ```
  repl-diskless-sync yes
  ```

  This reduces sync time and improves performance during full syncs, especially useful in high-throughput environments.

  > **Note:** Diskless replication can increase memory pressure during full syncs, so ensure sufficient RAM is available on the primary.

- **Increase Replication Backlog to Avoid Full Resyncs**

  The replication backlog is a circular buffer where Redis keeps recent write operations. If a replica disconnects temporarily, it can catch up using this buffer (**partial resync**).

  If your backlog is too small and gets overwritten before the replica reconnects, Redis must do a full **sync (expensive!)**.

  Best practice:

  ```
  repl-backlog-size 10mb  # or larger, depending on your write volume
  ```

  Larger backlogs help **avoid unnecessary full resyncs.**

- **Monitor Replication Lag Continuously**

  Replication lag can sneak up silently, causing stale reads or delayed failovers.

  Key metrics to monitor:

  - `master_last_io_seconds_ago`
  - `slave_repl_offset`
  - Compare with primary's `master_repl_offset`

  Example with Redis CLI:

  ```
  redis-cli -p 6380 INFO replication
  ```

  Set up alerts when lag exceeds your acceptable threshold (for example, 5 seconds).

- **Place Replicas in Different Availability Zones**

  If you are running Redis in the cloud (AWS, GCP, Azure), it is wise to spread replicas across different zones or regions.

  Why?

  - If a full zone outage happens, your replicas in other zones stay alive and can take over.

Trade-off: Cross-zone replication adds **network latency,** but it is a small price to pay for **disaster resilience.**

- **Automate Primary Reattachment after Failover**

  When a primary fails and later comes back online, it does not automatically know it should now be a replica.

  Best practice: Automate this with tools such as:

  - Redis Sentinel (which handles it for you)
  - Or custom scripts that reattach the old primary:

    ```
    redis-cli -p 6379 REPLICAOF new-master-ip new-master-port
    ```

This prevents split-brain situations.

- **Test Failover Regularly**

  Failovers are not "set-and-forget."

  Regular testing ensures that your replication + Sentinel setup works when disaster strikes.

  Example:

  - Kill the primary.
  - Confirm a replica is promoted.
  - Check if your application successfully reconnects to the new primary.

  Tip: Run failover tests during low-traffic windows.

- **Use Client Libraries that Support Sentinel**

  If you are using Sentinel, your app needs to discover the new primary automatically.

  Choose a Redis client that supports Sentinel natively, such as:

  - `ioredis` (Node.js)
  - `Jedis` (Java)
  - `redis-py` (Python)
  - StackExchange.Redis (C#)

- **Secure Replication Traffic**

  Replication traffic can expose sensitive data across the network. Protect it by:

  - Using private networks (VPCs, VPNs).
  - Enabling TLS/SSL (available in Redis 6+).
  - Setting **requirepass** and **masterauth** to enforce authentication between primary and replicas.

  Example:

  ```
  masterauth myStrongPassword
  ```

- **Log and Alert on Replication Failures**

  Replication failures may not stop your app immediately, but they silently degrade resilience.

  Set up logs/alerts when:

  - The replication link goes down.

    - Lag exceeds X seconds.
    - Sentinel triggers a failover.

  Use Prometheus, Datadog, or RedisInsight for deeper visibility.

- **Avoid Circular Replication**

  A common mistake:

  Setting up two masters to replicate to each other.

  Example:

    - **Master A** → `replica of` **Master B**
    - **Master B** → `replica of` **Master A**

  This creates infinite loops and corrupts data. Always keep replication one-way only.

- **Set Replica Priorities for Failover**

  When multiple replicas are available, Sentinel uses priority numbers to pick the next master.

  You can influence failover selection using:

  ```
  replica-priority 100
  ```

    - A lower number = higher priority.
    - Set to 0 to exclude a replica from being promoted.

Understanding `repl-diskless-sync` and `repl-diskless-sync-delay`:

Replication settings such as repl-diskless-sync and repl-diskless-sync-delay can look scary at first, but the idea behind them is simple.

- **`repl-diskless-sync yes`** tells the master:

  "When a replica needs a full sync, do not write an RDB file to disk first. Just stream the data directly over the network."

  This avoids extra disk I/O and is usually **faster**, especially when you have multiple replicas.

- **`repl-diskless-sync-delay` 5 says:**

  "When a full sync is about to start, wait up to 5 seconds to see if other replicas also need a full sync, and then serve them all in one go."

  This is helpful when you are starting several replicas at the same time, or after a restart.

A simple way to think about it:

- Without diskless sync:
    - **Master**: *"Let me write a big snapshot file to disk, then send it."*
- With diskless sync:
    - **Master**: *"I'll just pour the data straight from memory to the replicas."*

Summary

Advanced replication is not just about turning on a few settings; it is about **engineering your Redis system for resilience, performance, and long-term growth.**

With smart tuning (diskless sync, backlog sizing), proactive monitoring, solid security, and automated failover mechanisms, **you can build a Redis replication setup that just works even when the unexpected happens.**

Conclusion

Replication in Redis might seem straightforward at first, such as just copying data from a primary node to replicas, but as we explored in this chapter, it is much more than that. It is the heartbeat of systems that demand speed, reliability, and resilience. What starts as a simple sync mechanism turns into a powerful tool for building robust architectures that stay strong even when things go wrong.

Throughout this chapter, we looked closely at how replication works behind the scenes from the first handshake to the live updates that keep replicas in sync with the primary. We walked through setting up replication manually and through configuration files, making sure that your setup survives restarts, and is ready for real-world use.

We also learned how to keep an eye on replication health, catch issues early, and understand what is happening under the hood using simple Redis commands. Failover handling was another key topic, where we saw both manual promotion and fully automated recovery using Redis Sentinel, which can keep things running smoothly when servers go down unexpectedly.

Along the way, we talked about how replication is not just about redundancy; it also helps with scaling. Offloading reads to replicas can dramatically improve performance without putting extra load on the primary. And we did not shy away from the tougher parts either. We tackled real-world challenges like memory pressure, eviction policies, and network hiccups that can complicate replication in production environments.

If there is one thing to take away from this chapter, it is this: Redis makes it easy to get started with replication, but doing it right, doing it in a way that supports your system as it grows, takes care, and planning. It is not just about flipping a few config settings. It is about thinking ahead: placing replicas strategically, monitoring actively, testing failovers before they happen, and building security into your design from day one.

When done well, replication becomes more than just a safety net; it becomes a core strength. Whether your application runs in a single region or spans the globe, replication gives you the confidence to move fast, scale out, and recover from the unexpected.

In the next chapter, *Redis Clustering and Sharding for Scalability and Availability*, we will dive into how Redis takes things a step further, splitting data across multiple nodes to handle massive scale, while keeping performance high and downtime low. It is where Redis shows its muscle in distributed systems, and this is where we are headed to as our next step.

CHAPTER 10

Redis Clustering and Sharding for Scalability and Availability

Introduction

Redis Cluster offers a built-in way to scale Redis horizontally, while maintaining high availability. It goes beyond simple master-replica setups by distributing data across multiple nodes using a concept called **sharding**. Instead of storing all the data on a single server, Redis Cluster intelligently splits it across a group of nodes, ensuring better performance, fault tolerance, and the ability to grow with your needs.

In this chapter, we will dive deep into how Redis Cluster works. You will learn about its architecture, how data is partitioned using hash slots, and how Redis handles node communication and failovers. We will walk through a step-by-step guide to setting up your own cluster, adding and removing nodes, and handling client-side behaviors like redirection. We will also explore key trade-offs, limitations, and best practices, so that you are well-prepared to run Redis in a clustered, production-ready environment.

Structure

In this chapter, we will cover the following topics:

- Introduction to Redis Cluster
- Beyond Replication: Embracing Redis Clustering
- Understanding Redis Cluster Architecture
- Slots and Data Distribution (Sharding Explained)
- Setting up a Redis Cluster (Step-by-Step)
- Adding and Removing Nodes
- Failover and High Availability in Cluster Mode
- Securing Redis Cluster Communication
- Client-Side Behavior in Cluster Mode
- Handling Redirection (MOVED and ASK)
- Limitations and Trade-offs of Redis Cluster
- Monitoring and Maintaining a Redis Cluster
- Performance Tuning Tips for Large-Scale Clusters
- Best Practices

Introduction to Redis Cluster

When you first start using Redis, everything feels fast and simple. You can read and write data at lightning speed, set up replication for high availability, and even add replicas to scale your read traffic. For many applications, this setup works beautifully.

But as your system grows to millions of keys, thousands of concurrent users, and massive write volumes, you begin to hit the **limits of a single Redis instance.**

Maybe, memory usage starts creeping up. Maybe, your Redis instance cannot keep up with the write load. Or maybe, you just do not feel comfortable relying on one machine to hold all your critical in-memory data.

This is where **Redis Cluster** enters the scene, not as a replacement for what you have built so far, but as the **next logical step** when your system demands more **scalability, fault tolerance, and distribution.**

Terminology Note

Throughout this chapter, the terms master/slave and primary/replica may be used interchangeably, depending on context. This is intentional and reflects real Redis Cluster commands, logs, and outputs.

Please remember:

- Master = Primary
- Slave = Replica

The underlying Redis behavior and architecture remain the same, regardless of the terminology used.

So What is Redis Cluster?

Redis Cluster is a distributed implementation of Redis that allows you to:

- Split your dataset across multiple Redis nodes (a process called sharding).
- Continue operating even when some nodes fail (thanks to built-in replication and failover).
- Avoid a single point of failure. Each node in the cluster knows about the others.

In short, Redis Cluster helps you scale horizontally, distribute your workload, and build a more resilient data architecture, without needing external tools or services.

Why Not Just Use a Bigger Server?

That is a fair question, and one many teams ask.

You can scale vertically for a while. Maybe, you double the RAM. Move to a more powerful VM. Add more CPU cores. And yes, Redis will fly... for a time.

But eventually, you hit a point where:

- Memory limits become a bottleneck (you just cannot go higher).
- Even with replication, the master (primary) node still handles **all writes**, and often many reads as well. Over time, this central point of responsibility becomes a bottleneck. While replicas can help distribute read traffic, **writes remain a single-node concern**, making it hard to scale further or protect against overload.

Redis Cluster addresses these problems by spreading the data and the responsibility across multiple nodes.

What Makes Redis Cluster Different?

Unlike traditional Redis setups with one master and several replicas, Redis Cluster gives you:

Sharding Built-In

- Data is automatically distributed across nodes using a hash slot mechanism.
- No manual key partitioning required.

Multiple Masters

- Each node can be a master responsible for part of the keyspace.
- You are no longer limited to one node doing all the writing.

Automatic Failover

- If a master goes down, one of its replicas is promoted automatically.
- The cluster reconfigures itself with minimal disruption.

Peer-to-Peer Communication

- Redis nodes talk to each other directly.
- There is no central coordinator or manager.

Real-World Scenarios Where Redis Cluster Shines

Here are just a few examples of how Redis Cluster can help:

- You are running an e-commerce platform with millions of users and need a scalable way to store cart data, product metadata, and session state.
- Your analytics system ingests millions of events per second, and needs to cache aggregated counters by region, category, or time window.
- You are building a multi-tenant SaaS product, and want each customer's data spread across the cluster for performance and isolation.

In all of these cases, Redis Cluster enables scale, speed, and safety, all built directly into Redis itself.

But It is Not Magic

Redis Cluster is powerful, but it is not plug-and-play. You need to:

- Understand how data is sharded.
- Learn how failover works in cluster mode.
- Know how clients handle redirection (like **MOVED** and **ASK** errors).
- Carefully plan node placement, replication, and backups.

That is exactly what this chapter will help you do.

Beyond Replication: Embracing Redis Clustering

Redis replication is incredibly useful. It lets you create **exact copies of your Redis master (replicas)**, which can:

- Offload read traffic.
- Provide redundancy in case the master fails.
- Serve as a backup for disaster recovery.

But as powerful as replication is, it has some **fundamental limitations**, especially when your application starts growing rapidly in size, users, and complexity.

In this section, we will break down **why replication alone may not be enough**, and why Redis Cluster becomes the natural next step when you are aiming for serious scalability and resilience.

Why Redis Replication Works Well

Let us start with what replication gives you:

- **Read Scaling**: Replicas can handle read queries, reducing load on the master.
- **High Availability (to an extent)**: If the master fails, you can promote a replica manually, or use Redis Sentinel for automatic failover.
- **Real-Time Backup**: Replicas are near real-time mirrors of your master's data, so that they can help during recovery.

Hence, if your app is mostly read-heavy, replication might serve you well for a while.

But here is the catch: write operations still go through a single node.

These are the **core limitations of Redis replication:**

- Only the master can handle writes.
- All replicas are read-only.

That means:

- No matter how many replicas you add, **write performance does not improve**.
- If your app is **write-intensive** (for example, analytics, real-time updates, logs, metrics, and session state), the master becomes a **bottleneck**.
- Even if you are horizontally scaling reads, you are still **vertically scaling writes**, which hits a wall eventually.

The Problem of Dataset Growth

Another big challenge is **data size**. Redis is an **in-memory database**, and **storing everything in RAM has limits**.

- With replication:
    - Every replica holds a **full copy** of the master's dataset.
    - If your master stores 100 GB of data, each replica needs the same.

Now you need:

- **Big, expensive machines** with enough RAM.
- **Wasted memory** due to full dataset duplication across nodes.
- Still no relief for write overload.

How Redis Cluster Solves These Problems

Redis Cluster is designed to overcome the limitations of replication by **splitting your data across multiple masters,** which is called **sharding**.

Here is what changes:

1. **Write Scaling**
    - Redis Cluster spreads the keyspace across **multiple master nodes**.

- Each master handles **a slice of the data**, both reads and writes.
- More nodes = more write throughput.

2. **Memory Distribution**
   - Your dataset is divided across nodes.
   - If you have 3 masters and 90 GB of data, each might store only ~30 GB.
   - Now you can scale horizontally without maxing out memory on one server.
3. **Automatic Failover (Still Built-in)**
   - Each master in Redis Cluster has **one or more replicas**.
   - If a master fails, its replica is **promoted automatically**.
   - The cluster continues functioning with **minimal disruption**.
4. **No Single Point of Failure**
   - There is no central master; each node is aware of the others.
   - Clients can talk to any node, and will be redirected if needed.

When to Move from Replication to Clustering

Your Scenario	Recommended Redis Setup
Read-heavy workload, low write volume	Master + Replicas (Replication)
Moderate write volume, small dataset	Master + Replicas + Sentinel
High write volume, growing dataset	Redis Cluster (Sharding)
Large team/data/multi-tenant scale	Redis Cluster + Clients with cluster support

Table 10.1: *Recommended Redis Setup Based on Workload Characteristics*

Summary

Redis replication is a fantastic solution for read scaling and basic high availability, but when your system starts demanding more writes, more memory, and more fault tolerance, replication alone just cannot keep up.

Redis Cluster fills that gap by:

- Distributing data and traffic across multiple nodes
- Scaling writes and memory horizontally
- Offering built-in failover across shards

In the next section, we will dive into how Redis Cluster is architected, how it uses slots, masters replicas, and gossip protocols to balance load as well as maintain availability.

Understanding Redis Cluster Architecture

As applications grow, so do their demands, and eventually, a single Redis instance may no longer be enough to handle the load. **Redis Cluster is Redis's built-in solution** to this challenge, designed to provide both **scalability and high availability**. But it is not just about spreading data randomly across multiple nodes. **Redis Cluster follows a thoughtful and structured architecture** that ensures that your data is distributed efficiently and your system remains resilient, even in the face of node failures.

In this section, we will take a closer look at how Redis Cluster works, explaining, in simple terms, how it distributes data, how the nodes coordinate and communicate, and how it recovers from failures. By the end, you will have a clear understanding of what is happening behind the scenes, before you go on to build and manage your own Redis Cluster.

Core Concepts of Redis Cluster

Let us begin by understanding the basic building blocks of a Redis Cluster.

1. **Multiple Masters with Optional Replicas**

   In a Redis Cluster:

   - There are multiple master nodes, each holding a portion of the total data.
   - Each master can have one or more replicas (just like traditional Redis replication).

   For example, in a 6-node cluster:

   - You might have 3 masters and 3 replicas (each replica mirrors one master).
   - The data is sharded across the 3 masters.
   - The replicas are there for high availability to take over if a master fails.

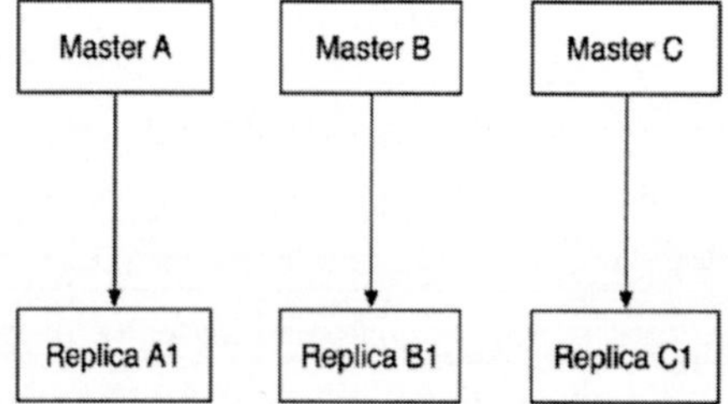

***Figure 10.1:** Redis Cluster with 3 Masters and 3 Replicas*

Figure 10.1: This diagram illustrates a 6-node Redis Cluster setup where data is evenly sharded across three master nodes. Each master has a dedicated replica to ensure high availability and automatic failover in case of node failure.

2. **Hash Slots: The Secret behind Sharding**

   Redis Cluster divides the entire keyspace into **16,384** hash slots.

   Each master is assigned a range of these slots, and is responsible for storing the keys that fall within them.

   Instead of storing a key randomly on any node, Redis Cluster uses a fixed hash slot system to determine where the data should go.

   - There are exactly 16,384 hash slots.
   - Each master node is responsible for a range of these slots.
   - When you insert a key, Redis computes a CRC16 hash of the key and maps it to a slot between **0 and 16383**.

Example:

```
SET user:1234 "Karnish"
```

Let us say the key user:1234 hashes to slot 8231.

If Master B owns slots 5000–9999, that key is stored on Master B.

So even if you have 10 million keys, the mapping always boils down to:

- Hash the key
- Find the slot
- Store/retrieve from the node responsible for that slot

This system ensures that:

- Even data distribution (if slots are balanced)
- Quick lookups without needing central metadata

3. **Gossip Protocol for Communication**

   All nodes in a Redis Cluster talk to each other using a lightweight gossip protocol.

   This allows nodes to:

   - Share state information (for example, which node is up or down).
   - Detect failures without a central coordinator.
   - Elect a replica to become the master, if needed.

   It is similar to how peer-to-peer networks or distributed databases such as Cassandra work.

   How Gossip Works:

   - Nodes exchange information periodically (every few hundred milliseconds).
   - If enough nodes agree that one node is down, it is marked as failed.
   - The cluster can then take action (like triggering failover).

4. **No Single Point of Failure**

   Redis Cluster is built to keep running, even if some nodes fail.

   Here is how:

   - Each master has one or more replicas.
   - If a master crashes, its replica is automatically promoted to master.
   - The other nodes update their state, and reroute requests accordingly.

   This makes Redis Cluster highly available, unlike a single-node Redis setup, where one crash means downtime.

5. **Minimal Client Redirection (Smart Clients)**

   When a client connects to a Redis Cluster, it may not know which node holds the key it wants.

   So, here is what happens:

   - The client sends a request to any node.
   - If that node does not have the key's slot, it replies with a `MOVED` message, pointing the client to the correct node.
   - The client remembers this mapping for future requests.

Most Redis clients today support this natively (for example, `ioredis`, `redis-py-cluster`, `Jedis`, and so on), so that the redirection is handled automatically and efficiently.

A Simple Example in Practice

Imagine this setup:

- Three masters, each with a replica:
  - Master A (slots 0–5460)
  - Master B (slots 5461–10922)
  - Master C (slots 10923–16383)

You insert:

```
SET product:2001 "Keyboard"
SET product:3002 "Monitor"
SET product:4003 "Mouse"
```

Each of those keys will hash to a specific slot, and Redis will:

- Route the command to the right master.
- Store the key only on that node (plus its replica).

Now, if Master B goes down:

- Replica B1 is promoted to the master.
- Other nodes update their cluster info.
- Clients are automatically redirected.

No data loss. Minimal disruption. No manual intervention. A small window of write loss is possible due to asynchronous replication.

Summary

Redis Cluster is a powerful distributed system built on a few simple yet brilliant principles:

- It uses hash slots to distribute data predictably.
- It relies on a peer-to-peer gossip protocol to manage the state, and detect failures.
- It supports automatic failover, ensuring high availability.
- It lets clients work with the entire cluster seamlessly, even as nodes go up or down.

Understanding this architecture is the key to deploying, managing, and troubleshooting the Redis Cluster with confidence.

In the next section, we will explore how sharding actually works, how slots are assigned, how keys are mapped, and how Redis ensures that the data is spread evenly across the cluster.

Slots and Data Distribution (Sharding Explained)

One of the most elegant features of Redis Cluster is how it handles sharding, the process of splitting data across multiple nodes. Instead of leaving sharding up to you, or relying on external coordination, Redis Cluster uses a built-in, transparent, and deterministic approach based on hash slots.

In this section, we will explore exactly how Redis Cluster distributes data, how keys are mapped to slots, and how these slots are assigned to nodes. We will use diagrams and examples to make the concept feel intuitive and easy to apply.

What are Hash Slots?

Redis Cluster uses a concept called hash slots to divide its keyspace. There are exactly 16,384 slots numbered from **0 to 16383**. Every key you store in Redis is assigned to one of these slots, using a hashing algorithm (CRC16) behind the scenes.

Redis then assigns each slot to a master node. A master may own a range of slots, and the sum of all slots across all masters makes up the full keyspace.

Think of It Like a Map

Imagine a world map divided into 16,384 zones. Each Redis master is responsible for certain zones:

- Master A owns slots 0 to 5460.
- Master B owns slots 5461 to 10922.
- Master C owns slots 10923 to 16383.

When a key is written, Redis computes a hash of the key, and checks which zone (slot) it belongs to. Then it routes the request to the corresponding master.

```
[Keys] --(CRC16 Hashing)--> [Slots] --(Range Mapping)--> [Master Node]
```

Real Example

Let us say, we store the following keys:

```
SET user:1001 "Karnish"
SET order:2002 "#XDR123"
SET product:3003 "Laptop"
```

Redis will internally compute the CRC16 hash of each key and map it to a slot:

- **`user:1001`** `might hash to slot 4302 → handled by Master A`
- **`order:2002`** `might hash to slot 7205 → handled by Master B`
- **`product:3003`** `might hash to slot 12120 → handled by Master C`

Your client does not need to know these details. Redis handles routing for you.

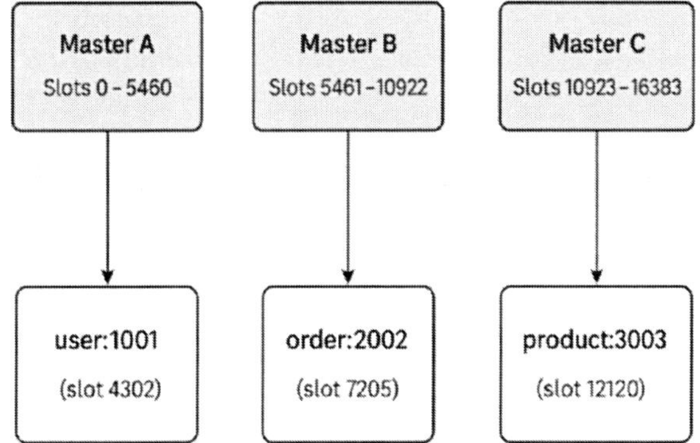

***Figure 10.2**: Key-to-Slot Mapping in Redis Cluster Using CRC16 Hashing*

Figure 10.2: Redis computes a CRC16 hash for each key, and maps it to one of 16,384 hash slots. In this example, keys such as user:1001, order:2002, and product:3003 are automatically assigned to different slots and distributed across Master A, B, and C, respectively.

Benefits of This Approach

- **Predictability:** You always know where a key will go based on its hash slot.
- **Scalability:** You can add or remove nodes and reassign slots.
- **No overlap:** Each slot is owned by only one master, avoiding confusion.
- **Resilience:** Each master can have replicas for failover.

Advanced Tip: Hash Tags for Related Keys

If you want **multiple related keys to live on the same node**, Redis lets you use **hash tags**:

```
SET user:{1001}:name "Karnish"
SET user:{1001}:email "alice@example.com"
SET user:{1001}:cart "5 items"
```

Only the part inside the braces (`{1001}`) is used for slot calculation. This ensures that all the three keys map to the same slot, and hence, the same master. This is useful for atomic operations like Lua scripts or transactions.

Summary

Redis Cluster's slot-based architecture allows for powerful, automatic sharding that is both efficient and easy to manage. By breaking the keyspace into 16,384 slots and evenly distributing them across nodes, Redis ensures that your data is:

- Well balanced
- Quickly accessible
- Ready to scale

In the next section, we will walk through setting up a Redis Cluster from scratch, including commands, tools, and best practices to see this architecture in action.

Setting up a Redis Cluster (Step-by-Step)

Now that we understand how Redis Cluster works internally with slots and sharding it is time to roll up our sleeves and actually build a cluster ourselves.

While Redis Cluster may sound complex, Redis has made it surprisingly straightforward to set up, especially for testing and development. In this section, we will walk through a complete step-by-step guide to setting up a basic Redis Cluster on a single machine using multiple instances.

You can use this as a learning lab before deploying Redis Cluster in production.

Before we begin, make sure you have:

- Redis installed (version 5.0 or later).
- A Linux/macOS environment or WSL (on Windows).
- A terminal with access to **`redis-server`**, **`redis-cli`**, and optionally **`redis-trib.rb`** (older) or **`redis-cli --cluster`** (newer)
- Ports 7000 to 7005 available (we will use six Redis nodes: 3 masters and 3 replicas).

Step-by-Step Setup

> **Note:** *This exercise is being performed on* **macOS**, *where the* **`sed`** *command behaves differently compared to* **Linux**. *Please account for these differences when executing commands.*

Step 1: Create Redis Configs for Each Node

We will simulate a 6-node Redis Cluster, each node running on a different port locally.

- Create a new folder to hold everything:

  ```
  mkdir redis-cluster
  cd redis-cluster
  ```

- Now, create 6 folders:

```
for port in 7000 7001 7002 7003 7004 7005; do
  mkdir $port
done
```

- Create a base configuration file (you can reuse this for all):

```
vim redis-cluster.tmpl

port PORT
cluster-enabled yes
cluster-config-file nodes-PORT.conf
cluster-node-timeout 5000
appendonly yes
protected-mode no
dir .
```

Note: This is for local testing only. Do not disable protected-mode in production without proper binding and authentication.

```
port PORT
cluster-enabled yes
cluster-config-file nodes-PORT.conf
cluster-node-timeout 5000
appendonly yes
protected-mode no
dir .
```

***Figure* 10.3:** *Base Redis Cluster Configuration Template*

Figure 10.3: This figure shows a reusable Redis cluster configuration file template (redis-cluster.tmpl). The placeholder PORT should be replaced with the actual Redis port when generating configuration files for each node in the cluster.

- Now, copy this template and replace **`PORT`**:

```
for port in 7000 7001 7002 7003 7004 7005; do
      sed "s/PORT/$port/" redis-cluster.tmpl > $port/redis.conf
done
```

Step 2: Start All Redis Instances

Use separate terminal tabs or background jobs to start each server:

```
for port in 7000 7001 7002 7003 7004 7005; do
  redis-server "$port/redis.conf" &
done
```

Now, you have six Redis nodes running locally, each with clustering enabled.

Check with the following code:

```
ps aux | grep redis
```

```
karnish          14885   0.1  0.0 411324832   4832 s005  SN   11:39AM   0:00.07 redis-server *:7004 [cluster]
karnish          14884   0.0  0.0 411323808   4608 s005  SN   11:39AM   0:00.07 redis-server *:7003 [cluster]
karnish          14883   0.0  0.0 411332000   4624 s005  SN   11:39AM   0:00.06 redis-server *:7002 [cluster]
karnish          14882   0.0  0.0 411078048   4576 s005  SN   11:39AM   0:00.08 redis-server *:7001 [cluster]
karnish          14881   0.0  0.0 411332000   4640 s005  SN   11:39AM   0:00.07 redis-server *:7000 [cluster]
karnish          14923   0.0  0.0 410724048   1328 s005  S+   11:39AM   0:00.01 grep redis
karnish          14886   0.0  0.0 411190688   4320 s005  SN   11:39AM   0:00.06 redis-server *:7005 [cluster]
```

Figure 10.4: *Verifying Redis Nodes Running with Clustering Enabled*

Figure 10.4: This figure demonstrates how to verify that all six Redis nodes are running locally with clustering enabled.

Step 3: Create the Cluster

Now comes the fun part: Telling Redis to treat these six instances as a cluster. Redis provides the command-line utility:

```
redis-cli --cluster create \
  127.0.0.1:7000 127.0.0.1:7001 127.0.0.1:7002 \
  127.0.0.1:7003 127.0.0.1:7004 127.0.0.1:7005 \
  --cluster-replicas 1
```

```
>>> Performing hash slots allocation on 6 nodes...
Master[0] -> Slots 0 - 5460
Master[1] -> Slots 5461 - 10922
Master[2] -> Slots 10923 - 16383
Adding replica 127.0.0.1:7004 to 127.0.0.1:7000
Adding replica 127.0.0.1:7005 to 127.0.0.1:7001
Adding replica 127.0.0.1:7003 to 127.0.0.1:7002
>>> Trying to optimize slaves allocation for anti-affinity
```

Figure 10.5: *Output of redis-cli --cluster create Command*

Figure 10.5: This figure shows the output after running the **`redis-cli --cluster create`** command, confirming successful creation of the cluster. It lists node assignments, slot distributions across masters, and replica pairings for high availability.

What this does:

- Creates a cluster with 3 masters and 3 replicas.
- Assigns slots automatically.
- Pairs each replica with one master.

It will ask for confirmation. Type **yes** to proceed.

Step 4: Verify the Cluster

Run:

```
redis-cli -c -p 7000 cluster info
```

You should see something like:

```
cluster_state:ok
cluster_slots_assigned:16384
cluster_known_nodes:6
```

```
cluster_state:ok
cluster_slots_assigned:16384
cluster_slots_ok:16384
cluster_slots_pfail:0
cluster_slots_fail:0
cluster_known_nodes:6
cluster_size:3
cluster_current_epoch:6
cluster_my_epoch:1
cluster_stats_messages_ping_sent:197
cluster_stats_messages_pong_sent:210
cluster_stats_messages_sent:407
cluster_stats_messages_ping_received:205
cluster_stats_messages_pong_received:197
cluster_stats_messages_meet_received:5
cluster_stats_messages_received:407
total_cluster_links_buffer_limit_exceeded:0
```

Figure 10.6: *Output of the Cluster Info Command in Redis Cluster*

Figure 10.6: This output confirms that the Redis Cluster is active and healthy. It shows the key information such as **`cluster_state:ok`**, all **`16384`** slots assigned, and the number of known nodes in the cluster.

To view individual nodes:

```
redis-cli -c -p 7000 cluster nodes
```

You will see node IDs, roles (master/replica), IPs, and slot ranges.

```
e8054aac91250cda0ecabd824f61991341c7b198 127.0.0.1:7003@17003 slave 459c1e68ad9ed95209a62b59468b290defcffd9a 0 1747376092000 3 connected
36827d5f08a71f3f57bd8c7d90f7015e76c85585 127.0.0.1:7004@17004 slave e6d8d605e0c5adb37966f89833459486f6b83e42 0 1747376092000 1 connected
7f4651ac0411930e355fc8b5e8931a3ebb4bbd57 127.0.0.1:7001@17001 master - 0 1747376091873 2 connected 5461-10922
459c1e68ad9ed95209a62b59468b290defcffd9a 127.0.0.1:7002@17002 master - 0 1747376092884 3 connected 10923-16383
5f7d8fc0c7441ea8ec37244a0200e4172e3d54e7 127.0.0.1:7005@17005 slave 7f4651ac0411930e355fc8b5e8931a3ebb4bbd57 0 1747376091000 2 connected
e6d8d605e0c5adb37966f89833459486f6b83e42 127.0.0.1:7000@17000 myself,master - 0 1747376091000 1 connected 0-5460
```

Figure 10.7: *Output of the Cluster Nodes Command in Redis Cluster*

Figure 10.7: This output lists all nodes in the cluster, along with their unique IDs, roles (master or replica), IP addresses, connection states, and the hash slot ranges, each master is responsible for.

Step 5: Test Data Sharding

Now try inserting some keys using a clustered client (**`-c` flag** tells **`redis-cli`** to follow redirections):

```
redis-cli -c -p 7000 set user:1001 "Karnish"
redis-cli -c -p 7000 set product:2002 "Keyboard"
```

Redis will automatically route these keys to the appropriate master, based on their slots.

To check slot mapping:

```
redis-cli -c -p 7000 cluster keyslot user:1001
```

This returns a slot number (for example, **`5712`**). You can then see which node owns that slot.

```
(integer) 5712
```

Figure 10.8: *Output of the Cluster Keyslot Command in Redis Cluster*

Figure 10.8: This figure shows the slot number assigned to the **`key user:1001`**. Redis calculates the CRC16 hash of the key, and maps it to one of the 16,384 hash slots, helping to determine which node stores the key.

Step 6: Simulate Failure and Observe Behavior

Kill a master node:

```
pkill -f "redis-server.*7000"
```

Now run:

```
redis-cli -c -p 7001 cluster nodes
```

You should see that the replica of the failed node has been promoted to the master automatically.

```
e6d8d605e0c5adb37966f89833459486f6b83e42 127.0.0.1:7000@17000 master,fail - 1747376940598 1747376938000 1 disconnected
459c1e68ad9ed95209a62b59468b290defcffd9a 127.0.0.1:7002@17002 master - 0 1747377001000 3 connected 10923 16383
5f7d8fc0c7441ea8ec37244a0200e4172e3d54e7 127.0.0.1:7005@17005 slave 7f4651ac0411930e355fc8b5e8931a3ebb4bbd57 0 1747377002133 2 connected
e8054aac91250cda0ecabd824f61991341c7b198 127.0.0.1:7003@17003 slave 459c1e68ad9ed95209a62b59468b290defcffd9a 0 1747377001121 3 connected
36827d5f08a71f3f57bd8c7d90f7015e76c85585 127.0.0.1:7004@17004 master - 0 1747377002000 7 connected 0-5460
7f4651ac0411930e355fc8b5e8931a3ebb4bbd57 127.0.0.1:7001@17001 myself,master - 0 1747377001000 2 connected 5461-10922
```

Figure 10.9: *Output after Simulating Master Node Failure in Redis Cluster*

Figure 10.9: This figure shows the result of stopping a master node (port 7000) and running **cluster nodes** from another node. Redis Cluster automatically promotes the associated replica to the master, ensuring high availability and continuity of service.

Redis Cluster detects the failure, elects a new master, and re-routes slots, all without your manual intervention.

Summary

Setting up a Redis Cluster is not difficult, but it is incredibly powerful. In just a few steps, you created:

- A distributed Redis environment
- With automatic sharding
- Built-in replication
- And hands-free failover

This setup is perfect for testing and learning. In production, you would deploy nodes across **multiple servers or data centers**, secure connections, and monitor cluster health closely.

In the next section, we shall explore **how to add or remove nodes**, and **how Redis handles slot reassignments** when the topology changes.

Adding and Removing Nodes

As your application evolves, so will your Redis Cluster. Thus, whether you are scaling up to handle more traffic or scaling down for cost efficiency, Redis makes it possible to dynamically add or remove nodes from a running cluster.

In this section, we will walk through how to:

- Add a new master node to expand capacity.
- Add a new replica for increased redundancy.
- Remove a node safely from the cluster.
- Rebalance slots when your cluster topology changes.

All of this can be done without bringing the cluster down, thanks to Redis Cluster's flexible and dynamic design!

Why Add Nodes?

Adding a node might be needed when:

- A particular master is handling too many slots or too much traffic.
- You want to increase **write capacity** (more masters).
- You need more **replicas** for failover safety or regional redundancy.

Adding a New Master Node

Let us say your current cluster has 3 masters and 3 replicas. You want to add a **fourth master**.

Step 1: Start the New Redis Instance

Choose a port not in use (for example, 7006):

```
mkdir 7006 && cp 7000/redis.conf 7006/
sed -i '' 's/7000/7006/' 7006/redis.conf
redis-server 7006/redis.conf
```

```
33436:M 17 May 2025 12:53:40.016 * Ready to accept connections tcp
```

Figure 10.10: *Output Showing Redis Server Startup with redis.conf for Port 7006*

Figure 10.10: This figure displays the Redis server initialization output using the configuration file for node 7006. It confirms that the node is starting with the correct settings, and is ready to join or operate within the Redis Cluster.

Step 2: Add the Node to the Cluster

```
redis-cli --cluster add-node 127.0.0.1:7006 127.0.0.1:7000
```

This adds 7006 to the cluster. It joins as a master, but with no slots assigned.

```
[OK] New node added correctly.
```

Figure 10.11: *Output of --cluster add-node Command Adding Node 7006*

Figure 10.11: This figure shows the result of adding a new node (port 7006) to the Redis Cluster using redis-cli --cluster add-node. The node successfully joins the cluster as a master but initially has no hash slots assigned.

Reconfirm by executing the command:

```
redis-cli -c -p 7000 cluster info
```

```
cluster_state:ok
cluster_slots_assigned:16384
cluster_slots_ok:16384
cluster_slots_pfail:0
cluster_slots_fail:0
cluster_known_nodes:7
cluster_size:3
cluster_current_epoch:7
cluster_my_epoch:7
cluster_stats_messages_ping_sent:1698
cluster_stats_messages_pong_sent:1743
cluster_stats_messages_sent:3441
cluster_stats_messages_ping_received:1742
cluster_stats_messages_pong_received:1698
cluster_stats_messages_meet_received:1
cluster_stats_messages_update_received:7
cluster_stats_messages_received:3448
total_cluster_links_buffer_limit_exceeded:0
```

Figure 10.12: *Output of Cluster Info after Adding a New Node*

Figure 10.12: This output confirms that the new node (7006) has joined the Redis Cluster. The cluster state remains ok, and the total node count increases, though slot distribution remains unchanged until rebalancing.

Step 3: Rebalance the Cluster to Distribute Slots

Now you need to move some slots to the new master:

```
redis-cli --cluster rebalance 127.0.0.1:7006
```

Redis will analyze the slot distribution, and move some from the existing masters to the new one.

Adding a Replica Node

Suppose, you want to add a replica for the new master at port 7006.

Step 1: Start Another Redis Instance

```
mkdir 7007 && cp 7006/redis.conf 7007/
sed -i '' 's/7006/7007/' 7007/redis.conf
redis-server 7007/redis.conf
```

Step 2: Add It as a Replica of 7006

First, get the node ID of 7006:

```
redis-cli -p 7006 cluster nodes
```

Copy the node ID of the master. Then run:

```
redis-cli --cluster add-node 127.0.0.1:7007 127.0.0.1:7000 --cluster-slave --cluster-master-id <NODE_ID>
```

```
887545dc023988494faa8237224ebb185b02bf62 127.0.0.1:7006@17006 myself,master - 0 1747468806000 0 connected
```

Figure 10.13: *Output of Cluster Nodes Command to Retrieve Node ID of 7006*

Figure 10.13: This figure displays the result of running redis-cli -p 7006 cluster nodes, showing detailed information about the node, including its unique node ID, role, connected peers, and cluster status needed to attach a replica.

```
redis-cli --cluster add-node 127.0.0.1:7007 127.0.0.1:7000 --cluster-slave --cluster-master-id 887545dc023988494faa8237224ebb185b02bf62
```

This tells Redis to join **`7007`** as a **replica of `7006`**.

```
[OK] All nodes agree about slots configuration.
>>> Check for open slots...
>>> Check slots coverage...
[OK] All 16384 slots covered.
>>> Send CLUSTER MEET to node 127.0.0.1:7007 to make it join the cluster.
Waiting for the cluster to join

>>> Configure node as replica of 127.0.0.1:7006.
[OK] New node added correctly.
```

Figure 10.14: *Output of Adding Node 7007 as a Replica of Node 7006*

Figure 10.14: This figure captures the output after using the **`--cluster add-node`** command with the **`--cluster-slave`** option to attach node 7007 as a replica of master 7006. The command uses the node ID of 7006, and the output confirms successful replica assignment within the cluster.

Removing a Node from the Cluster

You may need to remove a node due to:

- Hardware decommissioning
- Maintenance
- Downsizing the cluster

Step 1: Migrate Slots off the Node (if it is a master)

If you are removing a master, migrate its slots first:

```
redis-cli --cluster reshard 127.0.0.1:7002
```

Follow the prompts to:

a. Move all the slots to other masters.

```
How many slots do you want to move (from 1 to 16384)?
```

Figure 10.15: *Prompt Asking for Number of Slots during Resharding*

Figure 10.15: This figure shows the Redis CLI prompt displayed during the resharding process using redis-cli --cluster reshard. It asks how many hash slots the user wants to move from source nodes to the target node, initiating the rebalancing of data across the cluster.

b. Receiving **node ID**

```
What is the receiving node ID?
```

Figure 10.16: *Prompt Asking for Receiving Node ID during Resharding*

Figure 10.16: This figure shows the Redis CLI prompt where the user is required to enter the receiving node ID, the master node that will receive the hash slots being moved as part of the resharding process.

c. Select the target nodes

```
Please enter all the source node IDs.
  Type 'all' to use all the nodes as source nodes for the hash slots.
  Type 'done' once you entered all the source nodes IDs.
```

Figure 10.17: *Prompt Asking for Source Node IDs during Resharding*

Figure 10.17: This figure displays the prompt where Redis asks the user to enter one or more source node IDs, the master nodes currently holding the slots that will be migrated to the receiving node during the resharding operation.

Step 2: Remove the Node

Once the node has **no slots**, run:

```
redis-cli --cluster del-node 127.0.0.1:7002 <NODE_ID>

redis-cli --cluster del-node 127.0.0.1:7002 459c1e68ad9ed95209a62b59468b290defcffd9a
```

```
>>> Removing node 459c1e68ad9ed95209a62b59468b290defcffd9a from cluster 127.0.0.1:7002
>>> Sending CLUSTER FORGET messages to the cluster...
>>> Sending CLUSTER RESET SOFT to the deleted node.
```

Figure 10.18: *Output of the del-node Command to Remove Node 7002 from the Cluster*

Figure 10.18: This figure shows the result of executing the **`redis-cli --cluster del-node`** command, which removes node 7002 from the cluster after all its hash slots have been migrated. The output confirms successful removal using the node's unique ID.

You can find <NODE_ID> with:

```
redis-cli -p 7002 cluster nodes
```

```
459c1e68ad9ed95209a62b59468b290defcffd9a 127.0.0.1:7002@17002 myself,master - 0 1747469753000 3 connected 10923-16383
```

Figure 10.19: *Output of Cluster Nodes Command to Retrieve Node ID of 7002*

Figure 10.19: This figure displays the output of redis-cli -p 7002 cluster nodes, which provides the unique node ID required to remove the node from the cluster, using the del-node command. It also shows role, slot ownership (if any), and connectivity status.

If the node is a **replica**, you can skip the resharding step.

Rebalancing the Cluster

Any time you add or remove masters, your cluster might end up with **uneven slot distribution**.

Use this to redistribute evenly:

```
redis-cli --cluster rebalance 127.0.0.1:7000
```

Redis will automatically analyze and move slots to ensure a balanced cluster.

```
>>> Performing Cluster Check (using node 127.0.0.1:7000)
[OK] All nodes agree about slots configuration.
>>> Check for open slots...
>>> Check slots coverage...
[OK] All 16384 slots covered.
*** No rebalancing needed! All nodes are within the 2.00% threshold.
```

Figure 10.20: *Output of --cluster Rebalance Command in Redis*

Figure 10.20: This figure shows the result of running **`redis-cli --cluster`** rebalance, which automatically redistributes hash slots across master nodes to achieve balanced data distribution after nodes have been added or removed from the cluster.

Summary

Redis Cluster is designed to grow or shrink with your system. Adding or removing nodes does not require downtime; you can do it live with a few commands.

Key takeaways:

- Use **`--cluster`** `add-node` and **`--cluster del-node`** for topology changes.
- Always rebalance slots after adding/removing masters.
- Replicas can be added easily for high availability.

In the next section, we will see **how Redis Cluster handles failover and recovery**, and how replicas are promoted when a master fails.

Failover and High Availability in Cluster Mode

One of the standout strengths of Redis Cluster is its ability to maintain availability, even when things go wrong. Redis Cluster is designed with built-in mechanisms for automatic failover and self-healing, which allow it to detect failures, promote replicas, and keep your data flowing with minimal disruption.

In this section, we will explore:

- What happens when a master fails

- How Redis detects and handles failures
- How replicas are promoted to masters
- How the cluster reconfigures itself automatically

So, let us walk through this in a way that is both practical and easy to understand.

What Happens When a Master Fails

In a Redis Cluster, each master should have at least one replica. If a master crashes due to hardware failure or a network outage, Redis Cluster steps in to minimize the impact.

Here is what happens:

1. **Other nodes notice the failure** using the cluster's built-in gossip protocol.
2. If enough nodes (the majority) agree that a master is unreachable, it is marked as **`FAIL`**.
3. One of the master's replicas is automatically promoted to become the new master.
4. The rest of the cluster updates their internal maps to reflect the change.

All of this typically happens in **under 10 seconds** (configurable with **cluster-node-timeout**).

Example: Simulating a Master Failure

Let us say we have this cluster:

- `Master A → Replica A1`
- `Master B → Replica B1`
- `Master C → Replica C1`

Each master handles a portion of the keyspace (via hash slots), and each replica mirrors its master.

Now, suppose **`Master B (port 7001)`** crashes.

Step 1: Stop the Master Manually

```
pkill -f "redis-server.*7001"
```

Step 2: Observe What Happens

Use any other node to monitor:

```
redis-cli -p 7000 cluster nodes
```

You will see something like:

```
28812:S 25 May 2025 11:41:30.240 # Cluster state changed: fail
28808:M 25 May 2025 11:41:30.240 # Cluster state changed: fail
28810:M 25 May 2025 11:41:30.240 * FAIL message received from 8d010eaddb6e8f65d8f604e028816df18350c900 () about 9b6c1d18119d39eec84abe5b
ff5a1ba98896d731 ()
28810:M 25 May 2025 11:41:30.240 # Cluster state changed: fail
28813:S 25 May 2025 11:41:30.240 * FAIL message received from 8d010eaddb6e8f65d8f604e028816df18350c900 () about 9b6c1d18119d39eec84abe5b
ff5a1ba98896d731 ()
28813:S 25 May 2025 11:41:30.240 # Cluster state changed: fail
28812:S 25 May 2025 11:41:30.336 * Start of election delayed for 705 milliseconds (rank #0, offset 672).
28812:S 25 May 2025 11:41:31.046 * Starting a failover election for epoch 7.
28808:M 25 May 2025 11:41:31.058 * Failover auth granted to 38f5034ea79bdf33718bfe6eea2dd4394a409afa () for epoch 7
28810:M 25 May 2025 11:41:31.058 * Failover auth granted to 38f5034ea79bdf33718bfe6eea2dd4394a409afa () for epoch 7
28812:S 25 May 2025 11:41:31.069 * Failover election won: I'm the new master.
28812:S 25 May 2025 11:41:31.069 * configEpoch set to 7 after successful failover
28812:M 25 May 2025 11:41:31.069 * Discarding previously cached master state.
28812:M 25 May 2025 11:41:31.069 * Setting secondary replication ID to 6e34639b9e56ab12e212a3f25d2a04f34b7571e6, valid up to offset: 673
. New replication ID is 7a641015ca2ac1071a0c195150646eec074f1676
28812:M 25 May 2025 11:41:31.069 * Cluster state changed: ok
28813:S 25 May 2025 11:41:31.076 * Cluster state changed: ok
28808:M 25 May 2025 11:41:31.076 * Cluster state changed: ok
28811:S 25 May 2025 11:41:31.077 * Cluster state changed: ok
28810:M 25 May 2025 11:41:31.077 * Cluster state changed: ok
```

Figure 10.21: *Output of Simulating a Master Failure in Redis*

Figure 10.21: This figure shows the output captured after simulating a failure of the Redis master node.

Redis automatically promotes **Replica B1 (port 7004)** to master. All other nodes update their cluster metadata, and route the traffic to the new master.

Automatic Reconfiguration

Redis Cluster uses a decentralized approach; there is no single coordinator. Instead:

- Nodes communicate with each other regularly.
- They share information about node health and slot ownership.
- When a failure is confirmed, the cluster reorganizes itself.

This means you do not need to step in manually. Clients that support clustering will also automatically re-route to the new master.

What If There is No Replica?

If a master fails **and has no replicas**, the cluster cannot serve the slots it owned. Those slots are considered **unavailable**, and any request involving those keys will fail with a `CLUSTERDOWN` error.

That is why Redis recommends that **every master has at least one replica** for high availability.

Configuration Note:

The responsiveness of failover is controlled by:

```
cluster-node-timeout 5000 # milliseconds
```

This defines how long Redis waits before declaring a node unreachable. You can fine-tune this for faster detection or slower environments.

Summary

Redis Cluster handles failover in a fast, automatic, and self-healing manner. When a master node fails:

- Its replica is quickly promoted.
- The cluster reconfigures itself.
- Clients are redirected to the new master.

This ensures that your application remains available with minimal impact.

In the next section, we will look at how clients behave in cluster mode, and how they deal with things like redirects and slot awareness.

How Redis Detects Failures Internally

Redis Cluster relies on a gossip-based communication mechanism to continuously monitor the health of all nodes in the cluster. Each node exchanges small heartbeat messages with others at regular intervals. These messages help nodes share information about which peers are reachable, which appear unresponsive, and the overall cluster state.

When a node fails to respond within the time defined by the **cluster-node-timeout** parameter, it is temporarily marked as `PFAIL` (Possible Failure) by the node that detected it. This alone does not trigger a failover - Redis waits for confirmation from other master nodes. If a majority of masters also report the same node as unreachable, the node's status changes to `FAIL` (Confirmed

Failure). At this point, one of its replicas is automatically promoted to master and maintains data availability.

This distributed decision-making process prevents false positives, and ensures that failovers are quick, reliable, and coordinated across the cluster. Typically, detection and promotion take only a few seconds, depending on network latency and timeout settings.

Note: *You can fine-tune the failover speed by adjusting the* ***`cluster-node-timeout`*** *value. Lower values detect failures faster but may increase the risk of false detection in unstable networks.*

Securing Redis Cluster Communication

When deploying Redis in cluster mode, it is important to secure both client and node-to-node communication. Each cluster node exchanges topology, slot, and replication data with other nodes, so that any unsecured link can expose the sensitive information or allow unauthorized access.

Redis supports **TLS (Transport Layer Security)** to encrypt all the traffic between clients and nodes, as well as among cluster members themselves. To enable TLS, start Redis with the **`--tls-port`** option, and provide your certificate as well as key files using **`tls-cert-file, tls-key-file`**, and **`tls-ca-cert-file`**. Disable the plain-text port (**`port 0`**) to ensure only encrypted communication.

You should also enable **password-based authentication** using **`requirepass`** (for clients) and **`masterauth`** (for replica nodes). For clusters, add the following options to ensure that all **cluster bus and replication traffic** is encrypted and authenticated:

Example:

```
# redis.conf
tls-port 6379
port 0
tls-cert-file /etc/ssl/redis.crt
tls-key-file /etc/ssl/redis.key
tls-ca-cert-file /etc/ssl/ca.crt
requirepass MySecurePass123
masterauth MySecurePass123
tls-cluster yes
tls-replication yes
```

Note: In Redis 6+, ACLs (user default on >password) are preferred over requirepass.

With this configuration:

- Client ↔ Node, Node ↔ Node, and Master ↔ Replica communications are all encrypted.
- Unauthorized nodes cannot join the cluster or replicate data, without proper credentials.
- It is safe to deploy the cluster across different servers or cloud environments.

Client-Side Behavior in Cluster Mode

So far, we have focused on how Redis Cluster distributes data, handles failover, and manages node operations. But there is one critical piece left: How clients interact with a Redis Cluster. Understanding this is key to building robust, scalable applications that talk to Redis efficiently and safcly.

In this section, we will explain:

- How Redis Cluster-aware clients behave.
- What happens when a client connects to the wrong node.
- How clients handle redirections like MOVED and ASK.
- What to look for when choosing or configuring a Redis client library.

Redis Cluster Requires Smart Clients

In a single-node Redis setup, a client can connect to one endpoint and work just fine. In a Redis Cluster, however, the data is split across multiple nodes.

This means your client needs to:

- Know **which node owns which slot.**
- Automatically follow **redirections**, if it asks the wrong node.
- Retry on failover when a node goes offline.

Many modern Redis clients have built-in **cluster mode support**, often called **cluster-aware clients.**

Example: Redirection in Action

Let us say your app connects to **`127.0.0.1:7000`** and tries to run:

```
GET user:1234
```

But that key hashes to slot **`15814`**, which belongs to a different master (for example, on **`127.0.0.1:7002`**). Here is what happens:

- Redis on port 7000 replies with:

  ```
  MOVED 15814 127.0.0.1:7002
  ```

  ```
  127.0.0.1:7000> GET user:1234
  (error) MOVED 15814 127.0.0.1:7002
  127.0.0.1:7000>
  ```

  Figure 10.22: *MOVED Redirection Error in a Redis Cluster*

  Figure 10.22: This figure illustrates what happens when a client sends a command (GET user:1234) to a Redis node that does not own the key's hash slot. In this example, the key hashes to slot 15814, which belongs to another master (127.0.0.1:7002).

- A cluster-aware client will:
  a. Learn that slot 15814 is handled by 7002.
  b. Redirect the request automatically.
  c. Cache this mapping for faster routing in the future.

This keeps the application fast and resilient even as data and roles move around.

Popular Redis Clients with Cluster Support:

Here are some client libraries that support Redis Cluster natively:

- **Node.js:** **`ioredis`**
- **Python:** **`redis-py / legacy:redis-py-cluster`**
- **Java:** **`Jedis, Lettuce`**

- **Go**: `go-redis`
- **.NET**: `StackExchange.Redis`

These libraries manage connections to all the cluster nodes, and automatically handle redirection and reconnection.

What is an `ASK` Redirection?

In addition to **`MOVED`**, you may see an **`ASK`** redirection during resharding, when a slot is temporarily in transit.

Example:

```
ASK 8123 127.0.0.1:7003
```

This means:

- The slot is being moved to a new master.
- The receiving node (7003) is ready to serve it *temporarily*.
- The client should send the next command with `ASKING` prepended, like:

```
ASKING
GET user:1234
```

Cluster-aware clients handle this automatically.

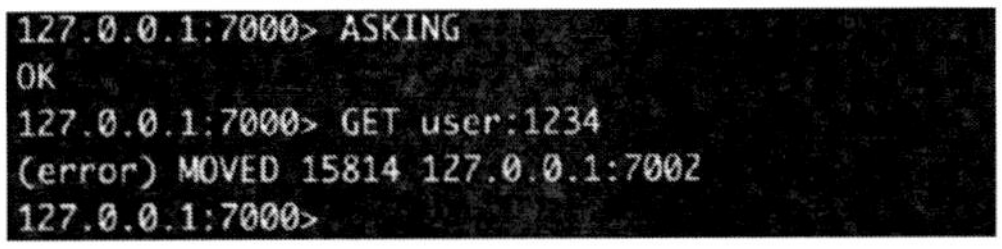

```
127.0.0.1:7000> ASKING
OK
127.0.0.1:7000> GET user:1234
(error) MOVED 15814 127.0.0.1:7002
127.0.0.1:7000>
```

***Figure* 10.23:** *Output of `ASKING` Command Followed by MOVED Error*

Figure 10.23: This figure shows the output when using the ASKING command in a Redis Cluster, followed by a MOVED error. In this case, the key hashes to slot 15814, which is managed by a different node (127.0.0.1:7002).

Summary

Redis Cluster clients must be aware of slot mappings, and ready to follow redirections. Choose a client that:

- Supports automatic redirection for **`MOVED`** and **`ASK`.**
- Can connect to multiple cluster nodes.
- Handles failover and retries gracefully.

In the next section, we will look at **how Redis Cluster handles redirections internally**, and explore the difference between **`MOVED`** and **`ASK`** in greater detail.

Let us now dig deeper into **error handling and command redirection** inside the cluster.

Handling Redirection (MOVED and ASK)

In Redis Cluster, **redirection is the mechanism that ensures clients always talk to the correct node**, even as the cluster topology changes or slots are in transit. While redirection may seem like a low-level detail, understanding it helps developers troubleshoot issues, interpret errors, and fine-tune their applications for high availability.

In this section, we will explore:

- What **MOVED** and **ASK** redirections mean.
- Why they happen.
- How cluster-aware clients handle them.
- Real-world scenarios where these are useful.

What is a Redirection?

In a Redis Cluster, every key belongs to one of 16,384 hash slots, and each slot is assigned to a specific master (primary) node. When a client sends a command to a node that does not own the slot for that key, Redis will respond with a **redirection message**, telling the client where it should retry the request.

There are two types of redirection:

- **MOVED**
- **ASK**

Let us explore both.

MOVED Redirection

A **MOVED** response indicates that the slot has been permanently assigned to a different node.

Example

Suppose the key user:1001 hashes to slot 7123, which is now assigned to node 127.0.0.1:7002, but your client sends the command to 127.0.0.1:7000, instead.

Redis responds with:

```
MOVED 7123 127.0.0.1:7002
```

This tells the client:

- *"You are talking to the wrong node."*
- *"The correct node for slot 7123 is 7002."*

A smart client will:

1. Forward the request to 7002.
2. Update its internal slot-to-node mapping to avoid the same redirection again.

ASK Redirection

An **ASK** response is different. It happens **during resharding**, when a slot is in the process of moving from one node to another.

In this case, Redis responds with:

```
ASK 7123 127.0.0.1:7003
```

This means:

- "Slot 7123 is being transferred to 7003."
- "7003 is temporarily allowed to serve requests for this slot."

The client must:

1. Connect to 7003.
2. Prepend the next command with **ASKING**.

Example:

```
ASKING
GET user:1001
```

After the resharding is complete, a `MOVED` redirection would apply instead.

Why the Difference Matters

- `MOVED` is **permanent**. It indicates a stable change in slot ownership.
- `ASK` is **temporary**. It only applies during slot migration.

This distinction ensures that clients can continue to operate even when the cluster is actively balancing itself.

How Clients Handle Redirection

Cluster-aware clients like `ioredis`, `Jedis`, or `redis-py/legacy:redis-py-cluster` handle redirections automatically.

- On a `MOVED`, the client retries and updates the slot map.
- On an ASK, the client sends the command again with `ASKING` prepended.

However, `non-cluster-aware clients will fail`, making them unsuitable for use in cluster mode.

Common Redirection Issues

1. **The client connects to only one node:** If the connected node does not own the slot and the client is not cluster-aware, commands will fail with `MOVED` or `ASK` errors.

   Fix: *Use a cluster-aware client, and connect to multiple nodes.*

2. **Outdated slot cache:** If a client has stale slot mapping (for example, after failover or resharding), it may initially hit the wrong node.

   Fix: *Good clients auto-refresh the slot map after `MOVED` responses.*

Summary

Redirection is Redis Cluster's way of ensuring clients always route commands to the correct node, even when the cluster is changing. There are two key types:

- `MOVED` - Permanent slot reassignment
- `ASK` - Temporary forwarding during slot migration

Cluster-aware clients handle these smoothly, allowing your application to stay responsive and accurate even under dynamic conditions.

In the next section, we will explore the limitations of Redis Cluster and the trade-offs to consider before deploying it in production.

Limitations and Trade-offs of Redis Cluster

Redis Cluster is a powerful solution for scaling Redis horizontally, but like all distributed systems, it comes with a few **limitations and trade-offs** that developers and architects need to be aware of. While Redis Cluster shines in terms of scalability and high availability, it is not a drop-in replacement for every single use case.

In this section, we will explore the most important limitations of Redis Cluster, explain why they exist, and provide examples and workarounds where applicable.

1. **No Multi-Key Operations across Slots:** In standalone Redis, you can perform operations involving multiple keys in a single command, for example, `MGET`, `MSET`, or transactions using `MULTI/EXEC`.

   But in Redis Cluster:

   - Multi-key operations work only if all keys belong to the same hash slot.

   Example:

   ```
   MGET user:1 user:2
   ```

   This will **fail** if `user:1` and `user:2` are mapped to different slots.

   Workaround:

   Use **hash tags** to force keys into the same slot. A hash tag is a part of the key enclosed in `{}`. Redis will hash only that part.

   ```
   MGET user:{1001}:name user:{1001}:email
   ```

   Both the keys hash to the same slot (`{1001}`), allowing multi-key commands to work.

2. **No Automatic Rebalancing: Redis Cluster does not automatically rebalance slots** when you add or remove nodes. If you add a new node to the cluster, it will not automatically get a share of the keyspace.

   You must run:

   ```
   redis-cli --cluster rebalance ...
   ```

   Redis leaves this task manual so that you have more control, but it does add complexity during scaling events.

   > **Note:** *Plan slot migrations during low-traffic periods and test resharding on staging before production.*

3. **Limited Client Compatibility:** Not all Redis clients support cluster mode. Some older or minimal Redis clients do not handle redirection (`MOVED`, `ASK`) or slot-awareness properly.

   Even among cluster-aware clients, features like pipelining, transactions, and Lua scripting can behave differently in cluster mode.

   > **Note:**
   >
   > Use mature, `cluster-aware` libraries:
   >
   > - `ioredis (Node.js)`
   > - **`redis-py/legacy: redis-py-cluster`** `(Python)`
   > - `JedisCluster (Java)`
   > - `StackExchange.Redis (C#)`

4. **Replication and Failover are not Instant:** Redis Cluster handles failover automatically, but not instantly. There is a short window (typically a few seconds) where:

   - The master is considered unreachable.
   - A replica is promoted.
   - Clients are redirected.

   During this time, any commands to the failed master's slot range may fail with a `CLUSTERDOWN` or `MOVED` error.

> **Note:** *Use retry logic and exponential backoff in your application to gracefully handle failovers.*

5. **Complex Topology Management:** Compared to standalone Redis or Redis with Sentinel, managing a cluster is more involved:
   - You need to understand and manage **slot allocation.**
   - Adding/removing nodes requires **resharding.**
   - Each node needs open ports (Redis + cluster bus port).
   - All nodes must be able to **talk to each other.**

   Example:

   To run a 6-node cluster with 3 masters and 3 replicas, you need at least:
   - Ports 7000 to 7005
   - Cluster bus ports 17000 to 17005 (each node uses port + 10000)

   This can be overwhelming for newcomers.

6. **No Support for Pub/Sub across Slots:** The Redis `PUBLISH/SUBSCRIBE` feature does not work across cluster nodes. A message published to a channel on one node will not be received by subscribers connected to other nodes.

   Alternatives:
   - Use a central Redis instance just for Pub/Sub.
   - Use a dedicated message broker such as **RabbitMQ**, **Kafka**, or **NATS**.

7. **Consistency is Eventual, Not Strong:** Redis Cluster offers **eventual consistency** during failovers and slot migration. There might be short windows where:
   - A key is not available because it is in transit.
   - Reads are inconsistent across replicas.

   It is **designed for high availability**, not strict consistency.

> **Note:** *If your application demands* **strong consistency** *(e.g., for financial systems), Redis Cluster may need to be supplemented with transaction-safe data layers or used carefully within known consistency boundaries.*

Summary

Redis Cluster is a remarkable tool for scaling Redis across nodes, but it's not magic. Here's what to keep in mind:

Limitation	Impact	Mitigation
Multi-key ops are limited to the same slot	Can't use `MGET`, `MSET` across slots	Use hash tags
No auto-rebalancing	Slots do not move automatically	Use `--cluster rebalance`
Limited client compatibility	Older clients may break	Use cluster-aware clients
Short failover downtime	Temporary errors during failover	Implement retries
Complex topology	More nodes, ports, and configs to manage	Use scripts and monitoring tools

Limitation	Impact	Mitigation
No cross-node Pub/Sub	Messages don't reach all nodes	Use central Redis or an external pub/sub system
Eventual consistency	Reads might be stale during failover	Use for tolerant workloads or tune app logic

***Table 10.2:** Redis Cluster Limitations, Their Impact, and Mitigation Strategies*

Understanding these trade-offs helps you design Redis-backed systems that are not only fast but also **robust and maintainable** at scale.

In the next section, we will explore how to monitor and maintain a Redis Cluster in production, ensuring that it stays healthy, balanced, and fast.

Monitoring and Maintaining a Redis Cluster

Once a Redis Cluster is up and running, your job shifts from **setup to ongoing operations,** making sure that the cluster stays healthy, well-balanced, and fault-tolerant over time.

Unlike standalone Redis, managing a Redis Cluster involves additional responsibilities such as **slot tracking**, **node state monitoring**, **resharding**, and **handling failover gracefully**. In this section, we will focus only on Redis Cluster-specific tasks and tools that help keep your deployment stable.

1. **Verifying Cluster Health with Built-in Commands**

   To check the overall state:

   ```
   redis-cli -p 7000 cluster info
   ```

   Sample output:

   ```
   cluster_state:ok
   cluster_slots_assigned:16384
   cluster_slots_ok:16384
   cluster_known_nodes:6
   ```

   `cluster_state:ok` = The cluster is functioning properly.

   `cluster_slots_ok` should match `cluster_slots_assigned` = All slots are covered.

   To inspect individual node roles and health:

   ```
   redis-cli -p 7000 cluster nodes
   ```

   Look for:

   - `Role:` **`master`** or **`slave`**
   - Slot ownership range
   - Flags: **`fail, handshake, noaddr`**, and so on.

2. **Regular Slot Distribution Checks**

   A healthy cluster **must always have all 16,384 slots assigned across the master nodes**. If you add a new master or remove one, you must **manually rebalance slots** to ensure an even workload.

   Check slot distribution:

   ```
   redis-cli -p 7000 cluster nodes
   ```

Count how many slots each master holds. If one master owns significantly more slots than others, performance will be uneven.

To rebalance slots after adding a node:

```
redis-cli --cluster rebalance 127.0.0.1:7000
```

You can review slot ownership before and after the rebalance using:

```
redis-cli -p 7000 cluster nodes
```

3. **Node Replacement and Slot Reassignment**

   If a master node becomes permanently unavailable (hardware failure, decommissioned VM), you must remove it, and reassign its slot responsibility.

   Steps:

   1. **Migrate its slots to other masters:**

      ```
      redis-cli --cluster reshard 127.0.0.1:7000
      ```

   2. **Once the node owns no slots, safely remove it:**

      ```
      redis-cli --cluster del-node 127.0.0.1:7000 <node-id>
      ```

   3. **Optionally add a new node, and assign slots or replicas:**

      ```
      redis-cli --cluster add-node 127.0.0.1:7006 127.0.0.1:7000
      ```

   4. **Detect and Fix Slot Inconsistencies**

      Unexpected shutdowns or improper resharding can leave some hash slots unassigned or assigned incorrectly.

      To detect:

      ```
      redis-cli -p 7000 cluster info
      ```

      `If cluster_slots_fail or cluster_slots_pfail` is greater than 0, there is a problem.

      To automatically fix uncovered slots:

      ```
      redis-cli --cluster fix 127.0.0.1:7000
      ```

      Redis will try to reassign missing or misaligned slots.

   5. **Routine Cluster Maintenance Tasks**

Task	Recommended Frequency	Command/Check
Check cluster state	Daily	**`cluster info`**
Validate slot distribution	Weekly or after changes	cluster nodes, manual count
Reshard and rebalance	After scaling events	**`--cluster reshard`**, rebalance
Node health check	Daily or automated	Look for fail, disconnected
Backup cluster configs	With RDB/AOF snapshots	Save nodes.conf per node
Test failover	Periodically (staging)	Kill a master, monitor promotion

Table 10.3: *Routine Maintenance Tasks for a Redis Cluster*

Note: *Redis Cluster uses a gossip protocol for internal health checks. If a node thinks another node is down, but others disagree, you may see inconsistent behavior or delays in failover.*

To confirm agreement, check multiple nodes:

```
redis-cli -p 7000 cluster nodes
redis-cli -p 7001 cluster nodes
```

Look for consistent flags (for example, no node shows `fail` if others show `connected`).

Summary

Managing a Redis Cluster means more than just watching CPU and memory – you are responsible for:

- Ensuring that slots are evenly distributed
- Keeping replicas aligned with masters
- Reacting quickly to failovers
- Periodically cleaning up the old nodes

Thus, by integrating cluster-specific checks into your operational workflows, you ensure that your cluster remains performant, balanced, and production-ready, even as your application scales.

In the next section, we will wrap up this chapter with a set of best practices, and a final recap of everything you have learned about Redis Cluster.

Performance Tuning Tips for Large-Scale Clusters

When running Redis Cluster in large or high-traffic environments, a few well-chosen configuration adjustments can significantly improve performance and stability. The following tips help optimize throughput, and reduce latency under heavy load.

- **Optimize Node Resources:** Allocate sufficient CPU and memory to each node. Redis is single-threaded, so dedicating a CPU core per node ensures better responsiveness. Keep background processes minimal on Redis hosts.
- **Tune Network Parameters:** Use low-latency and high-bandwidth networks. **Increase the tcp-backlog value** (for example, to **511**) and update system parameters such as net.core.somaxconn to allow more concurrent connections.
- **Manage Client Buffers:** For clusters serving thousands of clients, tune **client-output-buffer-limit** to prevent disconnections caused by slow or blocked consumers.
- **Handle Partial Failures Gracefully:** Set `cluster-require-full-coverage no` to avoid complete unavailability if one or more nodes are temporarily down. This helps to maintain continuity in large distributed environments.

  > **Note:** *Setting cluster-require-full-coverage no favors availability over consistency. Reads and writes may continue even when some slots are unavailable.*

- **Use Pipelining and Batching:** Encourage client applications to use pipelining to reduce round trips and network overhead, especially for write-heavy workloads.
- **Monitor and Adjust:** Regularly track key metrics such as `used_memory`, `connected_clients`, and `cluster_state, and replication lag (via INFO replication)`. Small adjustments to parameters, such as `cluster-node-timeout`, can prevent unnecessary failovers.

Parameter	Recommended Adjustment	Purpose
tcp-backlog	511	Increases queue size for pending connections
client-output-buffer-limit	Adjust based on client type	Prevents disconnections under high load
cluster-node-timeout	10,000–15,000 ms (recommended for large or unstable networks)	Balances responsiveness with stability
cluster-require-full-coverage	no	Avoids a complete outage during minor failures

Table 10.4: *Key Configuration Parameters for Cluster Performance Tuning*

These lightweight optimizations can make a noticeable difference when scaling Redis Cluster to handle high workloads. Always benchmark any change in a staging setup, before applying it to production.

Best Practices

Building a Redis Cluster is not just about getting it to work; it is about making it **robust, scalable, and production-ready**. After going through the fundamentals of clustering, slot allocation, resharding, failover, and client behavior, it is important to close with the **principles and patterns** that ensure your cluster remains healthy and high-performing over time.

In this final section, we will highlight the **most important best practices** you should follow, along with a concise wrap-up of what you have learned.

Best Practices for Redis Cluster in Production

1. **Always Use an Odd Number of Masters with Replicas**
    - A Redis Cluster requires a **majority of masters to remain available** to avoid a complete shutdown.
    - For high availability and failover, each master should have **at least one replica**.

    Example: For a resilient setup, use **3 masters + 3 replicas (total 6 nodes)**. This setup tolerates one full master node failure, and allows automatic promotion.

2. **Balance Slots Evenly across Masters**
    - Redis Cluster does not auto-balance slots after adding a new node.
    - Use `--cluster rebalance` to ensure that each master handles a similar number of hash slots, preventing one node from becoming a bottleneck.

      Command:

      ```
      redis-cli --cluster rebalance 127.0.0.1:7000
      ```

3. **Do Not Perform Writes to Replicas**
    - Replica nodes are meant for **read-scaling and failover**, not for direct writes.
    - Writing to replicas can lead to inconsistencies, and loss of data during failover.

    How to avoid: Ensure that clients are aware of the cluster topology, and direct all writes to the master nodes.

4. **Use Cluster-Aware Clients**

- Not all Redis clients support clustering.
- Use libraries or drivers that support automatic redirection (handling **`MOVED`** and **`ASK`** replies) and slot awareness.

Example: `ioredis` (Node.js), `Jedis` (Java), and `redis-py/legacy: redis-py-cluster` (Python) are cluster-aware.

5. **Avoid Multi-Key Operations across Slots**
   - Redis Cluster does not allow multi-key operations, unless all keys are in the **same hash slot**.
   - Use **hash tags** (`{}`) to place related keys in the same slot.

   Example: Keys **`order:{123}:item`** and **`order:{123}:status`** both hash to the same slot due to **`{123}.`**

6. **Monitor and Rotate Node Config Files**
   - Each Redis node stores its view of the cluster in a file (for example, **`nodes.conf`**).
   - Back up this file regularly, especially before restarting nodes, to avoid sync issues.

7. **Automate Backups**
   - Although Redis Cluster is distributed, it is **not a backup mechanism**.
   - Use RDB or AOF to back up data regularly, and consider offloading snapshots to cloud storage or a backup server.

8. **Simulate Failover in Staging**
   - Practice failover scenarios in non-production environments.
   - Simulate master failures and verify that:
     - Replicas are promoted.
     - Clients reconnect.
     - No data is lost.

9. **Set Appropriate Timeout Values**
   - Tune **`cluster-node-timeout`** to balance responsiveness and false positives.
   - Too low = false failovers, too high = slow recovery.

   Default:

   ```
   cluster-node-timeout 5000 # milliseconds
   ```

10. **Scale Horizontally but with Planning**
    - Adding more masters improves write throughput and memory capacity.
    - Rebalancing is not automatic; always plan and monitor when scaling out.

Conclusion

Redis Cluster offers a robust and scalable solution for applications that require high availability, fault tolerance, and both read and write scalability. However, this power comes with added complexity. Managing a Redis Cluster means working with a distributed system, rather than a single node. In this chapter, we explored the need for clustering beyond simple replication, examined how Redis distributes data using hash slots, and walked through the steps to set up, scale, and maintain a cluster. We also discussed how clients interact with a clustered setup, including handling redirections and designing keys with clustering in mind. Operational aspects such as failover, node management, and rebalancing were also covered in detail.

Thus, by gaining a solid understanding of how Redis Cluster works, and adhering to the best practices, you are now equipped to deploy and manage Redis at scale with confidence.

In the next chapter, *Troubleshooting Redis Issues*, we will dive into common problems you may encounter in real-world Redis environments. Hence, from connection errors and performance bottlenecks to replication and memory issues, we will provide actionable insights and diagnostic techniques to help you identify and resolve issues effectively.

CHAPTER 11

Troubleshooting Redis Issues

Introduction

Redis is known for its speed, simplicity, and reliability. However, as your system scales and becomes more complex, so does the potential for encountering operational issues. Hence, whether you are dealing with connection errors, memory bottlenecks, or unexpected data loss, troubleshooting Redis effectively requires a structured approach and an understanding of both common pitfalls and subtle edge cases.

In this chapter, we will take you through a clear and practical approach to **diagnosing and fixing Redis issues**. You will learn how to spot and resolve connection or authentication problems, track down performance bottlenecks, and manage your resources, so that Redis can keep running smoothly. We will also talk about protecting data integrity, whether challenges come from persistence, replication quirks, or unexpected client behavior, and show you how to make sense of Redis logs and runtime metrics to catch trouble before it grows. Finally, we will share the best practices to help you stay ahead of problems in production. By the time you finish this chapter, you will be well prepared to keep your Redis environment healthy, stable, and performing its best, even under pressure.

Structure

In this chapter, we will cover the following topics:

- Introduction to Troubleshooting Redis
- Connection and Authentication Issues
- Performance and Resource Problems
- Data Integrity and Consistency Issues
- Troubleshooting Cluster and Advanced Scenarios
- Analyzing Redis Logs and Metrics

Introduction to Troubleshooting Redis

Troubleshooting Redis effectively starts with understanding how Redis works under the hood. **Redis is a single-threaded, in-memory key-value store**, which means:

- It is extremely fast, but also sensitive to resource constraints like CPU and memory.
- One misbehaving command (for example, `KEYS *` or `FLUSHALL`) can impact the entire instance.
- There is no built-in query optimizer, so performance depends heavily on data modeling and access patterns.

Note: *Redis executes commands in a single thread, while I/O and background operations may use additional threads.*

To troubleshoot Redis, you will typically rely on:

- Redis logs (**redis-server.log)**
- Runtime commands (such as **`INFO`**, **`MONITOR`**, **`SLOWLOG`**, and so on)
- Client error messages
- System-level monitoring tools (like **top, netstat, iostat**)

So, let us now dive into the specific categories of issues and how to troubleshoot them.

Connection and Authentication Issues

Redis is known for being lightweight, fast, and relatively easy to get started with. However, even in the most well-planned deployments, users often encounter basic but critical roadblocks **while connecting to Redis or authenticating against it**. These are among the **first challenges developers and administrators face**, especially in distributed or production environments.

This section is dedicated to helping you understand, identify, and resolve **connection-related issues** and **authentication errors** in Redis.

One of the most common categories of Redis issues involves **problems connecting to the Redis server**. These issues can manifest as:

- "*Could not connect to Redis at 127.0.0.1:6379: Connection refused*"
- "NOAUTH *Authentication required.*"
- "READONLY *You cannot write against a read-only replica.*"

These errors may stem from a variety of reasons - misconfigurations, network firewalls, client behavior, or authentication settings. Let us walk through how to troubleshoot and fix them.

Common Connection Errors and What They Mean

- **Connection Refused:** This usually means Redis is not listening on the specified address and port.

```
$ redis-cli -h 127.0.0.1 -p 6379
Could not connect to Redis at 127.0.0.1:6379: Connection refused
```

```
Could not connect to Redis at 127.0.0.1:6379: Connection refused
not connected>
```

Figure 11.1: *Connection Refused Error in Redis*

Figure 11.1: This figure shows the error message encountered when attempting to connect to Redis, but the server is either not running or not reachable on the specified host and port.

Troubleshooting Steps:

- **Is Redis running?**

```
$ ps aux | grep redis-server
```

```
karnish          45662   0.0  0.0 410732240   1440 s011  S+   10:23PM   0:00.01 grep redis-server
```

Figure 11.2: *Output of ps aux | grep redis-server*

Figure 11.2: This figure displays the result of running the **`ps aux | grep redis-server`** command, which lists the Redis server process, along with its details. The grep command itself may also appear in the output.

If not, start Redis:

```
$ redis-server /etc/redis/redis.conf
```

- **Check the bind configuration**

  By default, Redis only binds to 127.0.0.1 (localhost). In **`redis.conf`**:

```
bind 127.0.0.1
```

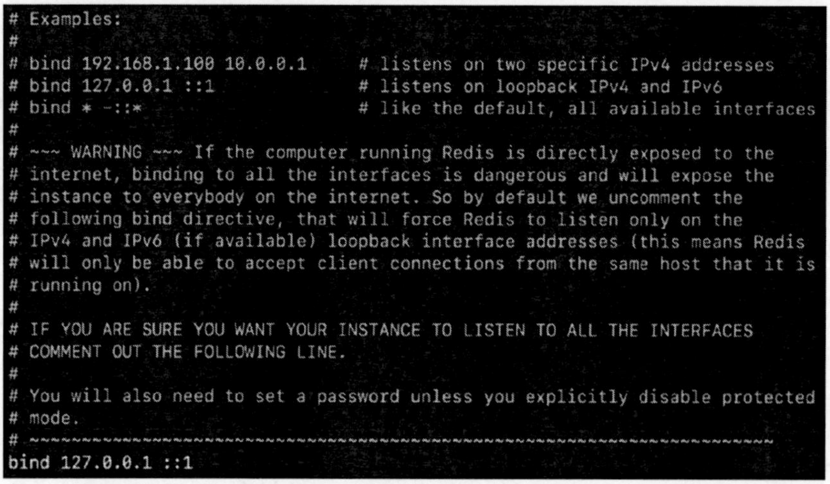

```
# Examples:
#
# bind 192.168.1.100 10.0.0.1     # listens on two specific IPv4 addresses
# bind 127.0.0.1 ::1              # listens on loopback IPv4 and IPv6
# bind * -::*                     # like the default, all available interfaces
#
# ~~~ WARNING ~~~ If the computer running Redis is directly exposed to the
# internet, binding to all the interfaces is dangerous and will expose the
# instance to everybody on the internet. So by default we uncomment the
# following bind directive, that will force Redis to listen only on the
# IPv4 and IPv6 (if available) loopback interface addresses (this means Redis
# will only be able to accept client connections from the same host that it is
# running on).
#
# IF YOU ARE SURE YOU WANT YOUR INSTANCE TO LISTEN TO ALL THE INTERFACES
# COMMENT OUT THE FOLLOWING LINE.
#
# You will also need to set a password unless you explicitly disable protected
# mode.
# ~~~~~~~~~~~~~~~~~~~~~~~~~~~~~~~~~~~~~~~~~~~~~~~~~~~~~~~~~~~~~~~~~~~~~~~~~~~~~~~~
bind 127.0.0.1 ::1
```

Figure 11.3: *bind Configuration in Redis*

Figure 11.3: This figure shows the **bind directive in the Redis configuration file**. By default, it is set to **127.0.0.1**, which restricts Redis to accept connections only from localhost.

To allow remote access (cautiously!):

```
bind 0.0.0.0
protected-mode no
```

> **Note:** *Do not expose Redis to the public internet without firewalls and authentication.*

- **Verify the port number**

  Ensure that the client is connecting to the correct port. If Redis is running on a custom port (for example, 6380):

```
$ redis-cli -p 6380
```

- **`NOAUTH` Authentication Required**

  Redis requires a password, but the client has not supplied it.

```
(error) NOAUTH Authentication required.
```

```
127.0.0.1:6379> ping
(error) NOAUTH Authentication required.
127.0.0.1:6379>
127.0.0.1:6379>
```

Figure 11.4: *NOAUTH Error in Redis*

Figure 11.4: This figure shows the **NOAUTH Authentication required error** encountered when running the **PING** command without authenticating. It indicates that Redis is configured with a password, and the client must authenticate before issuing commands.

Fix by running:

```
$ redis-cli
127.0.0.1:6379> AUTH yourpassword
OK
```

```
127.0.0.1:6379>
127.0.0.1:6379>
127.0.0.1:6379> AUTH yourpassword
OK
127.0.0.1:6379>
127.0.0.1:6379>
127.0.0.1:6379> ping
PONG
```

Figure 11.5: *Successful Authentication and PING in Redis*

Figure 11.5: This figure demonstrates how to authenticate with Redis using the AUTH command. After providing the correct password, the **PING** command responds with PONG, confirming a successful connection.

Or pass it directly:

```
$ redis-cli -a yourpassword
```

In redis.conf (Redis 5.x and earlier), to set your password:

```
requirepass yourpassword
```

```
# IMPORTANT NOTE: starting with Redis 6 "requirepass" is just a compatibility
# layer on top of the new ACL system. The option effect will be just setting
# the password for the default user. Clients will still authenticate using
# AUTH <password> as usually, or more explicitly with AUTH default <password>
# if they follow the new protocol: both will work.
#
# The requirepass is not compatible with aclfile option and the ACL LOAD
# command, these will cause requirepass to be ignored.
#
requirepass yourpassword
```

Figure 11.6: *requirepass Setting in Redis Configuration*

Figure 11.6: This figure shows the requirepass directive in the Redis configuration file. The setting enforces password-based authentication, requiring clients to authenticate before executing any commands.

> **Note:** *Always use a strong password in production.*

- **READONLY Error**

  This means you are trying to write to a replica, **which is read-only by default.**

  ```
  (error) READONLY You can't write against a read-only replica.
  ```

```
127.0.0.1:6380>
127.0.0.1:6380> SET user:10021 "testreplicawrite"
(error) READONLY You can't write against a read only replica.
127.0.0.1:6380>
127.0.0.1:6380>
```

Figure 11.7: READONLY *Error on Redis Replica*

Figure 11.7: This figure shows the READONLY error message encountered when attempting to execute a write command on a Redis replica. Replicas are read-only by default and do not accept write operations.

Fix:

- Either connect to a **master node**,
- Or promote the replica to master using **`SLAVEOF NO ONE / REPLICAOF NO ONE`** (if you are deliberately promoting it).

Using Tools to Test Connection

If you are unsure whether Redis is even reachable, try (for basic connectivity testing only):

```
$ telnet 127.0.0.1 6379
```

> ***Note: In macOS, the main alternative to the telnet command is*** **`nc`**, *which stands for* **`netcat`**. *nc is a versatile tool that can be used for various network operations, including testing port connectivity, sending and receiving data, and acting as a telnet client. Additionally,* **`ssh`** *(Secure Shell) can be used for secure remote logins and file transfers, offering a more secure alternative to the unsecured telnet protocol.*

```
$ nc -vz 127.0.0.1 6379
```

If the connection succeeds and you see:

```
Connection to 127.0.0.1 port 6379 [tcp/*] succeeded!
```

Figure 11.8: *Successful Connection to Redis Using the nc Command*

Figure 11.8: This figure shows the output of the **`nc -vz 127.0.0.1 6379`** command, indicating a successful TCP connection to the Redis server running on localhost at port 6379.

`v - Verbose` mode - shows detailed output

`z - Zero-I/O` mode - used for scanning; it doesn't send any data, just checks if the port is open

Then, Redis is accepting connections. You can also use **`ping`** from **`redis-cli`**:

```
$ redis-cli ping
PONG
```

Remote Connection Issues

If connecting from a different machine, and you see this error:

```
Could not connect to Redis at <IP>:6379: Connection timed out (Linux)

nc: connectx to <IP> port 6379 (tcp) failed: Operation timed out (macOS)
```

```
nc: connectx to 127.12.34.56 port 6379 (tcp) failed: Operation timed out
```

Figure 11.9: *Connection Timeout While Using nc from a Remote Machine*

Figure 11.9: This figure shows the **operation timed out error** encountered when attempting to connect to the Redis server from a remote machine using the nc (netcat) command. This typically indicates that the Redis server is not accessible remotely, possibly due to firewall settings or binding only to 127.0.0.1.

Check the following:

1. **Firewall Rules:** Make sure port **6379** is open on the server:
2. **Bind Configuration:** In **/etc/redis/redis.conf**, ensure Redis binds to the correct interface:

   ```
   bind 0.0.0.0
   ```

   Note: *If you make changes in the redis conf file, make sure to restart redis:*

   ```
   $ sudo systemctl restart redis
   ```

3. **Cloud Provider Rules:** If Redis is hosted in the cloud (for example, AWS EC2 or Azure VM), update security group rules to allow inbound access on port **6379**.

Secure Setup: Do It Right

While it may be tempting to expose Redis for convenience, it is not recommended unless:

- Redis is protected by a firewall.
- Authentication is enforced.
- TLS is enabled (Redis 6+ with tls-port and certificates).
- Access is restricted to internal networks only.

Here is a safer minimal config for a remote-accessible Redis:

```
bind 0.0.0.0
protected-mode yes
requirepass MyStr0ngP@ssw0rd
port 6379
```

Recap Checklist:

Symptom	Likely Cause	Suggested Fix
Connection refused	Redis is not running, or the wrong port is specified	Start Redis, verify the port, and `bind` configuration
NOAUTH	Password not supplied	Use `AUTH` or `-a` flag
READONLY	Connected to a replica	Connect to the master or reconfigure the replica
Connection timeout remotely	Firewall or bind issue	Open port, change bind to `0.0.0.0`

Table 11.1: *Common Redis Connection Issues, Causes, and Solutions*

Table 11.1: This table outlines frequent connection-related errors in Redis, their likely causes, and recommended actions to resolve them.

Real-World Tip

Thus, you are deploying in a container or Kubernetes, always double-check:

- The container port is exposed.
- The service or ingress rules route traffic to the correct internal port.
- You are not accidentally connecting to a read-only replica in HA setups.

The Human Side of These Errors

Most Redis connection problems are not due to bugs - they are due to **small gaps in setup knowledge**. Maybe:

- The Redis process was not started with the correct config.
- Testing from a different environment than your config expects.
- Connecting to a replica and trying to write the data.
- After upgrading Redis, and now security defaults are stricter.

This chapter aims to bridge those gaps. You will learn **how Redis thinks** when it comes to connections, and how you can align your configurations and clients accordingly.

Performance and Resource Problems

Redis is famous for its speed, **sub-millisecond response times**, **millions of operations per second,** and **a minimal memory footprint**. However, as your application grows or your infrastructure changes, Redis can hit **performance bottlenecks**. In this section, we will walk through common causes of slowdowns and resource issues, and how to detect, debug, and resolve them.

Whether it is a spike in latency, high memory usage, or rejected commands, we will explore these with **real-world examples**, **step-by-step techniques**, and **practical best practices**.

Identifying Performance Problems

Before jumping to conclusions, you need to ask:

- Is Redis actually slow, or is it a symptom of something else?
- Are the issues *occasional* or *persistent*?
- What do the Redis metrics tell us?

You can begin your diagnosis using:

```
redis-cli INFO stats
```

Sample output:

```
instantaneous_ops_per_sec:12859
total_commands_processed:1405063
keyspace_hits:204302
keyspace_misses:21489
```

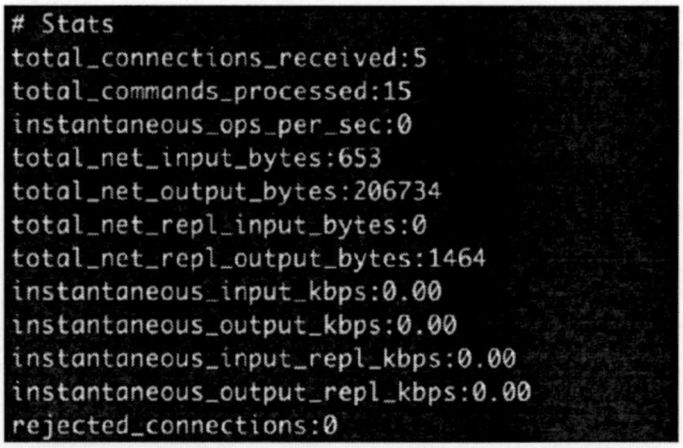

```
# Stats
total_connections_received:5
total_commands_processed:15
instantaneous_ops_per_sec:0
total_net_input_bytes:653
total_net_output_bytes:206734
total_net_repl_input_bytes:0
total_net_repl_output_bytes:1464
instantaneous_input_kbps:0.00
instantaneous_output_kbps:0.00
instantaneous_input_repl_kbps:0.00
instantaneous_output_repl_kbps:0.00
rejected_connections:0
```

Figure 11.10: *Output of redis-cli INFO stats Command*

Figure 11.10: This figure displays the result of running the **`INFO stats` command** using the Redis CLI. It provides the key statistical metrics such as the number of connections, commands processed, rejected connections, and so on, which are useful for monitoring Redis performance.

This gives a quick overview of what is happening internally.

Other useful sections:

```
redis-cli INFO memory
redis-cli INFO cpu
redis-cli INFO latency
```

CPU Bottlenecks

Problem: Redis is single-threaded for command execution (though modern Redis supports some multithreaded I/O). If your CPU usage hits 100%, it becomes a bottleneck.

Symptoms:

- Commands are queued but slow to execute.
- High **`latency`** in monitoring.
- **`top`** or **`htop`** shows Redis consuming 100% CPU

What You Can Do:

1. **Use faster disks/network:** Even with in-memory data, network I/O matters.
2. **Avoid slow commands:** Commands like **KEYS ***, **SMEMBERS**, and **ZRANGE** on large sets can be costly.
3. **Offload reads with replicas.**
4. **Split workloads** using Redis Cluster.

Memory Issues

Since Redis is an in-memory database, memory is often the most important resource.

Symptoms:

- Redis crashes with **`OOM`** **(Out of Memory)** errors.
- Redis starts evicting keys (check **`evicted_keys`** in **`INFO stats`**).
- Unexpectedly high memory usage even for small datasets.

Diagnosing:

Run:

```
redis-cli INFO memory
```

Look for:

- **`used_memory`**

```
# Memory
used_memory:1313664
used_memory_human:1.25M
```

Figure 11.11: *Output of redis-cli INFO memory – used_memory and used_memory_human*

Figure 11.11: This figure displays the result of the INFO memory command in Redis CLI, focusing on the **`used_memory`** and **`used_memory_human fields.used_memory`** shows the total memory used by Redis in **`bytes.used_memory_human`** presents the same value in a more readable format (for example, MB or GB), making it easier to interpret at a glance.

- **maxmemory**

Figure 11.12: *Output of redis-cli INFO memory – maxmemory and maxmemory_human*

Figure 11.12: This figure shows the output of the INFO memory command in Redis CLI, highlighting the **maxmemory** and **maxmemory_human** fields. maxmemory indicates the maximum amount of memory Redis is allowed to use, specified in **bytes.maxmemory_human** provides the same value in a human-readable format (for example, Bytes, MB, or GB), making it easier to understand memory limits at a glance.

- **evicted_keys**

Figure 11.13: *Evicted Keys in Output of INFO Memory*

Figure 11.13: This figure highlights the **evicted_keys** field from the **INFO memory** command in Redis CLI. This field indicates the number of keys that have been removed from the dataset to free up memory, typically when the maxmemory limit is reached, and an eviction policy is in place.

No Eviction Policy: If your **maxmemory-policy** is set to no eviction, Redis will reject commands that would cause the memory limit to be exceeded, rather than evicting keys. This means no keys will be evicted, and the **evicted_keys** count in **INFO** will remain at zero.

- **mem_fragmentation_ratio**

```
mem_fragmentation_ratio:2.25
mem_fragmentation_bytes:1604720
```

Figure 11.14: *mem_fragmentation_ratio and mem_fragmentation_bytes in Output of INFO memory*

Figure 11.14: The figure displays the **mem_fragmentation_ratio** and **mem_fragmentation_bytes** fields from the **INFO** memory command in Redis CLI. The **mem_fragmentation_ratio** shows the ratio between the memory allocated by the operating system and the memory used by Redis, while **mem_fragmentation_bytes** indicates the actual number of bytes lost due to fragmentation. These metrics help assess memory efficiency and identify potential memory overhead issues.

What You Can Do:

1. Set a memory limit in **redis.conf:**

   ```
   maxmemory 2gb
   maxmemory-policy allkeys-lru
   ```

2. Use efficient data types: Avoid large strings or deeply nested structures.
3. Compress data before storing(if applicable and only if CPU overhead is acceptable; benchmark).
4. Periodically monitor large keys using:

   ```
   redis-cli --bigkeys
   ```

```
# Scanning the entire keyspace to find biggest keys as well as
# average sizes per key type.  You can use -i 0.1 to sleep 0.1 sec
# per 100 SCAN commands (not usually needed).

[00.00%] Biggest string found so far '"user:1001:logins"' with 3 bytes
[00.00%] Biggest string found so far '"report:region:sales"' with 5 bytes
[00.00%] Biggest string found so far '"user:1001:last_seen"' with 10 bytes
[00.00%] Biggest hash   found so far '"user:profile"' with 2 fields
[00.00%] Biggest string found so far '"user:1:email"' with 23 bytes
[00.00%] Biggest hash   found so far '"sales:region:north"' with 4 fields

-------- summary -------

Sampled 16 keys in the keyspace!
Total key length in bytes is 212 (avg len 13.25)

Biggest   hash found '"sales:region:north"' has 4 fields
Biggest string found '"user:1:email"' has 23 bytes

0 lists with 0 items (00.00% of keys, avg size 0.00)
2 hashs with 6 fields (12.50% of keys, avg size 3.00)
14 strings with 118 bytes (87.50% of keys, avg size 8.43)
0 streams with 0 entries (00.00% of keys, avg size 0.00)
0 sets with 0 members (00.00% of keys, avg size 0.00)
0 zsets with 0 members (00.00% of keys, avg size 0.00)
```

Figure 11.15: *Output of redis-cli –bigkeys*

Figure 11.15: This figure shows the result of running the **redis-cli --bigkeys** command, which scans the Redis database to identify the largest keys by type. It provides valuable insights into memory usage patterns by highlighting keys that consume the most space, helping with optimization and cleanup efforts.

Or even better:

```
redis-cli --memkeys
```

```
# Scanning the entire keyspace to find biggest keys as well as
# average sizes per key type.  You can use -i 0.1 to sleep 0.1 sec
# per 100 SCAN commands (not usually needed).

[00.00%] Biggest string found so far '"user:1001:logins"' with 72 bytes
[00.00%] Biggest string found so far '"user:1001:last_seen"' with 88 bytes
[00.00%] Biggest hash   found so far '"user:profile"' with 120 bytes
[00.00%] Biggest string found so far '"user:1001:email"' with 104 bytes

-------- summary -------

Sampled 16 keys in the keyspace!
Total key length in bytes is 212 (avg len 13.25)

Biggest   hash found '"user:profile"' has 120 bytes
Biggest string found '"user:1001:email"' has 104 bytes

0 lists with 0 bytes (00.00% of keys, avg size 0.00)
2 hashs with 240 bytes (12.50% of keys, avg size 120.00)
14 strings with 1072 bytes (87.50% of keys, avg size 76.57)
0 streams with 0 bytes (00.00% of keys, avg size 0.00)
0 sets with 0 bytes (00.00% of keys, avg size 0.00)
0 zsets with 0 bytes (00.00% of keys, avg size 0.00)
```

Figure 11.16: *Output of redis-cli --memkeys*

Figure 11.16: This figure shows the output of the **redis-cli --memkeys** command, which analyzes the Redis dataset to report memory usage for individual keys. It helps identify keys that consume the most memory, enabling better memory management and performance tuning.

Slow Commands

You can enable **Redis's `slowlog`** to detect sluggish commands.

```
redis-cli CONFIG SET slowlog-log-slower-than 10000
redis-cli SLOWLOG GET
```

This logs all commands slower than 10ms.

Sample output:

```
1) 1) (integer) 157
   2) (integer) 1692754085
   3) (integer) 22052
   4) 1) "ZRANGE"
      2) "leaderboard"
      3) "0"
      4) "-1"
```

```
2) 1) (integer) 13
   2) (integer) 1749048486
   3) (integer) 14839
   4) 1) "EVAL"
      2) "-- Save as mass_insert.lua\nfor i = 1, 100 do\n    redis.call(\"SET\", \"test_slow:key:\" .. i, i)\nend\n\n"
      3) "0"
   5) "127.0.0.1:59191"
   6) ""
```

Figure 11.17: *Output of redis-cli* SLOWLOG GET

Figure 11.17: This figure displays the output of the **`SLOWLOG GET`** command in Redis CLI, which retrieves recent entries from the Redis Slow Log. Each entry includes the unique log ID, timestamp, execution time in microseconds, and the command that was executed. This helps in identifying long-running commands that may be affecting Redis performance.

Best Practices:

- Avoid using **`KEYS *`** in production, use **`SCAN`** carefully with small **`COUNT`** values instead.
- Break large operations into smaller batches.
- Use pipelining for multiple operations.

Network Latency

Sometimes, Redis itself is not slow, but the connection between Redis and your client is.

Symptoms:

- Ping times are high.
- Occasional dropped packets.
- Lag in monitoring tools.

What You Can Do:

- Use Redis closer to your application server (same availability zone or region).
- Use persistent connections, not frequent open/closes.
- Avoid long-running Lua scripts or large responses.

Run basic latency diagnostics with:

```
redis-cli --latency
```

```
min: 0, max: 24, avg: 0.33 (3288 samples)
```

Figure 11.18: *Output of redis-cli --latency*

Figure 11.18: This figure shows the output of the **redis-cli --latency** command, which measures and reports the real-time latency of Redis commands. It continuously samples the round-trip time between the client and the server, helping to identify network delays or performance bottlenecks affecting Redis responsiveness.

Or use `redis-cli --latency-dist` to get distribution curves.

```
---------------------------------------------
. - * #               .01 .125 .25 .5 milliseconds
1,2,3,...,9           from 1 to 9     milliseconds
A,B,C,D,E             10,20,30,40,50  milliseconds
F,G,H,I,J             .1,.2,.3,.4,.5       seconds
K,L,M,N,O,P,Q,?       1,2,4,8,16,30,60,>60 seconds
From 0 to 100%:
---------------------------------------------
```

Figure 11.19: *Output of redis-cli --latency-dist*

Figure 11.19: This figure presents the output of the **redis-cli --latency-dist** command, which provides a latency distribution histogram for Redis commands. It helps visualize how frequently certain latency ranges occur, making it easier to detect spikes, delays, or patterns that may affect the overall performance. This tool is useful for long-term latency monitoring and identifying irregularities in command execution times.

Evictions and Data Loss

When Redis runs out of memory, eviction policies kick in, potentially deleting the data.

Run:

```
redis-cli INFO stats
```

Look at:

```
evicted_keys:4238
```

If this number keeps increasing, Redis is deleting keys.

How to Fix:

- Increase memory or add more Redis nodes.
- Use smarter eviction policies (for example, **volatile-lru**).
- Persist critical data using AOF or RDB backups.

Example: Real-World Performance Tuning

Scenario: Your application uses Redis to cache product prices. Users report slowdowns.

Investigation:

- You find 100,000 keys in one hash (**product:prices**).
- **HGETALL** is taking 250 ms on average.

Solution:

- Refactor large hash into smaller, category-wise hashes (for example, **prices:electronics, prices:books**).

- Use pipelining to fetch only the required keys.

Result: Latency drops to ~20ms.

Final Thoughts

Performance problems can be subtle, but Redis gives you **all the tools you need** to identify them:

- `INFO` commands to inspect stats
- `MONITOR` to watch live commands
- `SLOWLOG` to catch bottlenecks
- Redis CLI latency tools for quick checks

Understanding Memory, Replication, and Persistence Internals

Troubleshooting Redis effectively requires understanding how it manages memory, replication, and data persistence under the hood. These areas often explain performance dips, unexpected latency, or data anomalies.

Memory Fragmentation

Redis uses system memory directly, rather than a managed heap. Over time, as keys are created and deleted, memory can become fragmented - meaning free memory exists but is spread unevenly, preventing efficient reuse.

Fragmentation can be observed using the `mem_fragmentation_ratio` metric from the `INFO memory` command. A ratio near 1.0 is ideal, while values above 1.5 indicate wasted space.

To mitigate this:

- Restart nodes during maintenance to allow clean memory allocation.
- Use `maxmemory-policy` settings such as `volatile-lru` or `allkeys-lru` to manage eviction effectively.
- Monitor `used_memory_rss` versus `used_memory` to detect fragmentation trends early.

Replication Internals

Redis uses **asynchronous replication**, where replicas pull updates from their masters using the `PSYNC` mechanism. During a reconnect, replicas can perform partial or full resynchronization depending on the replication offset and backlog size. Common replication issues, such as lag or frequent full syncs - are usually caused by small replication backlog buffers or slow networks. Increasing `repl-backlog-size` and ensuring adequate network bandwidth can help replicas stay in sync efficiently.

> **Tip:** *Monitor replication offsets via* `INFO replication`; *consistent offsets across nodes indicate healthy synchronization.*

Impact of Persistence Methods

Redis supports **RDB (snapshotting)** and **AOF (Append Only File)** persistence modes. While RDB creates compact point-in-time snapshots, AOF logs every write operation for durability. Using both together provides balance between speed and reliability, but may increase I/O load.

For troubleshooting:

- High disk I/O or latency during RDB saves can pause the server briefly - schedule snapshots during low activity.
- AOF rewriting can temporarily increase CPU usage; monitor **`aof_rewrite_in_progress`** to avoid stacking writes during rewrite cycles.
- In critical systems, consider disabling persistence on replicas to offload disk pressure.

Data Integrity and Consistency Issues

It is important to ensure that the **data stored in Redis remains accurate and consistent.** In this section, we will dive into the challenges of maintaining data integrity and consistency in Redis, especially in complex deployments involving persistence, replication, and failover.

We will explore real-world issues such as **data loss after crashes**, **replication lag**, and **unexpected overwrites**, and provide hands-on examples to help you detect and resolve them.

Understanding What "Consistency" Means in Redis

Redis is eventually consistent in certain setups, particularly when used with replication and clustering. That means replicas may temporarily have outdated data compared to the master.

Redis is **not ACID** like traditional databases. Instead, it focuses on performance and simplicity. So, when we talk about consistency here, we mean:

- Ensuring data changes propagate correctly to replicas
- Preventing partial writes or data corruption
- Avoiding data loss during crashes or restarts

Risk: Data Loss after Crashes

If Redis crashes or the system powers down suddenly, some data might not be saved, especially if persistence is misconfigured.

Reproduce the Scenario:

1. Start Redis with only RDB persistence enabled (default setting):

```
redis-server --save 900 1
```

2. Run the following command to write data:

```
redis-cli set crash_test "important_value"
```

3. Immediately kill the process (simulating a crash):

```
pkill -9 redis-server # only on a local test machine
```

> ***Warning:*** *Run this only on a local test machine. Never kill Redis processes like this on production systems.*

4. Restart Redis and run:

```
redis-cli get crash_test
```

You may find the key is missing.

***Figure 11.20**: Missing Key While Using the GET Command*

Figure 11.20: This figure shows the output of the GET command in Redis when attempting to retrieve a key that does not exist. Redis returns (nil), indicating that the specified key is missing or has expired. This is a common response when querying the non-existent data.

Solution:

- **Enable AOF (Append Only File) for better durability:**

```
appendonly yes
appendfsync everysec
```

```
appendonly yes
appendfsync everysec
```

***Figure 11.21**: appendonly Set to Yes and appendfsync Set to everysec in the Redis Configuration*

Figure 11.21: This figure shows the Redis configuration where appendonly is enabled by setting it to "*yes*", ensuring that all write operations are logged to the append-only file for durability. The appendfsync option is set to everysec, meaning Redis will sync the AOF to disk every second, providing a good balance between performance and data safety.

- **Combine RDB + AOF for the best coverage:** In Redis, **RDB (Redis Database)** and **AOF (Append Only File)** are two complementary persistence mechanisms used to store data on disk. The **RDB** approach creates point-in-time snapshots of the dataset at configured intervals, offering efficient backups with minimal overhead. In contrast, **AOF** logs every write operation as it occurs, providing a more durable and accurate reconstruction of data in the event of a crash or restart.
- **Use `BGREWRITEAOF` periodically to compact logs:** In Redis, the **`BGREWRITEAOF`** command triggers a background process to rewrite the **Append Only File (AOF)**, which is used for data persistence. This rewrite operation generates a more compact and optimized version of the AOF, significantly reducing disk space usage and improving the overall performance without interrupting normal operations.

Risk: Replication Lag

When a replica lags behind its master, reads from the replica might return the stale data.

Diagnose:

Run on replica:

```
redis-cli INFO replication
```

Look at:

```
master_link_status:up
```

```
master_last_io_seconds_ago: 3
slave_repl_offset: 9860
```

```
# Replication
role:slave
master_host:127.0.0.1
master_port:6379
master_link_status:up
master_last_io_seconds_ago:0
master_sync_in_progress:0
slave_read_repl_offset:6099807
slave_repl_offset:6099807
slave_priority:100
slave_read_only:1
```

***Figure 11.22:** Replication Section in Output of redis-cli INFO Replication on a Replica Node*

Figure 11.22: This figure shows the replication section from the **`INFO replication`** command executed on a Redis replica node. It indicates that the current node is acting as a replica (formerly referred to as a "**`slave`**"), and includes details such as the master host and port, replication state, link status, and replication lag. This information is essential for monitoring the health and connectivity of the replica in a Redis replication setup.

Now check on the master:

```
redis-cli INFO replication
```

Compare master_repl_offset. If there is a large difference, the **replica is lagging**.

```
# Replication
role:master
connected_slaves:1
min_slaves_good_slaves:1
slave0:ip=127.0.0.1,port=6380,state=online,offset=6099933,lag=0
master_failover_state:no-failover
master_replid:500766d55cf16795ca272c032af8cd92a1f0a8b0
master_replid2:35a2c78d793b7ff090a6c92a562658ae397b5d3e
master_repl_offset:6099933
```

***Figure 11.23:** Replication Section in Output of redis-cli INFO Replication on a Master Node*

Figure 11.23: This figure displays the replication section from the output of the **`INFO replication`** command executed on a Redis master node. It confirms the node's role as master and lists connected replica nodes. This section is crucial for monitoring replication status and ensuring that replicas are properly synchronized with the master.

Solution:

- Monitor **`master_last_io_seconds_ago`** to catch slow replicas.
- Avoid serving critical reads from replicas during failover.
- Tune the network, and check the disk speed on replicas.

Risk: Conflicts after Failover

In Redis replication, writes should only happen to the master. If an app accidentally writes to a replica, that data is overwritten after resynchronization.

Try This:

1. Sct up **`master-replica`**

2. Connect to the replica and run:

```
redis-cli -p 6380 set accidental_write "oops"
```

3. Restart the replica to trigger **sync**

```
redis-cli -p 6380 slaveof 127.0.0.1 6379
or
redis-cli -p 6380 REPLICAOF 127.0.0.1 6379
```

4. Now run:

```
redis-cli -p 6380 get accidental_write
```

Result: nil - the replica has resynced and dropped the write

```
(nil)
```

Figure 11.24: *Attempt to Retrieve Data Returning Nil*

Figure 11.24: This figure shows the result of using a Redis command (such as **GET**) to retrieve the data for a key. Redis returns (**nil**), indicating that no value is associated with the specified key at the time of the request.

How to Prevent:

- Set replicas to **read-only**:

```
redis-cli -p 6380 CONFIG SET slave-read-only yes # legacy
```

or

```
redis-cli -p 6380 CONFIG SET replica-read-only yes
```

```
slave_read_only:1
```

Figure 11.25: *slave-read-only Setting Enabled (1) in Redis Configuration*

Figure 11.25: The figure shows the Redis configuration where the slave-read-only parameter is set to 1, meaning the replica (slave) node is in read-only mode. In this mode, the replica does not accept write operations and only serves read requests, helping maintain data consistency with the master.

Always ensure that the clients are writing to the correct master (use Sentinel or Cluster).

Data Overwrites in Lua Scripts

A careless script can overwrite or delete multiple keys. Since Lua scripts run atomically, there is no rollback.

Example:

```
-- script.lua
redis.call("del", KEYS[1])
redis.call("set", KEYS[1], ARGV[1])
```

If the set fails (low memory, wrong type), the key is still deleted.

Better script (with check)

```
-- script.lua
if redis.call("type", KEYS[1]).ok == "string" then
  return redis.call("set", KEYS[1], ARGV[1])
```

```
else
  return "Type mismatch!"
end
```

Use EVAL to run:

```
redis-cli EVAL "$(cat script.lua)" 1 key1 value1
```

Preventing Key Conflicts

Key naming conflicts can arise when multiple apps use the same Redis instance.

Best Practice:

Use namespaces (**prefixes**) for each module or service:

- `user:1001:name`
- `session:token:abc123`

Or enable Keyspace Isolation using separate databases (with the SELECT command) - though this is limited in Cluster mode.

Securing Sensitive Data

Inconsistent or missing security can expose confidential values.

Always:

- Use ACLs (`redis.conf` or ACL `SETUSER`).
- Never store plaintext passwords or tokens.
- Enable TLS for encrypted data in motion.

Final Thoughts

Maintaining data integrity in Redis requires:

- **Proper persistence setup** to prevent data loss.
- **Replica monitoring** to avoid reading stale data.
- **Careful scripting** to prevent accidental deletions.
- **Client-side discipline** to avoid conflicting writes.

These practices will help you build a **robust and reliable Redis deployment**, where speed and correctness go hand in hand.

Troubleshooting Cluster and Advanced Scenarios

While most Redis issues stem from connectivity, authentication, or performance bottlenecks, production environments often present more advanced challenges. These scenarios usually involve **Redis Cluster behavior**, **complex Lua Scripting**, or **Network Anomalies** that require deeper investigation. Understanding these edge cases helps administrators maintain stability, even under unexpected conditions.

Handling Network Partitions in Cluster Mode

Redis Cluster relies on continuous inter-node communication using a **gossip protocol**. Each node exchanges heartbeat messages with peers to detect failures. During a **network partition**, some nodes may temporarily lose visibility of others, causing inconsistent states. You may see nodes marked as **PFAIL** (Possible Failure) or **FAIL** (Confirmed Failure), and clients may receive "**MOVED**" or "**ASK**" redirection errors.

To troubleshoot:

- Use the command **redis-cli --cluster check <ip:port>** to verify node reachability and slot distribution.
- Review the **`cluster_state in INFO cluster`** output - if it shows **fail**, check the affected nodes' connectivity and firewall rules.
- Ensure that **`cluster-node-timeout`** is appropriately tuned. Setting it too low can cause false failovers; too high can delay recovery.

> **Tip:** *In environments prone to transient network drops, consider setting* **`cluster-require-full-coverage no`** *to prevent complete unavailability until connectivity is restored.*

Replica Synchronization and Resync Issues

Heavy write loads or slow networks can cause replica lag, leading to data inconsistency or missed updates. Use **`INFO replication`** to monitor **`master_repl_offset`** and **`slave_repl_offset.`** A large offset difference indicates a delay. Restarting a replica may trigger a full resynchronization (**PSYNC**), which is resource-intensive in large clusters.

To minimize such issues:

- Optimize network throughput and latency between the master and replica nodes.
- Use **`repl-backlog-size`** large enough to handle replication bursts.
- Avoid restarting multiple replicas simultaneously.

Lua Scripting Pitfalls

Redis executes Lua scripts atomically in a single thread. Complex or long-running scripts can block all other operations, appearing as temporary freezes or timeouts. If Redis becomes unresponsive after script execution:

- Use **`SCRIPT KILL`** to terminate the running script safely (if not performing writes).
- Review script logic to avoid deep loops or large data iteration.
- Keep scripts idempotent and bounded in execution time.
- Monitor logs for **BUSY** or **BUSYKEY** errors, which indicate scripting overload.

Issue	Likely Cause	Resolution
MOVED/ASK errors	Network partition or slot migration	Recheck cluster state; verify connectivity
Replica lag	Network latency or backlog too small	Increase **`repl-backlog-size`**, improve bandwidth
BUSY error	Long-running Lua script	Use **`SCRIPT KILL`** and optimize script logic
FAIL status	Node unreachable or misconfigured	Verify cluster bus ports and firewall rules

Table 11.2: *Common Advanced Redis Issues and Quick Fixes*

Table 11.2 summarizes common advanced Redis issues and their quick resolutions. These cases are often encountered in large-scale or clustered environments where network stability, replication lag, or Lua scripting behavior can impact the overall performance. Identifying the root cause early using tools like **`redis-cli --cluster`** and **`check`** and monitoring commands such as **`INFO replication`** helps maintain cluster health, and prevent downtime.

By addressing these scenarios systematically, you can prevent extended downtime and ensure smooth Redis operation even in distributed or high-load deployments. Many of these checks can be automated using monitoring tools discussed in the next section.

Analyzing Redis Logs and Metrics

Just like any complex system, Redis provides a wealth of information through its logs and runtime metrics. Knowing how to read and interpret these can be the difference between **catching an issue early vs. letting it turn into a full-blown outage**.

In this section, we will break down:

- How to find and interpret Redis logs?
- Key runtime metrics you should track.
- How to troubleshoot issues using these insights?

Everything will be illustrated with **real, executable examples** so that you can try them in your environment.

Redis Log Basics

By default, Redis logs are sent to a file or standard output, depending on the configuration. Check your log destination in your **`redis.conf`**:

```
logfile /var/log/redis/redis-server.log
loglevel notice
```

You can verify it live with:

```
cat /var/log/redis/redis-server.log | tail -f
```

Note: *If running via Docker or in a service manager like* **`systemd`**, *use* **`journalctl`** *or* **`docker logs`**.

Example Log Snippet:

```
3274:M 05 Jun 2025 10:23:42.982 * Background saving started by pid 8743
8743:C 05 Jun 2025 10:23:43.189 * DB saved on disk
3274:M 05 Jun 2025 10:23:43.190 * Background saving terminated with success
```

```
73967:M 09 Jun 2025 11:56:22.689 * Background saving started by pid 74219
74219:C 09 Jun 2025 11:56:22.697 * DB saved on disk
74219:C 09 Jun 2025 11:56:22.698 * Fork CoW for RDB: current 0 MB, peak 0 MB, average 0 MB
73967:M 09 Jun 2025 11:56:22.783 * Background saving terminated with success
```

Figure 11.26: *Redis Log Snippet*

Figure 11.26: This figure displays a snippet from the Redis log file, which includes important runtime information. Redis logs are a valuable resource for monitoring server activity, troubleshooting issues, and understanding system behavior over time.

This shows Redis triggered an RDB snapshot and completed it successfully.

Interpreting Log Levels

Set the level in **`redis.conf`**:

```
loglevel notice
```

```
# Specify the server verbosity level.
# This can be one of:
# debug (a lot of information, useful for development/testing)
# verbose (many rarely useful info, but not a mess like the debug level)
# notice (moderately verbose, what you want in production probably)
# warning (only very important / critical messages are logged)
# nothing (nothing is logged)
loglevel notice
```

Figure 11.27: *Log Level Set to Notice in Redis Configuration File*

Figure 11.27: This figure shows the Redis configuration where the loglevel is set to notice.

Available levels:

- **`debug`**: very verbose (use during development or deep troubleshooting).
- **`verbose`**: a bit more than **`notice`**.
- **`notice:`** the default includes events like replication, persistence, and so on.
- **`warning:`** only critical problems.

Temporarily change log level at runtime:

```
redis-cli CONFIG SET loglevel debug
```

Note: Remember to set it back to notice/warning after troubleshooting to avoid noisy logs.

Real-Time Runtime Metrics: `INFO` Command

Redis's **`INFO`** command is your built-in dashboard. You can call it like:

```
redis-cli INFO
```

Or target specific sections:

```
redis-cli INFO memory
redis-cli INFO stats
redis-cli INFO replication
```

Common Use Cases with `INFO`

1. **Check memory usage**

   ```
   redis-cli INFO memory
   ```

   ```
   used_memory_human:963.39K
   ```

   Figure 11.28: *used_memory_human Field from INFO Memory Command*

   Figure 11.28: This figure displays the **`used_memory_human`** field from the output of the **`INFO`** memory command in Redis CLI. This field represents the amount of memory used by Redis in a human-readable format, making it easier to quickly assess memory consumption.

```
mem_fragmentation_ratio:5.75
```

***Figure 11.29**: mem_fragmentation_ratio Field from INFO Memory Command*

Figure 11.29: This figure shows the **`mem_fragmentation_ratio`** field from the output of the **`INFO`** memory command in Redis CLI. This metric indicates the ratio between the memory allocated by the operating system and the memory actually used by Redis, helping identify inefficiencies or memory overhead due to fragmentation.

Look for:

```
used_memory_human:12.78M
mem_fragmentation_ratio:1.05
```

`A high fragmentation_ratio (like >1.5)` may suggest memory bloat.

2. **Track command stats**

```
redis-cli INFO commandstats
```

Sample output:

```
cmdstat_get:calls=134500,usec=1839400,usec_per_call=13.7
cmdstat_set:calls=56700,usec=1340000,usec_per_call=23.6
```

This helps to identify expensive or overly-used commands.

```
# Commandstats
cmdstat_set:calls=1,usec=50,usec_per_call=50.00,rejected_calls=0,failed_calls=0
cmdstat_ping:calls=2,usec=5,usec_per_call=2.50,rejected_calls=0,failed_calls=0
cmdstat_get:calls=1,usec=6,usec_per_call=6.00,rejected_calls=0,failed_calls=0
cmdstat_command|docs:calls=3,usec=3490,usec_per_call=1163.33,rejected_calls=0,failed_calls=0
cmdstat_info:calls=9,usec=689,usec_per_call=76.56,rejected_calls=0,failed_calls=0
cmdstat_bgsave:calls=1,usec=1239,usec_per_call=1239.00,rejected_calls=0,failed_calls=0
```

***Figure 11.30**: Output of redis-cli INFO commandstats*

Figure 11.30: This figure displays the output of the **`INFO commandstats`** command in Redis CLI, which provides statistics on the usage of each Redis command. It includes metrics such as the number of calls, total execution time, and average execution time per command. These insights help analyze command patterns and identify potential performance bottlenecks.

3. **Replication health**

```
redis-cli INFO replication
```

Look at:

- **`role`** → `should be master or slave`
- **`connected_slaves`** → `check expected count`
- **`master_link_status: up`** → `means replica is in sync`

```
# Replication
role:slave
master_host:127.0.0.1
master_port:6379
master_link_status:up
master_last_io_seconds_ago:7
master_sync_in_progress:0
slave_read_repl_offset:224
slave_repl_offset:224
replica_full_sync_buffer_size:0
replica_full_sync_buffer_peak:0
slave_priority:100
slave_read_only:1
replica_announced:1
connected_slaves:0
master_failover_state:no-failover
master_replid:6eab1af43f336bbd95fe3e707a77e414c50411e4
master_replid2:0000000000000000000000000000000000000000
master_repl_offset:224
second_repl_offset:-1
repl_backlog_active:1
repl_backlog_size:1048576
repl_backlog_first_byte_offset:15
repl_backlog_histlen:210
```

Figure 11.31: *Replication Section from redis-cli INFO Replication*

Figure 11.31: This figure shows the replication section from the output of the **`INFO replication`** command in Redis CLI. It provides comprehensive details about the replication setup. This information is essential for monitoring the health and synchronization status of Redis replication.

Monitor Slow Queries: `SLOWLOG`

Redis tracks long-running commands using **`SLOWLOG`**.

How to see slow queries:

```
redis-cli SLOWLOG get 5
```

Output:

```
1) 1) (integer) 92
   2) (integer) 1717573501
   3) (integer) 1200
   4) 1) "zrangebyscore"
      2) "leaderboard"
      3) "0"
      4) "100"
```

This tells us a **`ZRANGEBYSCORE`** took 1200 microseconds.

Configure what is considered "`slow`":

```
redis-cli CONFIG SET slowlog-log-slower-than 1000   # in microseconds
redis-cli CONFIG SET slowlog-max-len 128
```

```
127.0.0.1:6379> CONFIG SET slowlog-log-slower-than 1000
OK
```

Figure 11.32: *Setting slowlog-log-slower-than to 1000 from the Redis CLI*

Figure 11.32: This figure shows how to configure the slowlog-log-slower-than parameter using the Redis CLI. Setting it to 1000 (microseconds) means any command that takes longer than 1 millisecond to execute will be logged in the Redis Slow Log, helping to identify and analyze slow-performing operations.

```
127.0.0.1:6379> CONFIG SET slowlog-max-len 128
OK
```

Figure 11.33: *Setting slowlog-max-len to 128 from the Redis CLI*

Figure 11.33: This figure shows how to configure the slowlog-max-len parameter using the Redis CLI. By setting it to 128, Redis will retain up to 128 entries in the Slow Log, allowing you to review recent slow commands and analyze performance trends over time.

Real-Time Monitoring with Redis CLI

You can use:

```
redis-cli monitor
```

This logs every single command hitting the Redis server in real time.

Note: *Only use in development or during troubleshooting; it is very verbose and slows Redis down.*

Sample output:

```
"172.17.0.1:51542" "GET" "user:1001"
"172.17.0.1:51542" "SET" "user:1001" "Karnish"
```

```
1749480634.447692 [0 127.0.0.1:51470] "COMMAND" "DOCS"
1749480642.575275 [0 127.0.0.1:51470] "get" "user:1001"
1749480664.050484 [0 127.0.0.1:51470] "set" "user:1001" "karnish"
```

Figure 11.34: *Output of redis-cli MONITOR Command*

Figure 11.34: This figure displays the output of the **`MONITOR`** command in Redis CLI, which streams every command received by the Redis server in real time. It is a powerful debugging and auditing tool that helps observe live interactions with the Redis instance, including client activity and executed commands.

Final Tips

- Use **`INFO`** as your first stop when something feels off.
- Regularly monitor **`SLOWLOG`** to keep queries fast.
- Tail logs when restarting Redis or debugging failovers.
- Combine logs + metrics to trace the full picture.

Summary: What to Watch

Metric/Log	Why It is Important
`used_memory`	Helps identify leaks or bloat
`connected_clients`	Sudden spikes could indicate misuse
`instantaneous_ops_per_sec`	Command throughput
`slowlog`	Identify poorly performing queries
`master_link_status`	For replication health
`Log entries` (* RDB saved on disk, etc.)	Track persistence
`expired_keys` and `evicted_keys`	Cache health

Table 11.3: *Key Redis Metrics and Logs for Monitoring and Diagnostics*

Table 11.3: This table highlights essential Redis metrics and log entries, explaining their significance in maintaining system performance, reliability, and stability.

Best Practices for Preventing Issues

Troubleshooting is important - but preventing issues in the first place is even better.

In this final section, we will cover practical, time-tested strategies to prevent common Redis problems. These best practices are drawn from real-world experience and will help ensure that your Redis environment stays healthy, high-performing, and easy to manage.

Thus, let us look at the key areas where prevention makes all the difference:

Secure Your Redis Installation

A poorly secured Redis server is a disaster waiting to happen.

Best Practices:

- Bind to localhost (or secure network):

  ```
  bind 127.0.0.1
  ```

- Set a strong password:

  ```
  requirepass StrongRedisP@ssw0rd
  ```

- Use Redis ACLs (v6.0+) to restrict command access:

  ```
  user readonly on >readonly_pass ~* +get +info
  ```

- Never expose Redis directly to the public internet. Use firewalls or tunnels.

Use Proper Persistence Settings

Avoid data loss by configuring persistence properly.

Recommended:

- Enable both **RDB** and **AOF** for a good balance:

  ```
  save 900 1
  save 300 10
  appendonly yes
  ```

- Regularly test RDB backups by restoring them on a different server.
- Use **`BGREWRITEAOF`** periodically to compact the AOF file and reduce disk usage.

Monitor Regularly

We have seen the power of metrics in the previous section. Now, let us make it proactive.

Best Practices:

- Set up a monitoring dashboard (RedisInsight, Prometheus + Grafana).
- Track **slow queries** weekly and optimize.
- Set alerts for:
  - High memory usage
  - Replica lag
  - Client connection spikes
  - **`expired_keys`** or **`evicted_keys`**

Use Proper Data Structures

Misusing data types can cause **wasteful memory usage** or **performance drops**.

Do's:

- Use **Sets** instead of **Lists** when uniqueness matters.
- Use **Hashes** for grouped key-values (for example, user objects).
- Use **Streams** for real-time log/event data (instead of List abuse).
- Avoid keys that grow **unbounded** (for example, massive Lists).

Note: *Think of Redis as a data structure server, not a general key-value store.*

Set Timeouts and Limits

To keep Redis from being overrun by stale data or noisy clients:

Use:

- TTL (Time to Live) for cache keys:

```
SET user:1001 "Karnish" EX 600
```

```
127.0.0.1:6379> SET user:1001 "Karnish" EX 600
OK
127.0.0.1:6379>
```

Figure 11.35: *Setting TTL to 600 for a Cache Key in Redis*

Figure 11.35: This figure shows how to set a Time to Live (TTL) of 600 seconds for a cache key using the `EXPIRE` command in Redis. Setting TTL ensures that the key will automatically expire and be removed from memory after the specified duration, which is necessary for managing cache lifecycle and memory usage efficiently.

- `maxmemory` settings to cap usage:

```
maxmemory 2gb
maxmemory-policy allkeys-lru
```

- `client-output-buffer-limit` to prevent memory spikes from chatty clients.

Plan for High Availability

You do not want to learn about HA the hard way - during a failure.

Choose based on scale:

Scale	Recommendation
Small	Replication + Sentinel
Medium	Replication + Sentinel + Persistent Storage
Large	Redis Cluster with replicas

Table 11.4: *Redis Deployment Recommendations Based on Scale*

Table 11.4: This table provides guidance on choosing the appropriate Redis architecture depending on the size and demands of your deployment environment.

Always have at least one replica per master.

Use:

```
replica-read-only yes
```

```
# Since Redis 2.6 by default replicas are read-only.
#
# Note: read only replicas are not designed to be exposed to untrusted clients
# on the internet. It's just a protection layer against misuse of the instance.
# Still a read only replica exports by default all the administrative commands
# such as CONFIG, DEBUG, and so forth. To a limited extent you can improve
# security of read only replicas using 'rename-command' to shadow all the
# administrative / dangerous commands.
replica-read-only yes
```

Figure 11.36: *replica-read-only Set to yes in the Redis Configuration File*

Figure 11.36: This figure shows the Redis configuration where the replica-read-only directive is set to "yes". This setting ensures that the replica node operates in read-only mode, disallowing any write operations to maintain consistency with the master, and prevent accidental data modifications.

Automate Backups and Validations

Setup:

1. Nightly RDB backups to external storage.
2. Run a restoration test weekly to validate backups.
3. Schedule Redis CLI sanity checks via cron:

   ```
   redis-cli INFO replication
   redis-cli SLOWLOG get 5
   ```

Test before Deploying Config Changes

Always restart Redis in staging with new config files before pushing to prod.

Use:

```
redis-server /etc/redis/redis.conf --test-memory 2048
```

This command performs a memory allocation test to verify system memory reliability, not Redis configuration validity.

Use Descriptive Keys and Name Spacing

This helps with debugging, maintenance, and memory planning.

Use:

```
user:123:name
product:456:price
session:token:abcd1234
```

Summary: Preventive Checklist

Area	Best Practice
Security	Require password, bind to localhost, disable unsafe commands
Memory	Set limits and eviction policy
Monitoring	Enable **SLOWLOG**, **INFO** checks, and set alerts
Structure	Use correct data types for your use case
HA	At least 1 replica per master, or use Redis Cluster
Persistence	Use both **RDB** and **AOF**, test backups
Automation	Use cron, scripts, and dashboards
Testing	Always validate the config before applying

Table 11.5: *Redis Best Practices across Key Operational Areas*

Table 11.5: This table summarizes the best practices for effectively managing Redis, covering security, performance, high availability, persistence, automation, and more to ensure a stable and optimized deployment.

Conclusion

Redis is beloved for its simplicity and speed, but when things go wrong, that simplicity can sometimes make it feel like Redis is a black box. This chapter aimed to open that box, shine a light inside, and help you become confident in diagnosing and fixing issues that arise in real-world environments.

We began by understanding the mindset of troubleshooting - not just reacting to errors, but proactively recognizing symptoms, using the right tools, and thinking systematically. Thus, whether it is a connection problem due to a misconfigured bind address or authentication failures because of missing credentials, we now know where to look and how to fix it.

As we explored performance bottlenecks, we saw how a single slow command, a bloated key, or an unbounded data structure can quietly degrade system health. With tools like **SLOWLOG**, **MONITOR**, and memory statistics from **INFO**, you now have a Redis diagnostic toolbox at your fingertips.

In the section on data integrity and consistency, we covered real-world problems such as race conditions, incomplete writes, and replication delays, along with examples showing how to spot them and what steps to take. So, if you have ever lost sleep wondering, "*Did that value really get saved?*", you now know how to find the answer.

We also walked through log analysis, key metrics, and how to interpret them. In fact, *Redis speaks - through its logs, statistics, and CLI responses, and the goal was to help you listen effectively.*

Finally, we shifted the focus from fixing issues to preventing them, such as setting timeouts, enabling persistence, watching memory use, and adopting naming conventions. Prevention is not glamorous, but it is the most powerful form of troubleshooting if there is an error.

CHAPTER 12

Running Redis on Cloud Platforms

Introduction

As your application grows, so does the pressure on Redis - it is expected to stay fast, available, and easy to manage, no matter how much traffic you throw at it. That is where the cloud comes in. Running Redis on a cloud platform is not just about keeping up with modern infrastructure trends; it is about making life easier for developers and operations teams alike.

Imagine not having to worry about setting up servers, dealing with failovers, or scrambling to scale when traffic spikes. With cloud-based Redis, those challenges are handled for you. High availability, built-in monitoring, and one-click scaling come baked in, letting you focus on what really matters: building features your users love. Thus, whether you are a scrappy startup racing to launch or a global company serving millions, **Redis on the cloud gives you the speed, simplicity, and flexibility to grow without slowing down**.

Structure

In this chapter, we will explore how to set up and configure Redis across major cloud platforms. Specifically, we will cover the following:

- Introduction to Redis in the Cloud
- Amazon Web Services (AWS) via ElastiCache
- Google Cloud Platform (GCP) via MemoryStore
- Microsoft Azure via Azure Cache for Redis
- Comparing Managed vs. Self-Hosted Redis in the Cloud

AWS ElastiCache for Redis

AWS ElastiCache for Redis is **Amazon's fully managed Redis service**. It takes the heavy lifting out of running Redis yourself. Hence, instead of manually installing Redis, worrying about version upgrades, setting up replication, or configuring backups, you simply choose your Redis setup in the AWS Management Console, and AWS handles the rest behind the scenes.

Think of **ElastiCache** as **Redis with superpowers**: it is faster to set up, automatically scales, (ElastiCache Serverless) and is integrated with Amazon's cloud infrastructure for reliability and performance.

Here is what ElastiCache does for you:

- **Server Setup and Maintenance:** You do not have to install or configure Redis manually. AWS provisions the Redis instances for you, sets up networking, applies updates, and handles day-to-day maintenance.

- **Automatic Backups and Failover:** If your primary Redis instance fails, ElastiCache can automatically detect the issue and promote a replica to become the new master, keeping your application up and running with minimal downtime. You can even configure daily snapshots for backup and restore.
- **Built-in Monitoring and Alerts:** ElastiCache is tightly integrated with **Amazon CloudWatch**, giving you real-time metrics like memory usage, CPU load, number of connections, evictions, and much more. You can set up alarms to get notified if something looks off, such as high memory usage or slow command response.

If you want to use Redis in your **AWS-based application without the operational burden of managing the infrastructure**, **ElastiCache is the way to go**. It lets you enjoy the benefits of Redis, while AWS takes care of installation, scaling, and keeping it healthy.

Step-by-Step: Setting Up Redis with ElastiCache

Setting up Redis via AWS ElastiCache is straightforward- thanks to AWS's managed service features. Here is how you can get Redis running on ElastiCache in just a few steps!

Step 1: Log in to the AWS Console

a. Go to *https://console.aws.amazon.com*, and log in with your credentials.

b. Make sure that you are in the **right AWS region,** as this is important because your Redis cache will be deployed in that region.

Figure 12.1: *Region Selection: Asia Pacific (Mumbai)*

Figure 12.1: This figure illustrates the region being set to **Asia Pacific (Mumbai)**. Choosing a region close to your user base helps minimize latency and improve the overall performance.

Step 2: Open the ElastiCache Dashboard

a. In the AWS Management Console, **search for ElastiCache** in the search bar, and select `ElastiCache` from the results.

b. On the `ElastiCache` home page, click on "`Redis`" in the left panel (**ElastiCache supports both Redis and Memcached**).

Figure 12.2: ElastiCache Home Page in AWS

Figure 12.2: This figure displays the AWS ElastiCache home page, which serves as the starting point for creating and managing Redis and Memcached clusters in your AWS environment.

Step 3: Click "`Redis OSS caches`."

a. Click the "**`Create cache`**" button.

b. You will now see the deployment option:

- Serverless
- Design your own cache

Figure 12.3: *Selecting "Design Your Own Cache" in AWS ElastiCache*

Figure 12.3: This figure shows the selection of the "*Design Your Own Cache*" option during the creation of a standalone Redis cache in Amazon ElastiCache. This option enables you to configure the essential settings, such as node type, engine version, and network placement, according to your specific application needs.

Step 4: Choose the creation method

- Easy create
- Cluster cache
- Restore from backup

Step 5: You will now see two setup options:

- **Cluster mode disabled (Single Node or Primary-Replica):** Good for simpler use cases.
- **Cluster mode enabled (Sharded Cluster):** Recommended for high-scale, distributed applications.

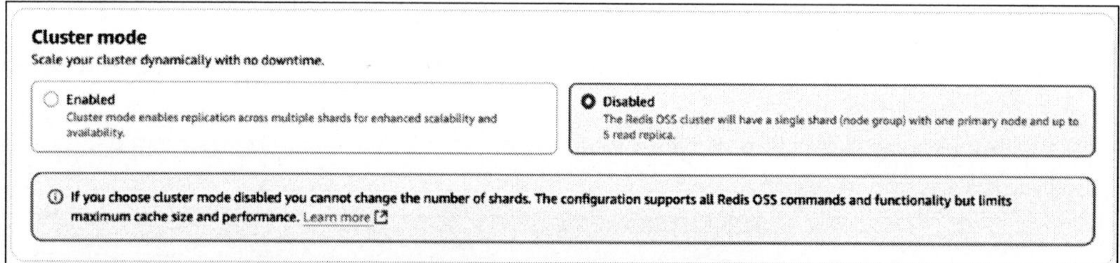

Figure 12.4: *Selecting Cluster Mode: Disabled in AWS ElastiCache*

Figure 12.4: This figure illustrates the step where Cluster Mode is set to "**`Disabled`**" during Redis cache creation in Amazon ElastiCache. Disabling cluster mode configures Redis to operate in standalone mode, which is ideal for simpler deployments that do not require data sharding across multiple nodes.

Note: *Choose* **"`Cluster mode disabled`"** *if you are just testing or getting started.*

Step 6: Configure Redis Cache Details

Setting	Recommended Value
Name	`my-redis-cache`
Engine version	Choose the latest stable Redis version
Port	Leave default as 6379
Parameter group	Default is fine, or create your own for fine-tuning Redis
Node type	Choose as per the requirement
Number of replicas	Set to 1 or more, depending on your redundancy needs

Table 12.1: *Configuration Settings for Creating a Redis Instance in AWS ElastiCache*

Table 12.1: This table lists the key settings filled in during the creation of a Redis instance using Amazon ElastiCache. These fields define the core properties of the deployment, such as its identity, size, and behavior.

Note: *You can enable Multi-AZ with Auto-Failover to improve availability.*

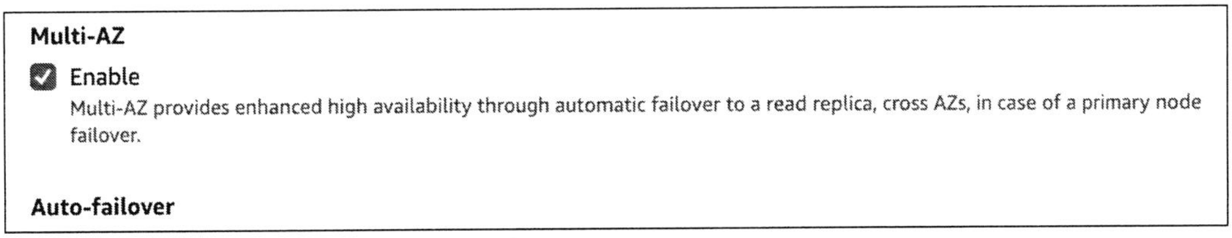

Multi-AZ

☑ Enable

Multi-AZ provides enhanced high availability through automatic failover to a read replica, cross AZs, in case of a primary node failover.

Auto-failover

Figure 12.5: *Enabling Multi-AZ in AWS ElastiCache*

Figure 12.5: This figure shows the option to enable Multi-AZ during the Redis cache setup in Amazon ElastiCache. Enabling Multi-AZ allows Redis to automatically distribute primary and replica nodes across multiple Availability Zones, enhancing fault tolerance and ensuring high availability in case of zone-level failures.

Step 7: Choose Network Settings

a. **VPC**: Choose the same VPC as your application or create a new one.
b. **Subnet group**: If this is your first time, you may need to create a **subnet group**:
    i. Go to **"`Subnet groups`"** > **`Create Subnet Group`**
    ii. Give it a name, select the VPC, and add at least two subnets from different Availability Zones.

Note: A Virtual Private Cloud (VPC) is an isolated network inside the cloud where your Redis instance and application servers can communicate securely.

Ensure that your application (for example, EC2 instance, Lambda, and so on) is in the **same VPC**, so that it can access the Redis instance.

Step 8: Set Access Controls

- **Security Group**: You can either create a new security group or select an existing one.
    - Make sure that the security group allows **inbound access to port 6379** from your application's IP or security group.

> **Note:** If you want to **secure Redis, ElastiCache now supports Redis `AUTH`**. You can enable this under the "`Access Control`" section by setting a password. For more granular security control, it is recommended to use Access Control Lists (ACLs) or IAM-based authentication mechanisms.

Step 9: Enable automated backup, if required

- You have the option to enable automated backup.
- You can specify a retention period and a backup window.

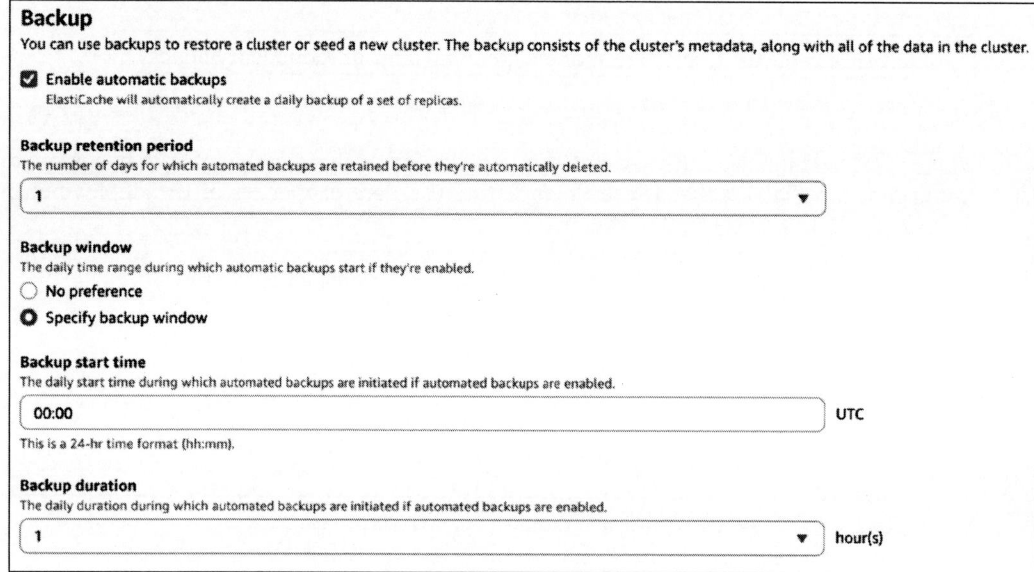

Figure 12.6: *Enabling Automatic Backups in AWS ElastiCache*

Figure 12.6: This figure demonstrates how to enable automatic backups during Redis cache creation by specifying parameters such as the backup retention period and the preferred backup window. Enabling this feature ensures that Redis snapshots are taken regularly, allowing for point-in-time recovery and enhancing data durability in production environments.

Step 10: Enable Logs, if required

- You have the option to enable slow and engine logs.

Home > Azure Cache for Redis >

New Redis Cache ...

Project details

Select the subscription to manage deployed resources and costs. Use resource groups like folders to organize and manage all your resources.

Subscription * Azure subscription 1

Resource group * redis_demo_rg

Create new

Instance Details

Name * redis-demo-v1

.redis.cache.windows.net

Region * Central India

Cache SKU (View full pricing details) * Basic (No SLA)

See which features are available on each Azure Cache for Redis tier Learn more

Cache size * C1 (1 GB Cache)

Review + create < Previous Next : Networking >

Figure 12.7: *Options to Enable Slow Log and Engine Log in AWS ElastiCache*

Figure 12.7: This figure highlights the option to enable slow log and engine log while configuring a Redis cache in Amazon ElastiCache. These logs provide valuable insights into slow-running commands and internal engine behavior, making them necessary for performance monitoring and troubleshooting in production environments.

Step 11: Finalize and Launch

a. Review all your settings.

b. Click "**`Create`**".

c. It will take a few minutes to launch your Redis cache.

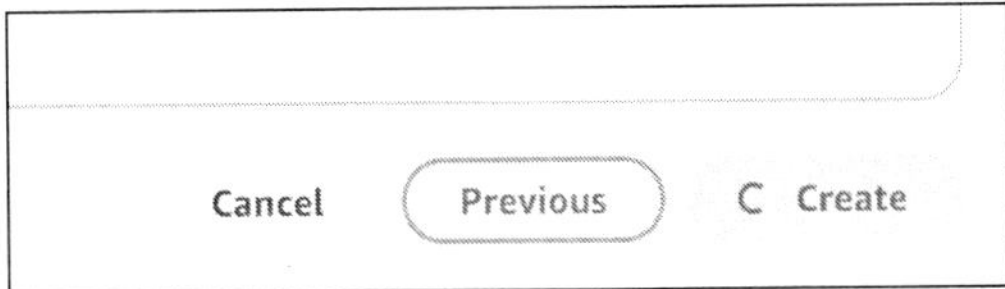

Figure 12.8: *Final Step: Click "Create" after Reviewing Configuration*

Figure 12.8: This figure shows the final step in the Redis cache setup process in Amazon ElastiCache, where you click the "**`Create`**" button after thoroughly reviewing all the selected configuration settings. This action initiates the creation of your standalone Redis instance based on the specified parameters.

Step 12: Connect to Your Redis Cache

Once your cluster is up and running:

a. Go to the Clusters section under ElastiCache.

b. Click on your Redis cache name.

c. You will find the Primary Endpoint (hostname + port), for example:

```
master.my-redis-cache.xyz123.aps1.cache.amazonaws.com:6379
```

Replica endpoint, for example:

```
replica.my-redis-cache.xyz123.aps1.cache.amazonaws.com:6379
```

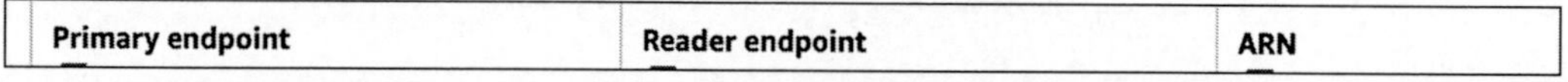

Figure 12.9: *Viewing Primary and Replica Endpoints in AWS ElastiCache*

Figure 12.9: This figure displays the section where **primary and replica endpoints** are shown after the Redis cache has been successfully created in Amazon ElastiCache. These endpoints are used by applications to connect to the correct Redis node. Writes go to the primary, while reads can be directed to replicas for load distribution and improved performance.

Use these endpoints to connect to Redis from your application or testing machine.

Figure 12.10: *Connection Options for Redis Cache in AWS ElastiCache*

Figure 12.10: This figure highlights the various options to connect to your Redis cache, including using AWS CloudShell, AWS CLI, or other supported clients. These tools provide flexible ways to interact with your Redis instance for testing, configuration, or operational tasks directly from within the AWS environment.

Step 13: Connect Using `redis-cli` (from EC2)

To connect using the Redis CLI:

a. Launch an EC2 instance in the same VPC.

b. SSH into it.

c. Install Redis tools:

```
sudo yum install -y redis
```

d. Connect using:

```
redis-cli -h <endpoint> -p 6379
```

e. If you have enabled Redis AUTH, add:

```
redis-cli -a <your_password> -h <endpoint>
```

Using AWS CloudShell to Connect to ElastiCache

In addition to using an EC2 instance, AWS also provides a browser-based terminal environment called CloudShell, which is perfect for running administrative commands without launching a separate server.

What is AWS CloudShell?

AWS CloudShell is a browser-based shell that comes pre-authenticated with your AWS credentials. It allows you to run AWS CLI commands, install utilities, and interact with your AWS services, without setting up a separate EC2 instance.

This makes it a convenient tool for quickly testing or managing services like ElastiCache.

Why Use CloudShell?

- No need to manage EC2 instances.
- Pre-authenticated with your IAM permissions.
- Useful for quick commands, diagnostics, or education/testing purposes.
- Secure and isolated per user.

Note: *CloudShell is ideal for hands-on learning or when you do not want to provision an EC2 instance just for a CLI session. For production-level access or automation, an EC2 instance or container is still the more scalable approach.*

Monitoring

- Use **CloudWatch** metrics for `CPUUtilization`, `CurrConnections`, and `Evictions`.
- Set up alerts for spikes or slowdowns.

GCP Memorystore for Redis

Google Cloud Platform (GCP) offers **Memorystore**, a fully managed in-memory data store compatible with Redis and Memcached. In this section, we will focus on using Memorystore for Redis, which lets you leverage Redis without worrying about infrastructure, failover, or patching.

Why Use GCP Memorystore for Redis?

When you choose Memorystore, GCP takes care of:

- Provisioning and scaling Redis instances
- Ensuring high availability (with automatic failover)
- Patch management and upgrades
- VPC-based private networking (secure access)
- Monitoring and logging through GCP's operations suite

If you are already hosting your app on GCP or using Kubernetes Engine (GKE), Memorystore integrates naturally and reduces operational overhead.

Step-by-Step: Deploying Redis on GCP with Memorystore

Let us walk through the process of creating and connecting to a Memorystore Redis instance.

Step 1: Open the Google Cloud Console

Go to:

https://console.cloud.google.com

Step 2: Enable the Required APIs

Before you begin, make sure that the **Memorystore API** is enabled.

a. Navigate to `APIs and Services > Library`

b. Search for "**Google Cloud Memorystore for Redis API**"

c. Click **Enable**

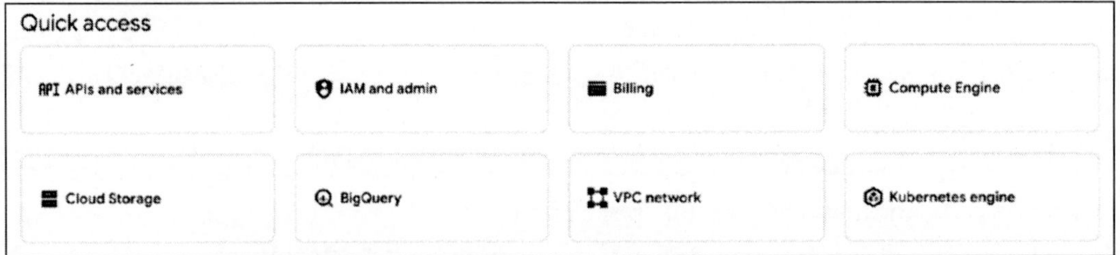

Figure 12.11: *Quick Access Section in Google Cloud Platform* (GCP)

Figure 12.11: This figure shows the Quick Access section within the Google Cloud Platform console.

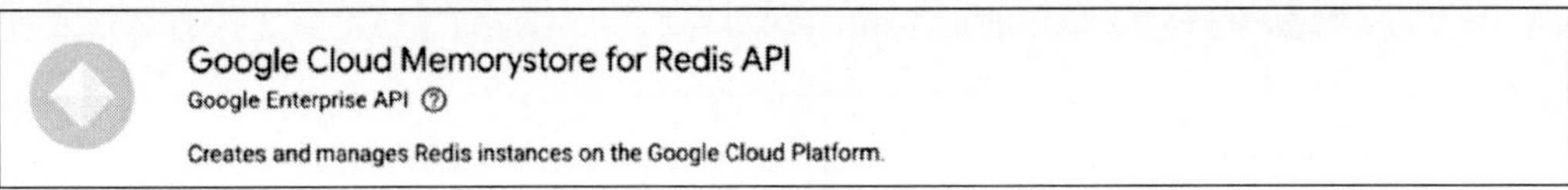

Figure 12.12: *Google Cloud Memorystore for Redis API Section in Google Cloud Platform* (GCP)

Figure 12.12: This figure displays the Memorystore for Redis API section within the Google Cloud Platform console. This section allows users to enable and manage the Redis API, which is required to provision and interact with Redis instances using Google Cloud's managed Memorystore service.

You can also do this from Cloud Shell:

```
gcloud services enable redis.googleapis.com
```

Step 3: Create a Redis Instance

Now, let us create a Redis instance using the Console:

a. Go to **Memorystore** > **Redis**

b. Click **Create Instance**

c. Fill out the form:

Field	Example
Instance ID	Provide a unique identifier for your Redis instance.
Display Name (Optional)	Give your instance a more descriptive name.
Tier	Choose between the Basic or Standard tier, depending on your needs.
Region and Zone	Select the appropriate region and zone for your instance.
Redis Version	Choose the latest version supported in your selected region.
Capacity	Specify the desired memory capacity for your instance (1-300 GB).
Enable AUTH (Optional)	Enable authentication for your Redis instance.
Enable In-transit Encryption (Optional)	Enable encryption for data in transit.

Table 12.2: *Key Configuration Fields for Creating a Redis Instance in Google Cloud Memorystore*

Table 12.2: This table outlines the essential and optional fields you will encounter when creating a Redis instance in Google Cloud Memorystore. Each field plays a critical role in defining the behavior, performance, and security of your Redis deployment. Understanding these options ensures that you provision the right instance for your workload.

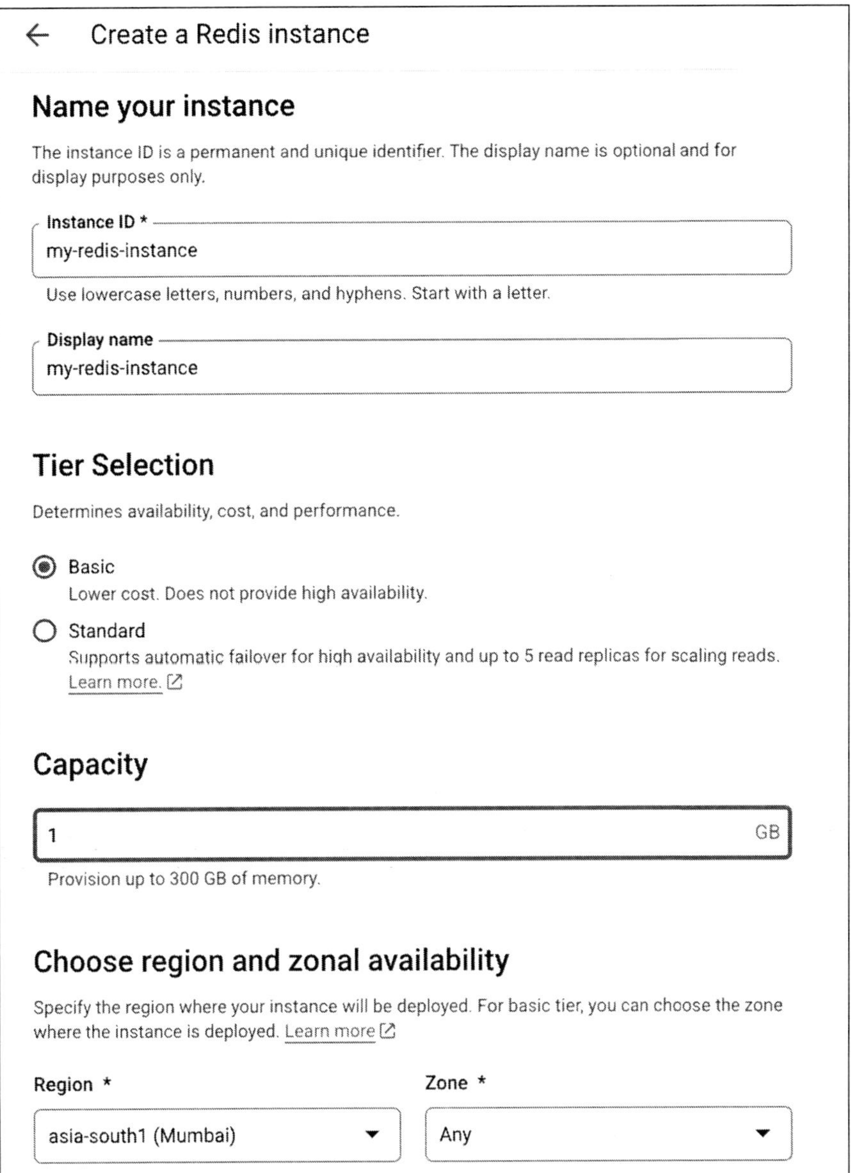

Figure 12.13: *Creating a Redis Instance by Specifying Name, Tier, Capacity, and Region*

Figure 12.13: This figure illustrates the process of creating a Redis instance in Google Cloud Memorystore by filling in key configuration details such as the instance name, service tier (Basic or Standard), capacity, and region. These inputs define the performance, availability, and geographic location of the Redis deployment.

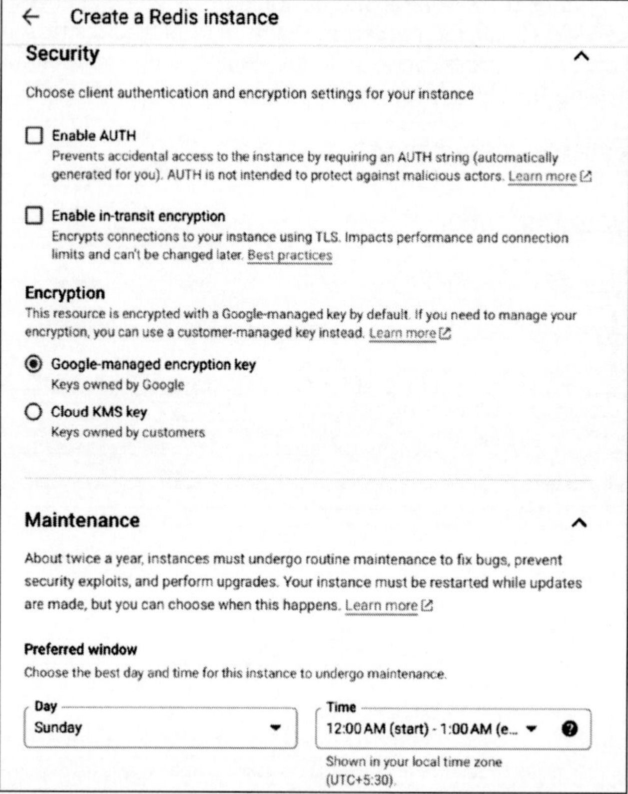

Figure 12.14: *Configuring Security and Maintenance Settings during Redis Instance Creation*

Figure 12.14: This figure shows the step where you configure security-related options, such as Redis **AUTH** password, along with maintenance settings during the creation of a Redis instance in Google Cloud Memorystore. These settings help to secure access to the instance and define preferred time windows for maintenance operations, ensuring both safety and stability in production environments.

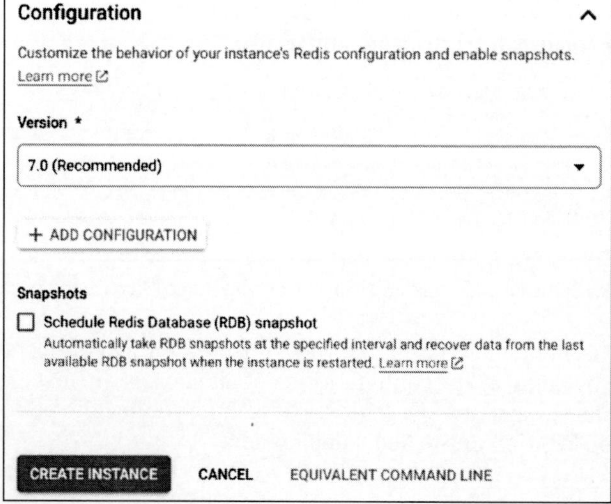

Figure 12.15: *Configuring Redis Version and Finalizing Instance Creation*

Figure 12.15: This figure displays the final configuration step in Google Cloud Memorystore, where you select the desired Redis version before proceeding to create the instance. Choosing the appropriate version ensures compatibility with your application's features as well as stability requirements. Once reviewed, clicking the "**Create**" button launches the Redis instance with the specified settings.

Click `Create`: It may take a couple of minutes to provision the instance.

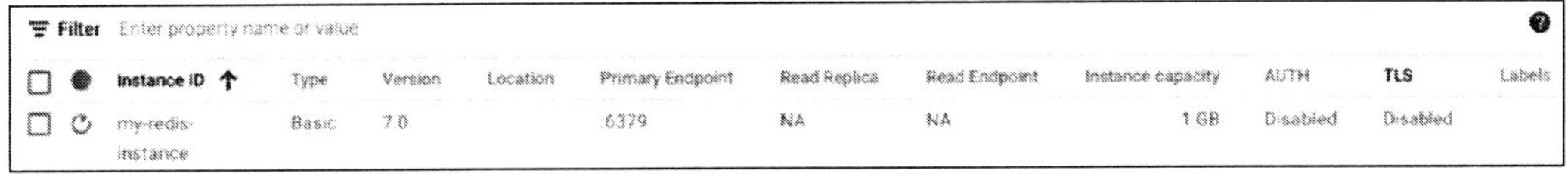
Filter Enter property name or value

Instance ID ↑	Type	Version	Location	Primary Endpoint	Read Replica	Read Endpoint	Instance capacity	AUTH	TLS	Labels
my-redis-instance	Basic	7.0		:6379	NA	NA	1 GB	Disabled	Disabled	

Figure 12.16: *Memorystore Redis Instance in Creation Progress*

Figure 12.16: This figure captures the Memorystore Redis instance immediately after the creation process has started in Google Cloud Memorystore. At this stage, essential details such as the endpoint and connection information are not yet populated, indicating that the instance is still being provisioned.

Equivalent command line:

```
gcloud redis instances create --project=my-gcp-project-id my-redis-instance
--tier=basic --size=1 --region=asia-south1 --redis-version=redis_7_0
--network=projects/<PROJECT_ID>/global/networks/<VPC_NAME>
--connect-mode=DIRECT_PEERING --display-name="my-redis-instance"
--maintenance-window-day=SATURDAY --maintenance-window-hour=18
```

Obtain Connection Details:

Once the instance is created, navigate to the instance details page.

Find the "**Host**" (IP address) and "**Port**" information.

For example: **`XX.XXX.XXX.XXX:6379`**

Step 4: Connect to the Memorystore Redis Instance

Check projects: gcloud projects list

```
PROJECT_ID: bold-potential-463214-t1
NAME: My First Project
PROJECT_NUMBER: 361574433298
```

Figure 12.17: *Output of the gcloud Projects List Command*

Figure 12.17: This figure shows the output of the **`gcloud projects list`** command, which displays a list of Google Cloud projects associated with the active account. The output includes details such as project ID, name, and project number, helping users identify and manage available projects from the command line.

`Set project : gcloud config set project "bold-potential-463214-t1"`

GCP Memorystore uses **private IPs**, so you must **connect to Redis from a VM or GKE pod inside the same VPC.**

Option A: From a Compute Engine VM

a. **Spin up a VM in the same VPC and region:**

```
gcloud compute instances create redis-client-vm \
  --zone=asia-south1-c \
  --machine-type=e2-micro \
```

```
--image-family=debian-11 \
--image-project=debian-cloud \
--tags=redis-client \
--network=default \
--project=bold-potential-463214-t1
```

Error: API **`[compute.googleapis.com]`** not enabled on project **`[calm-method-424105-n1]`**. Would you like to enable and retry (this will take a few minutes)?

Enabling via Cloud Shell (recommended): Simply type '**y**' or '**yes**' and press '*Enter*' in the Cloud Shell. The system will then enable the API and retry the command.

```
karnish16@cloudshell:~ (bold-potential-463214-t1)$ gcloud compute instances create redis-client-vm \
  --zone=asia-south1-c \
  --machine-type=e2-micro \
  --image-family=debian-11 \
  --image-project=debian-cloud \
  --tags=redis-client \
  --network=default \
  --project=bold-potential-463214-t1
```

Figure 12.18: *Creating a Virtual Machine via Google Cloud Shell*

Figure 12.18: This figure illustrates the process of creating a Virtual Machine (VM) using Google Cloud Shell, a browser-based terminal provided by GCP. Using Cloud Shell, users can provision VM instances directly from the command line, without leaving the web console, streamlining development and testing workflows.

b. **SSH into the instance:**

```
gcloud compute ssh redis-client-vm
```

c. **Install the Redis CLI:**

```
sudo apt update
sudo apt install -y redis-tools
```

d. **Connect to Redis using the internal IP (found on your instance page):**

```
redis-cli -h 10.193.83.123
```

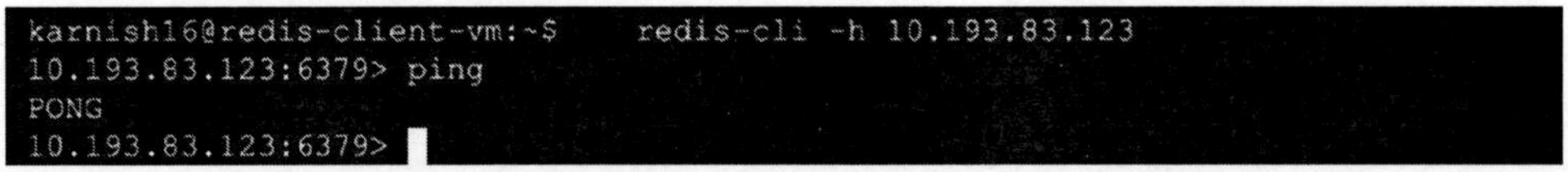

```
karnish16@redis-client-vm:~$    redis-cli -h 10.193.83.123
10.193.83.123:6379> ping
PONG
10.193.83.123:6379>
```

Figure 12.19: *Connecting to Redis from a Virtual Machine in Google Cloud*

Figure 12.19: This figure demonstrates how to connect to a Redis instance from a virtual machine within the same Google Cloud environment. The connection is typically established using the Redis CLI and the instance's internal IP address, enabling secure and low-latency communication between the application and the Redis server.

Step 5: Set and Get a Value

Now that you are connected, try the basics:

```
SET book "Redis in GCP"
OK
```

```
10.193.83.123:6379> SET book "Redis in GCP"
OK
10.193.83.123:6379>
```

Figure 12.20: *Executing the SET Command in Redis*

Figure 12.20: This figure shows a simple example of using the **SET** command in the Redis CLI to store a key-value pair. This confirms a successful connection to the Redis instance and demonstrates how to write the data into the Redis data store from the virtual machine.

```
GET book
"Redis in GCP"
```

```
10.193.83.123:6379> GET book
"Redis in GCP"
10.193.83.123:6379>
```

Figure 12.21: *Executing the GET Command in Redis*

Figure 12.21: This figure demonstrates the use of the **GET** command in the Redis CLI to retrieve the value of a previously stored key. It confirms that the data has been successfully written and can be read back, verifying the basic functionality of the Redis instance.

You have successfully deployed and connected to Redis on GCP!

Additional Features and Tips

Scaling Memory: You can **scale the memory** of your instance anytime:

1. Go to **Memorystore > Redis**
2. Select your instance
3. Click **Edit**
4. Increase the memory size

Memorystore will **resize the node**, without affecting your data (though there may be brief reconnections).

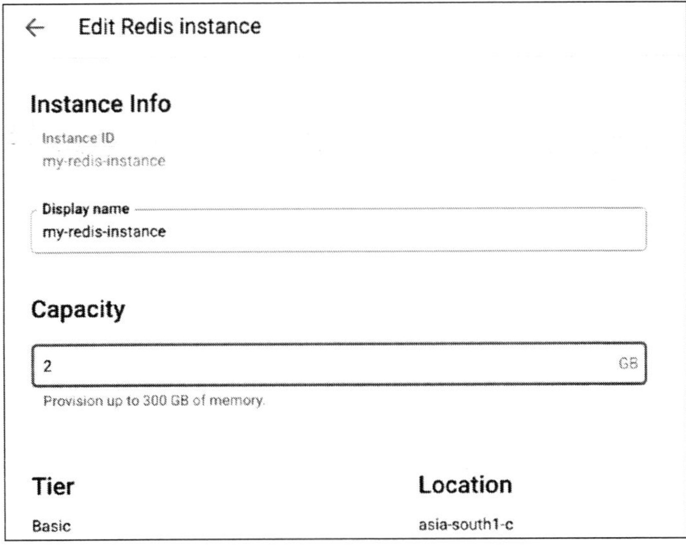

Figure 12.22: *Editing and Resizing the Capacity of an Existing Redis Instance*

Figure 12.22: This figure illustrates the process of modifying an existing Redis instance in Google Cloud Memorystore by resizing its capacity. Adjusting the memory allocation allows you to scale the instance based on changing workload requirements, ensuring optimal performance and cost-efficiency.

Monitoring and Logs

1. Go to **`Operations > Monitoring`** to see charts for latency, memory usage, and command rate.
2. Redis logs are viewable under **`Operations > Logging`**.

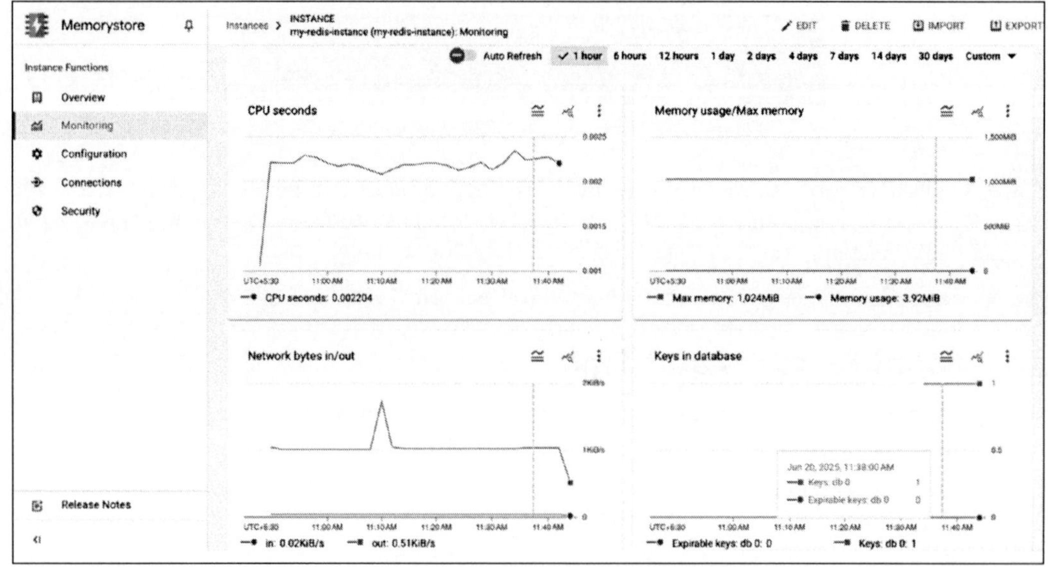

Figure 12.23: *Viewing the Monitoring Page of Redis Memorystore*

Figure 12.23: This figure displays the Monitoring page of a Redis instance in Google Cloud Memorystore. It provides real-time insights into key performance metrics such as memory usage, operation throughput, and CPU utilization, helping users track system health and diagnose potential issues efficiently.

Security and VPC Access

- Memorystore instances are **not accessible via public IP**.
- You must be within the **same VPC network**.
- You can fine-tune access with **firewall rules**, **IAM roles**, and **Service Accounts**.

Summary

GCP Memorystore for Redis is ideal if you are looking for a low-maintenance, secure, and scalable Redis deployment. Thus, whether you are building analytics dashboards, caching layers, or real-time apps, Memorystore simplifies Redis in the cloud by offloading all the operational tasks to Google.

- Easy to create
- Private and secure
- HA support with automatic failover
- Seamless integration with GCP VMs, GKE, and App Engine

Azure Cache for Redis

Azure Cache for Redis is Microsoft's fully managed Redis service built on open-source Redis. It offers the power of Redis, without the overhead of managing Redis servers manually. Microsoft handles all the heavy lifting - patching, backups, monitoring, high availability, and scaling so that you can focus on building fast and responsive applications.

This service is ideal for use cases like:

- Caching web application data
- Session storage
- Leaderboards and real-time analytics
- Pub/Sub message broadcasting

Why Use Azure Cache for Redis?

When you use Azure's Redis service, you benefit from:

- Fully managed infrastructure (no setup or server maintenance)
- High availability with built-in redundancy
- Geo-replication support for global scale
- Private network access via VNet integration
- Integrated monitoring with Azure Monitor and Log Analytics

If your application is already running on Azure App Services, AKS, or Virtual Machines, using Azure Cache for Redis makes perfect architectural sense.

Step-by-Step: Deploying Redis on Azure Cache

Before deploying Azure Cache for Redis, make sure to create the **resource group** and **virtual network** in advance. Having these resources pre-configured will streamline the deployment process and help avoid unnecessary delays or configuration issues later.

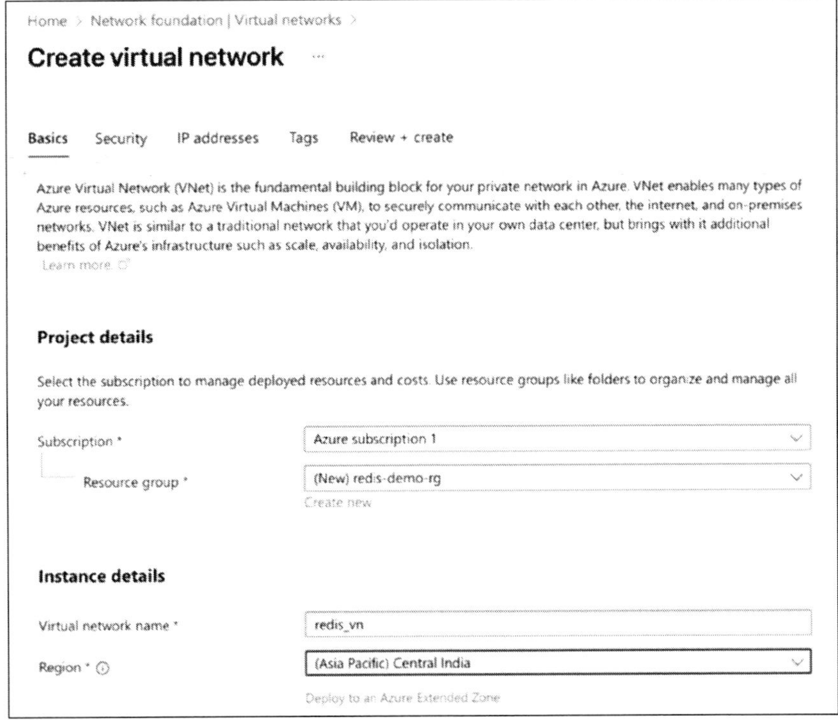

Figure 12.24: *Creating a Virtual Network in Microsoft Azure*

Figure 12.24: This figure shows the process of creating a **Virtual Network (VNet)** in Microsoft Azure. A VNet serves as the foundational networking layer, allowing secure communication between Azure resources like virtual machines, databases, and Redis instances within an isolated and customizable IP address space.

Navigate to Virtual Networks

1. On the left-hand side, click on "`Create a resource`."
2. In the search bar, type "`Virtual Network`."
3. Click on `Virtual Network` from the list.
4. Click "`Create`."

Basics Tab Configuration

1. `Subscription`: Select your active subscription.
2. `Resource Group`: Either select an existing one or click "`Create new`."
3. `Name`: Give a name to your VNet (for example, **redis-VNet**)
4. `Region`: Choose the region where you plan to deploy Redis.

IP Addresses Tab

1. Click on the "`IP Addresses`" tab.
2. By default, you will get an **address space** like **10.0.0.0/16**
    - You can modify it if needed.
3. Add at least one `subnet`.
    - Name: For example, `redis-subnet`
    - Subnet address range: For example, **10.0.1.0/24**

Security Tab

Leave the default options, unless you need specific configurations such as:

- Enabling `BastionHost`
- Custom `DDoS protection` or **Firewall**

Tags (Optional): You can tag your resources for easier management.

`Review + Create`

1. Click on `Review + Create`.
2. Azure will validate the settings.
3. If all looks good, click `Create`.

It may take a few seconds for the VNet to be deployed.

Let us walk through how to create and use Azure Cache for Redis via the **Azure Portal**, and also how to connect via CLI for a deeper understanding.

Step 1: Log in to the Azure Portal

Head over to: https://portal.azure.com

Make sure that you are logged into your **Azure subscription** and have selected the right **resource group** and **region**.

Step 2: Create an Azure Redis Instance

a. In the search bar, type "`Azure Cache for Redis`"

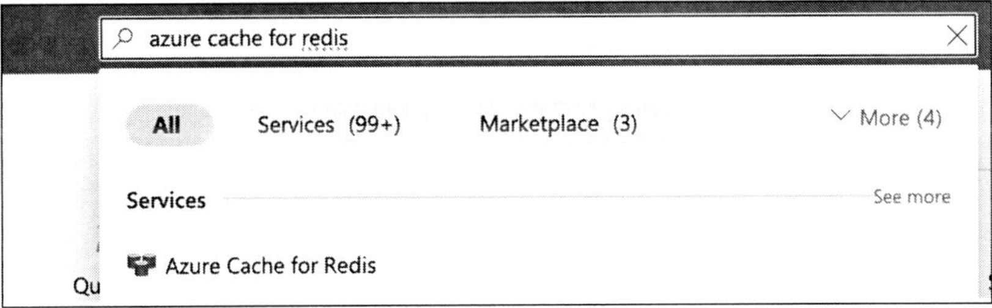

***Figure 12.25**: Searching for "Azure Cache for Redis" in the Azure Portal*

Figure 12.25: This figure illustrates how to locate the Azure Cache for Redis service by entering the term in the search bar at the top of the Azure Portal. This is the first step in creating or managing Redis instances within the Azure Cloud environment.

b. Click "`Create`"

***Figure 12.26**: Clicking "Create" to Start Redis Cache Deployment in Azure*

Figure 12.26: This figure shows the step where the "`Create`" button is clicked in the Azure Portal to initiate the deployment of a new Azure Cache for Redis instance. This begins the configuration process, where you define settings such as pricing tier, region, and networking.

c. Fill in the **following details**:

Field	Example
Subscription	Your Azure subscription
Resource Group	`redis_demo_rg` (create new or choose an existing one)
Name	`redis-demo-v1`
Region	Central India
Cache Size	Basic (C1: 1 GB Cache)
Connectivity method	Private Endpoint (Recommended)
Redis version	Latest available Redis version (varies by tier/region)

***Table 12.3**: Configuration Fields for Creating an Azure Cache for Redis Instance*

Table 12.3: This table highlights the key fields required when provisioning a Redis instance using Azure Cache for Redis. These settings help define the scope, scale, and security of your deployment, making it important to select values that align with your project's requirements.

Home > Azure Cache for Redis >

New Redis Cache ...

Project details

Select the subscription to manage deployed resources and costs. Use resource groups like folders to organize and manage all your resources.

Subscription * Azure subscription 1

Resource group * redis_demo_rg

Create new

Instance Details

Name * redis-demo-v1

.redis.cache.windows.net

Region * Central India

Cache SKU (View full pricing details) * Basic (No SLA)

See which features are available on each Azure Cache for Redis tier Learn more

Cache size * C1 (1 GB Cache)

Review + create < Previous Next : Networking >

Figure 12.27: *Providing Basic Configuration Details for Azure Cache for Redis*

Figure 12.27: This figure shows the form where you enter essential details to create an Azure Cache for Redis instance, including the name, region, cache size, and resource group. These settings define the identity, location, and capacity of your Redis instance within the Azure environment.

> **Note:** *Basic tier is suitable for development and testing. For production features such as persistence, replication, and advanced security, use Standard or Premium tiers.*

d. Click `Next` to configure the advanced settings, that is, Networking, Advanced, and so on.

> **Note:** *Add a Private Endpoint: To disable public network access, you must add a private endpoint. If you select "`Private endpoint`", without creating one, your resource will remain accessible via the public network. To resolve this, either add a private endpoint or change the connectivity method to a public endpoint.*

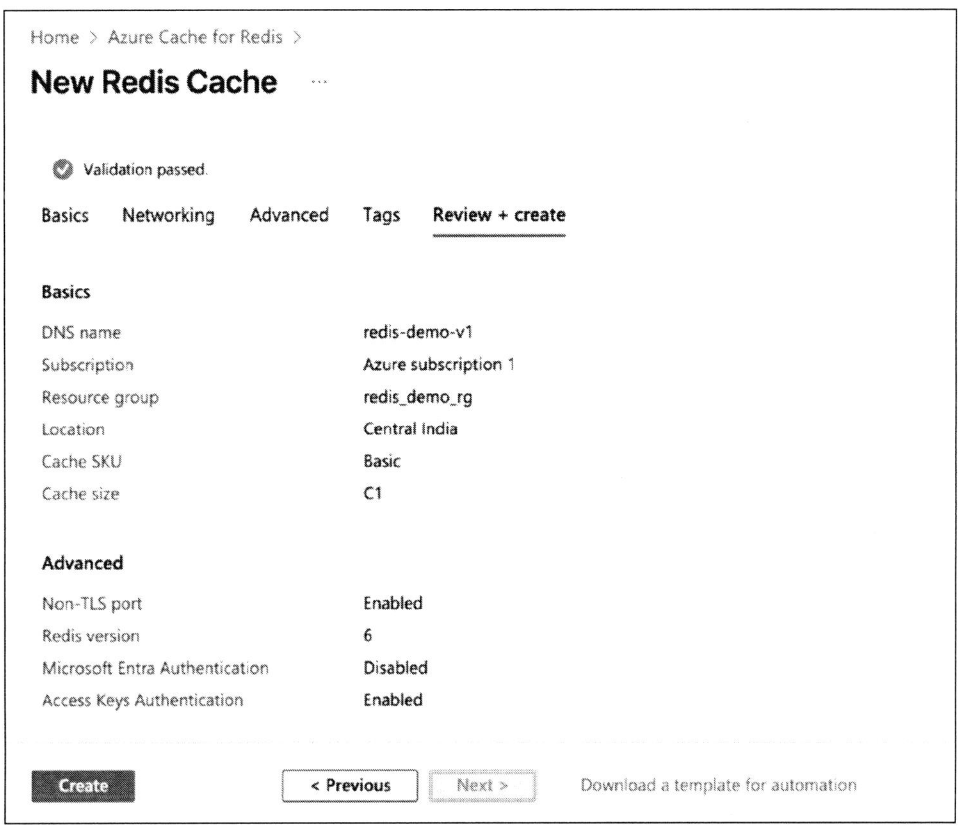

Figure 12.28: *Reviewing Configuration before Creating Azure Cache for Redis*

Figure 12.28: This figure displays the **`Review + Create`** step in the Azure Portal, where all the selected configurations - such as name, region, pricing tier, and networking are summarized. At this stage, Azure performs a validation check to ensure that the setup is correct before allowing you to proceed with the deployment.

e. After validation, hit **`Create`** to begin provisioning.

Note: *This may take a few minutes.*

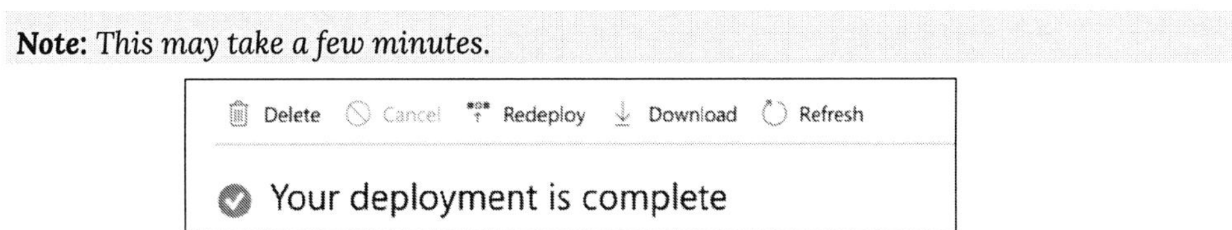

Figure 12.29: *Deployment Complete Confirmation in Azure Portal*

Figure 12.29: This figure shows the "**`Deployment complete`**" message in the Azure Portal, indicating that the Azure Cache for Redis instance has been successfully created. From here, users can navigate directly to the resource to begin configuration, monitoring, or connecting applications to the Redis cache.

Step 3: Connect to Redis from a Client

Once your instance is ready:

a. Go to the **`Overview`** tab.

b. Note down:

   a. **Host name** (for example, `redis-demo.redis.cache.windows.net`)

      `redis-demo-v1.redis.cache.windows.net`

   b. **Port** (usually 6379 or 6380)

      `Non-SSL port (6379) enabled`

   c. **Access Keys** under the **Authentication tab**

Connect using `redis-cli`

Create a Virtual Machine for testing purposes

a. **Search for a virtual machine in the search bar**

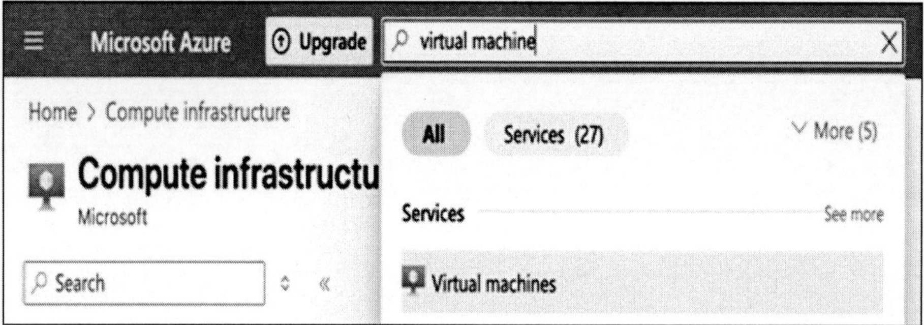

Figure 12.30: *Searching for "Virtual Machine" in the Azure Portal Search Bar*

Figure 12.30: This figure illustrates the use of the search bar in the Azure Portal to locate the Virtual Machines service. This is typically the first step when provisioning a new VM to interact with services such as Azure Cache for Redis or to host application components.

b. **Click "`Create`" and Select "`Virtual Machine`":**

   On the Virtual Machines page, click the + Add button to start creating a new virtual machine.

c. **Configure the Virtual Machine Basics:**

   - **Subscription:** Select the subscription you want to use (the one with billing and resource limits).
   - **Resource Group:** Choose an existing resource group or create a new one by clicking Create new.
   - **Virtual Machine Name:** Provide a unique name for your VM (for example, `MyVM`).
   - **Region:** Choose the Azure region where you want your VM to be hosted. For better performance, this could be a location close to your users.
   - **Availability Options:** You can select between:
     - No infrastructure redundancy required
     - Availability zone (for high availability)
     - Availability set (for fault tolerance across multiple VMs)
   - **Image:** Choose the OS you want to install on the VM. For example, Ubuntu 20.04 LTS, Windows Server 2019, Windows 10, and so on.
   - **Size:** Select the VM size based on your needs. You can either:

- Click Change size to select from predefined options (for example, General purpose, Compute optimized, and so on).
- Based on your choice, the cost will vary depending on the machine type, number of CPUs, RAM, and so on.

- **Authentication Type:** Choose the authentication method for accessing the VM:
  - Password: Set a username and password for access.
  - SSH public key (for Linux-based VMs): Upload your public SSH key.
- **Username and Password:** If you choose Password for authentication, provide a username and a strong password.
- **Configure Networking and Disks**
- **Review and Create**

d. **From your VM (or inside your private network), run:**

```
nslookup redis-demo-v1.privatelink.redis.cache.windows.net
```

It should return a **private IP (10.x.x.x)** if not:

Make sure that the Private Endpoint is linked to the **Private DNS Zone**: *privatelink.redis.cache.windows.net.*

```
# nslookup redis-demo-v1.privatelink.redis.cache.windows.net
Server:         127.0.0.53
Address:        127.0.0.53#53

Non-authoritative answer:
Name:   redis-demo-v1.privatelink.redis.cache.windows.net
Address: 10.0.0.4

#
```

Figure 12.31: *Running the nslookup Command to get the Private IP*

Figure 12.31: This figure shows the execution of the **nslookup** command from an Azure Virtual Machine to resolve the private endpoint DNS name of the Azure Cache for Redis instance. The command returns the private IP address, confirming internal network connectivity within the virtual network.

e. **Install the Redis CLI:**

```
sudo apt update
sudo apt install -y redis-tools
```

f. **Connect to the Redis instance from the VM**

```
redis-cli -p 6380 -h redis-demo-v1.redis.cache.windows.net -a accesskey --tls
```

Note:

i. Port **6380** is for TLS-secured connections.

ii. Use **--tls** for SSL encryption.

iii. TLS (Transport Layer Security) is the standard protocol used to encrypt data in transit between your application and Redis.

g. Once connected:

```
SET azure "works!"
GET azure
```

```
redis-demo-v1.redis.cache.windows.net:6380> SET azure "works!"
OK
redis-demo-v1.redis.cache.windows.net:6380> GET azure
"works!"
redis-demo-v1.redis.cache.windows.net:6380>
```

Figure 12.32: *Running SET and GET Commands after Connecting to Redis*

Figure 12.32: This figure demonstrates the successful execution of the **`SET`** and **`GET`** commands in the Redis CLI from an Azure Virtual Machine. It confirms that the VM is properly connected to the Azure Cache for Redis instance and can perform the basic read and write operations.

Summary

Azure Cache for Redis makes it easy to use Redis without worrying about infrastructure. It is perfect for caching, pub/sub, and session storage in cloud-native applications.

- Fully managed
- Scalable and secure
- Integrated with Azure monitoring
- Supports replication and persistence in premium tiers
- Easy integration with Azure App Services, AKS, and VMs

Comparing Managed vs. Self-Hosted Redis in the Cloud

As you explore putting Redis in the cloud, you will find two main routes:

- **Managed Redis** (for example, **AWS ElastiCache, GCP Memorystore,** and **Azure Cache** for Redis)
- **Self-Hosted Redis** (where you run Redis on your own virtual machines in the cloud)

Choosing between these paths depends on your **team's skills**, **budget**, and **operational responsibilities**. So, let us explore them in detail with practical examples.

Managed Redis Services

In managed services, the cloud provider handles nearly everything. You just click through a console or run a **`CLI`** command, and they provision Redis on your behalf.

What you get:

- **Automatic patching:** No worrying about CVEs
- **Monitoring built-in**: CloudWatch (AWS), Azure Monitor, and Stackdriver (GCP)
- **High availability**: Auto-failover and multi-zone replication
- **Backups and snapshots:** Schedule them with a checkbox
- **Scaling:** Add memory or nodes with a few clicks
- **Encryption:** Both in-transit and at-rest, handled for you
- **24×7 support:** In higher plans

Example:

AWS: If you set up ElastiCache for Redis, you can enable multi-AZ with auto-failover, have daily backups, get metrics in CloudWatch, and let AWS do the rest.

You simply connect to your Redis endpoint:

```
redis-cli -h mycache.abc123.use1.cache.amazonaws.com -p 6379
```

No package upgrades, no kernel tuning, and no worries about restarting after a security patch.

When to choose managed Redis?

- You do not want to manage servers.
- You need a fast time-to-market.
- Your team is small or lacks Redis tuning expertise.
- You have strict uptime/HA requirements.
- You can budget a bit higher for operational ease.

Self-Hosted Redis in the Cloud

With self-hosting, you spin up your own VM (for example, EC2, Compute Engine, and Azure VM) as well as install Redis directly.

What you get:

- Full **control** over every Redis setting
- Install Redis modules (for example, RedisJSON, RediSearch, and so on)
- Custom ACL rules
- Choose your OS, kernel, and tuning options
- Total flexibility in architecture (file systems, network layouts, and so on)
- Often, **lower infrastructure costs for large deployments**

But remember: You own everything, such as:

- Patch management
- Failover (via Sentinel or Cluster)
- Backups and snapshot rotation
- Security groups/firewall rules
- Scaling decisions
- Monitoring (via Prometheus, ELK, or similar)

Example:

You launch an Ubuntu VM, install Redis with `apt`, edit `redis.conf`, and manually configure:

```
bind 0.0.0.0 # inside private VPC only
requirepass "MySecurePass"
maxmemory 2gb,
```

and so on.

Then you need to handle:

- Backups via `cron` + `BGSAVE`
- Monitoring via a third-party stack

- Manually configuring Redis Sentinel or Redis Cluster for high availability

This is **great if you love deep customization**, but it can be risky if your team is short on Redis or Linux expertise.

When to choose self-hosted Redis?

- You want advanced Redis modules.
- You need very fine-grained control.
- You are comfortable managing failover and tuning.
- Your workloads are highly specialized.
- You want to optimize costs for very large-scale deployments.

Managed vs. Self-Hosted Side by Side

Feature	Managed Redis	Self-Hosted Redis
Setup Time	5 minutes	30–60 minutes
Scaling	Built-in, with a click	Manual
High Availability	Automatic (multi-AZ, failover)	Requires Sentinel/Cluster setup
Backups	Automated snapshots	Manual with cron or custom scripts
Monitoring	Cloud-native dashboards	DIY with Prometheus, ELK, and Grafana
Custom Modules	Limited (depending on cloud provider)	Full freedom
OS/Kernel Tuning	Not available	Fully controlled
Cost	Higher per GB/hour, but includes ops	Lower, but with more operational burden
Security	Cloud IAM, encryption out of the box	Your own firewalls, ACLs, and manual updates
Maintenance	Handled by the provider	Handled by you

Table 12.4: *Managed vs. Self-Hosted Redis: Side-by-Side Comparison*

Table 12.4: This table presents a side-by-side comparison of Managed Redis (such as AWS ElastiCache, Azure Cache for Redis, or Google Memorystore) and Self-Hosted Redis. It highlights the key differences across setup, scalability, maintenance, flexibility, and operational control, helping you to choose the model that best fits your team's needs and expertise.

Note: *If you want speed, ease, and reduced responsibility, go managed.*

If you want maximum control, customization, and can dedicate engineering resources, go self-hosted.

Real-World Perspective

In many production systems, teams start with managed Redis to launch quickly and with fewer headaches. Later, if workloads grow or specialized needs appear (like running Redis modules for graph databases or advanced data models), they may migrate to self-hosted Redis for full flexibility.

Some even hybrid these models:

- Managed Redis for caching (fast scaling, easy HA)
- Self-hosted Redis for specialized data (custom modules)

This hybrid approach is becoming more common in large enterprise environments.

In Summary

When it comes to running Redis in production, **there is no one-size-fits-all answer**. The right setup depends entirely on **what matters most to your team**, **your budget**, and **your technical strengths**.

If you value simplicity and speed, **managed Redis services** (like AWS ElastiCache, Azure Cache for Redis, or Google Cloud Memorystore) offer a near-zero-ops experience. You get built-in security, automatic backups, scaling options, and a faster path to production, all without worrying about infrastructure.

On the other hand, if you need maximum flexibility, **self-hosting Redis might be a better path**. It gives you full control over configuration, access to advanced Redis modules (such as RedisBloom, RedisSearch, or RedisGears), and can even reduce costs - especially at scale, if managed properly.

What is the good news? Redis is remarkably adaptable. Hence, whether you are running it on a managed cloud service or on your own bare-metal servers, Redis will perform reliably. And if your needs shift down the line, Redis makes it relatively painless to switch between hosting models.

Advanced Considerations: Persistence, Security, and Performance in the Cloud

Once Redis is running successfully in a managed cloud service like **AWS ElastiCache**, **GCP MemoryStore**, or **Azure Cache for Redis**, it is important to understand how persistence, security, and performance settings behave in these environments. While cloud providers handle much of the complexity, administrators should still be aware of how to optimize and secure their deployments.

Persistence Strategies

Managed Redis services typically allow you to choose between **RDB snapshots** and **AOF (Append Only File)** persistence:

- **DB snapshots** create periodic backups of your Redis data, and are ideal for quick recovery with minimal overhead.
- **AOF persistence** logs every write operation, providing stronger durability but slightly higher I/O usage.
- **Recommended approach:** For production systems, use both RDB and AOF together where supported by the cloud provider and service tier, to achieve a balance between performance and durability. In managed Redis services, persistence options are configured via the provider's console or API, and snapshots are typically stored in secure object storage (such as Amazon S3 or Google Cloud Storage).

Note:

1. In managed services, persistence settings are configured through the console or API rather than `redis.conf`, simplifying maintenance and recovery.
2. RDB creates periodic snapshots of data, while AOF logs every write operation for stronger durability.

Security Hardening

Cloud-managed Redis can be isolated using VPC/private networking, but **additional precautions are still essential:**

- **Enable encryption in transit and at rest:** All major providers support TLS-based encryption and key management through KMS or CMEK.
- **Restrict network access:** Use VPC security groups or firewall rules to limit inbound connections only to trusted applications.
- **Use AUTH for additional protection:** Even in private networks, always enable authentication to avoid accidental exposure.

Note: In AWS **ElastiCache**, **GCP MemoryStore**, and **Azure Cache for Redis**, security options can be managed directly via the console under "`Access Control`" or "`Security Settings.`"

Performance Optimization

While managed Redis automatically scales hardware resources, fine-tuning parameters can improve responsiveness:

- **Choose the right node size and tier:** Larger instance types offer better CPU and network throughput.
- **Enable clustering** when dealing with large datasets to distribute the load across multiple nodes.
- **Monitor key metrics** such as memory usage, cache hit ratio, and network throughput using native tools like **CloudWatch**, **Google Cloud Operations Suite**, or **Azure Monitor**.
- **Eviction policies** such as `volatile-lru` or `allkeys-lfu` can help manage memory pressure under heavy load.

Area	Example Setting	Purpose
Persistence	RDB + AOF	Balanced durability and speed
Security	TLS + AUTH	Protects data in transit and access
Memory	LRU/LFU Eviction	Prevents memory exhaustion
Scaling	Cluster Mode Enabled	Improves throughput and availability

Table 12.5: *Key Cloud Redis Optimization Settings*

Table 12.5 represents the key configuration areas that influence the durability, security, and performance of Redis deployments in cloud environments. These parameters help administrators balance reliability with speed while ensuring that the data remains protected and the memory usage stays efficient across different managed platforms.

Therefore, these configurations ensure that Redis remains fast, resilient, and secure even in dynamic cloud environments. The managed platforms abstract away infrastructure complexity, but understanding these core principles helps administrators fine-tune performance and safeguard data effectively.

Further Reading and Resources

If you want to go beyond the basics covered in this chapter, the following resources can help:

- Official documentation for AWS ElastiCache for Redis, GCP MemoryStore, and Azure Cache for Redis.
- Redis documentation on persistence (RDB and AOF), security hardening, and performance tuning.
- Cloud provider's best-practice guides for securing and scaling Redis in production.

Conclusion

Running Redis on the cloud is not just about convenience - it is about unlocking speed, scalability, and resilience, without getting bogged down in infrastructure overhead. In this chapter, we explored how Redis fits seamlessly into major cloud ecosystems such as AWS, Google Cloud Platform, and Microsoft Azure. Thus, whether you are spinning up a managed instance with a few clicks or customizing your own virtual network and VM-based deployment, Redis remains incredibly adaptable!

Hence, we walked through step-by-step setups for each provider, reviewed options for performance tuning, high availability, security, and monitoring, all with a clear focus on real-world deployment. One key takeaway? Cloud platforms offer multiple paths to success with Redis, and you are free to choose the model that best fits your project's scale, speed, and budget.

Managed or self-hosted, Redis proves time and again that it can thrive in the cloud, efficiently and reliably.

Now that you have seen how to run Redis in the cloud, it is time to elevate your Redis skills even further. In the next chapter, *Best Practices and Advanced Use Cases*, we will shift gears from setup to strategy. You will also learn how real-world teams use Redis to solve complex problems from blazing-fast caching and leaderboard tracking to event streaming, session management, rate limiting, and much more.

We shall also cover architectural patterns, design decisions, and pro-tips that help keep Redis performant, secure, and production-grade, even under heavy load. It is where the theory meets the real world - and where Redis really starts to shine. So, let us dive in and level up your Redis game.

CHAPTER 13
Best Practices and Advanced Use Cases

Introduction

Congratulations, you have made it to the final chapter of your Redis journey! That is no small accomplishment. Together, we have gone from understanding the simplest key-value commands to exploring Redis's powerful data structures, replication, persistence, clustering, Lua scripting, and cloud deployments.

If you have followed along chapter by chapter, you now hold an in-depth, practical, and well-rounded understanding of what Redis can do and why it has become one of the world's most **respected data platforms**. You should feel proud of the skills you have built so far, because Redis may look simple at first glance, but beneath the surface, it is a robust and complex system that rewards curiosity, experimentation, and thoughtful design.

This final chapter is about tying all that learning together. We will look at the production best practices, share advanced patterns used by real-world teams, and recent and upcoming Redis enhancements (including Redis 8), so that you can stay ahead of the curve. We will also take a closer look at backups, one of the most vital yet often overlooked parts of managing Redis, and make sure you know how to protect your data with confidence.

Finally, we will wrap everything up with a practical, down-to-earth checklist that you can keep nearby whenever you are planning or troubleshooting Redis in production. Think of this last chapter as your Redis owner's manual: a resource to revisit whenever you need a refresher, inspiration, or simply some friendly advice on running Redis reliably.

Take a moment to appreciate how far you have come, and get ready to build your skills even further, because this is where your Redis knowledge becomes truly production-grade.

Structure

The following topics will be covered:

- Redis Advanced Use Cases
- Best Practices for Production Redis
- Redis 8: New Features and Enhancements
- Backing Up Redis: Protecting What Matters Most
- Final Words: Closing the Book, Opening Possibilities

Redis Advanced Use Cases

Redis is far more than a simple cache; it has evolved into a versatile data platform that can solve real-world, high-performance problems. Let us walk through some of the more advanced, creative ways people use Redis today. Think of these as inspiration for your own projects.

Rate Limiting

Imagine you are building a public API, and you want to protect it from spam or accidental overload. Redis's atomic commands are perfect for this because they let you increment counters and apply timeouts, all in a single, fast operation.

Example: Limit 10 requests per minute

```
INCR user:1001:requests
EXPIRE user:1001:requests 60
GET user:1001:requests
```

If that key hits more than 10 times, you block the user. The counter automatically resets after 60 seconds.

> **Note:** *This is exactly how big companies or any rate-limited API protect themselves; it is simple, predictable, and battle-tested.*

Simple Example Application Flow

```
import redis

r = redis.StrictRedis(host='localhost', port=6379, decode_responses=True)

user_key = "user:1001:requests"
current = r.incr(user_key)

if current == 1:
    r.expire(user_key, 60)

if current > 10:
    print("Too many requests! Please try again later.")
else:
    print("Request allowed.")
```

> **NOTE:** *StrictRedis is deprecated in modern versions of redis-py. Use the Redis class instead, as it provides the same functionality and is the recommended client interface going forward.*

```
Too many requests! Please try again later.
```

Figure 13.1: Output: "Too many requests" – *Rate Limiting Using Redis with a Simple Python Script*

Figure 13.1: This figure displays the output of a Python-based rate-limiting script using Redis. When the user exceeds 10 requests within a 60-second window, the script triggers a limit condition and outputs, "*Too many requests! Please try again later.*"

Why does this work well?

Redis guarantees atomic execution for individual commands like INCR and EXPIRE.

Leaderboards

Competitive applications, whether they are games, trivia contests, sports leagues, or even corporate performance dashboards, often need to track and rank scores in real-time. Redis Sorted Sets make this easy by automatically maintaining a ranked list as scores change.

Example use case: A trivia app where each correct answer earns you points, and the leaderboard updates instantly.

Example:

- **When a player answers correctly, you increment their score:**

```
ZINCRBY game:scores 50 player42
```

This increases player42's score by 50 points in the game:scores sorted set.

```
ZRANGE game:scores 0 9 WITHSCORES
```

This retrieves the bottom 10 players (lowest scores first). To fetch top scorers, use **`ZREVRANGE`**:

```
ZREVRANGE game:scores 0 9 WITHSCORES
```

Why Sorted Sets?

Sorted Sets store each member with an associated numeric score, and automatically keep them ranked. That means every time a score changes, Redis handles reordering instantly, no manual sorting needed.

Your trivia app shows a live, accurate leaderboard, where players move up as they answer questions correctly, making for an engaging, real-time, competitive experience.

Pub/Sub Messaging

Sometimes, you need to push updates to many clients instantly - think of sending a live sports score update, a stock price alert, or a push notification when an order status changes in an e-commerce system. That is where Redis's **Publish/Subscribe (Pub/Sub) feature shines**. It lets you broadcast messages to multiple subscribers in real time, acting almost like a lightweight message broker for simple, fast notification patterns.

Example: Imagine you are building a live sports updates app. When a match starts, you want to notify all the connected clients right away.

Publisher side (for example, a backend service when the match kicks off):

```
PUBLISH sports "Match started"
```

Subscriber side (for example, each user's app listening for updates):

```
SUBSCRIBE sports
```

Any client subscribed to the sports channel will instantly receive the message, "*Match started*" without polling or delays.

This pattern is ideal for simple, real-time applications, such as broadcasting live events, sending order status updates, or coordinating updates between microservices. Redis handles the distribution for you, delivering messages to all active subscribers the moment they are published.

A fast, easy-to-implement push mechanism that keeps all your clients in sync in real time, without building a complex queuing or messaging system from scratch.

Session Storage

Web applications, whether built with Django, Flask, Spring Boot, or almost any modern framework, often need to manage user sessions quickly and reliably. Redis is a popular choice for this because it delivers blazing-fast in-memory lookups, supports automatic key expiration, and can easily scale with replicas for higher availability.

Imagine a user named Karnish logs into your web app. You want to keep their session active for 30 minutes so that they do not have to re-authenticate on every click. Redis makes this seamless:

Example:

```
SETEX session:abcd123 1800 '{"user":"Karnish"}'
```

Here, the key session:abcd123 represents the user's session token. The **SETEX** command sets the session data, and automatically expires it after 1800 seconds (30 minutes). Redis handles the expiration behind the scenes, so there is no need to clean up stale sessions manually.

```
127.0.0.1:6379> SETEX session:abcd123 1800 '{"user":"Karnish"}'
OK
127.0.0.1:6379>
```

***Figure* 13.2:** *Using SETEX for Session Management in Redis*

Figure 13.2: This figure shows the use of the **SETEX** command to store a user session in Redis with an expiration time. This approach is commonly used in web applications to manage user sessions efficiently, ensuring that stale sessions are automatically cleared without additional cleanup logic.

Your application gets a simple, high-performance way to store and expire user sessions, keeping logins fast, secure, and hassle-free, whether you have hundreds or millions of active users.

Event Streaming

If you are building an event-driven system but do not need the heavy setup of tools like Kafka, Redis Streams provide a powerful, lightweight alternative. Streams let you store a continuous sequence of messages, while supporting multiple consumers who can read and process those messages at their own pace. This makes them perfect for tasks like logging, tracking user activity, or processing purchase events in real time.

Example: Imagine you are running an e-commerce platform and want to capture every new purchase for things like fraud detection, receipts, or analytics. With Redis Streams, you can store each purchase event as soon as it happens:

```
XADD purchases * item_id 567 amount 200
```

Here, purchases is the stream name, and you are adding a new message with details about the purchased item and amount. The * tells Redis to auto-generate a unique ID for this entry.

Later, you could build **consumer groups** to process these events in parallel, for example, one group that sends receipts to customers, and another that checks for suspicious transactions. Redis Streams ensure that all those consumers get reliable, ordered delivery without missing data.

A fast, flexible, and easy-to-manage event streaming system that gives you some Kafka-like capabilities for lightweight use cases, but with the simplicity and performance Redis is known for.

Best Practices for Production Redis

Running Redis in production is where your skills truly shine, because a fast, powerful data store is only as good as how securely you operate it. Redis's simplicity makes it easy to get started, but it also means that it can be dangerously easy to leave it exposed if you do not take proper precautions. There have been countless stories of Redis instances hacked because someone left them wide open on **port 6379**, with no authentication and no network restrictions. Please do not be that person!

Security: Too many Redis hacks happen because Redis is left open on port 6379 with no password. Please do not be that person!

Checklist:

- Set a Strong Password or Use ACL Users. Always set the **`requirepass`** directive in your **`redis.conf` file** to a strong, unique password. Even better, use Redis's Access Control Lists (ACLs) to define different users with precise permissions, limiting who can read or write to critical keys.

  Example:

  ```
  requirepass "S3cureP@ssw0rd!"
  ```

- Bind Redis to a private IP address or a VPC subnet. By default, Redis can listen on all network interfaces, which is risky. Instead, explicitly bind Redis to a private IP address, or to a secure VPC subnet, so that only your trusted infrastructure can reach it.

  Example in redis.conf:

  ```
  bind 10.0.0.5
  ```

- Do not send passwords or sensitive data over plain-text TCP connections. Configure Redis to use TLS on port 6380, so the data is encrypted in transit. Most modern clients fully support Redis over TLS.

  Example config snippet:

  ```
  port 0
  tls-port 6380
  tls-cert-file /etc/redis/cert.pem
  tls-key-file /etc/redis/key.pem
  tls-ca-cert-file /etc/redis/ca.pem
  ```

  - Rotate Passwords and Tokens Regularly. Just like any other critical system, change your Redis passwords or ACL tokens on a regular schedule. This reduces the impact if a secret ever leaks. Automate this rotation, if possible, to make it less painful.

  - Control which IPs can connect with a firewall. Set up strict firewall rules or network security groups so that only trusted IPs and ports can connect to your Redis server. This is a crucial second line of defense in case authentication fails or credentials leak.

  - In cloud-managed Redis, use IAM roles for even tighter security. If you deploy Redis through a cloud provider (like Azure Cache for Redis or AWS ElastiCache), take advantage of built-in IAM roles and policies to tightly control who can administer or connect to your Redis service, rather than relying only on passwords.

  By following these practices, you dramatically reduce the chances of someone hijacking your Redis instance, stealing your data, or taking down your application. Redis is lightning-fast, but it is also unforgiving if misconfigured. Take the time to secure it properly, and you will sleep much better knowing your data is safe.

- **Persistence and Backups:** Because Redis is an in-memory data store, it is incredibly fast - but that speed comes with a risk. If the server crashes or loses power, anything stored only in memory could vanish instantly. That is why enabling persistence and building a solid backup routine is absolutely critical for production. Think of it as an insurance policy to protect you from the unexpected.

Recommended Persistence Settings

A good starting point for most environments combines both **RDB snapshots** and **AOF (Append-Only File)** to balance durability and performance:

```
save 900 1
appendonly yes
appendfsync everysec
```

This means:

- Redis will take an RDB snapshot every 15 minutes if at least one key has changed (the `save 900 1` rule).
- The append-only file (`AOF`) will log every write command, giving you a rolling transaction log.
- With `appendfsync everysec`, Redis will flush those writes to disk every second - a great balance between data safety and performance.

Backup routine example: Persistence helps, but you still need to **back up** the data externally, so that you can recover from catastrophic events (like disk corruption or operator mistakes).

Here is a simple, practical example:

1. **Trigger a manual save.**

   ```
   redis-cli SAVE
   ```

   This forces Redis to write the current in-memory dataset to the RDB file.

   > **Note:** *Prefer* BGSAVE *in production to avoid blocking Redis during snapshot creation.*

2. **Copy the snapshot file.**

   ```
   cp /var/lib/redis/dump.rdb /backups/dump-$(date +%F).rdb
   ```

   Save a timestamped backup copy in a separate directory.

3. **Upload the backup to cloud storage.** Or move it to a dedicated backup server, so that you are protected even if the Redis machine itself is lost.

4. **Automate with cron.** Schedule this process to run regularly using a cron job, so that backups do not rely on manual intervention.

5. **Test your backups.** Every so often, actually restore a backup into a staging environment to confirm it works. A backup you never test is worse than no backup at all, because it gives you false confidence.

   Thus, by combining persistent storage (RDB + AOF) with a regular, tested backup routine, you can be confident that your Redis data will survive crashes, reboots, or even full machine failures. It is a small investment in peace of mind that pays off the moment something goes wrong.

   Performance: One of Redis's greatest strengths is its incredible speed, but even the fastest tools can break down if you overload them with poor design or careless data growth. Running Redis in production means thinking ahead about memory use, data structures, and query patterns to keep things running smoothly.

Recommended Performance Settings

Start by setting a memory ceiling and a sane eviction policy, so that Redis does not run out of RAM in unpredictable ways:

```
maxmemory 2gb
maxmemory-policy allkeys-lru
```

This means Redis will use up to 2 GB of memory, and if it runs out, it will evict the **least recently used keys** across all keys, which is a good general-purpose strategy for many workloads.

What to Monitor

Keeping an eye on these metrics will help you spot trouble early:

- `used_memory`: How close you are to your memory ceiling
- `evicted_keys`: Whether keys are being automatically evicted\
- `connected_clients`: So you can detect sudden spikes in traffic or stuck connections

Profiling Slow Commands

Redis is generally lightning-fast, but a badly written query or giant key can still slow things down. Use the built-in slow query log to see the top offenders:

```
redis-cli SLOWLOG get 10
```

This shows the last 10 slowest commands, so that you can tune or fix them.

Use the Right Data Structures

Picking the right data structures is a superpower in Redis. Here are some practical tips:

- **Hashes** work great for representing objects with multiple fields (like user profiles).
- **Sorted Sets** are perfect for leaderboards or ranked scores.
- **Strings** are ideal for simple counters or flags.

Hence, by setting smart memory policies, monitoring actively, profiling slow commands, and choosing the best data structures for your use case, you will keep Redis fast and efficient, ready to handle production traffic gracefully.

Remember: Redis is incredibly fast, but even the best tools will struggle if you throw huge, poorly-managed data at them without discipline. Design carefully, monitor continuously, and Redis will serve you well for years to come.

High Availability: Planning for Failure

A single-node Redis server is fast and simple, but let us be honest, it will fail eventually. Disks die, network links go down, and power cuts happen. That is why you need to build for **high availability** from day one, so that you are ready for the moment things go wrong.

Minimum High-Availability Setup

A solid starting point includes:

- **One master(primary)** to handle all writes.
- **One replica** to take over if the master fails.
- **Redis Sentinel** to monitor the master and replica, and perform automatic failover if the master goes down.

With Sentinel in place, your system can promote the replica to master, without you having to wake up in the middle of the night to fix it manually.

Scaling Horizontally

If you need to handle more data than a single master can store, or if you want even greater resilience, **Redis Cluster is your next step**. It automatically shards your data across multiple masters, while maintaining replication and failover support for each shard. This gives you fault tolerance and horizontal scalability in one elegant package.

Practice Makes Perfect

Even with a strong high-availability setup, it is crucial to test it. Simulate failovers before you go live to see how your applications respond. Watch how clients reconnect, verify that data stays consistent, and make sure Sentinel or the cluster can recover smoothly.

Think of it as a **fire drill** for your Redis environment. Practicing failure scenarios ahead of time means you will know exactly what to do, and your system will be ready when the real thing happens.

Therefore, by designing with high availability in mind, you protect yourself from downtime and data loss. Redis gives you the building blocks for master-replica replication, Sentinel, and Cluster so that you can keep serving users with confidence, even when servers crash or networks fail.

Monitoring: Monitoring your Redis server is absolutely essential. Too many teams treat Redis like a "just works" black box until it fails, taking their entire application down with it. In production, Redis should be treated as a mission-critical part of your stack, not an afterthought.

Recommended Monitoring Tools

Integrate Redis with a solid monitoring stack, so that you get full visibility into its health and performance. Some great options include:

- **Prometheus + Grafana** for flexible, detailed metrics and visual dashboards.
- **RedisInsight** is a Redis Labs–supported tool with a user-friendly interface.
- **Cloud-native monitoring** solutions are offered by your provider, such as Azure Monitor or AWS CloudWatch.

What to Track

Keep a close eye on these key metrics to stay ahead of trouble:

- **Memory usage:** So that you know when you are nearing your configured limits.
- **Replication lag:** To confirm that replicas are keeping up with the master.
- **Slow commands:** To catch poorly performing queries before they snowball.
- **Client count:** To detect traffic spikes, client leaks, or stuck connections

Set Smart Alerts

Monitoring is only half the battle - you also need to *act on what you see. Set up alerts for critical events, including:*

- **High latency** - Commands are taking too long to respond.
- **Link down** - Broken replication or Sentinel connections.
- **Memory exhaustion** - Hitting your memory ceiling and evicting keys unexpectedly.

In this way, you will be warned about issues before they spiral into outages. Thus, a well-monitored Redis server gives you confidence in its stability and performance.

Remember: *If you cannot measure it, you cannot trust it*. Good monitoring makes Redis predictable, reliable, and safe, exactly what you want for production systems.

Comparing Managed Redis Solutions (High-Level View)

In earlier chapters, we explored how to run Redis on different cloud platforms such as AWS ElastiCache, GCP MemoryStore, and Azure Cache for Redis. In practice, many teams struggle with choosing which managed option is best for their use case. Instead of going deep into provider-specific details again, the following table gives a simple, high-level comparison.

Aspect	AWS ElastiCache for Redis	GCP MemoryStore for Redis	Azure Cache for Redis
Typical use case	AWS-centric workloads and microservices	Workloads already running on GCP	Applications built on Azure Stack
Management model	Fully managed (nodes, failover, scaling)	Fully managed	Fully managed
Cluster support	Yes, supports sharding and replicas	Yes, cluster mode is available	Yes, with multiple pricing tiers and SKUs
Security integration	VPC, Security Groups, KMS, IAM	VPC networks, firewall rules, CMEK	VNets, NSGs, Key Vault, RBAC
Monitoring and observability	CloudWatch metrics and alarms	Cloud Monitoring (Stackdriver)	Azure Monitor and alerts
When it fits best	When most of your stack runs in AWS	When your data and services are already on GCP	When your core workloads are hosted on Azure

Table 13.1: *High-Level Comparison of Managed Redis Solutions*

Table 13.1 represents a simplified comparison of major managed Redis offerings. The focus is on how well each option fits into its native cloud ecosystem, rather than minor feature differences. In real projects, the "`best`" choice is usually the one that integrates most smoothly with where the rest of your infrastructure already exists.

Redis 8: New Features and Enhancements

Redis 8 takes Redis's reputation for simplicity, speed, and flexibility to a whole new level. While Redis 8's core engine strengthens its core features such as observability, functions, and protocol improvements, it is best understood as the **foundation of Redis Stack**, which bundles official modules for **JSON, vector indexing, search, and advanced probabilistic data structures.**

This means Redis 8 + Redis Stack together provide a full data platform that is production-ready and deeply modern. Let us now explore **exactly what Redis 8 offers**, which parts belong to Redis Stack, and how you can use them with working, copy-paste-ready commands.

Native Features in Redis 8 Core

These features work directly in Redis 8, no modules needed:

Enhanced Server-Side Functions

Building on Redis 7's Lua-based functions, Redis 8 adds:

- hot-reloading functions on the fly
- per-tenant function isolation
- detailed error tracing

Example:

Write a Lua script (**`safe_divide.lua`**):

```
#!lua name=math_utils
redis.register_function('safe_divide', function(keys, args)
  local num = tonumber(args[1])
  local den = tonumber(args[2])
  if den == 0 then
    return "divide-by-zero error"
  end
  return num / den
end)
```

Then load it from redis-cli:

```
redis-cli FUNCTION LOAD "$(cat safe_divide.lua)"
```

Call it:

```
redis-cli FCALL safe_divide 0 100 5
```

Serverless Optimization

Redis 8's multi-threaded I/O (significant throughput improvements) handles the bursty traffic patterns of serverless architectures like AWS Lambda and Azure Functions exceptionally well. Client connection pooling becomes more efficient with Redis 8's improved I/O threading; no configuration changes needed on the Redis server side.

Advanced Pub/Sub

Redis Pub/Sub provides a lightweight, real-time messaging mechanism that allows publishers to broadcast messages to multiple subscribers instantly. It is designed for low-latency, fire-and-forget notifications, not for durable or replayable messaging.

Key characteristics of Redis Pub/Sub:

- Messages are delivered only to currently connected subscribers
- There is no message persistence or replay
- If a subscriber is offline, messages published during that time are lost
- Filtering is channel-based (no built-in topic hierarchies or wildcards beyond pattern subscriptions)

Example:

```
redis-cli PUBLISH notifications "New update available!"
```

```
Subscriber:
```

```
redis-cli SUBSCRIBE notifications
```

Any client subscribed to the notifications channel will receive the message immediately, provided it is connected at the time of publication. For durable messaging, message replay, consumer acknowledgements, or advanced filtering, Redis Streams should be used instead. Streams provide persistent storage, replayable history, and consumer groups, making them a better fit for event-driven architectures and reliable message processing.

Better Observability

Redis 8 improves monitoring with:

- OpenTelemetry hooks
- Better metrics for Prometheus
- Histogram-style **slowlog** summaries
- Richer eviction reporting

Example:

```
redis-cli INFO stats
or
redis-cli SLOWLOG GET 5
```

```
to track slow commands and evictions.
```

RESP4 Protocol

RESP4 is the next-generation Redis wire protocol, enabling richer metadata and better data framing. Your Redis client libraries will upgrade to it automatically, and you do not have to do anything manually, but be aware that it is a part of Redis 8 under the hood.

Redis Stack Features (Modules on Top of Redis 8)

While Redis 8 on its own provides amazing performance, advanced data structures like JSON, vector indexing, secondary search, and probabilistic data structures come from **Redis Stack**, which wraps up these capabilities into a single package of official Redis modules.

On macOS, you can easily install Redis Stack using Homebrew. Hence, let us go step by step.

Installing Redis Stack on macOS

- If you have not installed Homebrew yet, install it:

  ```
  /bin/bash -c "$(curl -fsSL https://raw.githubusercontent.com/Homebrew/install/HEAD/install.sh)"
  ```

- Add the Redis Stack tap to Homebrew:

  ```
  brew tap redis-stack/redis-stack
  ```

- Install Redis Stack:

  ```
  brew install redis-stack
  ```

- Stop Redis if already running:

  ```
  brew services stop redis
  ```

- Run Redis Stack Server (do not use plain redis-server):

  ```
  redis-stack-server
  ```

- Connect with redis-cli as usual:

  ```
  redis-cli
  ```

- Check that Modules are Loaded:

  ```
  redis-cli MODULE LIST
  ```

```
127.0.0.1:6379> MODULE LIST
1) 1) "name"
   2) "RedisCompat"
   3) "ver"
   4) (integer) 1
   5) "path"
   6) "/opt/homebrew/Caskroom/redis-stack-server/7.4.0-v6/lib/rediscompat.so"
   7) "args"
   8) (empty array)
2) 1) "name"
   2) "ReJSON"
   3) "ver"
   4) (integer) 20809
   5) "path"
   6) "/opt/homebrew/Caskroom/redis-stack-server/7.4.0-v6/lib/rejson.so"
   7) "args"
   8) (empty array)
3) 1) "name"
   2) "search"
   3) "ver"
   4) (integer) 21020
   5) "path"
   6) "/opt/homebrew/Caskroom/redis-stack-server/7.4.0-v6/lib/redisearch.so"
   7) "args"
   8) 1) "MAXSEARCHRESULTS"
      2) "10000"
      3) "MAXAGGREGATERESULTS"
      4) "10000"
4) 1) "name"
   2) "timeseries"
   3) "ver"
   4) (integer) 11206
   5) "path"
   6) "/opt/homebrew/Caskroom/redis-stack-server/7.4.0-v6/lib/redistimeseries.so"
   7) "args"
   8) (empty array)
5) 1) "name"
   2) "bf"
   3) "ver"
   4) (integer) 20807
   5) "path"
   6) "/opt/homebrew/Caskroom/redis-stack-server/7.4.0-v6/lib/redisbloom.so"
   7) "args"
   8) (empty array)
6) 1) "name"
   2) "redisgears_2"
   3) "ver"
   4) (integer) 20020
   5) "path"
   6) "/opt/homebrew/Caskroom/redis-stack-server/7.4.0-v6/lib/redisgears.so"
   7) "args"
   8) 1) "v8-plugin-path"
      2) "/opt/homebrew/Caskroom/redis-stack-server/7.4.0-v6/lib/libredisgears_v8_plugin.so"
```

Figure 13.3: *Output of redis-cli MODULE LIST Command*

Figure 13.3: Redis modules are currently loaded into the server, including their names, versions, and unique identifiers. This is especially useful when working with Redis Stack or custom modules such as RedisJSON, RedisBloom, or RediSearch, as it helps verify that the necessary extensions are active and ready for use.

Vector Search with RediSearch

Redis Stack enables approximate nearest neighbor vector search, perfect for AI embeddings or recommendation systems.

Example flow:

- Create a vector index:

  ```
  FT.CREATE products_idx ON HASH PREFIX 1 product: SCHEMA embedding VECTOR FLAT
  6 DIM 4 TYPE FLOAT32 DISTANCE_METRIC COSINE
  ```

- Add a product with an embedding:

  ```
  HSET product:101 name "Running Shoe" embedding "\x3f\x80\x00\x00\x3f\x00\x00\
  x00\x3f\x40\x00\x00\x3f\x20\x00\x00"
  ```

- Search for similar products:

  ```
  FT.SEARCH products_idx "*=>[KNN 2 @embedding $vec AS score]" PARAMS 2 vec "\
  x3f\x80\x00\x00\x3f\x00\x00\x00\x3f\x40\x00\x00\x3f\x20\x00\x00" DIALECT 2
  ```

```
127.0.0.1:6379>
127.0.0.1:6379> FT.CREATE products_idx ON HASH PREFIX 1 product: SCHEMA embedding VECTOR FLAT 6 DIM 4 TYPE FLOAT32 DISTANCE_METRIC COSINE
OK
127.0.0.1:6379> HSET product:101 name "Running Shoe" embedding "\x3f\x80\x00\x00\x3f\x00\x00\x00\x3f\x40\x00\x00\x3f\x20\x00\x00"
(integer) 2
127.0.0.1:6379> FT.SEARCH products_idx "*=>[KNN 2 @embedding $vec AS score]" PARAMS 2 vec "\x3f\x80\x00\x00\x3f\x00\x00\x00\x3f\x40\x00\x00\x3f\x20\x00\x00" DIALECT 2

1) (integer) 1
2) "product:101"
3) 1) "score"
   2) "1.15036964417e-05"
   3) "name"
   4) "Running Shoe"
   5) "embedding"
   6) "?\x80\x00\x00?\x00\x00\x00?@\x00\x00? \x00\x00"
127.0.0.1:6379>
```

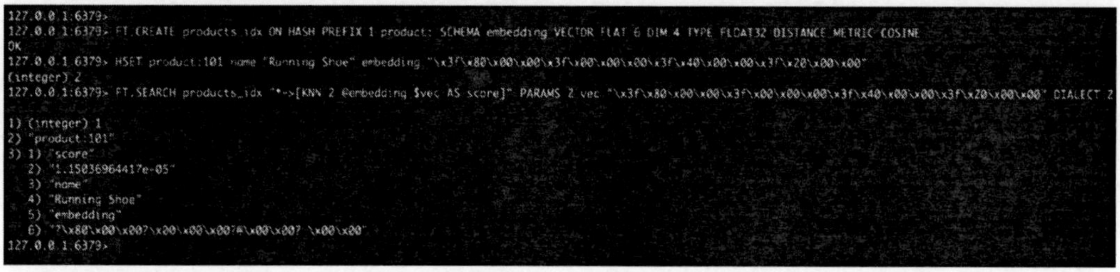

Figure 13.4: *Output of FT.CREATE, HSET, and FT.SEARCH Commands Using RediSearch Module*

Figure 13.4: This figure demonstrates how the RediSearch module enables full-text indexing and querying in Redis. It shows the output of three key commands: FT.CREATE to define a searchable index on hash fields, HSET to populate documents with data, and FT.SEARCH to retrieve matching results using full-text queries. This powerful feature transforms Redis into a lightning-fast search engine for structured and unstructured data.

JSON with RedisJSON

Store flexible JSON documents directly in Redis.

Example:

```
JSON.SET user:1 $ '{"name":"Karnish","age":35,"email":"karnish@databasegyan.com"}'
JSON.GET user:1 $
```

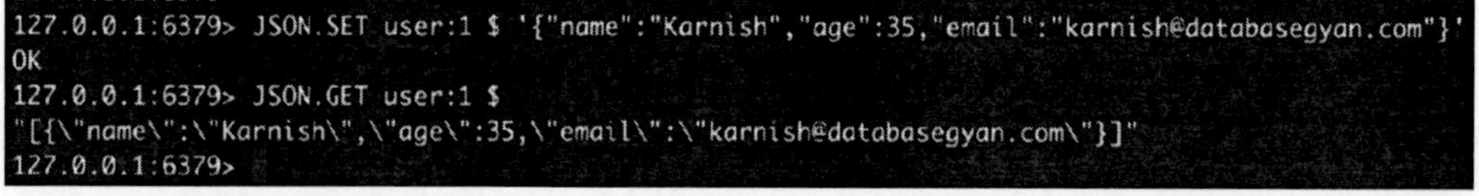

```
127.0.0.1:6379>
127.0.0.1:6379> JSON.SET user:1 $ '{"name":"Karnish","age":35,"email":"karnish@databasegyan.com"}'
OK
127.0.0.1:6379> JSON.GET user:1 $
"[{\"name\":\"Karnish\",\"age\":35,\"email\":\"karnish@databasegyan.com\"}]"
127.0.0.1:6379>
```

Figure 13.5: *Executing JSON.SET and JSON.GET Commands Using RedisJSON Module*

Figure 13.5: This figure shows the execution and output of RedisJSON commands used to store and retrieve structured JSON data in Redis. The **`JSON.SET`** command stores a user object under the key user:1 with fields like name, age, and email. The **`JSON.GET`** command then retrieves the complete JSON document. RedisJSON allows native manipulation and querying of JSON data, making Redis a powerful option for document-style storage, alongside traditional key-value operations.

You can also search over JSON data:

```
FT.CREATE user_idx ON JSON PREFIX 1 user: SCHEMA $.name AS name TEXT $.age AS age
NUMERIC
FT.SEARCH user_idx "@name:Karnish"
```

```
127.0.0.1:6379>
127.0.0.1:6379> FT.CREATE user_idx ON JSON PREFIX 1 user: SCHEMA $.name AS name TEXT $.age AS age NUMERIC
OK
127.0.0.1:6379> FT.SEARCH user_idx "@name:Karnish"
1) (integer) 1
2) "user:1"
3) 1) "$"
   2) "{\"name\":\"Karnish\",\"age\":35,\"email\":\"karnish@databasegyan.com\"}"
127.0.0.1:6379>
```

Figure 13.6: *Full-Text Search on JSON Data Using RediSearch and RedisJSON*

Figure 13.6: This figure shows the execution of **`FT.CREATE`** and **`FT.SEARCH`** commands to perform full-text search on JSON documents stored in Redis. This powerful combination of RedisJSON and RediSearch enables efficient querying over structured JSON data directly within Redis.

Probabilistic Data Structures with RedisBloom

Modern applications often need to analyze large, fast-moving streams of data, such as billions of user clicks, millions of fraud events, or error codes from massive logs. Storing every individual value would be far too heavy on memory and storage.

Probabilistic data structures solve this by trading off *perfect accuracy for extremely small memory footprints and near-instant speed.* They answer questions like:

- *Have I seen this item before?*
- *How many times has this event occurred?*
- *What are the most common things?*
- *What is the 95th percentile of this metric?*

All while using kilobytes of memory, instead of gigabytes.

RedisBloom is an official Redis module that brings these advanced probabilistic data structures to Redis. You load it as part of Redis Stack, and then you get these powerful tools:

Bloom Filter

What is it?

A Bloom filter is a compact data structure that answers:

"*Might this element be in my dataset?*"

It guarantees no false negatives (if it says "not present," it really is not present), but allows a small false positive rate (it might say "yes" when the item was never added).

This is perfect for use cases like spam filters, leaked password lists, or blocking known bad IPs, where it's okay to double-check if you get a "maybe" match.

Example

- **Reserve a Bloom filter**:

  ```
  BF.RESERVE known_spammers 0.01 1000000
  ```

This creates a Bloom filter with a 1% false positive rate, capable of tracking up to 1 million items.

- **Add elements**:

```
BF.ADD known_spammers "bot@databasegyan.com"
```

- **Check membership**:

```
BF.EXISTS known_spammers "bot@databasegyan.com"
```

If it returns 1, the element probably exists; if 0, you know for sure it does not.

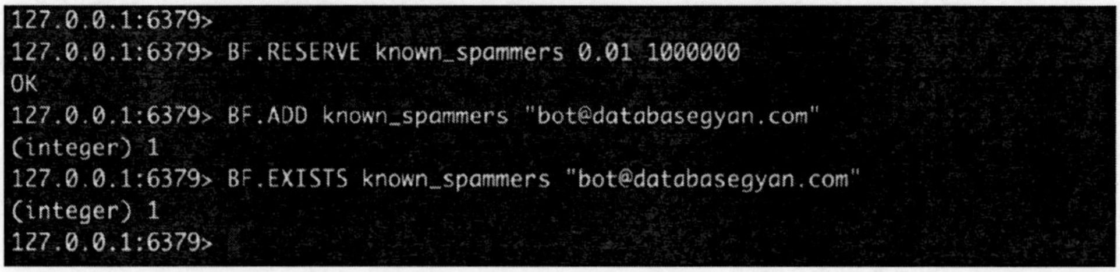

```
127.0.0.1:6379>
127.0.0.1:6379> BF.RESERVE known_spammers 0.01 1000000
OK
127.0.0.1:6379> BF.ADD known_spammers "bot@databasegyan.com"
(integer) 1
127.0.0.1:6379> BF.EXISTS known_spammers "bot@databasegyan.com"
(integer) 1
127.0.0.1:6379>
```

Figure 13.7: *Creating and Querying a Bloom Filter Using RedisBloom*

Figure 13.7: **`BF.RESERVE known_spammers 0.01 1000000`** command initializes a Bloom filter named **`known_spammers`** with a 1% false positive rate and capacity for 1 million items. The command **`BF.ADD known_spammers "bot@databasegyan.com"`** adds an email address to the filter. Finally, **`BF.EXISTS known_spammers "bot@databasegyan.com"`** checks whether the item exists in the filter. A return value of 1 means it probably exists, while 0 confirms, it definitely does not. Bloom filters are ideal for scalable membership checks with minimal memory usage.

Cuckoo Filter

What is it?

A **Cuckoo Filter is like a Bloom Filter**, but even more advanced. It **allows deletions**, which Bloom filters cannot do.

This is useful when you want a *dynamic filter* that changes over time, for example:

- Temporary user bans
- Temporary discount codes
- Lists that expire

How it works

It uses a more advanced hashing scheme that supports the removal of items without rebuilding the entire structure.

Example

- **Reserve a Cuckoo filter**:

```
CF.RESERVE temp_bans 100000
```

- **Add elements**:

```
CF.ADD temp_bans user:1234
```

- **Check membership**

```
CF.EXISTS temp_bans user:1234
```

- **Delete elements**:

  ```
  CF.DEL temp_bans user:1234
  ```

```
127.0.0.1:6379> CF.RESERVE temp_bans 100000
OK
127.0.0.1:6379> CF.ADD temp_bans user:1234
(integer) 1
127.0.0.1:6379> CF.EXISTS temp_bans user:1234
(integer) 1
127.0.0.1:6379> CF.DEL temp_bans user:1234
(integer) 1
127.0.0.1:6379>
```

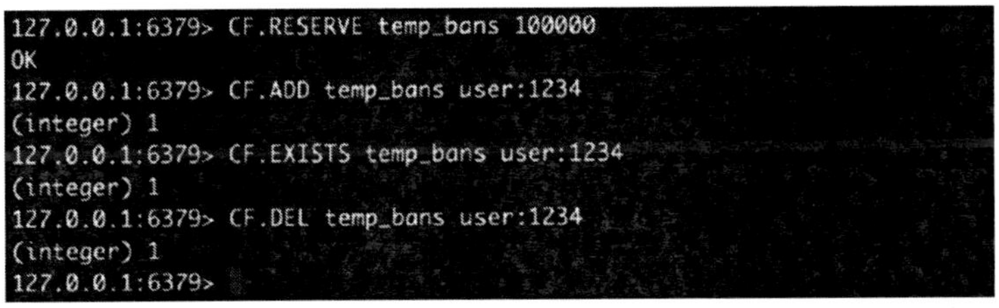

Figure 13.8: *Using a Cuckoo Filter with RedisBloom for Membership Management*

Figure 13.8: This figure illustrates how to use RedisBloom's Cuckoo filter to manage temporary or dynamic sets with insertions, lookups, and deletions. The command **`CF.RESERVE temp_bans 100000`** creates a Cuckoo filter named **`temp_bans`** with a capacity of 100,000 entries. The **`CF.ADD temp_bans user:1234`** command adds a user ID to the filter and **`CF.EXISTS temp_bans user:1234`** checks for its presence. Unlike Bloom filters, Cuckoo filters allow deletions, demonstrated with **`CF.DEL temp_bans user:1234`**. This makes them ideal for use cases such as tracking temporary bans, session IDs, or other revocable states with high efficiency.

Count-Min Sketch

What is it?

Count-Min Sketch is a compact counter for answering:

"How many times has this item occurred?"

It is approximate, but highly memory-efficient, especially for thousands or millions of distinct counters.

Why use it?

Perfect for:

- Counting error codes
- Counting website clicks per ad
- Counting product views
- Counting logins by country

Example

- Initialize a sketch:

  ```
  CMS.INITBYPROB error_counts 0.001 0.99
  ```

  This sets a 0.1% error rate with 99% confidence.

- Increment counts:

  ```
  CMS.INCRBY error_counts "404" 5
  ```

- Query counts:

  ```
  CMS.QUERY error_counts "404"
  ```

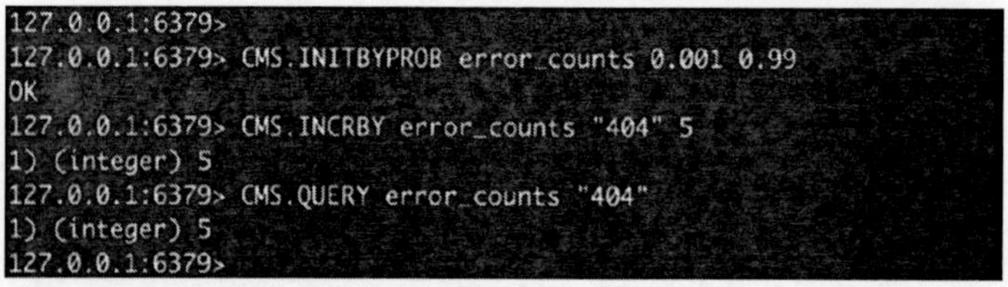

```
127.0.0.1:6379>
127.0.0.1:6379> CMS.INITBYPROB error_counts 0.001 0.99
OK
127.0.0.1:6379> CMS.INCRBY error_counts "404" 5
1) (integer) 5
127.0.0.1:6379> CMS.QUERY error_counts "404"
1) (integer) 5
127.0.0.1:6379>
```

Figure 13.9: *Counting Events with Count-Min Sketch Using RedisBloom*

Figure 13.9: This figure showcases how to use RedisBloom's Count-Min Sketch to track approximate frequencies of events in a memory-efficient way. The **`CMS.INITBYPROB error_counts 0.001 0.99`** command initializes a sketch named **`error_counts`** with a 0.1% error margin and 99% confidence level. Using **`CMS.INCRBY error_counts "404" 5`**, we increment the count of "**`404`**" errors by 5. Finally, **`CMS.QUERY error_counts "404"`** returns the approximate count. Count-Min Sketch is particularly useful for tracking high-volume metrics like error codes, API hits, or page views without storing each event individually.

Top-K Sketch

What is it?

Top-K Sketch is a probabilistic structure for keeping track of the K most frequent items in a stream, think "*trending*" items, hashtags, or top search queries.

Why use it?

Traditional counters can grow indefinitely. Top-K uses limited memory to keep only the most frequent items, automatically evicting the less-frequent ones.

Example:

Reserve a Top-K:

```
TOPK.RESERVE trending_keywords 10 2000 7 0.9
```

This tracks the top 10 items with a 0.9 probability accuracy.

- Add items:

  ```
  TOPK.ADD trending_keywords "redis" "ai" "redis" "cloud"
  ```

- List the top items:

  ```
  TOPK.LIST trending_keywords
  ```

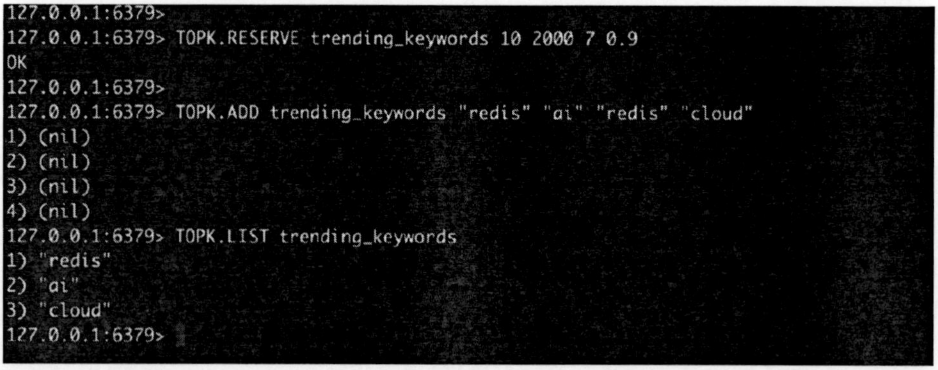

```
127.0.0.1:6379>
127.0.0.1:6379> TOPK.RESERVE trending_keywords 10 2000 7 0.9
OK
127.0.0.1:6379>
127.0.0.1:6379> TOPK.ADD trending_keywords "redis" "ai" "redis" "cloud"
1) (nil)
2) (nil)
3) (nil)
4) (nil)
127.0.0.1:6379> TOPK.LIST trending_keywords
1) "redis"
2) "ai"
3) "cloud"
127.0.0.1:6379>
```

Figure 13.10: *Tracking Top-K Frequent Items Using RedisBloom's Top-K Filter*

Figure 13.10: This figure demonstrates the use of RedisBloom's TOPK data structure to track the most frequent items in a stream. The command **`TOPK.RESERVE trending_keywords 10 2000 7 0.9`** initializes the filter to keep the top 10 most frequent items with high accuracy. Using TOPK.ADD, items like "**`redis`**", "**`ai`**", and "**`cloud`**" are added where repeated occurrences (for example, "**`redis`**") increase their rank. Finally, **`TOPK.LIST trending_keywords`** displays the current top items. This approach is excellent for identifying trending keywords, popular queries, or commonly accessed resources in real-time.

TDigest

What is it?

TDigest is a structure to estimate **quantiles and percentiles** in a stream.

Perfect for:

- p95/p99 API latency
- user spend distributions
- transaction amounts

How it works

Instead of saving every value, it keeps a compact summary that can accurately estimate percentile queries.

Example

- **Create a TDigest**:

  `TDIGEST.CREATE api_latency COMPRESSION 100`

  This creates a TDigest sketch named **`api_latency`** with a compression factor of 100, which balances accuracy and memory usage.

- **Add samples**:

  `TDIGEST.ADD api_latency 250 1`

  This adds the value 250 with a weight of 1 to the TDigest.

- **Query quantiles**:

  `TDIGEST.QUANTILE api_latency 0.95`

  This returns the approximate 95th percentile latency value from the **`api_latency`** distribution.

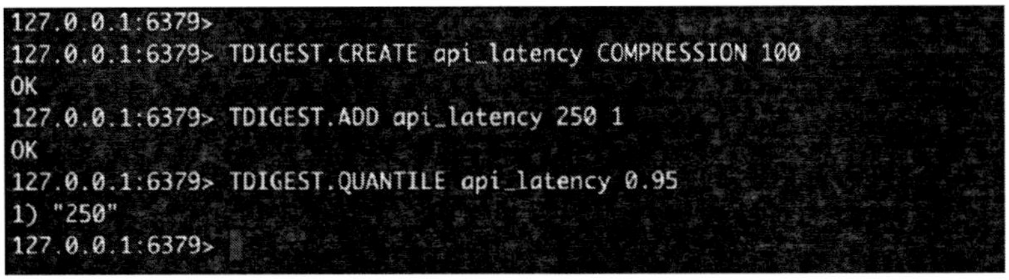

```
127.0.0.1:6379>
127.0.0.1:6379> TDIGEST.CREATE api_latency COMPRESSION 100
OK
127.0.0.1:6379> TDIGEST.ADD api_latency 250 1
OK
127.0.0.1:6379> TDIGEST.QUANTILE api_latency 0.95
1) "250"
127.0.0.1:6379>
```

Figure 13.11: *Estimating Percentiles with TDigest in RedisBloom*

Figure 13.11: This figure illustrates how the TDigest data structure in RedisBloom is used to estimate percentile values efficiently. A TDigest sketch named api_latency is created with a compression factor of 100 to balance accuracy and memory usage. A latency sample of

250 is then added to the sketch and the TDIGEST.QUANTILE command is used to retrieve the approximate 95th percentile latency. This approach allows Redis to compute p95 or p99 metrics accurately without storing every individual data point, making it ideal for real-time performance monitoring at scale.

Why Probabilistic Structures Matter

- They use tiny amounts of memory.
- They handle billions of events efficiently.
- They enable **real-time answers** without heavyweight data pipelines.

That is why **`RedisBloom`** + **`Redis Stack`** are game-changers for modern, data-driven engineering.

Recap

Before we wrap up, it is worth taking a step back to reflect on the various probabilistic data structures we explored in this chapter. Each of them is designed to solve specific problems efficiently, and at scale, without needing to store every single data point. Thus, whether you are filtering out spam users, tracking API error rates, or monitoring application latency percentiles, RedisBloom offers a tailored solution that saves memory and computation. The following table serves as a quick reference to help you choose the right tool for the job, based on your use case and performance goals.

Structure	Use Case	Notes
Bloom Filter	Membership check (no deletes)	fast, tiny, 1% false positives
Cuckoo Filter	Membership check with delete	supports removal
Count-Min	Approximate counters	tiny memory
Top-K	Find the most frequent elements	trending keywords, error codes
TDigest	Percentiles, quantiles	latency, amounts

Table 13.2: *Summary of Advanced Data Structures in Redis Stack*

Table 13.2: This table highlights several powerful data structures supported in Redis Stack, enabling developers to solve complex problems efficiently with minimal memory overhead. Hence, whether you are tracking frequent events, estimating counts, performing membership tests, or calculating percentiles, Redis Stack provides flexible tools that go beyond the core Redis data types. These structures are particularly useful in real-time systems where performance, scalability, and accuracy need to coexist.

Redis 8 vs. Redis Stack

As Redis evolves, developers are often faced with a choice between using the core Redis server (Redis 8) or adopting Redis Stack. This bundled, enhanced version brings extra capabilities out of the box. While Redis 8 delivers impressive performance and powerful new features such as server-side functions and enhanced observability via RESP4, Redis Stack takes things further by packaging advanced modules such as RedisJSON, RediSearch, and RedisBloom. These additions unlock use cases like full-text search, document storage, and vector similarity search, without needing to build custom extensions. The following table helps you quickly compare the native capabilities of Redis 8 with the extended power offered by Redis Stack, so that you can decide which version fits your project best.

Feature	Native Redis 8	Redis Stack
Server-Side Functions	Yes	Yes
Advanced Pub/Sub	Yes	Yes
Observability (RESP4)	Yes	Yes
Vector Search	No	Yes (with RediSearch)
JSON Document Store	No	Yes (with RedisJSON)
Search/Secondary Indexes	No	Yes (with RediSearch)
Probabilistic Structures	No	Yes (with RedisBloom)

Table 13.3: *Redis 8 vs. Redis Stack: Feature Comparison*

Table 13.3: This table offers a side-by-side comparison of Redis 8 and Redis Stack, helping you understand how their capabilities differ. Redis 8 provides a solid foundation with modern features like server-side functions, advanced Pub/Sub, and RESP4-based observability. However, Redis Stack significantly expands on this foundation by bundling additional modules such as RediSearch, RedisJSON, and RedisBloom, enabling support for vector search, document storage, secondary indexes, and probabilistic data structures. This makes Redis Stack an ideal choice for developers looking to build smarter, feature-rich applications with minimal external tooling.

Backing up Redis: Protecting What Matters Most

Before we conclude this book, we want to ask you to do something important: **go through Redis backups one more time, thoroughly**. While we have already touched on this topic earlier, we genuinely believe it deserves a dedicated section of its own.

Why? Because in Redis, just like in any production system, backups are just not a nice-to-have; they are **absolutely essential**. Redis is fast and powerful, but without a reliable backup and restore strategy, even a minor mistake or unexpected failure could result in serious data loss. And that is not a risk worth taking.

This section exists for a very specific reason: to **re-emphasize** how critical backups are, guide you through best practices, and make sure you not only understand how Redis handles persistence but also how to safeguard your data with confidence.

In-memory databases like Redis are known for their speed, but with that speed comes a crucial responsibility: making sure that your data does not disappear the moment something goes wrong. Therefore, whether you are running Redis in the cloud or hosting it yourself, backups are your safety net. They allow you to recover from disasters, human errors, or infrastructure failures without losing the critical data.

This section will walk you through how Redis handles persistence, the different backup mechanisms available, and how to implement reliable, production-ready backup strategies, both for managed Redis services and self-hosted deployments.

Understanding Redis Persistence First

Thus, before diving into backups, it is important to understand how Redis handles persistence internally. Redis supports two main persistence methods:

- **RDB (Redis Database Backups):** Point-in-time snapshots of the dataset are saved to disk at configured intervals. Great for fast restarts and compact storage.

- **AOF (Append-Only File):** Logs every write operation. Redis can replay these logs to restore the exact state. Slower to load than RDB, but more durable.

Many production setups use both RDB and AOF for a balance of performance and safety.

Backups in Managed Redis Services

If you are using a **managed Redis service** like:

- **Amazon ElastiCache**
- **Azure Cache for Redis**
- **Google Cloud Memorystore**

The good news is: **backups are built in** - but they still require understanding and configuration.

Backup Options in AWS ElastiCache

- **Snapshots**: You can enable automatic daily snapshots or trigger manual ones.
- **Retention Period**: Define how long snapshots are kept.
- **Restore**: Snapshots can be restored into new clusters with a few clicks.

Azure Cache for Redis

- Backups are available in the Premium tier.
- Azure Cache for Redis Premium and Enterprise tiers also offer geo-replication, which is a separate feature for disaster recovery. This actively replicates your entire cache across two Azure regions, creating an active-passive (Premium tier) or active-active (Enterprise tier) setup. This provides strong protection against regional failures for your live cache data, not just the backups. While distinct from "*geo-redundant storage for backups*," it achieves the goal of regional protection.
- Snapshot schedule and retention can be configured from the Azure portal.

Google Cloud Memorystore

- For Memorystore for Redis (standalone instances), RDB snapshots are available for both Basic and Standard Tiers.
- Backups are stored automatically and used during failover scenarios.
- Manual backup/restore functionality is more limited compared to AWS.

While managed services automate much of the backup lifecycle, it is still your responsibility to:

- **Verify that backups are enabled.**
- **Check backup frequency and retention settings.**
- **Periodically test restores in staging.**

Remember: **An untested backup is a false sense of security.**

Backups in Self-Hosted Redis

Thus, if you are managing Redis on your own (bare metal, VM, Docker, and so on), backups are 100% your responsibility. Here is how to do it right:

1. **RDB Snapshot Backups**

   You can trigger a backup manually:

   ```
   redis-cli SAVE
   ```

```
127.0.0.1:6379> SAVE
OK
127.0.0.1:6379>
```

Figure 13.12: *Triggering a Manual Redis Backup Using the SAVE Command*

Figure 13.12: This figure illustrates how to initiate a manual snapshot backup in Redis by executing the SAVE command via redis-cli. When this command runs, Redis writes the current in-memory dataset to disk in RDB format (usually in dump.rdb). It is, therefore, a simple yet effective way to capture a consistent backup of your data at a specific point in time, especially useful before performing critical changes or upgrades.

This saves the dataset to the **`dump.rdb`** file (usually in **`/var/lib/redis/ or /opt/homebrew/var/db/redis/ (Apple Silicon Macs)`**).

```
/opt/homebrew/var/db/redis
```

Figure 13.13: *Default Location of dump.rdb File in Redis*

Figure 13.13: This figure shows where Redis typically stores its RDB snapshot file, after a manual or automatic SAVE operation. On most Linux systems, the file is located at **`/var/lib/redis/`**, while on Apple Silicon Macs (using Homebrew), it's usually found under **`/opt/homebrew/var/db/redis/`**. Knowing the exact location is crucial when setting up backup routines or verifying that your persistence strategy is working correctly.

To automate:

- Use a cron job to copy **`dump.rdb`** at intervals:

  `cp /opt/homebrew/var/db/redis/dump.rdb /backups/dump-$(date +%F).rdb`.

- Upload backups to cloud storage solutions such as AWS S3, Azure Blob Storage, or Google Cloud Storage, or alternatively to a designated backup or archival server using automated scripts or backup agents.

2. **AOF Backups**

   If AOF is enabled (**`appendonly yes`**), make sure you:

   - Rotate AOF logs periodically.
   - Archive copies off-server.
   - Monitor AOF size to avoid disk overuse.

3. **Combining RDB + AOF**

   Many teams use **hybrid mode**: configure Redis to use both persistence types (**`appendonly yes`** `and` **`save`** `directives`). This gives you fast restarts (RDB) and high durability (AOF).

4. **Cold Backups**

   Another option is to shut down Redis and back up both the RDB and AOF files directly. This ensures data consistency but involves downtime, best for off-peak hours.

Backup Automation Strategy

To maintain a healthy Redis backup system:

- **Automate backups** using scripts, cron jobs, or cloud-native tools.
- **Monitor disk space**, backup success/failure, and file timestamps.
- **Encrypt** backups if they contain sensitive data.

- **Use versioned storage** to prevent accidental overwrites.
- **Test restores regularly** - recovery procedures should be documented and rehearsed.

Restoring a Backup (Self-Hosted)

To restore an RDB backup:

1. Stop the Redis server.
2. Replace `dump.rdb` in the data directory.
3. Restart Redis.

For AOF:

1. Replace the `appendonly.aof` file.
2. Ensure that AOF is enabled in your config.
3. Restart Redis and let it replay the log.

Always restore backups in a staging environment first to validate data integrity.

Validating Redis Backups

Taking regular backups is only half the story. A backup is truly useful only if it can be restored successfully when you need it. Validating your Redis backups helps you avoid the unpleasant surprise of discovering a corrupted or incomplete backup during a real incident.

You can think of backup validation in three simple steps.

1. **Check backup file integrity**

   For RDB and AOF files, Redis provides built-in tools to check basic consistency:

   - `redis-check-rdb backup.rdb`
   - `redis-check-aof appendonly.aof`

   Run these commands on a copy of your backup files. If the tool reports errors, treat that backup as unsafe and investigate the cause (disk issues, interrupted writes, and so on).

2. **Test-restore in an isolated environment**

   A more reliable way to validate backups is to **actually restore them** on a temporary Redis instance:

   a. Start a test Redis server on a non-production port.
   b. Place the RDB or AOF file in its data directory.
   c. Start Redis and let it load the data.
   d. Connect using `redis-cli` or a simple application script and verify:
      - `DBSIZE` (total keys) looks reasonable.
      - A few critical keys (configuration, user data, counters, and so on.) are present and correct.
      - Basic application flows work against this test instance (a small "`smoke test`").

   This gives you confidence that the backup can be used in a real recovery scenario.

3. **Automate periodic validation**

   Backup validation should not be a one-time exercise. You can schedule a **regular "`restore drill`"** (for example, weekly or monthly) where:

- The latest backup is restored to a test environment.
- A small script checks key counts, sample keys, and simple read/write operations.
- Any failure sends an alert so you can fix the backup pipeline early.

Note: *Treat backup validation like a fire drill.* *It might feel repetitive, but it ensures that when something goes wrong, you already know that your Redis backups are trustworthy.*

Conclusion

Thus, backups are one of those things that you hope you will never need, but when disaster strikes, they are your lifeline! So, whether you are running Redis in the cloud or on your own infrastructure, having a reliable, well-tested backup and restore process is non-negotiable. It is the difference between a minor hiccup and a catastrophic loss.

Your Redis deployment is only as safe as your last successful backup. Treat it with the same care as your application code, automate it, test it, and never assume it is "*just working*."

Final Words: While Closing the Book, Opening Possibilities

Writing this book has been a journey driven by a deep respect for the simplicity and power of Redis, and a desire to make it accessible to you, the engineer, builder, or curious learner who wants to run **Redis not just correctly, but confidently**.

You have learned how Redis stores data, scales horizontally, survives failures, and integrates with real-world applications. You have walked through cloud setups, tuned performance, locked down security, and prepared for disaster.

And now, you have got everything you need to take Redis from your terminal to production and beyond.

Thank you for making it to the end. We hope this book not only taught you Redis but also gave you the confidence to build systems that are fast, reliable, and ready for the real world.

To sum up, Redis is now in your hands, so use it well!

Index

K

L

M

N

S